NETWORKING
FUTURES

Experimental Futures:
Technological Lives, Scientific Arts, Anthropological Voices

A series edited by Michael M. J. Fischer and Joseph Dumit

JEFFREY S. JURIS

NETWORKING
FUTURES

THE MOVEMENTS

AGAINST

CORPORATE

GLOBALIZATION

Duke University Press   Durham and London   2008

© 2008 Duke University Press

All rights reserved

Printed in the United States of America

on acid-free paper ∞

Designed by Heather Hensley

Typeset in Minion Pro by Achorn

International

Library of Congress Cataloging-in-Publication

data and republication acknowledgments

appear on the last printed pages of this book.

For Mom

CONTENTS

LIST OF ILLUSTRATIONS
AND TABLES

Tables

ACKNOWLEDGMENTS

This book is the result of a long-term collaborative process involving activists, scholars, and friends from many sites around the world. I am perhaps most indebted to my former *companys* from the Movement for Global Resistance and allied groups in Barcelona, the activists around whom this book primarily revolves. Not only did they welcome me into their lives, allow me to participate in their ongoing networking and protest activities, and share with me their frustrations, hopes, and dreams, but many were important intellectual peers and interlocutors, engaging in collective discussions, generating common analyses, and taking part in collaborative writing projects. I would love to mention them all by name, but I have promised to maintain their anonymity. In any event, the list would go on for many pages. I would also like to extend my gratitude to several colleagues and friends in Catalonia and Spain whom I *can* name and who offered friendship, scholarly advice, and emotional support at key stages in this project: Amparo Simón, Carles Feixa, Francisco Ferrándiz, and Ken Dubin.

I am also indebted to many people in San Francisco and Berkeley, where this book project began, first as an inspiration following the protests against the World Trade Organization (wto) in Seattle, and later as a dissertation at the University of California, Berkeley ("Digital Age Activism: Anti–Corporate Globalization and the Cultural Politics of Transnational Networking," 2004). Once again I would like to thank my Bay Area activist friends who provided valuable ideas and support during both the pre-fieldwork phase and later the dissertation write-up. I am also deeply grateful to my graduate school mentors, Aihwa Ong, Manuel Castells, and Barbara Epstein, for their wisdom and guidance throughout the dissertation process. I owe a special debt of gratitude to my advisor Stanley Brandes, a fantastic role model in every way: intellectual, professional, and personal. Others at UC Berkeley who had a major influence on my thinking and writing include Laura Nader, Paul Rabinow, Nancy Scheper-Hughes, Nelson Graburn, Donald Moore, Alexei Yurchak, Lawrence Cohen, and Michael Watts. I would also like to thank two close friends who have been incredibly supportive of my work since our days in graduate school, particularly with respect to this project: Eric Klinenberg and Caitlin Zaloom. Moreover, this book would not have been possible without the love, care, and support of my partner, Carla Tejeda, and my closest Bay Area friends, Joe Elford, Anthony Littman, Steve Pockross, Jen Sarche, and Greg McCombs, who gave me strength and encouragement when needed most.

I would also like to thank numerous colleagues, mentors, and peers associated with institutions and research networks that have provided key forums for discussing and developing my work. These include Geoffrey Pleyers, Michal Osterweil, Giuseppe Caruso, Jai Sen, and the rest of the Explorations in Open Space organizing group; Arturo Escobar, as well as the other faculty and graduate students associated with the Social Movements Working Group at the University of North Carolina, Chapel Hill; Manuel Castells, Peter Monge, and Patricia Riley from the Annenberg Research Network on Globalization and Communication and the USC Annenberg School for Communication, where I spent a wonderful and productive year as a postdoctoral fellow; Ron Kassimir, formerly of the Social Science Research Council Working Group on Youth Activism and Citizenship; as well as Jackie Smith and the other participants in the North American Research Network on the World Social Forum. Moreover, the intellectual roots of this book date back to my time as an undergraduate at Wesleyan University, where Elizabeth Traube, Lincoln Keiser, Charles Lemert, Alex Dupuy, and Steven Gregory, as well as my good friend Mireille Abelin, all left an indelible mark on my thinking.

Most recently, my colleagues in the Department of Social and Behavioral Sciences at Arizona State University have provided an extremely supportive environment for the completion of this book. A special note of thanks goes out to two other ASU colleagues, Nora Haenn and Torin Monahan, who provided insightful readings on various parts of this manuscript. The final versions of several chapters were partly shaped by their helpful advice. In addition, Barbara Epstein, Arturo Escobar, Peter Waterman, and Sherry Ortner also contributed particularly helpful comments on various chapters and words of encouragement at critical junctures. At Duke University Press I would like to thank Ken Wissoker for his advice and guidance in bringing the book to fruition and Mandy Earley for her untiring patience in responding to my ceaseless questions while preparing the final manuscript, and Pam Morrison for her invaluable assistance during the production process. I am also grateful to two anonymous readers who provided particularly helpful and constructive readings of an early version of this manuscript. Last but not least I want to thank my family—Mom, the late Sandra Juris, to whom I dedicate this book; Dad, Gerald Juris; sisters, Andrea Juris and Sharon Ferraro; and nieces, Noa and Alyssa. I am also grateful to my closest childhood friends—Paul Sackaroff, Jonathan Philips, Jay Bauman, and Jonathan Grandin, among others, who have provided invaluable support over the years, and without whom I would never have completed this project.

Funding for fieldwork in Barcelona from June 2001 to August 2002 was provided by Dissertation Research Fellowships from the Social Science Research Council, with Andrew W. Mellon funding, and the Wenner-Gren Foundation for Anthropological Research. The dissertation write-up was supported, in part, by a Simpson Memorial Fellowship in International and Comparative Studies at the University of California, Berkeley. Finally, a postdoctoral fellowship from the USC Annenberg School for Communication provided the time, support, and resources needed to complete early revisions of the manuscript.

ABBREVIATIONS

A16   Protest against the World Bank and International Monetary Fund in Washington, D.C., April 16, 2000

AFL-CIO   American Federation of Labor and Congress of Industrial Organizations

ATTAC   Associatión pour la Taxatión des Transactións pour l'Aìde aux Citoyëns (Association for the Taxation of Transactions to Help Citizens, or International Movement for Democratic Control of Financial Markets and Their Institutions)

BSF   Barcelona Social Forum

CACIM   Critical Action: Center in Movement

CAE   Critical Art Ensemble

CCOO   Comisiones Obreras (Workers' Commissions)

CES   Confederation of European Syndicates

CGT   Confederación General de Trabajo (General Labor Confederation)

CNT   Confederación Nacional de Trabajo (National Labor Confederation)

CRIDA   Call for Solidarity in Defense of the Language and Culture of the Catalan Nations

CUT   Central Única dos Trabalhadores (Unified Workers Center)

D2K   Protest against the Democratic National Convention in Los Angeles, August 2000

DAN   Direct Action Network

DIY   do-it-yourself

DNC   Democratic National Convention

ECD   electronic civil disobedience

EDT	Electronic Disturbance Theater
EF!	Earth First!
ERC	Ezquerra Republicana de Catalunya (Republican Left of Catalonia)
ESC	European Social Consulta
ESF	European Social Forum
EU	European Union
EZLN	Ejército Zapatista de Liberación Nacional (Zapatista National Liberation Army)
FS	free software
FTAA	Free Trade Area of the Americas
G8	Group of Eight Nations (includes the top seven industrialized economies in the world: United States, Japan, Germany, United Kingdom, France, Italy, Canada; plus Russia)
GMO	genetically modified organisms
GSF	Genoa Social Forum
GATT	General Agreement on Trade and Tariffs
HB	Herri Batasuna (Unity of the People)
IC	Iniciativa per Catalunya (Initiative for Catalonia) (chapters 2 and 3)
IC	International Committee (chapter 7)
IC	internal consultation (chapter 8)
ICT	information and communication technology
IU	Izquierda Unida (United Left)
IFG	International Forum on Globalization
ILWU	International Longshore and Warehouse Union
IMC	Independent Media Center (Indymedia)
IMF	International Monetary Fund
INPEG	Initiative against Economic Globalization
IYC	International Youth Camp
J18	Global Day of Action against G8 Summit in Cologne, June 18, 1999
KRRS	Karnataka State Farmers Association
M16	Global Day of Action against G8 Summit in Birmingham, May 16, 1998

MAI   Multilateral Agreement on Investment

MIB   Mouvement de l'Immigratión et des Banlieues (Movement of
        Immigration and the Banlieues)

MOC   Movimiento de Objeción de Conciencia (Conscientious
        Objector Movement)

MRG   Movimiento para la Resistencia Global (Movement for Global
        Resistance)

MST   Movimento dos Trabalhadores Rurais Sem Terra (Landless
        Workers Movement)

N30   Global Day of Action against the World Trade Organization in
        Seattle, November 30, 1999

NAFTA   North American Free Trade Agreement

NATO   North Atlantic Treaty Organization

NGO   nongovernmental organization

NSM   new social movements

OC   organizing committee

PCC   Partit Comunista de Catalunya (Communist Party of
        Catalonia)

PCE   Partido Comunista de España (Communist Party of Spain)

PGA   Peoples' Global Action

PSOE   Partido Socialista Obrera de España (Socialist Workers' Party
        of Spain)

PSUC   Partit Socialista Unificat de Catalunya (Unified Socialist Party
        of Catalonia)

PUC   Pontifícia Universidade Católica (Pontifical Catholic
        University)

PT   Partido dos Trabalhadores (Workers Party)

R2K   Protest against the Republican National Convention in
        Philadelphia, July 2000

RCADE   Red Ciudadana para Abolir la Deuda Externa (Citizens
        Network to Abolish the Foreign Debt)

RNC   Republication National Convention

RTS   Reclaim the Streets

S26   Protest against the World Bank and International Monetary
        Fund in Prague, September 26, 2000

SIS   Schengen Information System
SWP   Socialist Workers Party
UGT   Unión General de Trabajo (General Labor Union)
UN   United Nations
UNICEF United Nations Children's Fund
USSF   United States Social Forum
WEDO   Women's Environment and Development Organization
WEF   World Economic Forum
WIDE   Women in Development Europe
WSF   World Social Forum
WTO   World Trade Organization

THE CULTURAL LOGIC
OF NETWORKING

Why would we no longer be capable of following the thousand paths, with their strange to-
pology, that lead from the local to the global
and return to the local? Is anthropology forever condemned to be reduced to territories,
unable to follow networks?[1]

After a day of intense planning for the upcoming actions against the G8, several Catalan activists and I eagerly waited for punk rocker cum international pop star Manu Chao to take the stage at the Piazza Kennedy in Genoa. Suddenly the crowd roared as Manu burst onto the scene with his band Radio Bemba Sound System, featuring musicians from France, Senegal, and North Africa. It was July 18, 2001, and the immigrant rights march was set for the next morning. The siege of the red zone would take place the following day, but we were soon lost in a frenzy of singing and dancing. As police helicopters circled overhead, the shoulder-to-shoulder contact helped release some of the building tension, though perhaps foreshadowing the violent clashes to come. On this evening, however, we would celebrate our spirit of global solidarity.

Born to Spanish parents in a working-class *banlieu* on the outskirts of Paris, Manu Chao has long enjoyed popularity among young European radicals. His former band, Mano Negra, was famed for staging surprise concerts at squatted activist social centers in France, Spain, and Italy,[2] and its lyrics dealt with hot-button political issues such as racism, police violence, and militarism. However, it was only after the release of his widely acclaimed solo debut album, *Clandestino*, that Manu became a truly global figure. Inspired by his travels in Latin America, where he came to know landless workers in Brazil, poor farmers and street children in Colombia, indigenous peasants in Chile and Bolivia, Zapatista communities in Chiapas, and undocumented border crossers in Tijuana, *Clandestino* provides an apt and touching portrait of the lives of those excluded from the global economy. Chao continued to give free concerts during political events and protests after taking residence in Barcelona, where he emerged as a hero among many anti–corporate globalization activists.

Manu Chao's popularity goes beyond political content. His rebellious character, hybrid style, and global vision reflect the ethos of a wave of protest against corporate globalization that achieved widespread visibility in Seattle but that many trace to the Zapatista uprising. Like his activist fans, Manu continually crosses borders, fusing sounds from North Africa, Latin America, and Europe while mixing traditional rhythms with ska, reggae, raï, rock, and punk. True to his diasporic roots, Chao exemplifies a grassroots genre called *musica mestiza*, popularized in the bars and squats of Barcelona, Madrid, and Bilbao. His lyrics combine Spanish, Portuguese, French, English, and Arabic while emphasizing marginal figures such as the immigrant. At the same time, Manu uses new digital technologies to create complex amalgams involving dubbed beats, melodies, and voice-overs. Indeed, like his anti–corporate globalization activist fans, Manu Chao reflects a seeming paradox: using the networking tools and logics of contemporary global capitalism to challenge global capitalism itself.

This book explores emerging norms, forms, and technologies within anti–corporate globalization movements based in Barcelona. Since November 30, 1999, when fifty thousand protesters converged on Seattle to shut down the World Trade Organization (WTO) meetings, anti–corporate globalization activists have organized protests against multilateral institutions in cities such as Prague, Barcelona, Genoa, Quito, and Cancún. Barcelona has emerged as a critical node, as Catalans have played key roles within the anarchist-inspired Peoples' Global Action (PGA) and the World Social Forum (WSF) process, both of which unite diverse movements in opposition to corporate globalization. Anti–corporate globalization movements involve an increasing confluence among network technologies, organizational forms, and political norms, mediated by concrete networking practices and micropolitical struggles. Activists are thus not only responding to growing poverty, inequality, and environmental devastation; they are also generating social laboratories for the production of alternative democratic values, discourses, and practices.

Grasping Networks in a Digital Age

I arrived in Barcelona on June 16, 2001, to conduct an ethnographic study of a network, an activist network to be precise. I had been organizing against corporate globalization for nearly two years, ever since the anti-WTO protests in Seattle. Before then I had also been a longtime Latin America solidarity activist working in support of grassroots struggles in El Salvador and Guatemala. My time in Central America had taught me about the dire consequences of free trade and neoliberalism for poor and indigenous communities, and when I learned about the WTO action, I was eager to join in. I was also a graduate student in anthropology at the time, searching for a dissertation project. I had since become interested in grassroots social movements in Spain and Catalonia and was familiar with previous anti–corporate globalization actions in Europe. But I never imagined the intense feelings of power, freedom, and solidarity I would experience on the streets of Seattle. When the WTO meetings were delayed and a major police riot broke out, I knew something big was happening. That was when I decided to study this emerging global phenomenon ethnographically.

Over the next few years, anti–corporate globalization activism would spread around the world as the local and regional networks we built during the protests in Seattle increasingly used digital technologies to communicate with activists in other countries. Computer-supported networks, including activist media projects, Listservs, and websites, were mobilizing hundreds of thousands of protesters, constituting "transnational counterpublics" (Olesen 2005) for the diffusion of alternative information. Indeed, media activism and digital networking more generally had become critical features of a transnational network of movements against corporate globalization, involving what Peter Waterman (1998) calls a "communications internationalism." Moreover, emerging networking logics were changing how grassroots movements organize, and were inspiring new utopian imaginaries involving directly democratic models of social, economic, and political organization coordinated at local, regional, and global scales.

Not surprisingly, digital networking facilitated my entry into the field. In May 2000 I joined a Spanish-language Listserv created to plan solidarity actions during protests against the World Bank and International Monetary Fund (IMF) meetings in Prague that September. The list was called *Resistencia-Mexico*, but most users were from Argentina and Spain, including activists from the Citizens Network to Abolish the Foreign Debt (RCADE) in Barcelona. "The Network," as it was known, had recently carried out a referendum against the debt during the March 2000 elections in Spain. Inspired by Seattle, RCADE would soon link up with Zapatista supporters, militant squatters, radical ecologists, and opponents of the European Union within a broad platform to mobilize for Prague called the Movement for Global Resistance (MRG). Barcelona, my primary field site, was quickly becoming a key locale within an emerging transnational anti–corporate globalization field. After I exchanged e-mails with Pau, whom I met on the *Resistencia* Listserv (and who would later become a key informant, colleague, and friend), MRG invited me to travel with them to Prague. I agreed, and after getting to know activists during the week of action, I decided to move forward with my plan to study anti–corporate globalization networks based in Spain and Catalonia.

My original idea was to examine transnational activism through ethnographic fieldwork among MRG-based activists involved with PGA, the transnational network that had inspired the first global days of action against capitalism, including the WTO protests in Seattle. Specifically, I would work with RCADE and also take part in broader networking activities with MRG and PGA. However, the situation soon proved more complicated. When I arrived in Barcelona, MRG was taking part in a larger campaign against a World Bank development conference, which also involved leftist parties, trade unions, and NGOs. At the same time, RCADE had splintered from MRG and many radical squatters had returned to their militant circles. I thus encountered a complex web of overlapping political spaces. MRG, my primary object of analysis, was seemingly coming undone.[3] Moreover, I soon learned that similar processes were occurring at the transnational scale. Just before leaving for the G8 protests in Genoa, Pau and I spoke to a Geneva-based PGA activist passing through Barcelona at the time:

> *Jeff*: How is PGA going?
> *Laurent*: It's the most interesting political process I've ever been a part of, but it's kind of ambiguous.

Jeff: What do you mean?

Laurent: Well, you never really know who is involved.

Jeff: How can that be?

Laurent: It's hard to pin down because no one can speak for PGA, and the ones who are most involved sometimes don't even think they are part of it!

Pau: Spanish networks are the same. This all started with RCADE. Then MRG formed during Prague, but now those who were most active in MRG are the main forces in the World Bank Campaign. The same people are at the center, but the networks keep changing around them.[4]

Now I was exasperated. I had taken excellent field notes during mobilizations in Seattle, Prague, and Barcelona, but I really wanted to study the networks behind these demonstrations during their visible *and* "submerged" phases (Melucci 1989). It seemed that if activists wanted to create sustainable movements, it was important to learn how newly emerging digitally powered networks operate and how periodic mass actions might lead to long-term social transformation. After several days, I finally realized what should have been apparent all along: my focus was not really a specific network, but rather the concrete practices through which such networks are constituted. Indeed, contemporary activist networks are fluid processes, not rigid structures. I would thus conduct an ethnographic study of transnational networking practices and the broader cultural logics, shaped by ongoing interactions with new digital technologies, that generate them. What is the cultural logic of networking, how is it distributed, and what kinds of resistances does it provoke? How do struggles over activist discourses, identities, strategies, and tactics constitute alternative networks within broader "movement fields" (Ray 1999)? How are activist networks embodied during mass actions, and to what extent have they made new struggles visible? How are networking logics expressed through experimentation with new digital technologies? Finally, what are the links among activist networking, political change, and social transformation?

To answer these questions, I turned to the traditional craft of the anthropologist: long-term participant observation within and among activist networks themselves. Indeed, rather than studying activist networks as an object, I wanted to understand how they were built in practice, which meant becoming an active practitioner. My entry into these networks was facilitated by my past activist experience and my fluency in Spanish and Catalan. Over the next year and a half, I attended hundreds of meetings, protests, and gatherings and also took part in online discussions and forums. I lived the passion, excitement, and fear associated with direct-action protest, and the exhilaration and frustration of working with activists from such diverse backgrounds. I also became embroiled in movement debates, at times aligning myself with certain groups and against others. This often made me feel uneasy, given my dual role as activist and observer, but I came to realize that only by taking clear positions could I grasp the complex micropolitical dynamics of transnational activist networking. At the same time, I hope this book will prove useful for activists. What impressed me most about so many of those I came to know and respect during my time in the field was their fierce dedication to egalitarian, collaborative process, which demanded of me a politically engaged mode of ethnographic research.

Contesting Globalization

"Antiglobalization" is not a particularly apt label for a movement that is internationalist in perspective, organizes through global communication networks, and whose participants travel widely to attend protests and gatherings. Moreover, most activists do not oppose globalization per se, but rather corporate globalization, understood as the extension of corporate power around the world, undermining local communities, democracy, and the environment.[5] Indeed, naming is an act of power, with profound implications for how activists see themselves and are understood. An ongoing debate has thus raged between those who identify as "anticapitalist" and others who reject corporate globalization, but not capitalism. At the same time, some activists and observers speak of the "global justice" or "alternative globalization" movements.[6] In this book, I refer to anti–corporate globalization movements in the plural, reflecting linguistic practice in Barcelona, while also distinguishing among various forms of globalization and recognizing the diversity of movement actors.

Globalization's cheerleaders, such as the *New York Times* columnist Thomas Friedman, have attempted to stigmatize anti–corporate globalization protesters as backward "flat earthers."[7] If globalization means growing interconnectedness based on technological innovation and the plummeting cost of communication and travel, who could be against that? Most activists would agree. Rather, they are specifically challenging a concrete political and economic project and a discourse that denies the possibility of an alternative (Weiss 1998). In examining anti–corporate globalization movements, it is thus important to consider how globalization operates along several distinct registers.

At the broadest level, globalization refers to a radical reconfiguration of time and space. It is thus a multidimensional process encompassing economic, social, cultural, and political domains.[8] With respect to the economic sphere, the current phase of globalization features several defining characteristics.[9] First, there has been an unprecedented rise in the scope and magnitude of global finance capital facilitated by digital technologies and market deregulation. Second, economic production and distribution are increasingly organized around decentralized global networks, leading to high-volume, flexible, and custom commercialization. Finally, the global economy now has the capability to operate as a single unit in real time. More generally, contemporary globalization generates complex spatial patterns as flows of capital, goods, and people have come unbound, even as they are reinscribed within concrete locales.[10]

At the same time, globalization should also be understood as a powerful discourse that produces specific effects.[11] On the one hand, globalization discourse is often used to legitimate neoliberal policies and practices, thus aiming "to propose the teleology of the market" as the dominant ideology of our times (Trouillot 2003, 48). Indeed, globalization discourse plays "a key role in defining and delimiting the terrain of practical action and the formation of political identities, thereby actively shaping the very processes they purport to describe" (Hart 2002, 12). On the other hand, globalization also provides a concrete enemy and symbolic framework, generating metonymic links among diverse struggles. In this sense, anti–corporate globalization networks such as PGA or the WSF help forge a global frame of reference. As the PGA slogan declares: "May the struggle be as transnational as capital!"

Finally, globalization can also be conceived as a concrete political and economic project enacted by governments, businesses, and financial elites. Specifically, corporate globalization or neoliberalism refers to a set of free market policies commonly referred to as the Washington Consensus, which are imposed through trade agreements and multilateral institutions including the World Bank, IMF, and WTO. These include privatization, trade liberalization, devaluation, deregulation, export-oriented production, and fiscal austerity measures, such as reductions in social expenditures and basic subsidies. Neoliberal projects have facilitated the penetration of corporate capitalism across space, bringing new areas into global production, consumption, and labor circuits while commodifying healthcare, education, the environment, and even life itself.

The results have been disastrous: growing poverty, inequality, social dislocation, and ecological destruction within and across developing and industrialized worlds. During the 1980s, many poor countries became trapped in an "infernal spiral of debt" (Toussaint 2005), as slow growth, devaluation, and falling commodity prices forced states to borrow increasing sums to meet their obligations. The situation improved little during the 1990s, when the number of people living in poverty around the world increased by nearly one hundred million, even as world income grew by 2.5 percent per year.[12] Meanwhile, the 1999 UN Human Development Report indicates that more than eighty countries had per capita incomes lower than in the previous decade.[13] Inequality has also increased between and within states. According to the 2003 World Bank Development Report, the average income in the richest twenty countries is thirty-seven times that in the poorest twenty, double the ratio of forty years ago. In the United States, the top 1 percent earns 17 percent of total income, a level not seen since the 1920s.[14] Moreover, 51 of the 100 largest economies in the world are transnational corporations.[15]

Over the past ten years, however, corporate globalization projects have faced increasing opposition. At least since the Zapatista uprising against the Mexican government on January 1, 1994, the day the North American Free Trade Agreement (NAFTA) went into effect, activists have forged an alternative project of "grassroots globalization" (Appadurai 2000), combining placed-based resistance and transnational networking (cf. Escobar 2001). Anti–corporate globalization movements have mounted a highly effective symbolic challenge to the legitimacy of neoliberalism. As the former World Bank chief economist Joseph Stiglitz (2002) suggests: "Until protesters came along there was little hope for change and no outlets for complaint. . . . It is the trade unionists, students, and environmentalists—ordinary citizens—marching in the streets of Prague, Seattle, Washington, and Genoa who have put the need for reform on the agenda of the developed world" (9).

Stiglitz is not alone among global elites in supporting activist demands. The international financier George Soros has consistently denounced "market fundamentalism" while the Harvard economist Jeffrey Sachs has been a vocal critic of the Bretton Woods institutions. Moreover, leftist political parties in France, Spain, Italy, Brazil, and elsewhere have embraced the popular slogan of the World Social Forum: "Another World Is Possible." On the other hand, as we shall see, the relationship between movement organizing and policy change is less clear. Panels at the World Economic Form (WEF) in Davos now routinely address the social impact of globalization, and the July 2005 G8 Summit in Scotland focused on debt relief and poverty reduction in Africa; but whether such rhetorical shifts translate into action, let alone structural change, remains to be seen.

However, this book is not about the politics of globalization. Rather, it explores emerging forms of organization among anti–corporate globalization movements, particularly in light of recent social, economic, and technological transformations. Although the activists explored in this book seek to influence contemporary political debates, they are also experimenting with new organizational and technological practices. In this sense, they enact a "dual politics" (Cohen and Arato 1992), intervening within dominant publics while generating decentralized network forms that "prefigure" the utopian worlds they are struggling to create.[16] In the 1960s, the New Left was similarly committed to building nonhierarchical structures that were consonant with its egalitarian values (cf. Polletta 2002). Indeed, as Wini Breines (1989) puts it, "prefigurative politics was what was new about the New Left" (xiv). At the same time, while these experiments in direct democracy were often successful at the local level, they were limited in scale. The rise of new digital technologies has profoundly altered the social movement landscape. Activists can now link up directly with one another, communicating through global communications networks without the need for a central bureaucracy. In what follows, I examine how activists are building local, regional, and global networks that are both instrumental *and* prefigurative, facilitating concrete political interventions while reflecting activists' emerging utopian ideals.[17]

Social movements are cyclical phenomena.[18] As discussed in chapter 1, anti–corporate globalization movements entered a highly visible phase starting with the anti-WTO protests in Seattle in November 1999. This stage of growing mobilization lasted through the siege of the G8 in Genoa in July 2001, when massive police violence produced a dampening effect. The attacks of September 11, 2001, complicated matters further, making confrontational protest increasingly risky. Since then activists have continued to organize large demonstrations, including the half-million-person march against the EU in Barcelona in March 2002, the anti-WTO action in Cancún in September 2003, and the anti-G8 protests in Gleneagles, Scotland, in July 2005; but the world and regional social forums and other grassroots networking processes have increasingly come to the fore. Although not as spectacular as direct actions, these projects have provided relatively sustainable platforms for generating alternative ideas, discourses, and practices, allowing activists to pursue their strategic and prefigurative goals in more lasting ways.

Technology, Norm, and Form

Shortly after the Bolshevik revolution, the Russian anarchist Voline outlined a bold vision for an alternative, directly democratic society: "Of course . . . society must be organized. . . . the new organization . . . must be established freely, socially, and, above all, from below. The principle of organization must not issue from a center created in advance to capture the whole and impose itself upon it but on the contrary, it must come from all sides to create nodes of coordination, natural centers to serve all these points."[19] What strikes today's reader about this passage is its resonance with the contemporary discourse of activist networking. Although the top-down Leninist model of organization won out in the Soviet Union, consolidating a revolutionary paradigm that would be exported around the world, the past few decades have witnessed a resurgence of decentralized, networked organization and utopian visions of autonomy and grassroots counterpower. As we will see, these emerging network forms and imaginaries have been greatly facilitated by the rise of new digital technologies. Shaped by the networking logic of the Internet and broader dynamics associated with late capitalism, social movements are increasingly organized around flexible, distributed network forms (Castells 1997; cf. Bennett 2003; Hardt and Negri 2004). Observers have pointed to the rise of "social netwars" (Arquilla and Ronfeldt 2001) or an "electronic fabric of struggle" (Cleaver 1995), but such abstract depictions tell us little about concrete networking practices. Manuel Castells has more generally identified a "networking, decentered form of organization and intervention, characteristic of the new social movements, mirroring, and counteracting, the networking logic of domination in the information society" (1997, 362). However, scholars have yet to explore the specific mechanisms through which decentered networking logics are produced, reproduced, and transformed within particular social, cultural, and political contexts.

This book outlines a practice-based approach to the study of networks, linking structure and practice to larger social, economic, and technological forces.[20] I employ the term "cultural logic of networking" as a way to conceive the broad guiding principles, shaped by the logic of informational capitalism, that are internalized by activists and generate concrete networking practices.[21] Networking logics specifically entail an embedded and embodied set of social and cultural dispositions that orient actors toward (1) the building of horizontal ties and connections among diverse autonomous elements, (2) the free and open circulation of information, (3) collaboration through decentralized coordination and consensus-based decision making, and (4) self-directed networking. At the same time, networking logics represent an ideal type. As we shall see, they are unevenly distributed in practice and always exist in dynamic tension with other competing logics, generating a complex "cultural politics of networking" within particular spheres.[22]

In what follows, I argue that anti–corporate globalization movements involve a growing confluence among networks as computer-supported infrastructure (technology), networks as organizational structure (form), and networks as political model (norm), mediated by concrete activist practice. Computer networks provide the technological infrastructure for the emergence of transnational social movements, constituting arenas for the production and dissemination of activist discourses and practices.[23] These networks are in turn produced and transformed by the discourses and practices circulating through them.[24] Such communication flows follow distinct trajectories, reproducing existing networks or generating new formations. Contemporary social movement networks are thus "self-reflexive" (Giddens 1991), constructed through communicative practice and struggle. Beyond social morphology, the network has also become a powerful cultural ideal, particularly among more radical activists, a guiding logic that provides a model of, and model for, emerging forms of directly democratic politics.

In *French Modern*, Paul Rabinow explores the "diverse constructions of norms and the search for forms adequate to understand and to regulate what came to be known as modern society" (1989, 9).[25] My own book is similarly concerned with norms and forms, but I am interested less in how specific configurations of knowledge and power produce and regulate society than in how contemporary norms and forms are shaped by technological change and, further, how they reflect emerging utopian imaginaries. The following chapters explore the complex interactions among these domains within diverse realms of anti–corporate globalization organizing, paying particular attention to how transnational activist networks are generated through communicative interaction and struggle. Different chapters place greater emphasis on one or another domain, but together they demonstrate a growing confluence among norm, form, and technology, mediated by activist practice.

Computer-Supported Social Movements

By enhancing the speed, flexibility, and global reach of communication flows, computer networks provide the technological infrastructure for the operation of contemporary transnational social movements. Barry Wellman (2001) has argued that "computer-supported social networks" are profoundly transforming communities, sociality, and interpersonal relations. Although the widespread proliferation of individualized, loosely bounded, and fragmentary social networks predates cyberspace, computer-mediated communication has reinforced such trends, allowing communities to sustain interactions across vast distances. The Internet is also being incorporated into more routine aspects of daily social life as virtual and physical activities are increasingly integrated.[26] The Internet thus facilitates global connectedness even as it strengthens local ties.

New technologies have also facilitated new modes of political engagement, including the emergence of computer-supported social movements. Powered by the Internet, anti–corporate globalization movements operate at local, regional, and global scales, while integrating online and offline activity. Building on the pioneering use of digital technologies by the Zapatistas, as well as early free trade campaigns,[27] anti–corporate globalization activists have used computer networks to organize actions and mobilizations, share information and resources, and coordinate campaigns by communicating at a distance. At the same time, the Internet complements and reinforces, rather than replaces, face-to-face interaction.[28]

Indeed, although the Internet circulates information rapidly and circumvents hierarchies, it also has disadvantages as a communications medium. Electronic distribution lists can become saturated with irrelevant posts, and nuances are often lost because of a lack of physical contact and interactivity. In addition, given the highly impersonal nature of e-mail lists, users tend to anger easily, which can lead to heated arguments and flame wars. The Internet can also produce a sense of information overload. Meanwhile, the digital divide remains a significant obstacle to the free flow of information in poorer regions, particularly in the Global South (see chapter 6). Computer-mediated communication is thus most effective when it is moderated, clearly focused, and used together with traditional modes of communication. Accordingly, activists generally use e-mail to stay informed about activities and perform concrete logistical tasks, while complex planning, political discussions, and relationship building occur within physical settings.

In addition to electronic Listservs, anti–corporate globalization activists have also used interactive web pages to facilitate planning and coordination. Particular networks, such as PGA or WSF, have their own home pages. At the same time, activists often create temporary websites during mobilizations to provide information, resources, and contact lists; post documents and calls to action; and, increasingly, house real-time discussion forums and chat rooms.[29] Moreover, activist networking projects, such as the Infospace in Barcelona, have begun to collectively produce and edit documents online using new wiki open editing technology, reflecting a growth in computer-based networked collaboration (Juris 2005a). Similarly, Independent Media Centers (IMC or Indymedia) have been established in hundreds of cities around the world, providing online forums that allow activists to post their own news stories, constituting a self-managed communications network that bypasses the corporate media.[30]

Network-Based Organizational Forms

Beyond providing a technological medium, the Internet's reticulate structure reinforces network-based organizational forms. New social movement (NSM) theorists have long argued that feminist, environmental, and student movements were structured around horizontal networks.[31] Similarly, the anthropologists Luther Gerlach and Virginia Hine pointed out in 1970 that grassroots movements are decentralized, segmentary, and reticulate. At the same time, digital technologies have significantly enhanced the most radically decentralized "all channel" formations (Kapferer 1973),[32] greatly facilitating transnational coordination and communication. Network designs are thus diffusing widely as digital technologies power the expansion of globally connected yet locally rooted social movements, which are increasingly organized around flexible all-channel patterns, rather than traditional top-down political formations.

Networking logics have given rise to what many activists in Spain and Catalonia refer to as a "new way of doing politics." By this they mean a mode of organizing involving horizontal coordination among autonomous groups, grassroots participation, consensus decision making, and the free and open exchange of information, although, as we shall see, this ideal is not always conformed to in practice. While the command-oriented logic of traditional parties and unions involves recruiting new members, developing unified strategies, pursuing political hegemony, and organizing through representative structures, network politics revolve around the creation of broad umbrella spaces, where diverse collectives, organizations, and networks converge around a few common principles while preserving their autonomy and identity-based specificity. The objective becomes enhanced "connectivity" and horizontal expansion by articulating diverse movements within flexible, decentralized information structures that facilitate transnational coordination and communication. Key "activist-hackers" (Nelson 1999) operate as relayers and exchangers, receiving, interpreting, and routing information to diverse network nodes. Like computer hackers, activist-hackers combine and recombine cultural codes—in this case political signifiers, sharing information about projects, mobilizations, strategies, and tactics within global communication networks.[33]

At the same time, discourses of open networking often conceal other forms of exclusion based on unequal access to information or technology. As a grassroots activist from India suggested to me at the 2002 WSF in Porto Alegre, "It's not enough to talk about networks; we also have to talk about democracy and the distribution of power within them." Furthermore, a given cultural logic always exists in dynamic tension with other competing logics. Even when particular cultural forms predominate, they never achieve complete hegemony. Indeed, what many observers view as a single, unified anti-corporate globalization movement is actually a congeries of competing yet sometimes overlapping social movement networks that differ according to issue addressed, political subjectivity, ideological framework, political culture, and organizational logic.

Social movements are complex fields shot through with internal differentiation (Burdick 1995). Struggles within and among specific movement networks shape how they are produced, how they develop, and how they relate to one another within broader movement fields. Cultural struggles involving ideology (antiglobalization versus anticapitalism), strategies (summit hopping versus sustained organizing), tactics (violence versus nonviolence), organizational form (structure versus nonstructure), and decision making (consensus versus voting), or what I refer to as the cultural politics of networking, are enduring features of anti–corporate globalization landscapes. In the following chapters, I thus emphasize culture, power, and internal conflict.[34] As we shall see, discrepant organizational logics often lead to heated struggles within broad "convergence spaces" (Routledge 2003), including the "unitary" campaigns against the World Bank and EU in Barcelona or the World Social Forum process more generally.

Networks as Emerging Ideal

Expanding and diversifying networks is more than a concrete organizational objective; it is also a highly valued political goal. The self-produced, self-developed, and self-managed network becomes a widespread cultural ideal, providing not only an effective model of political organizing but also a model for reorganizing society as a whole. As we shall see, the network ideal is reflected in the proliferation of decentralized organizational forms within anti–corporate globalization movements, as well as the development of new self-directed communication and coordination tools, such as Indymedia, or the countless electronic Listservs created over the past few years. The dominant spirit behind this emerging political praxis can broadly be defined as anarchist, or what activists in Barcelona refer to as libertarian.[35] Classic anarchist principles such as autonomy, self-management, federation, direct action, and direct democracy are among the most important values for today's radicals, who increasingly identify as anticapitalist, anti-authoritarian, or left-libertarian.

These emerging political subjectivities are not necessarily identical to anarchism in the strict ideological sense. Rather, they share specific cultural affinities revolving around the values associated with the network as an emerging political and cultural ideal: open access, the free circulation of information, self-management, and coordination based on diversity and autonomy. Despite popular conceptions, anarchism does not mean complete disorder. Indeed, anarchists specifically emphasize the importance of organization, but of a particular kind: organization based on grassroots participation from below rather than centralized command from above. As Bakunin once wrote: "We want the reconstruction of society and the unification of mankind to be achieved, not from above downwards by any sort of authority, nor by socialist officials, engineers, and other accredited men of learning—but from below upwards" (Ward 1973, 22).

The networking logic within contemporary movements involves precisely this conception of horizontal coordination among autonomous elements. In a similar vein, Arturo Escobar (2004) has drawn on complexity theory to argue that anti–corporate globalization movements are emergent in that "the actions of multiple agents interacting dynamically and following local rules rather than top-down commands result in visible macro-behavior or structures" (222).[36] This is a compelling depiction of how anti–corporate globalization networks operate from a distance, but a slightly different perspective emerges when we engage in activist networking firsthand. Transnational networking requires a great deal of communicative work and struggle. Complexity theory provides a useful metaphor, but given its emphasis on abstract self-organizing systems, it tends to obscure micropolitical practices.[37] Rather than reject the notion of self-organization, however, I recast it here as part of a wider network ideal, which inspires concrete networking practices within specific social, cultural, and political contexts.

In this sense, influenced by their interaction with new technologies, many activists view the Free and Open Source Software (FOSS) development process—where geographically dispersed computer programmers continuously improve, adapt, and distribute new versions of computer software code through collaborative networks—as a model of political organizing and a potential harbinger of postcapitalist forms of economic, social, and political organization. The self-generating network has thus become a powerful model for (re)organizing society based on horizontal collaboration, participatory democracy, and coordination through autonomy and diversity.[38] At the same time, activists increasingly express their emerging utopian imaginaries directly through concrete organizational and technological practice. As Geert Lovink (2002) suggests, "Ideas that matter are hardwired into software and network architectures" (34). This helps to explain why ideological debates are often coded as conflicts over organizational process and form.

Before moving on, it is important to sound a brief cautionary note regarding the liberatory potential of networks. Networks are not *inherently* democratic or egalitarian, and they may be used for divergent ends. The network technologies and forms explored in this book were initially developed as a strategy for enhancing coordination, scale, and efficiency in the context of post-Fordist capital accumulation. As we are reminded nearly every day, terror and crime outfits increasingly operate through global networks as well. Meanwhile, police and military forces are building their own transnational networks of surveillance, repression, and control (see chapter 5).[39] Despite their libertarian outlook, even the most radical activist networks thus have to contend with the state. The differences among these networks are related not so much to the technologies or forms as to the *norms*: their guiding values and goals. While capital is oriented toward maximizing profit and the state is concerned with maintaining order, activist networks employ similar tools and logics to build mass-based movements for social, economic, and environmental justice while emphasizing egalitarianism and openness. Unlike networks of capital, repression, and terror, anti–corporate globalization networks are committed, at least in principle, to democratic process, stressing the consonance between means and ends.[40]

Moreover, while networks more generally are not *necessarily* democratic or egalitarian, their distributed structure does suggest a *potential* affinity with egalitarian values—including flat hierarchies, horizontal relations, and decentralized coordination—which activists project back onto network technologies and forms. At the same time, networks should not be romanticized. In practice, activist networks involve varying degrees of centralization and hierarchy, ranging from relatively horizontal relations within radical networks like PGA to more centralized interactions in the context of the world and regional social forums. In addition, the absence of formal hierarchical designs does not prevent, and may even encourage, the rise of informal hierarchies. What many activists now call "horizontalism" is best understood as a guiding vision, not an empirical depiction (see chapter 6). In sum, given that this book is concerned with emerging network norms and forms, it must also confront their multiple contradictions.

Multiscalar Ethnography

The ethnographic approach developed here moves across various physical and virtual sites to examine transnational flows of people, ideas, strategies, and tactics while also remaining situated in a specific locale. It thus combines multisited and grounded ethnography to explore networking practices at local, regional, and global scales. On the one hand, my research involves what George Marcus calls "multi-sited" ethnography, which "moves out from the single sites and local situations of conventional ethnographic research designs to examine the circulation of cultural meanings, objects, and identities in diffuse time-space" (1995, 96). I specifically employ two tracking strategies: following activists to mobilizations and gatherings, and monitoring discourses and debates through electronic networks. However, whereas Marcus emphasizes the multiple, temporary, and discontinuous, my strategy is more rooted, as I situate myself within a specific locale, or node, and follow the network connections outward, constituting an example of what Burawoy (2000) calls a "grounded globalization."[41] I thus conducted long-term research at my primary field site, Barcelona, while traveling with activists to various protests and events. Since I am mainly concerned with networks that are locally rooted, yet globally coordinated, my research design reflects this tension as well. [42]

My primary stint in the field involved fourteen months of ethnographic research among MRG-based activists in Barcelona from June 2001 to September 2002. This allowed me to take part in local campaigns against the World Bank and EU as well as mobilizations and actions in Barcelona (World Bank, June 2001; EU, March 2002), Genoa (G8, July 2001), Brussels (EU, December 2001), Zaragoza (EU, March 2002), Madrid (EU, May 2002), and Sevilla (EU, June 2002). I also traveled with Barcelona-based activists as part of the MRG International Work Group to several international gatherings, including the

WSF in Porto Alegre (January–February 2002), Strasbourg No Border Camp (July 2002), and PGA European Conference in Leiden (September 2002). I had also previously conducted intermittent research from November 1999 to June 2001, including mobilizations in Seattle (WTO, November 1999), Los Angeles (Democratic National Convention, July 2001), and Prague (World Bank/IMF, September 2000), as well as ongoing organizing in San Francisco. Finally, I subsequently attended the European Social Forum in London in October 2004 and the WSF in Porto Alegre in January 2005.

During my time in the field, I employed diverse ethnographic methods. First, I conducted participant observation among activists at mass mobilizations, actions, and gatherings; meetings and organizing sessions; and informal social settings. Second, I made extensive use of the Internet, which allowed me to participate in and follow planning, coordinating, and political discussions within Catalan, Spanish, and English-language Listservs based in Europe, Latin America, and North America. Third, I conducted seventy qualitative interviews with Barcelona-based activists from diverse backgrounds. Fourth, I collected and examined movement-related documents produced for education, publicity, and outreach, including flyers, brochures, reports, and posters. Finally, I also collected articles and texts within mainstream and alternative media.

Practicing Militant Ethnography

As Marc Edelman suggests, the need to situate ourselves as authors within the research and writing process has more to do with the nature of fieldwork, particularly when studying social movements, "than from a preexisting or abstract commitment to reflexivity" (1999, 6). Edelman (36–7) thus turns to Bourdieu, for whom reflexivity refers to the "bending back of science upon itself," which reinforces rather than undermines "the epistemological security" of the social sciences (Wacquant 1992, 36). Another level of complexity emerges when our political and intellectual commitments coincide. What is the relationship between ethnography and political action? How can we make our work relevant to those (with whom) we study? I believe it *is* possible to produce ethnographic accounts that are rigorous *and* useful for activists. I also believe transnational networking and ethnographic practice are complementary. To illustrate this point, I address three areas of concern raised by

Bourdieu: the social origin of the researcher, intellectualism, and the relation of the researcher to the academic field (Wacquant 1992, 39).

As a white middle-class male activist and practicing anthropologist, I occupy a position of privilege, in many ways a typical one within northern academic and social movement circles.[43] Still, the opportunity to study activism in Barcelona allowed me to link my intellectual and political concerns. Since I had already spent a year living and conducting prior field research in Barcelona and spoke fluent Spanish and Catalan, the context was ideal. At the same time, I was anxious about being accepted within Catalan and Spanish movement circles. However, my past anti–corporate globalization organizing experience facilitated a relatively smooth transition. Moreover, because contemporary activists frequently cross borders, I was able to link up with an emerging network of political circulation and exchange among activists and researchers.[44]

The ethnographic methodology developed here, which I call "militant ethnography," is meant to address what Wacquant (1992) calls the "intellectual bias": how our position as outside observer "entices us to construe the world as a spectacle, as a set of significations to be interpreted rather than as concrete problems to be solved practically" (39). The tendency to position oneself at a distance and treat social life as an object to decode rather than entering the flow and rhythm of ongoing social interaction hinders our ability to understand social practice.[45] To grasp the concrete logic generating specific practices, one has to become an active participant. With respect to social movements, this means organizing actions and workshops, facilitating meetings, weighing in during strategic and tactical debates, staking out political positions, and putting one's body on the line during direct actions. Simply taking on the role of "circumstantial activist" (Marcus 1995) is not sufficient; one has to build long-term relationships of commitment and trust, become entangled with complex relations of power, and live the emotions associated with direct-action organizing and transnational networking. Militant ethnography thus refers to ethnographic research that is not only politically engaged but also collaborative, thus breaking down the divide between researcher and object.[46]

Furthermore, militant ethnography also generates embodied and affective understanding. As anyone who has participated in mass direct actions or demonstrations can attest, such events produce powerful emotions, involving alternating sensations of anticipation, tension, anxiety, fear, terror, solidarity, celebration, and joy. These affective dynamics are not incidental; they are central to sustained processes of movement building and activist networking. In this sense, I use my body as a research tool, particularly during moments of intense passion and excitement, to generate what Deidre Sklar (1994) calls "kinesthetic empathy."[47] As Margaret Meade once pointed out, "In matters of ethos, the surest and most perfect instrument of understanding is our own emotional response, provided that we can make a disciplined use of it" (Jacknis 1988, 172).

The relationship between the researcher and the broader academic (and social movement) field is more complicated. If ethnographic methods driven by political commitment and guided by a theory of practice largely break down the distinction between researcher and activist during the moment of fieldwork, the same cannot be said for the moment of writing and distribution, when one has to confront vastly different systems of standards, awards, selection, and stylistic criteria. As Paul Routledge (1996) suggests, "When it comes to researching resistance, there has traditionally been what de Certeau refers to as a gap between the time of solidarity and the time of writing. The former is marked by docility and gratitude toward one's hosts, while the latter reveals the institutional affiliations, and the intellectual, professional, and financial profit for which this hospitality is objectively the means" (402).

An anecdote illustrates the point. In January 2004, some of my former MRG-based colleagues organized a conference in Barcelona to explore the theory and practice of what they called "activist research." The idea was to create an open space for reflection and debate among activists and those conducting research within and for social movements. During one session, a British activist mounted a harsh attack on academics studying movements from the outside. He was somewhat appeased when we explained our politically engaged practice, but he remained skeptical about how the research would be used: "You go back to the university and use collectively produced knowledge to earn your degrees and gain academic prestige. What's in it for the rest of us?" The issue was not so much the kind of knowledge produced but rather how it is presented, for which audience, and where it is distributed. These questions cut to the heart of the network-based cultural logics and practices explored throughout this book.

Part of the issue has to do with how we understand the nature and role of the intellectual. In exploring the difference between academic and movement theorizing, for example, Barker and Cox (2002) have criticized traditional objectivist paradigms that are *about*, rather than *for*, social movements. They specifically distinguish between academic intellectuals, who operate according to dominant interests, and movement intellectuals, who write in support of subaltern groups. In my experience, however, this distinction breaks down in practice. Moreover, the relationship between activists and intellectuals within contemporary anti–corporate globalization movements is more complex. When so many activists practice their own theorizing, self-publishing, and electronic distribution, the traditional functions of Gramsci's organic intellectual—providing strategic analysis and political direction—are undermined.[48] In this sense, militant ethnography refuses to offer programmatic directives about what activists should or should not do. Rather, by providing critically engaged and theoretically informed analyses generated through collective practice, militant ethnography can provide tools for activist (self-) reflection and decision making while remaining pertinent for broader academic audiences. I thus hope to contribute to strategic debates, but always from the partial and situated position of the militant ethnographer.

Anthropologists have proposed several strategies for making ethnography useful for activists, which can be incorporated into a militant ethnographic praxis. Working with U.S.-based activists, for example, David Graeber (2004) similarly notes the embattled role of the vanguard intellectual, positing ethnography as a potential alternative, which would involve "teasing out the tacit logic or principles underlying certain forms of radical practice, and then, not only offering the analysis back to those communities, but using them to formulate new visions" (335). In this register, ethnography becomes a tool for collective reflection about activist practice and emerging utopian possibilities. Julia Paley (2001) enacts another kind of critically engaged ethnography, working with urban community groups in Chile to analyze power relations and political processes that shape and constrain their strategic options at particular historical junctures. In this mode, ethnography becomes a tool for collective analysis about the outside world. Finally, in his study of gender, race, and religion within Afro-Brazilian movements, John Burdick (1998) suggests that ethnography can help movements represent themselves in order to capture the social and cultural heterogeneity among mobilized and unmobilized constituencies. Practicing militant ethnography can thus help activists carry out their own ethnographic research.

For Burdick, this involves supporting movements in their efforts to reach out to a wider audience. But it might also mean helping activists analyze diverse movement sectors, understand how they operate, and learn how to most effectively work together. In my own case, for example, I spent hours talking to MRG-based colleagues about diverse movement sectors in Barcelona and elsewhere and how they might best coordinate through flexible, decentralized structures. I also participated actively in debates concerning protest tactics and violence, organizational forms, and political strategy. In this sense, transnational activist networking always already involves a form of militant ethnography, while practicing militant ethnography within contemporary local/global movements necessarily requires transnational networking.

Militant ethnography thus includes three interrelated modes: (1) collective reflection and visioning about movement practices, logics, and emerging cultural and political models; (2) collective analysis of broader social processes and power relations that affect strategic and tactical decision making; and (3) collective ethnographic reflection about diverse movement networks, how they interact, and how they might better relate to broader constituencies. Each of these levels involves engaged, practice-based, and politically committed research carried out in horizontal collaboration with social movements.[49] I have tried to incorporate all these modes throughout the book. Indeed, many of the ideas presented here were developed collectively. At the same time, the resulting account involves a particular interpretation produced with the practical and theoretical tools at my disposal and offered back to activists, scholars, and others for further reflection and debate.

Finally, the question remains as to the most appropriate context for practicing militant ethnography and how to distribute the results. One obvious place is the academy, which, despite increasing corporate influence and institutional constraints, continues to offer a critical space for collective discussion, learning, and debate. Indeed, as Scheper-Hughes (1995) suggests, those of us within the academy can use writing and publishing as a form of resistance, working within the system to generate alternative politically engaged accounts. Moreover, as Routledge (1996) points out, there are no "pure" or "authentic" sites, as academia and activism both "constitute fluid fields of social action that are interwoven with other activity spaces." Routledge thus posits an alternative "third space," "where neither site, role, or representation holds sway, where one continually subverts the other" (400). The utopian alternative is suggested by the rise of free university projects and autonomous research networks, such as the activist research conference mentioned earlier. Indeed, such grassroots endeavors embody the networking logics and practices I explore throughout the book. By examining emerging network norms and forms within anti–corporate globalization movements, I thus hope to contribute to both academic and activist theorizing by exploring, as the Argentine Colectivo Situaciones (2001) puts it, the "emerging clues of a new sociability within concrete practices" (39).

The Book Ahead

The following chapters explore the complex interactions among network technologies, organizational forms, and political norms within diverse realms of anti–corporate globalization activism. Chapter 1 provides a historical account of anti–corporate globalization movements, examining their emergence as a transnational phenomenon. I begin with an ethnographic vignette from the WTO protests in Seattle and then shift backward to consider the genealogy of diverse processes that converged there, including grassroots struggles in the Global South, student-based anticorporate activism, campaigns against structural adjustment and free trade, anarchist-inspired direct action, and global Zapatista solidarity networks. I then go on to trace the growth and expansion of anti–corporate globalization movements after Seattle, before concluding with an analysis of their major defining characteristics.

Chapters 2 and 3 consider how anti–corporate globalization movements articulate with local dynamics, specifically examining the production of competing movement networks in Barcelona and the cultural politics surrounding them. Chapter 2 outlines diverse movement sectors in Barcelona and traces their historical roots, including the region's strong culture of opposition forged through decades of nationalist and anti-Franco struggle and its powerful anarchist legacy. Chapter 3 examines contemporary networking politics among anti–corporate globalization activists, revolving in part around two distinct forms of practicing democracy: one based on political representation within permanent structures, and another rooted in flexible coordination and direct participation through decentralized networks. The conflict between networking and traditional command logics forms part of a broader series of struggles involving competing visions, ideologies, and practices, leading to a complex pattern of shifting alliances driven by networking politics at local, regional, and global scales.

The following two chapters explore how alternative activist networks are embodied during direct-action protests, which provide physical spaces where activists meet, meanings are produced and contested, and political imaginaries are enacted through mass-mediated symbolic performance. Chapter 4 considers the affective and spatial dynamics of mass anti–corporate globalization mobilizations, paying particular attention to how networking politics are performed through activist bodies and inscribed onto urban space. Chapter 5 explores protest violence as a potential limit to network norms and forms through an ethnographic study of the G8 protests in Genoa. This chapter specifically examines the dynamic interplay between performative violence, state terror, media images, and activist tactical debates. Moreover, as we shall see, the prevailing "diversity of tactics" ethic among radicals reflects the cultural logic of networking itself.

Chapter 6 explores the transnational dimension of activist networking within Peoples' Global Action. PGA was founded in February 1998 as a flexible space for communication and coordination among grassroots struggles against free trade and corporate globalization, and activists have since defined the PGA network as anticapitalist, forging a more radical current within a broader movement field. In chapter 6, I examine how PGA activists in Europe have struggled to build horizontal organizational forms that correspond to their emerging political norms.

Since January 2001, when the World Social Forum was first organized in Porto Alegre, the WSF has provided a broader space for diverse movements and organizations to discuss, develop, and exchange information about alternatives. Local and regional forums have also been held in Europe, South Asia, and Latin America, transforming the WSF into a sustained process driven by NGOs, trade unions, and the traditional Left. Through ethnographic accounts of meetings and forums in Leiden, Porto Alegre, Barcelona, and London, chapter 7 analyzes how network norms and forms are reproduced and contested within and around the forums through alternative spatial discourses and practices.

Chapter 8 goes on to explore emerging forms of grassroots media activism within anti–corporate globalization movements. Activists have used e-mail lists, web pages, and open-editing software to organize actions, share information and resources, collectively produce documents, and coordinate at a distance. At the same time, Indymedia has provided an online forum for autonomously distributing news stories, constituting a self-managed communications network outside the corporate press. Activists have thus not only employed digital technologies as tools, they have also used them to practice what I call "informational utopics," physically embodying alternative political visions based on a horizontal network ideal.

Finally, the conclusion considers the impact of anti–corporate globalization movements. On the one hand, activists have pursued symbolic tactics, organizing mass actions to elicit media attention, make hidden conflicts visible, and challenge hegemonic meanings. Changes in media coverage and political rhetoric have not yet translated into concrete policy change, but they do indicate that tacitly accepted notions are increasingly subject to debate. On the other hand, activists are also seeking to build grassroots "counterpower" through strategic networking and experimentation with new technologies, which might one day lead to broader social and cultural transformation.

1

THE SEATTLE EFFECT

Let's make a network of communication among all our struggles and resistances. An intercontinental network of alternative communication against neoliberalism . . . (and) for humanity. This intercontinental network of alternative communication will weave the channels so that words may travel all the roads that resist. . . . (It) will be the medium by which distinct resistances communicate with one another. This intercontinental network of alternative communication is not an organizing structure, nor has a central head or decision maker, nor does it have a central command or hierarchies. We are the network, all of us who speak and listen.[1]

It was November 29, 1999, and three friends and I were speeding up Interstate 5 on the way to Seattle for the big protest against the wto. We had left San Francisco at dawn, hoping to make it before midnight. We had no idea what to expect, but we all had the feeling something big was about to happen, that we were somehow making history. We had not taken part in the previous weeks of direct-action training, but we were eager to join the fray. Shortly after passing through Eugene, I turned to my friend at the wheel, a longtime environmental activist, and asked him why he was going to Seattle. His face lit up and he responded, "This is going to be historic, radical environmentalists and organized labor are finally pulling it together. I don't know exactly what is going to happen, but this is going to be huge, there is no way I would miss this!" He seemed to be echoing a widely shared sentiment.

To be honest, at the time I had only a vague understanding of what the wto was. I knew about the globalization debates and had been active in Latin American solidarity movements for years. Having lived and worked in Guatemala in the early 1990s, I knew a lot about structural adjustment and the destructive environmental and economic policies of the World Bank and imf in Central America. During my first few years as a graduate student, I had worked with a local Latino employment cooperative in Oakland but had recently begun to collaborate with a San Francisco–based NGO supporting grassroots projects in the Global South. Moreover, as a student of social movements, I had also closely followed the Zapatista uprising, but I still had no sense of belonging to a grassroots movement against neoliberalism. The next few days would change all that. As for so many others, Seattle was my initiation into a new and inspiring world that would soon be known around the planet as the "antiglobalization" movement. Beyond street protests, each new mobilization would leave behind a new coalition of environmental, labor, solidarity, economic justice, women's, and indigenous rights networks, slowly weaving together the kind of decentralized intercontinental network—a broad transnational web of resistance—the Zapatistas had called for several years earlier.

Throughout this book, I move back and forth between the local and the global, between Barcelona and the distant locales that form part of the broader global networks Catalan activists have helped to produce. This chapter provides an overview of anti–corporate globalization movements, examining their emergence as a transnational phenomenon and analyzing their major defining characteristics. What are anti–corporate globalization movements? When and why did alternative networks emerge? How do different sectors articulate within broader movement fields? The rapid diffusion of network-based models has facilitated interaction among diverse political perspectives, reflecting a broader confluence among organizational forms, political norms, and new technologies. During the April 2001 protests against the Free Trade Area of the Americas (FTAA) in Quebec, radical activists proclaimed, "The movement didn't start in Seattle, and it won't end in Quebec!" My story begins in Seattle, however, because it was the first in a string of mass direct actions that were broadcast on a global scale and where so many diverse networks came together against a common enemy—corporate globalization—producing something larger than the sum of its parts.

The Battle in Seattle

We arrived in Seattle shortly before midnight. The streets were empty, and there was no indication of the gathering storm that would hit the following day. After a brief night's sleep, we made it down to the port for the action at

1. Affinity group locks down intersection during the anti-WTO protests in Seattle.
PHOTOGRAPH COURTESY OF OAKLEY MYERS.

7:30 the next morning. We quickly downed some fresh coffee at the pier and then decided to join a large, motley group of protesters heading toward the conference center. We saw colorful costumes, huge puppets depicting world leaders, and protesters dressed as giant green sea turtles.[2] The sound of drums was everywhere. Protesters wore backpacks stuffed with food, gas masks, and lemons, and many wore bandannas around their necks in preparation for the street battle to come. Just before reaching the conference center, we passed an intersection locked down by fifteen activists, blocking oncoming traffic. I would witness similar scenes around the world during the next few years, but this was my first mass direct action, and I had never seen anything like it. We were thoroughly unprepared.

As we approached the conference center, small groups began to break off from the larger crowd, taking up distinct positions around the perimeter. Activists communicated by cell phone, and everything seemed extremely well organized, but there was no central command. Indeed, the networked form of the various protest blocs reflected what I would come to recognize as an emerging networking logic, mirroring the decentered structure of the e-mail lists activists had used to mobilize for the action. All of a sudden, people began forming a human chain around the conference center. We decided to join in. It was cold and drizzling, but locking arms together with strangers united in common cause produced a feeling of human warmth. Fifteen minutes later, we caught word the building had been surrounded and most of the major downtown arteries shut down. Everyone cheered. Many clusters like the one we had joined that morning had gone out from different points around the city, some taking part in the blockade, others locking down intersections, still others occupying major bridges and overpasses.

For the next several hours, we held our position in front of the conference center, blocking delegate after delegate from entering the building. Some smiled and walked away, others protested violently, and some even tried to slip through by pretending to be protesters. As I would later learn through direct-action trainings, we had organized a flawless "hassle line." Activists organized similar scenes around the city, and many delegates remained blocked inside their hotels, including a reportedly furious Madeleine Albright (Cockburn and St. Clair, 2000, 31). As we held our position, chanting slogans such as "Whose Streets? Our Streets!" and "No Justice, No Peace!" giant turtles and butterflies occasionally passed by with colorful signs proclaiming "Teamsters and Turtles: Together at Last!" and "No Globalization without Representation!"

Everything appeared calm throughout the morning, and we even chatted with police officers stationed directly behind us. Little did we know the first tear gas canisters had already been fired at protesters around 10:00 a.m. (Hawken 2000, 21). Those first groups held their ground, but the city would soon be engulfed in a major police riot. After a while, we caught our first whiff of tear gas floating with the shifting winds from the other end of the convention center. As the tension began to mount, we soon saw our first "Black Bloc" contingent. Dressed in black, gas masks buckled to their waists, wearing hoods and bandannas to cover their faces, they moved swiftly and purposefully, darting in and out of a stunned group of dancing turtles. That afternoon they began smashing the windows at major corporate outlets in downtown Seattle: Nike, Starbucks, the Gap, and Bank of America.

At around 1:00 p.m. the massive labor march approached the conference center. I decided to walk over and have a look. In addition to the Teamsters, longshoremen, and steelworkers, there were colorful contingents of Korean workers, Latino immigrants, indigenous activists, and French farmers. Many activists later criticized the "lack of color" in Seattle, pointing to the predominantly white middle-class backgrounds of the protesters (cf. Martínez 1999; Starr 2004), but this charge was less evident at this particular intersection. Organizers had expected the labor marchers to join the direct action, but marshals directed them away from the conference center. Many of the thirty thousand labor marchers broke ranks, however, and joined the protesters in the streets, swelling our number to more than fifty thousand.

Before heading back to the blockade, I followed several activist groups who were playing cat and mouse with riot cops through the side alleys next to the Paramount Theater. The streets were overflowing with people, some playing instruments, others dancing and singing, still others holding puppets and banners. It felt like a huge street carnival, with the added excitement of periodic confrontations with the police. The tension was intoxicating. At one point, I walked over to a group of people holding a meeting next to a large fence. Someone had a sticker on his shirt that read "Direct Action Network," the coalition that had organized the protests.

Rumors had already begun circulating that the WTO ministerial had been canceled; the excitement was mounting. After reloading on coffee, we walked through the streets on the other side of the conference center, back down toward the pier. At one intersection, protesters had set up a makeshift stage with speakers blaring music and periodic speeches and spoken word performances. A large group began dancing circles around an affinity group locked down in the middle of the street. Occasionally, protesters would step up to the microphone and recite spoken-word poetry. Although I had been to many mass gatherings, I had never felt such ecstatic freedom and spontaneous *communitas* (Turner 1969). We had slipped into a time out of time, a moment when the prevailing order had been overturned, creating what the anarchist writer Hakim Bey (1991) calls a "temporary autonomous zone." This was highly charged carnival indeed.

It turns out we were in the midst of a two-hour hiatus when the police had run out of tear gas and pepper spray (Cockburn and St. Clair 2000, 30). But they soon refueled and initiated another round of indiscriminate assaults. Shortly before 4:00 p.m., we walked over to the next corner and witnessed riot cops launching tear gas canisters into the middle of an affinity group blockading an intersection. They soon began shooting pepper spray at protesters' faces and lobbing tear gas canisters into the crowd. My eyes started to burn

2. Guerrilla theater performance on the streets of Seattle. PHOTOGRAPH COURTESY OF OAKLEY MYERS.

violently. A woman offered us wet rags and lemon, but after the next loud bang, the crowd began to stampede. My friend and I quickly turned and ran to avoid being trampled. Over the next few hours, we darted through the streets, moving in toward police lines, only to run away frantically after more tear gas was fired. There was something eerily addicting about the whole experience, and during my field research over the next two years, I would relive similar encounters over and over again in cities like Prague, Barcelona, and Genoa.

After nightfall, looting began at Starbucks and other downtown stores. Many activists tried to intervene, shouting, "No violence! No violence!" but to no avail. The mayor of Seattle declared martial law, bringing a curfew into effect. The situation in the streets quickly deteriorated, so we went back to the hotel, as we were not planning to risk arrest. We met up with our friends and decided to have a drink at the bar next door. Exhausted, we watched the live scenes on the evening news, our eyes still burning. Images depicted looting and chaos, interspersed with an occasional festive scene. Meanwhile, broadcasters denounced the violent anarchists in black. Similar images were broadcast across the United States and around the world. Over the next few weeks, the WTO would become a household name, and globalization the center of an intense public debate. Although the protests continued for several more days, including continued mass arrests and jail solidarity actions, my friends and I headed back to San Francisco the next morning.

The Seattle Effect

Beyond direct action, the anti-WTO protests involved more than seven hundred organizations in daily forums, teach-ins, and demonstrations. The overall mobilization was organized by a broad coalition of direct-action groups, environmental organizations, NGOs, and labor unions, including the Direct Action Network, Public Citizen, the Sierra Club, and King County Labor Council.[3] The way these diverse elements came together and transformed the anti-WTO protests into a global media event produced what I call the "Seattle Effect." As images circulated around the world, similar protest convergences would soon take place in other cities, generating a growing transnational wave of protest against corporate globalization.[4] Moreover, the diverse networks that converged in Seattle represented key sectors within an emerging anti–corporate globalization field. The way they interacted on the streets mirrored how alternative movements and struggles would converge within transnational networks, as new technologies and emerging networking logics allowed activists to organize across distance, diversity, and difference.

Direct Action

The mass action was coordinated by a loose coalition called the Direct Action Network (DAN), which included Seattle-based activists and groups such as Art and Revolution, the Rainforest Action Network, Earth First!, the Ruckus Society, and Global Exchange.[5] The overall action strategy involved nonviolent civil disobedience, including blockades and lockdowns, consensus-based decision making, and an affinity group structure based on small, autonomous groups of five to fifteen activists, which formed larger clusters and organized via spokescouncil meetings.[6] The direct-action organizer and trainer Starhawk (2002) described the action in this way:

> The participants in the action were organized into small groups called "affinity groups." Each group was empowered to make its own decisions around how it would participate in the blockade. There were groups doing street theater, others preparing to lock themselves to structures, groups with

TABLE 1. Major sectors and protest activities during the mobilization against the WTO in Seattle, November 30, 1999

Sectors	Groups and networks	Main activities
Nonviolent direct action	Direct Action Network (DAN): Art and Revolution, Rainforest Action Network, Earth First!, Ruckus Society, Global Exchange	WTO Summit blockade
Organized labor	AFL-CIO	Labor rally at Memorial Stadium, downtown march; radicals later join blockade
Economic justice/ debt activism	International Forum on Globalization (IFG), Fifty Years Is Enough, Jubilee 2000, Public Citizen, Global Exchange	Forums and teach-ins on economic justice, debt, health, women, the environment, and biotechnology; some activists also take part in the labor march, blockade, and the human chain against the debt
Environmentalism	Radical networks: Earth First!, Rainforest Action Network; mainstream groups: Sierra Club, Friends of the Earth	Forums and teach-ins, public education, and network building; radicals take lead role in direct-action organizing
Women	Women's Environment and Development Organization (WEDO), Women in Development Europe (WIDE)	NGO-based activists and intellectuals take part in forums and teach-ins; radicals help plan and organize blockade
Farmers and indigenous peoples	Peoples' Global Action (PGA) caravan, French Farmers Confederation, Via Campesina	Labor march and rally, blockade, and smaller actions against McDonalds and genetically modified (GMO) foods
Black Bloc	Loose cluster of militant anti-capitalist affinity groups	Blockade, mobile tactics, property destruction, tossing tear gas canisters back at police
Grassroots media activism	Independent Media Center (IMC), or Indymedia	Independent reporting from the streets, multimedia production, development and maintenance of Indymedia website

banners and giant puppets, others simply prepared to link arms to non-violently block delegates. . . . Affinity groups were organized into clusters. The area around the Convention Center was broken down into thirteen sections, and affinity groups and clusters were committed to hold particular sections. As well, some groups were "flying squads"—free to move to wherever they were most needed. All of this was coordinated at spokes-council meetings. . . . In practice, this form of organization meant that groups could move and react with great flexibility during the blockade. . . . No centralized leader could have coordinated the scene in the midst of the chaos, and none was needed—the organic, autonomous organization we had proved far more powerful and effective. (17–8)

Although perhaps overstated, this flexible, decentralized strategy, which Arquilla and Ronfeldt (2001) call "swarming," physically embodied the de-centered networking logic that came to define anti–corporate globalization networks more generally. Indeed, many radical activists view this system as a model for organizing broader networks and social relations, facilitated on a larger scale by the introduction of the Internet, reflecting the increasing confluence among organizational forms, political forms, and new technologies.

Forums and Teach-Ins

Activists also organized diverse public education events in Seattle, including a teach-in sponsored by the International Forum on Globalization (IFG) and daily workshops on issues such as militarization, health, the environment, women's rights, democracy, sovereignty, development, agriculture, and bio-technology. These events featured public intellectuals from international NGOs and think tanks, including Walden Bello of Focus on the Global South; Martin Khor, president of the Third World Network; and Vandana Shiva, founder of the Research Foundation for Science, Technology, and Ecology in India. Such counterconferences would emerge as an integral part of later mobilizations, providing an early model for the World Social Forum (WSF).

Labor Rally and March

Despite the Teamster-Turtle alliance, the relationship between big labor and grassroots environmental activists was often strained. AFL-CIO leaders made a

conscious decision to stay away from the direct-action protesters by organizing their own labor rally at Memorial Stadium, well outside the downtown
area. Although they tried to keep the labor march apart from the direct action, many grassroots labor militants joined anyway. The International Long-
shore and Warehouse Union (ILWU) took a much more radical stance, shutting
down ports along the West Coast to push for the release of jailed protesters.
The split between labor and the more radical activists has also been a recurring feature among European movements, where the CES (Confederation of
European Syndicates) has organized its own marches and rallies.

Economic Justice and Debt Activism

Global solidarity activists also played a crucial role in Seattle. The Fifty Years
Is Enough network against the World Bank and IMF, which focused on the
WTO in Seattle, spearheaded the April 16, 2000, protests against the Bretton
Woods institutions in Washington, D.C. Meanwhile, Jubilee 2000, a transnational movement to cancel the debt of the world's poorest countries, organized a twenty-thousand-person human chain against the debt in Seattle
on November 29, 1999, and would have a major presence at future mobilizations, including Washington, D.C., Prague, and Genoa.[7] Among economic
justice networks in Europe, ATTAC (International Movement for Democratic
Control of Financial Markets and Their Institutions) has been particularly
influential. Created to promote and educate the public about the Tobin Tax,
a levy on international financial transactions that would regulate global financial markets and generate development funding, the network has since
broadened its scope, becoming a leading voice against corporate globalization more generally. Radicals often criticize moderate groups and large NGOs
for their "reformist" positions and top-down organizing practices, generating the kind of cultural politics of networking I explore further in subsequent
chapters.

Environmentalists

Environmental activists and organizations, including the more radical Earth
First! and Rainforest Action Network, which helped found DAN, and mainstream organizations such as the Sierra Club and Friends of the Earth, took
lead roles with respect to direct action, public education, and networking in

Seattle. Since then, U.S. environmental groups have continued to take part in antiglobalization mobilizations but have had a lower profile (see Gould, Lewis, and Roberts 2004). European activists from environmental networks such as Earth First! or Ecologists in Action in Spain and Catalonia have also played key roles within antiglobalization networks, contributing their direct-action experience and horizontal organizing models.

Women

Feminist networks such as Women in Development Europe (WIDE) and the Women's Environment and Development Organization (WEDO) also took part in Seattle (Moghadam 2005, 72). Beyond their organizational presence, however, women had a more profound impact. The consensus decision-making model used to coordinate direct action is an example of feminist process (Epstein 1991; Polletta 2002), and many direct-action organizers, particularly in the United States, and prominent movement intellectuals, such as Vandana Shiva, Helena Norberg-Hodge, and Susan George, are also feminist leaders (see Thomas 2001, 153–54). Moreover, the World March of Women, founded by the Quebec Women's Federation in 1998, held its first march in 2000 and has been active since within antiglobalization networks, particularly the WSF. The World March of Women's organizational principles include a plank that specifically challenges the policies of international financial, military, and economic institutions viewed as responsible for impoverishing and marginalizing women around the world.[8]

Farmers and Indigenous People

Peoples' Global Action organized a caravan to bring indigenous activists and peasant farmers to Seattle from South Asia and Latin America, and would later help grassroots activists from the Global South attend protests against the World Bank and IMF in Prague in September 2000. PGA has continued to provide a mechanism for coordination and communication among more radical anticapitalists, particularly in western Europe. However, Jose Bové, the charismatic figure from the French Farmers Confederation, was the big media star in Seattle.[9] The Farmers Confederation has been an active member of the international network Via Campesina, which has taken a lead role in global struggles against structural adjustment and free trade (see Edelman 2003).

Black Bloc

A loosely organized cluster of militant affinity groups employed "Black Bloc" tactics in Seattle, and the practice diffused quickly through transnational activist networks. Although specific tactics vary, Black Bloc contingents tend to wear black bandannas, black army surplus pants, black hooded sweatshirts, shiny black boots, and bandannas while carrying out targeted property destruction and defensive maneuvers, such as "de-arrests." Based on the aesthetics and practice of German *autonomen* (see Katsiaficas 2001), Black Blocs first appeared in the United States during anti–Gulf War protests in 1991. European Black Blocs have been more aggressive than their North American counterparts, viewing physical attacks against police as legitimate acts of resistance. The relationship between Black Blocs and other movement sectors has often been strained, involving an ongoing debate over protest violence (see chapter 5).

Indymedia

Media activists launched Indymedia to provide alternative news and information during the protests in Seattle. Activists covered events on the streets using various production formats and technologies, such as camcorders, web radio, streaming video, digital photography, and laptop journalism (Halleck 2002, 416). The IMC website received more than 1.5 million hits in its first week of operation, and the network has since spread to cities throughout the world.[10] Like the Internet and the larger movements of which it forms a part, the Indymedia network incorporates a horizontal networking logic. Each site is autonomous but remains connected to the global network for sharing ideas, resources, and information.

Rewind: A Genealogy of Anti–Corporate Globalization Activism

Although the WTO protests in Seattle took many casual observers by surprise, activists had been organizing against corporate globalization for years. The "antiglobalization movement" is actually a congeries of networks, practices, and ideas that came together to oppose a particular model of economic, social, and political organization. This complex articulation was made possible by the emergence of horizontal networking logics tied to the rise of

TABLE 2. Roots of anti–corporate globalization activism

Form of collective action	Time frame	Major activities	Contribution
Grassroots urban, peasant, and indigenous movements in the Global South	1970s to present	Austerity protests; actions and organizing against mining, oil drilling, dams, and other infrastructure projects; cross-border activism	Among first to challenge corporate globalization, front line of global struggles, grassroots base for transnational campaigns
Anticorporate activism	1990s to present	Student-based anti-sweatshop campaigns; anticorporate actions, protests, and boycotts; NGO-based research and public education; culture jamming and media activism	Focus on corporations as target, increased awareness of global division of labor and sweatshops, university activism, new media tactics
NGO and transna-tional advocacy networks, Northern civil society cam-paigns	1980s to present	Parallel forums and counter-summit protests; anti–free trade and multilateral development bank campaigns; research, education, and advocacy	Discursive critique of globalization, first to chal-lenge multilateral summits, resources and advocacy on behalf of grassroots groups, victories against free trade
Anarchist-inspired direct action	1970s to present	Direct-action protest against economic, environmental, and social injustice; nonviolent, creative, and militant tactics	Visibility, tactical and stra-tegic innovation, confronta-tional spirit, networking logics, creative use of media and new technologies
Zapatistas	1994 to present	Social netwar against Mexican government, grassroots autonomy in Chiapas, networking against globalization and neoliberalism	Inspiration, vision of global solidarity, new political language and model of or-ganizing, global networking and gatherings

informational capitalism. A brief historical overview of the diverse roots of anti–corporate globalization activism can thus help to shed light on how al-ternative political norms, forms, and practices have interacted in a context of rapid social, political, and technological change.[11]

IMF Riots and Southern Resource Struggles

The spread of structural adjustment in the 1970s and 1980s led to an explo-sion of popular protest throughout the Global South (see Walton and Sed-don 1994). Two-thirds of these austerity protests occurred in Latin America, increasing rapidly until 1985 and remaining steady during the nineties (106–7).[12] As Walton and Shefner (1994) suggest, "Before long, it was clear that the new phenomenon was an international protest wave—a recurring form consisting of large collective actions in opposition to state economic measures that stem from international pressures and aim at domestic market reforms to reduce foreign debt" (107). The Argentine financial crisis in 2001 sparked renewed anti-IMF sentiment in that country and throughout Latin America.

Grassroots indigenous and peasant movements have also arisen since the 1980s to challenge threats posed by mining and oil drilling, privatization, World Bank infrastructure projects, and genetically modified foods, while others have organized struggles for land reform.[13] Moreover, indigenous peoples such as the Ogoni in Nigeria, the U'wa in Colombia, and the Subanen in the Philippines have created links with organizations such as Amazon Watch, Rainforest Action Network, and Project Underground to forge both "transnational advocacy networks" (Keck and Sikkink 1998) and wider movements against multilateral institutions (cf. Fox and Brown 1998; O'Brien, Goetz, and Scholte 2000). In addition, powerful grassroots movements such as the Karnataka State Farmers in India and the Brazilian Landless Workers Movement (MST) helped found prominent anti–corporate globalization networks, including PGA, Via Campesina, and the WSF process.[14]

Student-Based Anticorporate Activism

In the late 1990s, U.S. students began staging protests, sit-ins, and other actions against the university apparel industry to protest against slave wages and atrocious working conditions in factories across the Global South. Anti-sweatshop activists later became active within emerging anti–corporate globalization networks, organizing teach-ins, World Bank bond boycott campaigns, and mass actions (Featherstone and United Students against Sweatshops 2002). The anti-sweatshop movement formed part of a broader wave of anticorporate activism, involving students and young people from around the world (see Klein 2000). During the same period, NGO networks such as U.S.-based Corp Watch, Corporate Europe Observatory in Amsterdam, and Corporate Watch in the United Kingdom began monitoring the harmful activities of transnational corporations. Meanwhile, political art groups such as Ad Busters started to organize guerrilla communication campaigns against corporate targets. By widening their focus, linking up with similar struggles, and joining mass actions against neoliberal capitalism, anticorporate activists helped spark the larger movement against corporate globalization.

NGO Campaigns against Structural Adjustment and Free Trade

For many activists, anti–corporate globalization activism began with a series of United Nations–related counterforums in the early 1990s, as well as civil society coalitions that formed to challenge multilateral institutions and free trade agreements around the same time. Indeed, NGO-based networks helped generate a discursive critique of economic globalization through alternative forums and conferences at the UN-sponsored World Summit for Children in 1990, the Rio Earth Summit in 1992, and the Beijing Conference on Women in 1995. Previously, economic justice, environmental, and human rights organizations had organized protests against the World Bank and IMF during the late 1980s, including a mass action in 1988 in Berlin (Fox and Brown 1998, 6; Gerhards and Rucht 1992). In 1994 a broad coalition of civil society actors founded Fifty Years Is Enough to mark the fiftieth anniversary of the Bretton Woods institutions. The new network organized a counterforum against the World Bank/IMF fall meetings in Madrid, which brought together activists from Europe, the United States, and the Global South.

Finally, citizen campaigns against free trade also helped pave the way for the anti-WTO protests in Seattle. Canadian activists led early campaigns against the General Agreement on Trade and Tariffs (GATT) and the U.S.-Canada Free Trade Area in the late 1980s, and U.S.-based coalitions, including Public Citizen's Global Trade Watch, the Sierra Club, Friends of the Earth, and United Auto Workers, organized against the North American Free Trade Agreement (NAFTA) in the early 1990s (Aaronson 2001, 118–19; see also Ayres 1998). The anti-NAFTA campaign generated a transnational alliance involving Mexican, Canadian, and U.S.-based activists, who used the Internet to link up with their counterparts elsewhere. This emerging global anti–free trade network, led by Public Citizen, the Council of Canadians, and the Third World Network, torpedoed the Multilateral Agreement on Investment (MAI) in 1996.[15] Two years later, activists and intellectuals founded the International Forum on Globalization (IFG), an alternative think tank that later expanded into a global network of organizations. IFG moved beyond the critique of free trade, introducing the concept "economic globalization" as a framework to unite diverse movements against neoliberalism (Lynch 1998, 155–56; Aaronson 2001, 173). Through publications, events, and forums, IFG helped develop and circulate a discourse challenging corporate globalization as a new phase of global economic and political organization.

Anarchist-Inspired Direct Action

Although NGO-based networks helped frame the globalization issue, produce insightful analyses, and organize transnational citizen campaigns, direct action caught the world's attention in Seattle. Direct action not only provided an effective protest strategy but helped infuse incipient anti–corporate globalization movements with a radical militancy and a decentralized, nonhierarchical form of organizing that corresponded to the cultural logic of networking I outlined in the introduction. As I argue in chapter 4, activists perform their networks during mass actions, reflecting competing political visions and organizational forms. The connections between norm, form, and technology are thus physically embodied through alternative direct-action practices.

The overall action strategy employed in Seattle came out of the U.S.-based "nonviolent direct-action movement," the radical wing of a series of struggles during the 1970s and 1980s, including antinuclear, peace, ecology, gay rights, and Central American solidarity movements (Epstein 1991, 1). Direct-action activists adapted the organizing model developed by the Quaker-based Movement for a New Society, combining civil disobedience in the spirit of Gandhi and Martin Luther King with consensus decision making and an affinity group structure inspired by the Iberian Anarchist Federation (Bookchin 2004; Kubrin 2001). Key organizers in Seattle, some of whom went on to provide direct-action training at countersummits in Europe, North America, and South America, had gained crucial experience in this earlier wave of protest.

Specific tactics employed in Seattle and subsequent actions have their own trajectories. Many lockdown, occupation, and banner-hang techniques came out of the radical environmental movement, particularly Earth First!, while groups such as Greenpeace and the Rainforest Action Network pioneered the staging of spectacular image events (DeLuca 1999). In 1995, environmental activists founded the Ruckus Society, which has trained thousands of activists in direct-action tactics and has sponsored camps to prepare for antiglobalization protests in North America. Meanwhile, political art groups such as Art and Revolution helped organize giant puppets and street theater in Seattle. Founded during an anarchist "convergence" at the 1996 Democratic National Convention in Chicago, Art and Revolution went on to help organize PGA Global Days of Action, starting with the anti-G8 protests in Birmingham in May 1998.[16]

Mass urban occupations and festive street party protests were most thoroughly developed in Britain, where Earth First! played a major role. Earth First! was established in the United Kingdom in 1991, operating as a decentralized network and thus helping to diffuse a horizontal networking logic throughout the British direct-action scene. During the early nineties, Earth First! UK spearheaded the anti-roads movement, which sought to stop the construction of major highways throughout Britain. The anti-roads movement brought environmentalists into contact with a do-it-yourself (DIY) counterculture involving antiauthoritarian punks, ravers, squatters, and New Age travelers (McKay 1998). DIY culture emphasized self-organization, action, festive resistance, reclaiming public space, and the innovative use of new digital technologies such as the Internet, camcorders, and digital sound systems to create independent media and computer-organized rave parties.

Activists organized the first anti-roads protest in 1992 against the M3 highway extension at Twyford Down, building a rural autonomous zone and direct-action camp. Similar protests spread throughout the United Kingdom, involving lockdowns, sabotage, tree-sits, and tunneling to stop road construction (Wall 1999, 65–87; see also Jordan 1998; McDonald 2006). In 1995, anti-roads campaigners tried to stop the M11 in east London, bringing ecological struggles to an urban social context. The police finally cleared the protest site, where activists had blocked the construction zone by hanging from large nets while their supporters danced to rave music, following a dramatic four-day standoff. That experience led to the rebirth of Reclaim the Streets (RTS), which organized impromptu street parties throughout the late 1990s against corporate-dominated consumer society, drawing thousands of people in London and other cities in the United Kingdom (Jordan 1998, 139–40).[17] In February 1998, RTS became a European convener of PGA and helped conceive the first Global Day of Action in May 1998. Since then, anti–corporate globalization activists have organized RTS street parties around the world in cities such as New York, San Francisco, and Barcelona (Chesters and Welsh 2004, 328).

Militant forms of direct action, including Black Bloc or Tute Bianchi (White Overalls) tactics, are rooted in the tradition of European autonomous Marxism (Katsiaficas 1997).[18] In Italy, the "Invisibles" collective in Rome first used White Overalls during an action in 1997, inspired by the Zapatista idea of bringing visibility to hidden struggles. A year later, the Milan-based Ya Basta! combined White Overalls with foam, inner tubes, and heavy padding during a migrant detention center protest in Trieste.[19] Together with a broader network of squatted social centers, Ya Basta! decided to continue using the Tute Bianchi symbol, developing a unique form of action where orderly blocs of protesters wearing white overalls, rubber tubes, foam padding, shinguards, and masks or goggles advance behind large plastic shields toward heavily armed police lines, where they initiate "nonviolent" contact (della Porta et al. 2006, 135). Activists push, but do not punch, kick, use weapons, or throw stones. In 1999, Ya Basta! helped organize a twenty-thousand-person "siege" of a detention center in Milan, involving nearly four thousand White Overalls (Ya Basta! 2001, 187–88), before achieving worldwide recognition during protests against the World Bank and IMF in Prague in September 2000 (see also Hardt and Negri 2004, 264–67).[20]

The autonomist tradition in Germany took a more aggressive turn as German squatters who had previously been active in movements against nuclear power, the arms race, patriarchy, and urban speculation forged a broad movement for autonomy based on antiauthoritarianism, decentralization, self-management, direct action, and independence from political parties (see Katsiaficas 1997). German autonomen often engaged in pitched street battles with police during anti-eviction actions, wearing black, military-style attire, which inspired the use of similar styles and tactics among anarchists in the United States and radical squatters around Europe. Militant anarchists and autonomists have continued to organize Black Blocs during anti–corporate globalization mobilizations, including Seattle, Prague, and Genoa (see chapter 5).[21]

The Zapatista Uprising

Many radicals trace the origins of anti–corporate globalization activism to the Zapatistas, who introduced what was widely perceived as a new kind of revolution based on grassroots participation from below as opposed to capturing state power. Indeed, the Zapatistas invented a new political language, leaving behind the age-old imagery of the proletariat and calling instead for global solidarity based on diversity and autonomy. In addition, their emphasis on consultations, or "asking as we walk," foreshadowed the widespread concern with directly democratic process and horizontal relations among anti–corporate globalization activists. Zapatista solidarity networks were also among the first to use new digital technologies to facilitate an innovative model of organizing involving locally rooted, yet globally linked, struggles as network technologies, norms, and forms increasingly coincided.[22]

The EZLN (Zapatista National Liberation Army) rose up on January 1, 1994, the same day NAFTA went into effect. Although fighting against political and economic exploitation of the Mayan Indians, the Zapatistas understood that free trade agreements, and neoliberalism more generally, contributed to the dire situation in Chiapas (Nash 2001). Twelve days later, the EZLN signed a cease-fire agreement with Mexican president Carlos Salinas. The Zapatista rebellion was not a traditional insurgency, but rather a prime-time media event, constituting what Manuel Castells (1997, 72) has called the "first informational guerrilla movement." Moreover, although Zapatista leaders initially envisioned a classic guerrilla struggle, they were transformed through their interaction with the Mayan communities of Chiapas and the NGOs and human rights groups that descended on the region to support the uprising. Within days, a global network of Zapatista support groups had formed, using phones, fax machines, and the Internet to share updates and information (Cleaver 1995). The EZLN spokesman Subcomandante Marcos proved adept at transforming these digital networks into an arena for instantly circulating communiqués around the world, generating a modern-day "social netwar" (Ronfeldt and Arquilla 1998).[23]

Significantly, the Zapatista uprising began a long chain of events culminating with the anti-WTO protests in Seattle. In January 1996, the Zapatistas sent out a call for a series of intercontinental encounters to challenge neoliberalism and begin forming a global network of resistance. Coordinated via e-mail and several face-to-face meetings, the first Intercontinental Gathering against Neoliberalism and for Humanity brought three thousand participants to the Lacandon jungle in 1996 (Cleaver 1998, 630). Activists organized a second intercontinental Zapatista encounter the following year in Spain, attracting four thousand activists from around the world, including indigenous people and farmers. During a workshop on agriculture and land struggles, various grass-roots movements, including the Zapatistas, the MST, and the Karnataka State Farmers, launched the idea for a global network to fight free trade. This led to the first PGA conference in Geneva in February 1998, which involved roughly three hundred delegates from seventy-one countries around the world.[24]

At the Geneva conference, activists decided to call for the first Global Day of Action against Capitalism on May 16, 1998, in conjunction with the G8 summit in Birmingham, and just two days before the WTO ministerial in Geneva. In early May, hundreds of thousands of peasant farmers in Hyder-abad demanded India's withdrawal from the WTO, and on May 15, ten thou-sand fisherfolk marched against the WTO in Manila. On May 16, five thousand people took part in a mobile street party against the G8 in Birmingham, while Reclaim the Streets parties were held in cities around the globe, including Helsinki, Finland, San Francisco, Toronto, Brussels, Lyon, Berlin, and Prague. Just days later, more than ten thousand converged on Geneva from all over Europe to protest against the WTO. In addition to the peaceful marches, activ-ists smashed bank windows, overturned the WTO director's car, and clashed with the police. Three days of rioting ensued, creating images of tear-gas filled streets that would be repeated a year later in Seattle.[25]

In spring 1999, PGA organized the Inter-continental Caravan for Solidar-ity and Resistance, bringing five hundred farmers, city dwellers, and activ-ists from India and other parts of the Global South to Europe for a series of protests, meetings, and debates. The Karnataka State Farmers promoted the project in South Asia, while European anarchists, punks, squatters, peaceniks, feminists, immigrant rights supporters, and anti-GMO activists organized the logistics on the ground, helping to consolidate an emerging PGA network in Europe (Cucci 2001, 475). The final days of the caravan coincided with the second PGA-coordinated Global Day of Action on June 18, 1999, (J18) against global financial and business centers during the G8 summit in Cologne. Se-attle became the third Global Day of Action just five months later when the overwhelming success of J18 encouraged U.S.-based activists to shut down the WTO. John Jordan, a London-based activist and artist, later recalled, "On that cold misty new years day in 1994, when the Zapatista rebels surged out of the mountains and jungles of Chiapas to occupy the towns, they probably had little idea their local revolt would eventually transform itself into the beginnings of a global revolution. No one realized that the breath of inspiration would travel so far so quickly. No one believed that so many different people and cultures could share their struggles so easily."[26]

Anti–Corporate Globalization Movements Develop and Expand

After Seattle, activists who had been instrumental in coordinating the direct action began traveling throughout the United States to help organize local DAN chapters in cities such as San Francisco, Chicago, New York, and Los Angeles, giving rise to a loosely organized continental DAN structure. Although the continental DAN was difficult to sustain, local DANs flourished in many cities, particularly where there had been weak activist infrastructures, providing physical and virtual spaces for activists from diverse movements to converge around common actions and campaigns. Similar networking processes began to emerge around the world, including RCADE, and later MRG, in Spain, while global and European PGA networks continued to expand. At the same time, Indymedia blossomed into a global alternative news and information project. Beyond providing communication tools, these decentralized network architectures allowed activists to coordinate across space without central command, reflecting their broader egalitarian ideals.

At the same time, anti–corporate globalization movements largely developed through the generation of mass-mediated images and affective ties during mass mobilizations and actions. Seattle not only energized networking processes around the world, it provided a new model for future mass mobilizations against multilateral financial and political institutions. Before the anti-WTO protests had concluded, plans were already in the works for protests against the World Bank and IMF in Washington, D.C., the following April 16 (A16), while European activists were busy planning a response to the World Bank and IMF fall meetings scheduled for Prague that September. The flurry of electronic activity that facilitated organizing for the Seattle protests moved over to a new national Listserv to coordinate A16, and new e-mail lists would soon be up and running to plan for the summer 2000 mobilizations against the Republican National Convention in Philadelphia and the Democratic National Convention in Los Angeles. Meanwhile, European-based activists created a series of English-language Listservs in early May 2000 to plan for Prague.

TABLE 3. Major anti–corporate globalization protests and events, May 1999 to July 2007

Event	Place	Date	Significance
Protest against G8 Summit in Birmingham (1st PGA Global Day of Action)	Decentralized	May 16, 1998 (M16)	Thousands participate in "Reclaim the Streets" parties in Birmingham and around the world; 10,000 converge on Geneva ten days later to protest against the WTO
Protest against G8 Summit in Cologne (2nd PGA Global Day of Action)	Decentralized	June 18, 1999 (J18)	Tens of thousands take part in protests against global financial and business centers around world, including mass action in City of London
Protest against WTO (3rd PGA Global Day of Action)	Seattle	Nov. 30, 1999 (N30)	50,000 shut down the WTO; largest U.S. anti–corporate globalization protest; anti–corporate globalization networks energized around the world
Protest against World Bank/IMF	Washington	Apr. 16, 2000 (A16)	First action in cycle against World Bank and IMF; draws 25,000 protesters
Protest against Republican National Convention	Philadelphia	July 31–Aug. 3, 2000 (R2K)	Tens of thousands denounce influence of corporate money on democratic process; convergence center raided by police; random arrests
Protest against Democratic National Convention	Los Angeles	Aug. 14–17, 2000 (D2K)	Similar themes as R2K; emphasis on mobilizing grassroots activists of color; massive police presence
Protest against World Bank and IMF	Prague, Czech Republic	Sept. 26, 2000 (S26)	15,000 protesters organized into color-coded blocs shut down the World Bank/IMF meeting a day early; leads to anti–corporate globalization boom in Europe, particularly in Spain and Catalonia

TABLE 3. (continued)

Event	Place	Date	Significance
Protest against European Union (EU)	Nice, France	Dec. 6–7, 2000	Draws 75,000, including strong presence of NGOs, trade unions, and traditional Left; Catalans organize several buses from Barcelona
World Social Forum (WSF)	Porto Alegre, Brazil	Jan. 25–30, 2001	Space for developing, discussing, and sharing alternatives; first WSF draws 20,000 participants
Protest against Free Trade Area of the Americas (FTAA) Summit	Quebec City, Quebec (Canada)	Apr. 20–21, 2001	Largest anti–corporate globalization action in North America (80,000); police "wall of shame"; activists divide protest into color-coded blocs for diverse tactics
Protest against EU	Gothenburg, Sweden	June 14–16, 2001	25,000 protesters; police use live ammunition; protester shot in back and left in coma
Protest against World Bank	Barcelona, Catalonia (Spain)	June 22–25, 2001	First major anti–corporate globalization mobilization in Spain and Catalonia; World Bank conference canceled; unity march ends in massive police attack
Protest against G8	Genoa, Italy	July 19–21, 2001	80,000 protesters in July 20 siege; 300,000 march the following day; police violence unprecedented, leaving 600 injured and a protester shot dead; public sympathy for movement spreads
WSF II	Porto Alegre, Brazil	Jan. 31–Feb. 4, 2002	70,000 participants; same time as anti–World Economic Forum protest in New York
Protest against EU	Barcelona, Catalonia (Spain)	Mar. 15–16, 2002	500,000 protesters in unity march against EU on Mar. 16; largest anti–corporate globalization protest to date

Continued on next page

TABLE 3. (continued)

Event	Place	Date	Significance
Protest against FTAA	Quito, Ecuador	Oct. 27–Nov. 1, 2002	Indigenous people and peasants march on Quito from four directions; mass protest draws 30,000
European Social Forum (ESF)	Florence, Italy	Nov. 6–10, 2002	First ESF draws 60,000 participants; march against war in Iraq mobilizes nearly one million
Asian Social Forum	Hyderabad, India	Jan. 2–7, 2003	Among first regional forums outside Europe; helps solidify India's place as site for fourth WSF
WSF III	Porto Alegre, Brazil	Jan. 23–27, 2003	Draws 100,000 participants; features opening-day address by Luiz Inácio Lula da Silva, newly elected president from the leftist Workers Party
Protest against G8	Evian, Switzerland	June 1–3, 2003	Hundreds of thousands of protesters descend on border of Switzerland and France to protest against corporate globalization and the war in Iraq
Protest against WTO	Cancún, Mexico	Sept. 9–13, 2003	Draws thousands of protesters from Mexico, the United States, and around the world; suicide of Korean farmer Lee Kyung Hae
ESF II	Paris	Nov. 6–10, 2003	Attracts 50,000 participants, and 150,000 for final march and rally
Protest against FTAA	Miami	Nov. 17–21, 2003	Draws thousands of U.S.-based activists; heavy police repression
WSF IV	Mumbai, India	Jan. 16–21, 2004	WSF takes place outside Porto Alegre for first time; 125,000 participants
Social Forum of the Americas	Quito, Ecuador	July 25–30, 2004	First ever Social Forum of the Americas; 10,000 participants

TABLE 3. (continued)

Event	Place	Date	Significance
Protest against Republican National Convention	New York	Aug. 29–Sept. 4, 2004	Nearly 500,000 antiwar, anti–corporate globalization, and social justice activists march against Republican National Convention
ESF III	London	Oct. 15–17, 2004	25,000 participants, 100,000 join final march; radicals organize autonomous spaces
WSF V	Porto Alegre, Brazil	Jan. 26–31, 2005	Largest WSF to date (150,000 delegates), organized in a more decentralized and grassroots manner than previous events
Protest against G8	Gleneagles, Scotland	July 2–7, 2005	Thousands of protesters swarm heavily fortified summit on July 6
WSF VI	Bamako, Mali / Caracas, Venezuela / Karachi, Pakistan	Jan. 19–23, / Jan. 24–29, / Mar. 24–29, 2006	First "Polycentric" WSF, held in three cities over a three-month period; draws tens of thousands of participants
ESF IV	Athens, Greece	May 4–7, 2006	35,000 participants; more than 100,000 join final antiwar march
Protest against G8	St. Petersburg, Russia	July 15–17, 2006	First major anti–corporate globalization mobilization in Russia
WSF VII	Nairobi, Kenya	Jan. 20–25, 2007	Draws fewer participants (50,000) and has strong NGO presence, but is the first WSF held in Africa
Protest against G8	Heiligendamm, Germany	June 1–8, 2007	Tens of thousands march against the G8 on June 2; thousands participate in blockades on June 7–8, the largest mass action in years
U.S Social Forum (USSF)	Atlanta, Georgia	June 27–July 1, 2007	15,000 participants take part in the first USSF, one of the most diverse forums on race and class

Over the next few years, these virtual networks would expand and become physically embodied through a series of mass actions, countersummits, and forums.

Washington, D.C., April 16, 2000 (World Bank/IMF)

The a16 mobilization brought twenty-five thousand activists to Washington, D.C., to protest against the World Bank and imf. Coming on the heels of Seattle, a16 involved a significant drop in numbers, yet still represented a major change from the previous year, when a Fifty Years Is Enough action drew only twenty-five protesters (Danaher 2001, 7). The Mobilization for Global Justice, which organized the protest, was an extremely diverse coalition, although labor played a smaller role than in Seattle. Activists again adopted an affinity group, consensus-based organizing model and set for themselves a similar goal: "shut the meetings down." However, the police were prepared this time, and protesters failed to block the summit. Still, they brought thousands of people to the streets and caused widespread gridlock. Although the media called a16 a tactical failure, protesters managed to garner significant press coverage. Moreover, the former World Bank economist Joseph Stiglitz publicly supported activist demands, while World Bank and imf officials were largely on the defensive. Although widespread violence was avoided, a16 marked an increase in selective repression, including targeted surveillance and random arrests.

Prague, Czech Republic, September 26, 2000 (World Bank/IMF)

Prague was a key turning point, helping to strengthen and expand emerging antiglobalization activist networks in Europe and other parts of the world, as nearly fifteen thousand protesters succeeded in disrupting the World Bank/imf meetings. Moreover, roughly one thousand activists traveled to Prague from Catalonia and Spain. U.S.-based organizers played a key role in organizing the direct action; providing training in consensus process, nonviolent direct action, and affinity group formation; and establishing a local Indymedia center. Activists divided the action terrain into three color-coded zones, which allowed for a diversity of tactics, a strategy that would be reproduced at future protests (see chapter 4). When the meetings were canceled a day early, protesters declared Prague the "Seattle of Europe." More importantly, activists made new connections, expanding their networks around the continent.

Nice, France, December 6–7, 2000 (European Union)

Seventy-five thousand protesters descended on Nice to challenge the neoliberal policies of the European Council. Whereas Prague had involved mostly radical grassroots activists, in Nice labor unions, political parties, and NGO networks played important roles. The European Confederation of Syndicates (CES); the European Marches against Unemployment, Job Insecurity and Social Exclusions; ATTAC; and other forces of the traditional Left dominated the mass march, while the police brutally repressed the much smaller direct action the following day with tear gas and rubber bullets. Moreover, the Schengen agreements were suspended before the protests, and authorities retained 1,500 Italians at the French-Italian border. Catalan activists organized several buses from Barcelona, including a strong contingent of labor and political party militants.

Porto Alegre, January 25–30, 2001 (World Social Forum I)

The World Social Forum (WSF) provided a space for diverse movements and networks around the world to discuss, share, and develop concrete alternatives to corporate globalization. Held concurrently with the World Economic Forum, an annual gathering of global political and economic elites in Davos, the first WSF attracted more than twelve thousand participants. Building on the momentum created during the previous summer and the widespread opposition to increasing U.S. militarism around the world, the second edition[27] of the WSF surpassed all expectations, bringing almost seventy thousand people to Porto Alegre. The 2002 WEF was held in New York both as a symbolic statement of strength after the terrorist attacks of September 11, 2001, and because Swiss officials were eager to avoid mass protests. Still reeling from the recent terrorist attacks, U.S.-based networks managed to organize a demonstration and counterforum, which drew ten thousand protesters and surprisingly positive media coverage. The social forum process has since emerged as a broad global network largely dominated by NGOs, unions, and the traditional Left. Whereas mass actions are more confrontational in nature and are often dominated by radical sectors, the social forums involve a much wider array of groups and are primarily oriented toward constructive dialogue and debate.

Quebec City, Canada, April 20–22, 2001 (FTAA)

During the third Summit of the Americas, held in Quebec City from April 20 to 22, 2001, thirty-four heads of state met to discuss implementation of the Free Trade Area of the Americas (FTAA), which would extend NAFTA to the entire Western Hemisphere, creating the largest free trade zone in the world. Activists pointed to NAFTA's record, arguing that the FTAA would widen inequality between and within countries while harming the environment, human rights, health, education, and labor. Still, the FTAA provided an unprecedented opportunity for building strong multisector, cross-border social movement networks. A broad coalition of NGOs, community-based organizations, and radical networks organized the Quebec City mobilization, including the anarchist-inspired Anti-Capitalist Convergence. Direct-action activists followed the Prague strategy, establishing distinct color-coded zones for different levels of confrontation. The police erected a 3.8-kilometer-long "wall of shame" around the old city, a containment strategy that would be repeated in Genoa. More than eighty thousand protesters turned out for the mass action, the largest anti–corporate globalization action ever organized in North America.

Gothenburg, Sweden, June 14–16, 2001 (European Union), and Barcelona,
Catalonia (Spain), June 22–25, 2001 (World Bank)

The center of gravity among anti–corporate globalization activists shifted to Europe in 2001. Activists organized massive protests and countersummits in Gothenburg, Barcelona, and Genoa, while temporary border camps were set up in cities around Europe, including Tarifa, Spain; Bialystok, Poland; and Frankfurt.[28] Indeed, European activists referred to the summer protest season as "Freedom Summer." The first major antiglobalization action of the season took place in Gothenburg from June 14 to 16, where twenty-five thousand people came from around Europe to protest against the European Union. The police fired live ammunition for the first time, and a protester was shot in the back and left in a coma. European leaders insisted that continuing disruptions of important international meetings would not be tolerated.

Shortly after Prague, Catalan activists began planning for protests against a World Bank development conference scheduled for Barcelona in June 2001. The Prague action had received a great deal of media coverage around the Spanish state. The response in Spain and Catalonia to MRG's initial call for new protests against the World Bank was overwhelming among NGOs, network-based movements, and the traditional Left. Activists forged a broad unitary campaign called Barcelona 2001, which became the basis for the state-wide campaign against the European Union the following spring. Fearing major confrontation, the World Bank canceled its scheduled conference, but the mobilizations continued. Hundreds of civil society organizations signed on to the campaign manifesto, and the final demonstration drew more than forty thousand people. The march ended in a violent police attack against thousands of peaceful protesters, continuing the spiral of repression that had begun in Gothenburg.

Genoa, Italy, July 19–21, 2001 (G8)

Genoa was the largest and most confrontational anti–corporate globalization mobilization to date. Nearly eighty thousand protesters took part in a "siege of the red zone" on July 20 and the next day roughly three hundred thousand protesters turned out for the march against the G8. Altogether, three days of protest left more than one thousand people injured (Gubitosa 2003, 177ff., cited in della Porta et al. 2006, 5) and a young anarchist shot dead. The level of police violence was unprecedented, including indiscriminate attacks with tear gas and rubber bullets, beatings, agents provocateurs, a vicious midnight raid, and widespread prison torture (see chapter 5). As in Quebec, a large no-protest red zone was created, surrounded on all sides by a large metal fence, while the "battlefield" was divided into distinct zones to accommodate diverse tactics, including a festive Pink and Silver March, Black Blocs, a "Gandhian" sit-in, and a ten-thousand-person-strong White Overalls action. Beyond the extraordinary violence, Genoa represented a major turning point, particularly in Europe, where the movement gained widespread sympathy among broad sectors of the public. Moreover, the Genoa Social Forum (GSF) provided a model for other social forum networks, extending the WSF process to local and regional levels.

Barcelona, Catalonia (Spain), March 15–16, 2002 (European Union)

Nearly a half million protesters took to the streets on March 16 to protest against the European Union behind the slogan "Against the Europe of Capital."

Building on the strong local networks developed during the Barcelona 2001 campaign against the World Bank as well as the momentum from the WSF, organizers put together a decentralized day of actions, a video series and counterforum, an outdoor concert, and the demonstration itself. The militarization of the city and campaign to criminalize protesters on the part of the right-wing government backfired, as Catalans of all stripes came out overwhelmingly to show their support. Catalan Socialists even gave in to widespread pressure, giving their members the green light to join moderate protesters, who marched behind the banner "Another Europe Is Possible." In Spain and Catalonia, the anti–corporate globalization movement had become high-stakes politics indeed (see chapter 3).

Global Antiwar Movements and the Social Forum Process

European movements entered a submerged phase during summer 2002, as activists turned toward local organizing and consolidating their networks. Many European activists focused on the first edition of the European Social Forum (ESF) in Florence. Meanwhile, radicals concentrated on the Strasbourg Border Camp in July, which brought several thousand activists to a temporary encampment on the Rhine, and the second European PGA conference in Leiden, Holland, in late August and early September. During these encounters, radicals began discussing how to position themselves vis-à-vis the social forum process, while a growing sense had emerged that mass actions were becoming less effective and that it was time to start achieving tangible victories.

The first European Social Forum (ESF) was held in Florence in early November 2002, drawing sixty thousand people from around Europe (see della Porta et al. 2006). The final march against the Iraq war brought nearly one million to the streets of Florence, as antiwar and anti–corporate globalization movements converged. The second ESF was held in Paris in November 2003, involving 50,000 participants and 100,000 protesters at the final march. Finally, the third and fourth editions of the ESF drew 25,000 and 35,000 delegates to London and Athens respectively and 100,000 in each case at the final marches. Meanwhile, in June 2003, hundreds of thousands of anti–corporate globalization and antiwar activists descended on the border of France and Switzerland to protest against the G8 summit in Evian. Although European movements have largely shifted their focus toward the forum process, mass actions still play an important, if less central, role. For example, activists organized a rebel clown army during the heavily fortified G8 summit meetings in Scotland in July 2005, and Russian activists protested against the G8 in St. Petersburg the following year.

Activists have also organized regional social forums in Latin America and Asia. In October 2002, the Latin American Social Forum was held in Quito, including a mass march against the FTAA, which mobilized thirty thousand people, largely from rural indigenous and peasant communities. A few months later, in January 2003, the first Asian Social Forum was organized in Hyderabad, India. Activists have since held local and regional forums around the world, leading to the emergence of a truly global process. Moreover, the WSF itself has continued to grow in numbers and geographic reach. The third edition of the forum in Porto Alegre drew 100,000 activists and featured a massive opening-day address by newly elected president from the leftist Workers Party, Luiz Inácio Lula da Silva. The fourth WSF moved to Mumbai, India, where 125,000 people attended, and the fifth edition returned to Porto Alegre, expanding to 150,000 participants. In 2006 the WSF was organized in a "polycentric" fashion at three sites: Bamako, Mali; Caracas, Venezuela; and Karachi, Pakistan. Following the 2007 edition of the forum, which took place in Nairobi, Kenya, the WSF has shifted to a biannual format, with a decentralized "Global Day of Mobilization" envisioned during off years.[29]

U.S.-Based Movements after September 11, 2001

Meanwhile, anti–corporate globalization movements in the United States, which were severely disrupted by the shock of the September 11 attacks, finally began to recover during fall 2003. Many U.S.-based activists helped organize the direct action in Cancún against the WTO in September, which drew thousands of protesters, largely from Mexico. Trade talks collapsed again when a bloc of developing nations led by Brazil held out for greater concessions on the part of the United States. The protests will be remembered most for the dramatic suicide of the Korean farmer Lee Kyung Hae, who plunged a knife into his heart toward the end of a march of fifteen thousand indigenous people, farmers, and youths. Leader of the Korean Federation of Advanced Farmers Association, Lee had staged a hunger strike earlier that year at the

WTO headquarters in Geneva to protest the impact of WTO policies on his homeland. Several thousand North American anti–corporate globalization activists then converged to protest against the FTAA that November in Miami, where they faced an increased level of police repression. In August 2004, anti–corporate globalization and antiwar activists protested against the Republican National Convention in New York. Most recently, U.S.-based anti–corporate globalization activists and community-based organizations held the first U.S. Social Forum in Atlanta in the summer of 2007.

Conclusion: Defining and Mapping the Field

Rather than a single, unified movement, anti–corporate globalization activism involves a congeries of overlapping networks, each with its own particular history, political vision, and organizational forms. These sectors converge during mass mobilizations and within more sustained networking processes. Anti–corporate globalization movements thus involve several distinctive features. First, specific networks are locally rooted, yet *globally* connected. Coordinating and communicating through transnational networks, activists have engaged in institutional politics, including global campaigns to defeat the MAI or abolish the external debt, and extra-institutional strategies, such as Global Days of Action, international forums, and cross-border information sharing. Perhaps most importantly, activists *think* of themselves as belonging to global movements, discursively linking local events to diverse struggles elsewhere (cf. Seidman 2000). Anti–corporate globalization movements have thus emerged as transnational fields of meaning, where images, discourses, and tactics flow from one continent to another via global communication circuits.

Second, anti–corporate globalization movements are highly *mediated*. Despite emerging in different cultural contexts, various protest tactics all produce highly visible, theatrical images for mass-mediated consumption, including giant puppets and street theater, mobile carnivals (Reclaim the Streets), spectacular protest involving white outfits, protective shields, and padding (White Overalls), and militant attacks against the symbols of corporate capitalism (Black Bloc). Moreover, the horizontal, directly democratic process through which actions are organized, which involves decentralized coordination among autonomous affinity groups, as well as the prevailing "diversity of tactics" ethic, embodies the broader cultural logic of networking itself.

Third, more radical sectors view social transformation as an ongoing collective process. Rather than messianic visions or an already established project, radicals emphasize continuous elaboration and day-to-day practices. The interactive nature of new digital technologies is thus reflected in the rise of new political visions combining elements of anarchism, an emphasis on internal democracy and autonomy, and a commitment to openness and horizontal collaboration. Meetings, protests, actions camps, and other anti–corporate globalization gatherings thus provide spaces for experiencing and experimenting with direct democracy, grassroots participation, and alternative forms of embodied sociality within daily social life (cf. McDonald 2006).

Finally, anti–corporate globalization movements are organized as flexible, decentralized *networks*, including more hierarchical circle patterns, intermediate wheel formations, and more decentralized all-channel configurations (cf. Kapferer 1973). Real-time global activist networking is made possible by the emergence of new digital technologies, which facilitate coordination and communication among small-scale, autonomous units. Moreover, the network has also emerged as a widespread cultural ideal among radical sectors, reflecting the traditional values of anarchism and the logic of computer networking. Indeed, network norms, forms, and technologies increasingly mirror one another, as local networks can now link up without compromising their autonomy and specificity.

With respect to movement actors, the anti–corporate globalization field involves four competing spaces. First, *institutional movements* operate within formal democratic structures, aiming to establish social democracy or socialism at the national or global level. This sector primarily involves political parties, trade unions, and large NGOs organized around traditional command logics and representative structures. Second, *critical sectors* include movements that are populist in tone, internationalist in scope, and radical in orientation and that aim to build a global civil society. These include small NGOs, citizen campaigns, and far leftist currents, including Marxists and Trotskyists. Although these actors are often committed to bottom-up organizing, they tend to favor centralized coordination over horizontal, networked collaboration.

Whereas institutional movements and critical sectors involve traditional organizational practices and forms, *radical network-based movements* emphasize autonomy, direct democracy, and horizontal coordination. Reflecting an emerging networking logic, formations such as MRG, PGA, and the Zapatistas have generated new utopian visions of political and social interaction based on global coordination among diverse local struggles.[30] These networks have most clearly articulated the increasing confluence among network norms, forms, and technologies. Finally, *autonomous movements*, including militant squatters and certain indigenous and poor people's movements, primarily emphasize local forms of struggle (see Starr and Adams 2004) but sometimes engage in transnational networking. These movements are staunchly anticapitalist, assuming a posture of direct confrontation with, and working toward solutions beyond, the market and state.[31]

Despite their differences, activists within each sector are struggling to regain democratic control over their daily lives, wresting it back from transnational corporations and global financial elites. If social movements are signs that announce the existence of a conflict, as Melucci (1989) contends, anti–corporate globalization movements point to a democratic deficit in the current regime of globalization, where the market has become disembedded from society (Polanyi 1957). What makes contemporary anti–corporate globalization movements unique is their ability to coordinate across vast distances and high levels of diversity and difference, overcoming many of the political and geographic obstacles that stymied mass movements in the past. Indeed, emerging networking logics have reinforced political models based on horizontal coordination, open access, and direct democracy. Although these principles are sometimes violated in practice, often resulting in heated micro-level political struggles, broader networking logics and ideals have helped give rise to ongoing experimentation with new digital technologies, organizational structures, and radically democratic norms. Precisely how these diverse spheres interact will be explored in the chapters to come.

2

When Seattle happened in 1999, everyone thought, "Wow . . . people are taking back the streets!" There would soon be more opportunities; all this could be globalized. When the World Bank came we had our chance to do something here. Before that many of us had gone to Prague. We were becoming part of what we had seen on TV, building the antiglobalization movement, making it ours. This was our way of feeling part of history, making it together.[1]

ANTI–CORPORATE GLOBALIZATION SOLDIERS IN BARCELONA

Late one evening in September 2002, three months after the campaign against the World Bank had concluded, I sat down for a round of beers and tapas with a half-dozen activists from MRG and RCADE. We had just finished another marathon meeting—this time about creating a new squatted activist social center in the heart of Barcelona. After wandering through a maze of streets and alleys, we settled on a run-down bar not far from the world-renowned Palau de la Música. Regardless of how long the official meetings lasted, there was always an eager group of *colegas* ready to continue discussing the important issues of the day in a more intimate setting. Such tightknit friendship networks—a typical Spanish and Catalan institution—provided the social glue that kept more far-flung social movement networks together.[2] On this evening, we were debating whether or not Catalan anti–corporate globalization networks were stronger in the outlying pueblos surrounding Barcelona precisely because they facilitated stronger interpersonal ties. Indeed, this concern had led to the initial proposal for building a new squatted social center in Barcelona, which would provide a space where activists from RCADE and MRG could gather.

The collective discussion soon gave way to individual conversations, and I found myself chatting with Pascual. As I devoured olives and sipped from my *caña* (a small glass of beer), he explained that he had previously helped build a social center in Gracia, a neighborhood with a long history of anarchist *ateneos populares*, community spaces during the early 1900s that housed political debates, educational forums about issues such as women's rights, vegetarianism, and free love, and a variety of cultural events (A. Smith 2002, 32). Pascual viewed such ateneos as an important model for present-day projects. When I asked him why he was so committed to building activist social centers, he replied, "Because I'm an anarchist, and we have to create our own institutions! If the antiglobalization movement can do that, we'll be unstoppable!"

I was initially taken aback by his resoluteness, but I soon came to realize Pascual was passionate about almost everything he did. Although he did not believe in states, for example, he was firmly committed to Catalan "self-determination," and like so many young Catalan activists, he was a staunch supporter of grassroots struggles in the Global South, having worked with a community-based project in Nicaragua. Above all, Pascual believed in the right of people to collectively forge their own destinies, free from the constraints of the market and state. He saw anti–corporate globalization activism as a logical extension of his dedication to anarchism, Catalan autonomy, and global solidarity. I was also struck that evening by his powerful sense of historical destiny—that somehow we were reliving Barcelona's revolutionary past. For Pascual, the repression he had experienced during the June anti–World Bank protest was just a small taste of future battles to come. But he was not entirely convinced. When I suggested that authorities did not *really* view us as such a threat, he ironically replied by citing a headline from the Spanish papers, "Of course they do; we are the 'antiglobalization soldiers'!"

Since the first PGA Global Days of Action, Barcelona-based activists have played key roles within emerging anti–corporate globalization networks. Militant squatters and solidarity activists spearheaded early organizing efforts in Catalonia, but diverse political forces became involved after Prague, including traditional Marxists and institutional actors. Barcelona-based activists often share strikingly similar visions regarding politics, technology, and organization as their counterparts elsewhere. This can be partly explained by the increasing connections and forms of organization facilitated by the Internet, particularly among younger activists influenced by the global circulation of images, ideas, and tactics related to autonomy, grassroots resistance, direct action, and horizontal networking. Moreover, many European and U.S.-based activists and NGO workers had come into contact during previous solidarity projects and gatherings in places such as Nicaragua, Chiapas, Guatemala, Brazil, and other political hotbeds, particularly in Latin America. Meanwhile, the presence of a similar range of movement actors in so many countries suggests that during the late 1990s "antiglobalization" had emerged as a powerful transnational "master frame" (Snow and Benford 1992), providing a magnet attracting diverse political forces.

At the same time, Catalan anti–corporate globalization movements are also rooted within local social and political contexts. Transnational networking takes place not within abstract, undifferentiated global space but in the historically sedimented contours of concrete places. Instead of viewing place as necessarily opposed to the global, however, I join a growing chorus of scholars who follow Doreen Massey (1994) in conceiving place as always already entangled within a complex nexus of translocal ties and articulations (cf. Escobar 2001; Routledge 2003; Thayer 2001). In this sense, anti–corporate globalization activism articulates with diverse social, cultural, and political dynamics in specific locales, even as activists reach out beyond place to forge transnational connections.

In this chapter, I explore the role of place within anti–corporate globalization networks by advancing two principal arguments. First, I contend that networking logics in Catalonia have been profoundly shaped by the region's unique political culture and history, including a tradition of "unitary" mobilization forged through decades of nationalist and anti-Franco struggle and its anarchist legacy. Contradictions between deeply ingrained patterns of popular opposition and the perceived oligarchic nature of political parties and unions have accentuated recent conflicts between network-based and traditional organizing practices. Second, I suggest that alternative anti–corporate globalization movement networks in Barcelona involve distinct configurations of norms, forms, and technologies, which are influenced by their own specific genealogies.

Locating Anti–Corporate Globalization Movements in Catalonia

Organized by a new network called the Movement for Global Resistance (MRG), the Catalan mobilization against the World Bank and IMF meetings in

Prague in September 2000 was a key turning point for activists in Barcelona. Prague was an opportunity to re-create the Seattle experience closer to home, as Marc, a former squatter and MRG founder, recalled: "Seattle implied something much larger than we thought. Things were changing, and we had to introduce this here in Catalonia." Activists in Barcelona had organized previous anti–corporate globalization actions, but Prague led to an explosion in participation and media coverage. Prague also helped diffuse an anti–corporate globalization discourse and led to the emergence of MRG as a network linking local and global struggles. As Marta explained, "Prague was a huge step forward in terms of communicating a global message. It brought together sectors that had never worked together before. We created a network, and this could not have happened otherwise."

MRG specifically involved the convergence of two sectors: a radical anti-capitalist bloc, involving squatters, Zapatista supporters, and anti-EU organizers, and a less militant group of international solidarity and NGO-based activists, many of whom had taken part in RCADE. At the same time, although network-based movements such as MRG and RCADE precipitated anti–corporate globalization activism in Barcelona, the entire Catalan Left would join the fold during the campaign against the World Bank in spring 2001.[3] As we will see, Catalan anti–corporate globalization mobilizations would be organized around broad unitary spaces, recalling previous mass movements in Catalonia.

The dynamics of collective action in Barcelona have been influenced by the political, cultural, and social history of the region, including the broad-based opposition to Franco, the transition to democracy, and the emergence of new social movements in the 1970s and 1980s. Contemporary social movements also bear the mark of two pre–civil war political legacies: Catalan nationalism and anarchism. Nationalism became a unifying force within the democratic opposition to the dictatorship and remains hegemonic within the Catalan Left, while anarchism ceased to be a major political factor after the fall of the Second Republic (1931–39). At the same time, the values and practices associated with Catalan nationalism and anarchism helped forge a unique culture of opposition in Barcelona, whose distinctive features resonate with contemporary network norms and forms. It is no accident that Barcelona has become such an important center of anti–corporate globalization activity.[4]

Pre–Civil War Movements

Claims for cultural and political autonomy have long dominated the Catalan landscape, but full-fledged political nationalism emerged in the late 1800s, first as a conservative movement uniting traditional rural sectors with a rising urban bourgeoisie (Diez Medrano 1995, 96), and later as a progressive force in the second decade of the twentieth century (Carr 1966, 555). After his victory in the Spanish civil war, Franco repressed Catalan language and culture, sparking a nationalist resistance that would unite the democratic opposition. The anarchist-dominated labor movement represented the other major social struggle in the pre–civil war period, becoming a revolutionary force in Barcelona, Zaragoza, and certain rural areas of Andalusia and Aragon (Alvarez-Junco 1986, 191). Barcelona acquired its reputation as the "Rose of Fire" at the height of the anarchist bombings in the 1890s (A. Smith 2002, 3), but the movement achieved its fullest expression with the rise of the anarcho-syndicalist Confederación Nacional de Trabajo (CNT) during the Second Republic. Although anarchism would disappear as an organized force, many of the ideas, values, and practices it promoted—self-management, autonomy, decentralized coordination, and direct action—would significantly influence contemporary activists.[5]

The Anti-Franco Movement and the Transition to Democracy

Beginning in the late 1950s, workers helped foment a burgeoning movement against the dictatorship, spontaneously organizing shop floor assemblies. These formed the embryo of a new union movement, Comisiones Obreras (Workers' Commissions) (CCOO), whose formal structure emerged in the mid-1960s (Fishman 1990, 96–7). CCOO involved an innovative form of organization based on open, loose-knit, and participatory structures. Indeed, CCOO was viewed as a sociopolitical movement, not an organization (Molinero and Ysas 2002, 200). The absence of formal structure facilitated collective action under repressive circumstances, but leaders also believed they were building a new kind of union (*un sindicato de nuevo tipo*) characterized by grassroots assemblies, direct participation, and the defense of all workers (Fishman 1990, 100). Although the Communist Partit Socialista Unificat de Catalunya (PSUC) would become the leading force within CCOO, the movement remained open and participatory. This emphasis on participatory assemblies would become part of a wider culture of opposition in Spain and Catalonia.

Students, neighborhood activists, feminists, and ecologists also played key roles in the pro-democracy movement, which Catalan nationalism helped solidify.[6] The church provided an early haven for Catalan cultural resurgence, linguistic expression, and nationalist militancy under Franco (Conversi 1997, 127). Catalan culture and language were also reproduced through a network of voluntary associations, including societies of Sardana dancers, choir singers, Scouts, and football fans (133–35), many of which continue to promote nationalist identities.[7] As nationalism became more confrontational, it fused with Catholic and Marxist traditions to forge a counterhegemonic frame around anti-Francoism and democracy (Johnston 1991), reinforced by an oppositional culture based on Catalan language, symbols, and identity (Conversi 1997, 139).[8]

The anti-Franco movement had a significant impact on future grassroots struggles in Catalonia. First, Catalan nationalism became a dominant political force, which is still evident among social movements today. Second, the tradition of unitary campaigns, together with the unifying force of Catalan nationalism, produced a stronger and less divided oppositional culture in Catalonia than in other regions of the Spanish state. Indeed, the unitary model still forms the basic structure within contemporary campaigns and mobilizations. Finally, many contemporary grassroots leaders were radicalized through their participation in the movement against Franco.

Moreover, the transition to democracy also helped shape future grassroots struggles in Catalonia. According to some observers, leftist party leaders made a conscious effort to moderate mass protest after Franco's death in 1975 in order to create a more stable political environment (Tarrow 1995, 228).[9] The lingering perception among many activists that the transition was top-down and reformist reinforced strong anti-party feelings and an emphasis on civil society as the locus for social change.[10] In addition, by the end of the dictatorship, the Partido Comunista de España (PCE), and PSUC in Catalonia, had largely succeeded in imposing their leadership on the new political actors that emerged, including environmental, pacifist, feminist, and student groups (Alvarez-Junco 1994, 314), generating a widespread critique of political parties and a commitment to autonomy and diversity within subsequent movements.[11]

The 1990s and the Rise of Anti–Corporate Globalization Networks

The late 1980s to early 1990s was a period of relative quiescence, but several important movements formed during this time that would contribute to contemporary anti–corporate globalization networks. Antimilitarism arose as an organized resistance with the Conscientious Objector Movement (MOC) in the late 1970s (Pastor 1998, 82), growing substantially after 1989 as MOC began a campaign of "insubmission" to all forms of obligatory service, including social alternatives to the military (Equip d'Anàlisis 2002, 10).[12] Antimilitarists have been particularly active within Spanish and Catalan anti–corporate globalization movements, bringing with them their radical critique of the state, emphasis on decentralization, horizontal relations and self-management, and their experience with nonviolent direct action.

Squatters also played a particularly important role in the formation of MRG.[13] Inspired by the Italian tradition of converting squatted buildings into self-managed social centers housing diverse political, cultural, and social activities, Spanish and Catalan activists began squatting in cities such as Barcelona, Madrid, Valencia, and Bilbao in the mid-1980s (Herreros 1999, 14–8; Martínez López 2002, 95–109). The movement expanded particularly rapidly in Barcelona in the early 1990s (Martínez López 2002, 144–47). Squatting involves a radical critique of free market capitalism and urban speculation by reappropriating and collectively self-managing abandoned buildings.[14] Squatters reject all forms of hierarchy, promote self-management, and stress autonomy from political parties, trade unions, and representative institutions (Pallares, Costa, and Feixa 2002, 92–3). Social centers also provide spaces for generating countercultural values and practices (32).[15] Although ideologically diverse, squatting forms part of a wider group of "self-managed movements" that emerged in the 1990s together with antimilitarism, alternative communication (pirate radios, websites, counterinformation), and solidarity economics (fair trade, cooperatives) (123).

Finally, international solidarity activism also had a major influence on the development of Spanish and Catalan anti–corporate globalization networks.[16] In the early 1990s, international solidarity and grassroots labor activists created the 0.7 Platform, which pressured government institutions to designate 0.7 percent of their budgets to international development aid. During fall 1994 the platform organized an illegal campout along Barcelona's Diagonal Boulevard, together with similar actions around the Spanish state, leading to an increase in awareness about development and global economic justice issues (Laraña 1999, 351–52; Díaz-Salazar 1996, 39–43). Activists from 0.7 later founded RCADE, which incorporated the 0.7 movement's emphasis on grassroots participation and horizontal decision making (Xarxa Ciutadana 2001, 61). In March 2000, six months before Prague, RCADE organized a Zapatista-inspired "Consulta Social" against the foreign debt, which was among the first mobilizations organized along a network-based model in Spain and Catalonia. With the founding of MRG, solidarity activists' focus on participatory democracy and global solidarity would converge with an emphasis on local autonomy and grassroots self-management among militant squatters, antimilitarists, and Zapatista supporters alike, generating a unique form of activism guided by emerging networking logics and practices.

Network Norms, Forms, and Technologies in Catalonia

Anti–corporate globalization networks in Spain and Catalonia thus emerged through a complex interaction among local political and cultural traditions, wider global forces, and new technological practices. In this sense, networks such as RCADE and MRG reflected an increasing confluence among organizational forms, political norms, and digital technologies. For example, the RCADE-sponsored Consulta was organized through a statewide network of autonomous collectives, which coordinated through electronic Listservs and websites. At the same time, the decentralized structure of the Internet articulated with an emphasis on horizontal coordination and grassroots participation among RCADE activists. Although their libertarian ethic was shaped, in part, by the region's unique culture of opposition, it was significantly reinforced by their interaction with new technologies.

RCADE-based activists self-reflexively employed the terminology of computer networks to characterize their organizational structure. A new political language thus emerged as activists began experimenting with new organizational and technological practices.[17] The "Network," as RCADE was popularly known, was composed of local, regional, and statewide "nodes." Local nodes constituted the Network's organizational and political base and were defined as "self-defined, self-managed, and self-organized spaces." Local nodes further coordinated with their regional and statewide counterparts during periodic meetings and annual gatherings. As one early document explained: "We are building an organizational formation that is difficult to classify. We have called it a 'citizens network' formed by independent persons and collectives that adhere to the network and can take advantage of its structure. Many of these people are organized into local nodes, which determine the dynamic of collective action through assemblies. These connect to other nodes, creating intermediate spheres of coordination and/or decision."[18]

Moreover, activists communicated and coordinated through local, regional, and statewide Listservs and web pages between physical assemblies and mobilizations, allowing for exchange, coordination, and collective action beyond the local level.[19] In addition to using new digital technologies as tools, RCADE-based activists thus purposefully appropriated the structure and language of the Internet itself. As Joan explained: "We organized ourselves as nodes, using the nomenclature of the Internet. This was completely new, because we were thinking in network terms. The nodes were the spaces where information was produced and made public, the physical embodiment of the Internet, what we might call affinity groups today. We took the idea, not of a platform—we didn't want to work as a platform—but rather of a network."

Like RCADE before it, MRG was similarly founded as a loose, decentralized space for communication and coordination, designed to mobilize as many sectors, groups, and collectives as possible around specific objectives. As the network's manifesto declared, "We understand MRG as a tool for collective mobilization, education, and exchange, which at the same time, respects and preserves the autonomy of participating people and groups, reinforcing all the voices taking part in the action." The network's organizational structure reflected the emerging networking logic prevalent among many anti–corporate globalization activists, involving, as Pau suggested, "working as a network, through horizontal assemblies, and with local autonomy in order to reach people with a more open and less dogmatic style."

As with similar networks elsewhere, new digital technologies were central to the early development of MRG. After participating in global English and Spanish-language Listservs, Catalan activists created a statewide list in May

2000 to plan for the protests against the World Bank and IMF in Prague, out of which MRG emerged. As Mar recalled, "The Internet played a key role in the rise of the antiglobalization movement, both at the international level and in Catalonia." By communicating via Internet, activists from diverse groups and collectives were able to share information and coordinate in a flexible, decentralized manner without hierarchical structures. "Before the Internet," Pau explained, "horizontal assemblies were tied to our local activity. When we built statewide coordinating mechanisms, we had to use representatives, and this was much slower." According to Joan, the Internet also "favored decentralization and autonomy, which was fantastic in terms of participatory democracy." The Internet thus allowed activists to coordinate more rapidly; it also reinforced their broader libertarian ideals, as technology, norm, and form increasingly coincided.

At the same time, MRG-based activists were also keenly aware of the limitations of new technologies, particularly the threat of information overload. As Mateo suggested, "The Internet is an essential tool, but it's dangerous because it's easy to become overwhelmed." In this respect there was an important generational element, as many older activists found it difficult to keep up. Carme recalled, "Sometimes I'm saturated with too much information. I need to learn how to better identify what interests me and what doesn't. Lots of interesting things come through, but I have to archive them because I don't have time to read everything." Moreover, as Mar pointed out, "New technologies can't replace human interactions. If the movement was only about the Internet, it wouldn't have gone anywhere. Personal relations are still important."

In this sense, the Internet has complemented and facilitated face-to-face interactions, not replaced them. MRG-based activists have thus used electronic Listservs to stay informed about activities and perform concrete logistical tasks, while complex planning, political and strategic discussions, and relationship building have taken place during periodic assemblies, where virtual networks are embodied. At the same time, digital technologies have reinforced the proliferation of diffuse, loose-knit, and adaptable organizational forms in contrast to traditional modes of political organization based on stable structures, clear membership, and political representation. As Nuria and Pau argued in an early document outlining MRG's identity and structure, "MRG provides a space for integration and convergence among people and collectives against global

TABLE 4. Anti–corporate globalization movement sectors in Barcelona

Sector	Activist backgrounds	Organizational structure	Participation/ commitment	Decision making	Political vision
Institutional sectors (NGOS, political parties, unions)	Older activists with stable jobs and families; most are middle-class Catalan speakers	Formal member organizations with clear leadership, representative structures, and vertical chains of command	Traditional membership and strong organizational identification; paid staff carry out most day-to-day activities	Majority voting; leaders and staff make day-to-day political and administrative decisions	Reformist political orientation; global social democracy
Critical sectors (leftist sectors of major parties and unions)	Working-class activists from Marxist Left; Spanish and Catalan speakers; past experience in anti-Franco movement	Grassroots assemblies; emphasis on centralization	Open participation; strong movement identification	Consensus decision making; little meeting facilitation	Marxism, Trotskyism; reforms as steps toward socialism
Network-based movements (MRG, RCADE, Indymedia, etc.)	Younger, middle-class activists, mostly Catalan speaking	Diffuse, network-based structures; flat hierarchies (in theory); no formal leaders	Open participation; weak movement identification; extensive use of new digital technologies	Consensus decision making; strong meeting facilitation; collaborative process	Anarchism, ecology, and feminism; local autonomy and global networking
Militant anticapitalists (Squats, anti-militarist collectives, some radical nationalist groups)	Younger, middle-class activists, mostly Catalan speaking (but many also from outside Catalonia)	Small anti-capitalist collectives; flat hierarchies (in theory); no formal leaders	Informal participation; strong identification with local collectives; local self-management	Consensus decision making; strong meeting facilitation; collaborative process	Militant anti-capitalism, anarchism, autonomous Marxism; direct conflict with state

capitalism. It has a diffuse structure, and involves a diffuse sense of individual identification with the movement. MRG should therefore be understood as a movement 'without members'; membership leads to static, non-dynamic structures and a clear and distinct, rather than a more diffuse sense of belonging."[20]

Catalan anti–corporate globalization networks thus reflect an emerging networking logic, as activists express their political imaginaries directly through organizational and technological practice. As I pointed out in the introduction, however, networking logics are unevenly distributed and often provoke fierce resistance, giving rise to intense cultural politics, which I explore further in chapter 3. Before turning to these dynamics, I outline the principal sectors in the Catalan anti–corporate globalization movement field, emphasizing activist backgrounds, political visions, and alternative modes of organization, participation, and commitment. Who are the anti–corporate globalization activists in Catalonia? What do they believe? How do they organize? How do different sectors reflect alternative configurations of norms, forms, and technologies?[21]

Institutional Sectors

Institutional sectors involve a diverse array of political and civil society associations in Barcelona, such as leftist political parties, trade unions, and nongovernmental organizations (NGOS).[22] They are generally reformist in political orientation, vertically structured, and characterized by representative forms of participation. Institutional sectors initially took part in the Barcelona 2001 campaign but later split off from the unitary space to form the Barcelona Social Forum before the campaign against the EU. Formal organizations mobilize a more traditional base than networks such as MRG and RCADE and are in a better position to translate activist demands into specific policies. At the same time, grassroots actors often criticize formal organizations for their reformism and hierarchical structures and practices.

Activist Backgrounds

Formal institutions tend to involve older members and participants who have stable jobs and families. Like other activists in Catalonia, most come from middle-class Catalan backgrounds, although many rank-and-file union members are working-class Spanish speakers. Class and language are integrally related in Catalonia, as hundreds of thousands of workers have moved to the region from other parts of Spain during periodic waves of migration since the 1950s. Meanwhile, Catalan-speaking families are more likely to be middle- or upper-class (Woolard 1989).[23] At the same time, because Catalan was banned during the dictatorship, it is still widely viewed as a language of opposition even as it reflects class domination. Conflicts between Spanish speakers and Catalan speakers over language use during meetings and events are thus particularly common within contemporary social movements in Barcelona.[24]

However, when leftist parties, unions, and NGOs take part in grassroots coalitions, such as the campaigns against the World Bank and EU, they often assign younger members who have previous movement-related experience to serve as official delegates. For example, Estelle, from the Fons Catalá de Cooperació Desenvolupament, became politically active in the youth and student movements after the transition and went on to help found the Catalan nationalist organization CRIDA (Call for Solidarity in Defense of the Language and Culture of the Catalan Nations). She later helped organize the 0.7 campaign, becoming a primary organizer of the illegal campout. For his part, Arman, the movement representative from the Socialist Unión General de Trabajo (UGT), was in his early thirties, came from a middle-class Catalanist family, and was politically socialized within nationalist and antimilitarist circles. Nationalism was a critical factor in the political trajectories of many Barcelona-based activists, given its traditional role as a mobilizing force in Catalonia. Many anti–corporate globalization activists continue to view nationalism as a crucial aspect of their political identity. As Arman explained, "My conception of nationalism is more cultural. I feel all cultural identities, religions, and ethnicities have a richness that should be preserved. For example, in our debates around economic globalization, diversity is an important value. I am extremely committed to the preservation of diversity and cultural identity." Indeed, for many Catalan activists, nationalism is a logical extension of their critique of corporate globalization. However, others are more skeptical of nationalism, emphasizing cosmopolitanism, diversity, and openness *within* Catalonia.

Organization, Participation, and Commitment

Formal organizations incorporate traditional forms of political participation and commitment, involving clear leadership structures, vertical chains of command, and the selection of official delegates to "represent" the membership base. While networks such as MRG and RCADE attempt to create open spaces for communication and coordination, leftist parties, unions, and NGOs seek to recruit new members as a way to increase their base and leverage greater political influence. Adherents thus join institutions as official members, reflecting a stronger sense of organizational identification. Moreover, formal institutions often count large numbers of affiliates, but only a relatively small number of elected leaders or paid staff members carry out much of the ongoing work. In this sense, although formal organizations may point to significant levels of nominal support, the majority of members are excluded from day-to-day operations.

On the other hand, formal structure often translates into greater organizational stability, avoiding the cyclical pattern associated with grassroots movements. Members can still follow organizational activities from a distance and attend periodic events and demonstrations, but the organization continues to function during periods of demobilization, as formally elected officials and permanent staff carry out ongoing logistical and political activities. Finally, decision making usually involves majority voting rather than consensus. Although perhaps less democratic and participatory, voting is faster, making it easier for older people with stable jobs and families to participate.[25] Formal organizations privilege efficiency, stability, and efficacy, while grassroots activists claim this form of organizing stifles participation, creates a class of professional elites, and privileges the interests of specific organizations above the movement. On the other hand, institutional actors retort that open assemblies are chaotic and not sufficiently representative. Neus, the social movement liaison from Intermon (the Catalan affiliate of UNICEF), pointed out, "You can't treat an individual or collective with four people the same way as a large organization with many people behind it. During the World Bank campaign, for example, things were always changing from one day to the next. We decided something and then the next day someone else would come, and we would vote again. It was out of control!"

Enric, the social movement delegate from Iniciativa per Catalunya (IC), a major leftist party, further explained how activists with more time on their hands ended up making all the important decisions during the anti–World Bank campaign, which "isn't democratic either." Generation also plays an important role, as Enric pointed out: "I have friends who are forty or fifty years old, and they don't have a culture of assemblies, but they also have to have channels for participation. Otherwise this will only be a youth movement. Those from a representative culture won't take part." As we will see, debates over organizational process and form constitute an important aspect of the cultural politics of activist networking.

Political Vision

Institutional actors generally share a reformist political orientation, coinciding with their emphasis on representative modes of organization. In this sense, they promote concrete political and economic reforms through formal participation in electoral politics. For example, regarding the age-old debate between anticapitalism and reform, Enric of IC pointed out, "All the revolutions that happened overnight have failed. We need a much slower process, so as many people as possible can participate. If from inside the system we can create a more human face—the Tobin Tax or canceling the foreign debt, that's great, even if these are only reforms."

Following the same logic, the major transnational financial institutions—World Bank, IMF, WTO—should not necessarily be abolished. Rather, Enric told me, "We have to reform them. The financial and economic powers now want to do away with these institutions. We need to reform them while addressing broader inequalities." Rather than return to the nation-state, globally oriented reformists would create a transnational regulatory regime, which might ultimately lead to a form of global social democracy, as Arman of UGT argued: "The global economy today transcends the national scale. We have to move beyond the welfare state and regulate at an international level. The market has always existed and will always exist. I have a social democratic perspective. The conditions of the market are dangerous, not necessarily the market per se."

Others feel viscerally more anticapitalist but fail to see any realistic alternatives beyond specific policy-oriented reforms. "Capitalism is immoral, unjust, and mistaken," explained Neus of Intermon. "An economy that causes millions of people to live on one dollar a day is a failure, but I don't have a solution. We have to try to avoid the negative aspects of capitalism, save the positive ones, and bring as many people as possible into a debate about how we want to live."

Among institutional actors, ideological reformism thus goes along with a more traditional approach to political participation and organizational form. At the same time, such large member organizations are among the least innovative with respect to adapting new technologies. In part, this has to do with the time required to sort through such large amounts of information. Estelle explained, "The Internet is an important tool, and it allows for different kinds of struggle. It's part of the new political generation. But with all the work I have, I can't keep up. There is so much information and so many e-mails, I can't read everything." Moreover, whereas resource-poor actors, including network-based movements, often gain leverage by using new technologies to reorganize along decentralized lines, reflecting their libertarian ideals, formal organizations tend to incorporate new technologies into their bureaucratic structures (cf. Bennett 2003; Norris 2001). Once again, norm, form, and technology are intricately connected.

Critical Sectors

This category includes anticapitalist groups that organize within grassroots assemblies but favor centralized coordination, viewing the "sovereign" assembly as the primary decision-making body and expression of unity. Militants from this sector favor permanent coordinating structures, not around specific organizations, but rather involving wider coalitions. According to this view, social movements are unified subjects as opposed to open spaces of articulation among autonomous networks and collectives. This current specifically includes traditional tendencies on the extreme Left, including dissident Marxists and Trotskyists, many of whom organize within mainstream and leftist parties and unions, as well as grassroots networks such as ATTAC.[26]

Activist Backgrounds

Critical-sector activists are often middle-aged Catalan and Spanish speakers with stable jobs and families who came of age before the transition and were influenced by the assembly-oriented tradition of CCOO and the unitary model of the anti-Franco movement. For example, Albert of CCOO became politically active in the 1960s with the Communist PSUC and Catalan student movement. His past experiences significantly influenced his current outlook: "A common fascist enemy like Franco was a great help. An enemy like capitalism is not as clear; we have to build consciousness that we are all united against it." He specifically compared the assembly-based form of organization within contemporary anti–corporate globalization movements to the student movement of his youth: "There are equal conditions for large and small organizations, and everyone can convince the whole group, so we have reproduced the space we had created with the Democratic Student Union, where the less politicized base was more important than the leaders."

Jesús, a grassroots militant with CCOO and Izquierda Unida (IU), also began his activist career with the anti-Franco and student struggles of the 1970s. He subsequently took part in the anti-NATO and international solidarity movements, playing a lead role in the 0.7 mobilization in Barcelona. As a member of CCOO's critical sector, he supports open assemblies: "Early on, CCOO was a movement, more interrelated with pacifism and ecology, but it became a closed organization. It is no longer an open, assembly-based movement, but those of us from the critical sector still think [assemblies] are the best way to operate."

Organization, Participation, and Commitment

Although their particular organizations are often structured along representative lines, activists from the critical sector emphasize participation in broad assembly-based movements, which feature open participation, informal committee structures, and consensus decision making. Anyone can participate in an open assembly, take part in committees, and help make decisions, regardless of whether they belong to an organization, which increases grassroots participation and internal democracy. At the same time, assemblies have no paid staff or elected positions, making them relatively unstable over time. Traditional assemblies have influenced, but also differ from, contemporary networking practices in many important respects.

First, activists from network-based movements such as MRG and RCADE emphasize strong meeting facilitation, which enhances participation and consensus building. The classic assembly tradition involves relatively unstructured forums that privilege individual expression, leading to long speeches and uneven participation. Second, in traditional assemblies, activists attempt to persuade others rather than coordinate across diverse perspectives. Third, whereas newer movements stress decentralized interaction among autonomous working groups, traditional movements situate authority within the assembly itself. Finally, traditional Marxists privilege structure and continuity over fluid, contingent formations. For example, during one heated debate about whether to disband the campaign against the World Bank, Albert stated, "We have to take advantage of everything we have built together. It would be a grave error to destroy it, not to give continuity to our work. The channels and connections are our collective patrimony; they help people to feel part of the movement."

Contemporary mobilizations, including the Barcelona campaigns against the World Bank and EU, have evolved into a hybrid form, involving both traditional and contemporary elements. As Meri explained, "We have an assembly, but the commissions have autonomy; there is no voting, and everything is decentralized." In this sense, contemporary networking practices have articulated with traditional Catalan assemblies, generating a unique form of mobilization that integrates new organizational and technological practices with older political traditions.

Like other anti–corporate globalization activists in Barcelona, many traditional Marxists have incorporated digital technologies into their everyday routines. "We have to know how to use the Internet," suggested Albert. "It helps us make new connections. In my political work, the Internet allows me to communicate rapidly with my contacts around the world." Others, such as Meri, a Trotskyist linked to the United Kingdom–based Socialist Workers Party, are more skeptical: "The Internet allows for more horizontal communication and makes everything faster, but it isn't a panacea. When it comes down to it, if you want to organize an event, you have to call people, have face-to-face meetings, agitate in the streets, and talk to people directly." For Meri, the Internet thus complements and reinforces, but does not replace, traditional organizing activities.

Political Vision

Critical-sector activists are resolutely anticapitalist and are influenced by traditional revolutionary and state-centered Marxist strategies. For example, Jesús told me, "While capitalism still exists, there is no way to get rid of injustice in the world. As long as there are markets and competition, there is no solution." Regarding concrete reforms, Albert exclaimed, "NGOs don't confront the system. They apply band-aids, while we address root causes. The Tobin Tax is acceptable to the system. I'll struggle for anticapitalism before the Tobin Tax. I'm not against reforms, but reforms don't change the system."

Regarding the major global financial and political institutions, Albert further argued, "They will be destroyed automatically when we destroy capitalism; they are part of the system." Moreover, whereas activists within network-based movements often express anti-party and anti-state positions, traditional leftists view parliamentary politics as a legitimate terrain of struggle. "We have to vote," explained Meri. "I would prefer that IU have a seat in parliament than not. Even though I don't agree with everything they do, I want them to win more seats. The anticapitalist vote has to have more weight. If we don't have parliamentary connections, we'll die."

Consonant with their goal of taking state power, dissident Marxists and Trotskyists are not averse to parliamentary politics. However, their emphasis on building popular power from below and their radical rejection of the current political and economic system translate into a style of organizing based on grassroots assemblies. At the same time, whereas newer network-based movements emphasize horizontal coordination among autonomous elements, a political praxis reinforced by new digital technologies, assembly-based movements prioritize permanent structures, unity, and central control. Indeed, such political, organizational, and ideological differences drive the complex networking politics I explore throughout this book.

Network-Based Movements

Network-based movements involve activists associated with RCADE, MRG, Barcelona Indymedia, certain squatted social centers, student and antimilitarist assemblies, and other allied collectives. They are often critical of traditional forms of organizing, including both formal institutions *and* critical sectors. Beyond open assemblies, network-based movements emphasize decentralized coordination and flexible, diffuse structures. Activists in this sector are thus experimenting with new forms of political participation and "individualized" commitment (Furlong and Cartmel 1997; see also Lichterman 1996), reflecting the values associated with the network as an emerging ideal, rendering the links among norms, forms, and technologies particularly visible.[27]

Activist Backgrounds

During my time in the field, I established close relationships with several key figures out of a core group of roughly forty activists associated with MRG and

RCADE. Their stories are interwoven throughout this book. Here I briefly introduce their personal histories (and later their political visions) to provide additional social and political context, while further exploring the relationships among political norms, organizational forms, and new digital technologies. Despite important exceptions, these activists tend to be young (in their twenties to early thirties) middle-class Catalan speakers with high levels of education. As with the squatters explored later, many have irregular employment situations, given the economic restructuring and job instability that have particularly affected young people in Spain and Catalonia (Martínez López 2002, 137–38).[28] A significant number of the activists I worked with were university students, including many at the graduate level, while others held flexible, part-time jobs in the service sector. Another handful worked for NGOs or had precarious professional positions, including a new university professor, several journalists, and a lawyer. In terms of housing, some continued to live with their parents, while others shared collective apartments or lived in squatted social centers. Activists from network-based movements thus tended not to have families or full-time employment, allowing them ample time for grassroots political activities.

For example, Pau, whom we met in the introduction, comes from a fairly typical upper-middle-class Catholic background. His father had taken part in previous mobilizations against Franco but had moved away from politics after the transition. Pau was a sociology student but left the university after his first year and was able to live for a time on an independent source of income. He became politically active during the Consulta, where he first learned about what he calls "a new way of doing politics." "The Consulta for the Abolition of the Foreign Debt was my first campaign experience," Pau explained. "It helped us build and experiment with a new way of doing politics, which valued collective work over our individual organizations, as well as working together as a network in an assembly-based and horizontal manner."

Moreover, like many activists in Barcelona, Pau grew up in a Catalanist cultural milieu: "We spoke Catalan at home and had a strong but flexible Catalan identity." Mar of RCADE described a similar upbringing: "We were a middle-class family, but very Catalan. We always spoke Catalan. My family was nationalistic, but not in an exclusive sense. Speaking Catalan was just a way of defending our culture." Some activists became politically active within a more resolutely nationalist context. For example, Joan, one of the founders of RCADE who worked for a grassroots NGO, recalled, "My family was very nationalist, and my first militant experiences were violent, going to demonstrations on the Catalan national holiday with my separatist friends and throwing rocks at the police." More generally, widespread Catalanist sentiment has helped create an environment conducive to the development of "contradictory consciousness" (Gramsci 1971).

Beyond overtly nationalist spheres, many activists had previously participated in church-based or secular associations, including the Scouts, which provided a relatively safe space for reproducing Catalan language and culture during the dictatorship. To this day, the Scouts not only expose young people to the Catalan countryside; they also promote nationalist ideals, constituting a vehicle for political socialization. As Sergi from MRG pointed out, "I got involved in social activities through the church, but I didn't join any political groups until I was eighteen. I was in the Scouts, though, for nine years, and then six as a monitor. The Scouts are a typical Catalan tradition. They promote an ecological and Catalanist vision."

Sergi's activist history provides a revealing snapshot of the various waves of collective action that have periodically swept through the Catalan political landscape since the 1980s. For example, after leaving the Scouts, he took part in the antimilitarist movement and then became involved in the 0.7 campaign of the early 1990s. It was only a short jump from a general interest in international development to a more politicized critique of neoliberal capitalism and global inequalities:

> After becoming a scout leader, I traveled for a year, and began organizing around issues such as the war in Bosnia. I got involved in antimilitarism, and then joined Christian Engineers. After that, I became interested in North-South relations, especially with the 0.7 campouts. Many of us came out of the NGO boom in the 1990s. I came from a nonpolitical family, and the NGOs, such as Greenpeace, Amnesty, or Cooperació, were the most visible social forces at the time. But we lacked a clear political paradigm. Anticapitalism sounded ridiculous ten years ago, very sectarian, but this is changing.

Many activists from MRG and RCADE also spent time volunteering with community development projects in countries such as Nicaragua, where numerous Catalan municipalities had established sister cities during the Sandinista revolution in the 1980s. These experiences helped promote an emerging global political consciousness among many younger activists. For example, Nuria, a graduate student and MRG organizer, gained her first political experiences with student assemblies in high school, but she was radicalized during her time with a grassroots development project in Nicaragua: "In Nicaragua I worked in a community, and my blood began to boil from rage when I realized how difficult it was to change the situation because of the external structures. But I also learned a lot about the human condition."

Upon returning to Catalonia in spring 2000, Nuria continued her political work with the Catalan Unitary Platform for Peace, which mobilized against a Spanish military parade slated to take place in Barcelona despite widespread resistance.[29] Nuria's parents had not been activists, although her mother had come from a Catalanist milieu, while her father's family had migrated from Andalusia in the 1950s. However, she recalls strong anti-Franco sentiments at home: "My family was always against Franco, and I used to like talking about the civil war with my grandfather. The military parade was the last straw; saying no to the army just kind of welled up from inside." Moreover, she met many of her future friends and colleagues from MRG during a direct action against the military parade:

> Sometimes it feels like I haven't stopped since then. That's where I met Pau, who told me about the Consulta and RCADE. We later formed a participatory democracy group. Then I went to Prague with the collective we had formed during the parade, and with which I continued working around civil disobedience and antimilitarism. In June I began to follow all the e-mails from Pau, even when I couldn't make it to the assemblies because I was working on my thesis. I remember telling my friends at the university how it felt just like May '68. I wasn't sure if I could make it at first, but in the end, I had to go to Prague.

The Zapatistas were also an important influence among many anti–corporate globalization activists. For example, Sergi, who had spent time in Chiapas during a yearlong trip to Mexico, Guatemala, El Salvador, Nicaragua, Colombia, and Venezuela, was greatly affected by his experience: "We never expected the Zapatistas. We didn't lack the intellectual analysis at that point, but rather the sense of hope. They had a refreshing vision, extremely open, less dogmatic, more like environmentalists."

Indeed, the Intercontinental Zapatista Encuentros led to the formation of solidarity groups in Spain, Italy, and throughout Europe, which were instrumental in the emergence of future anti–corporate globalization networks. The Zapatista ideal of a global network of autonomous communities resonated widely among global activist networks. Joan from RCADE explained the Zapatista influence thus: "Zapatismo had an international impact, and part of that was the formation of numerous solidarity collectives in Europe, particularly in Spain and Italy, but also in France and Germany. Everyone read Marcos's texts, which for me were the philosophical foundation of the antiglobalization movement as we understand it today. In Seattle there were a lot of new tactics, but the underlying philosophy comes from the Zapatistas."

The squatter movement was another crucial politicizing experience for many MRG-based activists, providing an important arena for the development of network norms and forms, particularly in Barcelona, where activists have drawn on the city's strong culture of opposition, mistrust of central authority, and its powerful anarchist legacy. For example, Marc, a former squatter and early promoter of MRG, explained, "We occupied buildings to create social centers and were inspired by similar experiences in Valencia and Madrid, but also by the ateneos populars built by the anarchist workers' movement. Social movements needed open spaces, where people could come and teach classes, give talks, socialize in alternative ways, and create a new system of values."

Organization, Participation, and Commitment

Decentralized networks such as MRG and RCADE involve an organizational model based on flexible patterns of political commitment and participation. For example, as we saw with MRG, rather than identifying with a specific organization, activists are committed to a larger movement and set of guiding values. However, unlike the critical sectors, activists within network-based movements often prefer more temporary, ad hoc coalitions. In this sense, MRG and RCADE provide open spaces for communication and coordination around concrete projects rather than unified political identities. Moreover, activists from network-based movements are willing to work with other sectors but hesitate to create permanent coalitions.

With respect to commitment and belonging, network-based movements thus favor open forms of participation over rigid membership. In this sense, no one belongs to MRG; instead, people participate in network-related meetings, actions, and events. Rather than representing a particular group, participation is more individualized, although still concerned with achieving concrete objectives through collaborative practice. In addition, there are no formal hierarchies, elected positions, or paid staff, and decisions are made by consensus. Horizontal structure and democratic process are thus viewed as political ends, leading to a practical, dynamic, and flexible form of activism. At the same time, networks can be unstable, given the lack of structure and clear chains of responsibility. Moreover, despite a commitment to egalitarianism, informal hierarchies often emerge (cf. Freeman 1973; Polletta 2002).

But what does it actually mean to take part in such networks? What are the diverse modes of participation? First, core groups of activists often take responsibility for much of the detailed planning and logistical arrangements around specific meetings, actions, and events. Rather than relying on elected leaders or staff members, those who are most interested in a project become informal coordinators. For example, during the Prague mobilization, a small cohort arranged all the transportation details, while another took care of relations with the press, and yet another organized direct-action training. In this way, those with the most skills and interest in a particular area are empowered to assume more responsibility. At the same time, this can often reproduce the very sort of hierarchies activists are attempting to overcome.

Second, another larger group of activists may attend general meetings and take on more specific tasks as a particular event gets closer. This can involve more mundane activities such as putting up flyers, creating signs or costumes, or sending an e-mail notice, or more involved contributions, such as giving a talk or writing text for outreach materials. As we shall see, during the lead-up to a particular protest or campaign, activists often spend many hours in physical assemblies and online discussions, engaging in both political and logistical discussions. At the same time, younger activists also spend time together within more informal settings, drinking beer, going to parties, and hanging out in bars and squats. Third, a still larger number of people will follow from a distance, often via electronic Listservs, helping out at particular moments in a limited way. Finally, many others will assume more passive roles, attending protests and events, but not contributing to planning and coordination. Once again, horizontal networking facilitates grassroots participation and democratic decision making among those who are the most informed and skilled or simply have more available time, but may exclude others who lack sufficient access, abilities, or information.

At the same time, activists from this sector are among the most optimistic regarding new technologies. Maria from MRG represents a fairly typical case: "I'm a member of ten Listservs, read 150 messages a day, and regularly visit websites such as Indymedia or the Forum home page." For his part, Joan recalled his experience with the Internet in this way: "I'm connected all day. The Internet has been vital for the articulation of our movements. It allows us to have real-time debates. You are discussing things all the time, coming into contact with diverse visions, seeing what the feminists say, seeing what the anarchists say. It gives you a better understanding, and it's fundamental for organizing actions."

Moreover, the Internet has helped to promote a global vision, particularly among network-based movements, as Mateo from RCADE pointed out: "I can rapidly find out what's happening around the world, in places like Venezuela or Palestine, without actually being there. It creates a feeling of global citizenship." However, extensive Internet use also requires a great deal of time, energy, and resources. As pointed out earlier, older activists with stable jobs and families, and those from poorer communities, particularly in the South, have a difficult time managing the large number of e-mails and Listserv messages, a situation many grassroots activists recognize. As Mateo told me, "There is a danger that only those who have access to the Internet or who know how to use the Internet can join our movements, which can distance us from many of the sectors we want to reach." For Joan, the important thing is to find a productive balance: "I remember when we celebrated everything about the Internet, and then another period when we criticized everything. Between those two extremes, we've reached a balance, recognizing the Internet has its problems, but that it provides an opportunity to connect with one another and organize in a different, more horizontal way, at least among middle-class activists from Northern countries."

Political Vision

As we have seen, many younger activists from network-based movements in Barcelona have been particularly influenced by anarchist ideas and practices.

Indeed, anarchists have long viewed self-generating networks as a model for organizing society beyond the market and state. For example, Kropotkin argued in 1905 that in a society without government, social order and harmony would arise by "an ever-changing adjustment and readjustment of equilibrium between the multitudes of forces and influences," organized as "an interwoven network, composed of an infinite variety of groups and federations of all sizes and degrees, local, regional, national, and international."[30] Colin Ward (1973) more recently described anarchist federations as decentralized networks composed of communes and syndicates that "federate together not like the stones of a pyramid where the biggest burden is borne by the lowest layer, but like the links of a network, the network of autonomous groups" (26).

New technologies have thus reinforced traditional anarchist models of organization within contemporary network-based movements. This growing confluence among norm, form, and technology is reflected in the rise of the network as a metaphor for grassroots democracy and horizontal coordination. For example, RCADE's political goals involved not only abolishing the foreign debt but also expanding the Network and its directly democratic modus operandi: "The Network is a tool for creating social fabric in our local contexts. Participatory democracy is not only a transversal theme in our work; it constitutes our model of operation."[31] This network ideal would become an important part of a broader ethos among MRG-based activists. For example, when I asked Nuria to define how she identifies herself politically, she explained:

I am close to the anarchist position, particularly around self-organization. I have a lot of conflict with the issue of power, obedience, and injustice. I can't give a precise definition, that I'm a communist for this reason, or an anarchist for that reason. It's more about how I was educated, my way of thinking—that you can build the world you want. For me, the twenty-first century, with the discourse of postmodernity, people are always talking about the "network of networks of networks," but for me building these networks is actually the world we want to create.

Many younger anti–corporate globalization activists in Barcelona hesitate to classify themselves according to rigid ideologies. Openness and flexibility have given rise to a new anticapitalism shaped by an emerging cultural logic of networking. Despite differences among specific networks (RCADE-based activists are more likely to support reforms, electoral politics, and revamped global financial institutions than their counterparts in MRG), activists increasingly define themselves as anticapitalist. As Joan explained, " 'Anticapitalism' was a prohibited word five or six years ago, but capitalism has become so brutal. Until recently I used to talk about neoliberalism, but today we all use anticapitalism to characterize a diversity of positions." Sergi explicitly linked his conception of anticapitalism to an emerging network ideal: "The revolution is also about process; the way we do things as social movements is also an alternative to capitalism, no? Horizontalism is the abstraction we want, and the tools are the assembly and the network."

Specifically contrasting parliamentary and assembly-based politics with the network ideal, Pau explained: "We are promoting decentralized participation, making each group responsible for their part so decisions are taken among many people as opposed to the old politics where a small group has all the information and decides everything." Pau further suggested that networks are the most effective way "to balance freedom and coordination, autonomy with collective work, self-organization with effectiveness." At the same time, innovative networking tools, such as Indymedia, Listservs, web pages, the European Social Consulta, and the Infospace project, are designed to help people "build networks at whatever rhythm possible" (see chapter 8).

Moreover, the rise of anti-party sentiment among younger activists has accompanied their increasing emphasis on autonomous, self-directed networking. Marc explained, "Political parties are filled with people who have objectives and modes of organizing radically different from ours. The division between institutional politics and social movements is becoming more and more evident." As we have seen, this critique of formal democracy goes back, at least in part, to the transition.[32] When combined with emerging networking logics, anti-party sentiment increasingly means that grassroots activists view social movements as directly democratic alternatives to representative democracy.[33]

For example, like many Catalan activists, Pau stopped voting after he began participating in grassroots movements. "I am building an alternative political system," he maintained, "which is much more important." He later explained how such an alternative requires the development of technological and social tools to enhance the capacity for building horizontal connections and self-organization among social movements. "We lacked a few elements in order to become truly coherent: tools, technological mechanisms, and specific affinity groups that could assume concrete tasks and promote decentralized coordination." This networking logic resonates with a broader political vision among many younger activists, which involves what Nuria described as a world composed of "small, self-organized, and self-managed communities, coordinated among them on a worldwide scale." Sergi posited a similar ideal:

> Exchange is prioritized over commercial products or monetary relations. It would be a world without exploitation, with much more collaborative work, less competition among people and communities, something much more organic. And these regions wouldn't be so nationalist, religious, messianic, or dependent on labor markets. There wouldn't be banana republics. Regions would be self-sufficient and would have food sovereignty, but they wouldn't close themselves off. Instead, they would articulate and work together through a kind of anarcho-eco-regionalist global government.

Sergi's vision not only recalls traditional anarchist principles of autonomous federation, it also reflects emerging network norms and forms within anti–corporate globalization movements and the new technologies that facilitate them. As Pau explained, "The Internet makes it possible to really talk about international coordination from below. It allows us to interact according to models that have always existed but weren't realistic before." Rather than generating entirely new political and cultural models, the Internet thus articulates with existing structures and ideals, including grassroots participation from below and horizontal coordination across diversity and difference. In this sense, new digital technologies reinforce traditional anarchist principles, which have influenced many activists within network-based movements, generating new organizational forms that reflect their emerging political norms.

Autonomous Movements

Autonomous movements encompass an informal network of militant anticapitalist collectives, including squatters, antimilitarists, and media activists who primarily emphasize autonomy, self-management, and confrontation with the state. As pointed out earlier, militant squatters were among the first groups to engage in anti–corporate globalization activism. However, since the entry of more reformist networks, parties, and unions into the wider field, some militants have developed a critical perspective toward broader anti–corporate globalization movements. Many of these collectives have organized alternative anticapitalist platforms during mobilizations in Barcelona, using diverse names such as "Anti-Capitalist Resistance," "Coordination against Military Occupation," or "Barcelona Trembles."

Activist Backgrounds

Militant anticapitalists occupy similar socioeconomic positions as their counterparts from network-based movements, although many were politicized at an earlier age. For example, Manel, an antimilitarist whose family was active in the anti-Franco and nationalist movements, came from an extremely political home. His activist career began with Esquerra Republicana de Catalunya's nationalist youth when he was fourteen. He was a conscientious objector at seventeen and later became an Insumiso. For his part, Fernando, an independent journalist and activist with a local anticapitalist collective, was influenced by his mother, who was active in the labor and nationalist movements in the Basque Country, before moving to Barcelona, where she joined PSUC. He joined the student assembly movement while still in high school and helped organize a regional strike against the Gulf War in 1991.

Although Fernando joined a local youth group associated with the Partido Comunista de Catalunya (PCC), he has since moved toward the autonomous Left. He is now extremely critical of institutional politics; as he pointed out, "Leftist parties won't bring more democracy or social change. It's more important to work in my neighborhood with grassroots projects and try to influence things from the outside." Contrasting two very different views of democracy, Manel explained, "I'm a democrat, but in a much more radical way. It's not about voting every four years, but rather doing politics in the street on a daily basis." Such views are becoming more and more prevalent among younger activists, both within network-based movements and among more radical anticapitalists.

Organization, Participation, and Commitment

Regarding organizational dynamics, militant anticapitalists tend to emphasize communal self-organization within intimate spheres of daily life. As Martínez

López (2002, 120) points out, they can be distinguished from similar movements by their concern for self-management *within* each collective, rather than among the larger network. Regarding the unitary antiglobalization campaigns in Barcelona, for example, Manel suggested, "It's easy to coordinate around concrete tasks. We built an interesting network, but I don't feel the need to maintain it. I work with my friends in my own spaces, and when I have to coordinate, I do, but I have a lot of work."

Moreover, militant anticapitalists tend to prioritize local struggles over open networking, and they are often skeptical of countersummit mobilizations. Manel pointed out, "I have never gone to Prague, Genoa, or Davos. Countersummits are important, but not as much as our day-to-day organizing." In addition, militant anticapitalists stress ideological and practical coherence over broad spaces of convergence, which include organizations and networks with significantly different values, objectives, and methodologies. For example, in response to a question about whether he feels he is part of the anti–corporate globalization movement, Fernando responded, "I guess so, in terms of consciousness, as part of my local collective, but I feel much more part of an emerging anticapitalist critique. I have no problem saying I'm part of the antiglobalization movement, but around the world, as in Porto Alegre, movements from the institutional Left are entering the antiglobalization terrain. I don't identify with them. If they are the antiglobalization movement, then I don't feel part of it, not for sectarian reasons, but in terms of ideological coherence."

With respect to new digital technologies, militant anticapitalists tend to use the Internet extensively, although they are often more skeptical of it than are their counterparts from network-based movements. For example, Fernando explained, "I use the Internet a great deal, mainly to send documents and organize logistics, not so much to chat. It's an important tool, but it also has advantages and disadvantages. It was an important leap forward for social movements in Catalonia, but there is always a risk of information overload." Gaizka was even more dubious, suggesting that "the Internet is often romanticized. It's an important tool, but it can't substitute for physical gatherings, assemblies, and common struggles. Very few people around the world are connected. When I go to Mexico, not even 10 percent of the people I see have access."

Political Vision

Militant anticapitalists also tend to express a more complete rejection of the political and economic system than their RCADE- or MRG-based counterparts. As Fernando explained, "I'm struggling to end all inequalities and injustice. I believe strongly in direct, self-managed action. You might call this libertarian communism, beyond the market and the state." He identified with the German and Italian autonomous movements, and the writings of Antonio Negri, pointing out that "in the case of Italy, workers became an autonomous force outside the political and union structures." Fernando was also strongly influenced by Catalan anarchism: "During the civil war there were cultural houses, ateneos populars, and cooperatives. We haven't come close to that, but we are saying similar things. When I talk about autonomy, we have the example of the workers' movement here and their experiences with popular, direct, and self-managed democracy."

Ricart, who had taken part in many high-profile squats around Barcelona, was committed to living completely outside capitalism: "I don't believe in the market, and I don't want to live inside it. But anticapitalists have to become grounded. It's the typical discussion. Should we spend our lives stealing from the supermarket? It's still a multinational, even if we rob the food. If we steal our electricity, the state still provides it, or Endesa [a private electric company]. We have to go further. If we want to defeat this system, we have to learn to live without it. The first thing is to self-manage our food, energy, transport, and begin creating networks of exchange."

Whereas network-based activists emphasize the use of new technologies to build broader ties and connections, thereby developing new anticapitalist visions from within the system, militant anticapitalists tend to favor local self-management in order to live completely beyond the market and state. Their smaller, more autonomous collectives thus correspond to a more radical anti-systemic critique. Likewise, at the tactical level, their more aggressive direct-action styles and practices embody their militant visions. In this sense, while network-based movements such as RCADE and MRG tend to carry out nonviolent forms of civil disobedience, militant anticapitalists often practice "self-defense" and violence against property, including sabotage against bank tellers and corporate storefronts. As Fernando explained, "Our collective accepts all forms of struggle, civil disobedience, street occupations, banner hangs, but when there is a situation in the neighborhood, such as an eviction, you respond however you can. Violence doesn't resolve anything, but as a form of self-defense, you have to be able to respond." Debates surrounding violence and nonviolence represent a crucial terrain in the cultural politics of anti–corporate globalization networking.

Conclusion: Political Cultures and Cultural Politics in Catalonia

Emerging network norms and forms among Barcelona-based anti–corporate globalization activists have been shaped by Catalonia's unique political and historical context, including the region's history of anarchism, nationalism, and assembly-based struggles. Moreover, diverse activist sectors in Barcelona have their own distinct trajectories characterized by alternative political norms, organizational forms, and technological practices. In this sense, the introduction of new technologies has reworked and reinforced traditional modes of popular mobilization involving grassroots organization, open participation, and decentralized coordination. At the same time, Catalan activists also bring their backgrounds and experiences to bear as they reach out across space to participate in larger regional and global processes. The specific cultural and political characteristics associated with concrete places, understood as nodes within regional and global networks of circulation and exchange, thus remain significant, even within transnational networks.

Indeed, given Catalonia's unique culture of opposition, it should come as no surprise that anti–corporate globalization movements have been so prominent in Barcelona, or that Catalans have played key roles in statewide, regional, and global networks. At the same time, the Catalan movement field is extremely diverse, involving competing organizations, groups, and collectives with vastly different political visions, traditions, and goals. Despite their political and cultural differences, however, competing sectors periodically converge within broad convergence spaces, reflecting a deeply established tradition of unitary mobilization in Catalonia. Nevertheless, struggles within and among distinct movement sectors, particularly those around organizational identity, structure, and process, have generated a complex micropolitics, involving perpetually shifting and often confusing political alliances. It is to these dynamics we now turn.

3

We understand freedom as our ability to think critically and intervene in the activities that most affect us. It is therefore necessary to rediscover the importance of democracy in politics—beyond the elitism and professionalism of today's political parties, and the value of a collectivized and cooperative economy . . . beyond capitalism.[1]

GRASSROOTS MOBILIZATION AND SHIFTING ALLIANCES

On January 26, 2003, MRG-Catalonia was "self-dissolved," two and a half years after it was founded to mobilize Catalan activists against the World Bank and IMF meetings in Prague. Rather than lament the occasion, activists pointed to their decision as an example of a new fluid network-based politics, explaining, "MRG was born as a network, a space of communication among collectives and struggles. But today it is becoming a fixed identity, a static structure, and we thought it was time to destroy it!"[2] Their public communiqué went on to describe how MRG had become an important symbol of the new radical activism within an emerging transnational anti–corporate globalization movement field. Indeed, the previous April, MRG had been invited to join the WSF International Council as a permanent member. However, for many grassroots activists, taking part in an international representative structure constituted a serious perversion of their networking logic. In its final collective statement, MRG thus declared, "Our definitive response is dissolution. We desert the boring politics of Porto Alegre, the false representations and micro-level struggles for power!"

MRG's deft political manifesto exhibited all the rhetorical virtuosity characteristic of its craft, yet as is often the case, it obscured as much as it revealed.

Over the past year, I had taken part in hundreds of face-to-face encounters and online discussions, which had suggested to me many other reasons why the network might dissolve: lagging participation, internal conflicts, the difficulty of sustaining diffuse network formations, or the emergence of new initiatives. Indeed, MRG was superseded by broader "unitary" spaces, including the Barcelona campaigns against the World Bank and the EU, culminating in mass mobilizations in June 2001 and March 2002, respectively. These campaigns included NGOS, parties, and unions in addition to grassroots networks. Beyond the politics of the forum, MRG's public self-dissolution can thus also be understood as a scathing critique of traditional Spanish and Catalan political and civil society institutions. Indeed, conflicts between networking and command logics form part of a larger set of struggles involving competing visions, ideologies, and practices, leading to evolving patterns of shifting alliances driven by a complex cultural politics of networking at multiple scales.

As we saw in chapter 2, anti–corporate globalization networks in Barcelona, such as MRG and RCADE, reflect a growing confluence among network technologies, organizational forms, and political norms. In this chapter, I explore how these domains are mediated in practice as activists build networks through communication and conflict. Chapter 2 further outlined the diverse sectors within Catalan anti–corporate globalization movements, emphasizing personal histories, alternative forms of participation and commitment, and competing political visions. Now I set networking in motion by exploring how networks are constructed and how they relate to one another within larger movements. I am primarily concerned here with the communicative interactions and shifting alliances that characterize anti–corporate globalization mobilizations in Catalonia. Indeed, building networks involves a great deal of communicative work and struggle, behind-the-scenes dynamics that facilitate mobilization during moments of greater visibility. In what follows, I argue that the fluid and shifting patterns of mobilization among Catalan anti–corporate globalization networks are generated by complex micropolitical struggles involving tensions between horizontal networking and vertical command logics. At the same time, given the growing confluence among political norms, organizational forms, and new digital technologies, such conflicts often revolve around network structure and identity.

Rhizomatic Networks

The mobilization to Prague was a key moment in the rise of anti–corporate globalization networks in Barcelona. After returning, many MRG-based activists hoped to consolidate their network as *the* "network of networks," a flexible tool for integrating the entire spectrum of grassroots groups and collectives opposed to corporate globalization in Catalonia. However, building and maintaining such a diffuse network proved more difficult than anticipated, and MRG soon became just one among many political spaces within a larger, constantly evolving movement field.[3] Indeed, after Prague many activists from RCADE decided to leave MRG. Differences between the networks remained subtle: both opposed neoliberalism, but MRG assumed a more radical, anticapitalist stance, while RCADE emphasized grassroots democracy and global economic reforms.[4] During the same period, many radical squatters also returned to their local activities. As we shall see, militants often hesitate to work with reformist groups, preferring instead to emphasize self-management within their immediate contexts. Many MRG-based activists subsequently began to organize within the Barcelona campaign against the World Bank, but often without identifying as MRG.

Throughout my time in the field, anti–corporate globalization networks in Barcelona thus constantly emerged, split, and morphed, alternatively fusing and separating through a fluid and dynamic process of interaction. As pointed out in the introduction, observers have characterized contemporary social movement networks more generally as "rhizomatic." This dynamic pattern of mobilization is often seen as an alternative to traditional static models of organizing. As Harry Cleaver suggests, "The rhizomatic pattern of collaboration has emerged as a partial solution to the failure of old organizational forms" (1995, 16). According to Deleuze and Guattari (1987), "Unlike a structure, which is defined by a set of points and positions, the rhizome is made only of lines: lines of segmentarity and stratification as its dimensions, and the line of flight or deterritorialization as the maximum dimension after which the multiplicity undergoes metamorphosis, changes in nature" (21).

This image does seem to reflect the dynamics of contemporary activist networking, at least in a metaphoric sense. Still, the question remains: how are such rhizomatic patterns actually generated in practice? Despite the constant shifting and transforming, which can be extremely confusing for activists and observers trying to make sense of a rapidly shifting movement field, certain key figures, the activist-hackers, were able to successfully negotiate this complex terrain. Activist-hackers served as relayers and exchangers, alternatively building and severing virtual and physical connections to maximize network "connectivity."[5]

For example, Pau conceived of social movement networking as a political art and social passion.[6] Having created and coordinated the Prague and Barcelona 2001 campaign Listservs, which helped diffuse antiglobalization activism throughout Spain and Catalonia, by June 2001 he was moderator of thirty-three Listservs and a member of fifty-five more, receiving several hundred e-mails a day.[7] However, Pau was not merely a virtual hacker. He also attended myriad face-to-face meetings to develop contacts, share ideas, and exchange information and resources, in short, to build networks. During one meeting, I witnessed a heated argument between Pau and an organizer for En Lluita, one of the leading Trotskyist groups in Barcelona:

> *Pau*: You only come to these meetings to sell newspapers.
> *Ignaci*: I don't even sell the papers during the meetings. I'd like to recruit members, but I'm more interested in contributing to the group.
> *Pau*: But your goal is still to recruit as many people as possible!
> *Ignaci*: Of course!
> *Pau*: But there is another idea, the network, like MRG or RCADE, where the goal isn't to recruit more members to your particular group, but to bring as many different groups, people, and nodes into the network as possible, so it expands outward, horizontally.

Rather than operating as discrete organizations, networks such as RCADE and MRG often serve as tools that mobilize activists within wider political spaces, giving rise to an extremely dynamic mode of activist participation. Pau explained the fluid nature of Catalan anti–corporate globalization networks in the following terms:

> There are always different people in these networks. I mean, it's often the same people, but they come and go. They are in the networks and they are not in the networks. It's very fluid. I keep joining new networks, like RCADE, MRG, and Barcelona 2001. I am still part of the old networks, and

I identify with the network that makes most sense at the time. The same networks function differently in different regions. In Barcelona, the campaign has become important, but MRG still functions more cohesively in Girona, Lleida, or Tarragona. Sometimes networks mean completely different things in different places. Sometimes the same people doing similar things see themselves as part of distinct networks. It's all mixed up, but you just have to understand how networks work!

Over time I began to see how such intersecting, splitting, and recombining resulted from concrete networking practices, as well as how activists negotiated complex strategic and political terrains. Beyond the poetics of Deleuze and Guattari, long-term ethnographic fieldwork allowed me to perceive how rhizomatic patterns were generated in practice through micro-level struggles over political vision, strategy, and tactics. At the same time, given the increasing confluence among network norms, forms, and technologies, political debates were often coded as conflict over organizational structure and process. Understanding activist networking in Barcelona thus required careful attention to the mechanisms through which networks are constructed and how alternative networks interact.

Constructing Networks in Barcelona

Building contemporary social movement networks involves diverse modes of interaction whereby activists communicate to one another while reaching out to potential supporters. This partly takes place in cyberspace, where activists exchange information about gatherings, protests, and events while debating the intricate details of network structure and identity.[8] Such electronic information sharing helps local networks articulate with wider regional and global processes. At the same time, these discourses do not merely circulate through networks; they produce and reproduce networks themselves.[9] On the other hand, constructing networks that can effectively coordinate actions and events also requires face-to-face interaction. Physical gatherings provide forums for generating personal trust and affective ties, complementing and reinforcing online engagement.

On the afternoon of June 19, 2001, several days before the unity march against the World Bank was set to begin, I sat in a circle with thirty activists in a tree-lined courtyard at the Central University of Barcelona. We were meeting as a coordinating group to prepare for an assembly scheduled for later that evening. Miquel was keeping stack (a list of people waiting to speak) and facilitating the meeting using the techniques Catalan activists had brought back with them from Prague. As we saw in the last chapter, Barcelona has a long tradition of consensus decision making, but this active facilitation process was new. Miquel not only called on speakers, he proactively guided discussions to help produce agreements. His task was relatively easy this time, as most participants were from MRG and RCADE and thus shared an orientation toward short, practical interventions. One by one, speakers suggested agenda items for the assembly. Participants then "twinkled" their fingers to signal agreement, a practice adopted by U.S. direct-action organizers and later transmitted to anti–corporate globalization activists elsewhere.[10]

The larger assembly would prove more complicated. This time there were 250 activists from diverse movement sectors in Barcelona, including delegates from NGOs, political parties, and unions, older Marxists, activists from MRG and RCADE, and a few squatters. Montse, from MRG, facilitated the assembly, but she had more difficulty managing the discussion. Whereas the afternoon's deliberation had remained relatively focused, many older participants insisted on making long declarations of political principle every time a new agenda item arose. A debate about what to do if the police raided the university thus sparked extended commentaries on the importance of defending Catalan universities as "safe havens," which have been off-limits to police actions since the transition to democracy. Montse tried to keep speakers on point, but she quickly became frustrated. The differences between the newer "consensus process" and the logic of traditional assemblies were becoming apparent.[11]

Throughout my time in the field, I attended hundreds of activist meetings and assemblies. As time went on, I learned how to "read" these gatherings ethnographically, recognizing various actors, pinpointing the underlying tensions, and interpreting the diverse interactions with respect to broader political visions and practices. As Maureen Mahon (2004, 60) suggests, meetings are not only goal-oriented affairs; they are forums where organizations and networks are constituted and imbued with meaning.[12] In the case of Catalan anti–corporate globalization networks, such meetings provided spaces for activists to express their emerging political ideals, not only through discourse but also directly through their political styles and organizational practices.

Social movement networks operate most effectively when activists focus on concrete tasks, such as organizing actions or logistics. At the same time, between mobilizations, internal struggles often become more frequent, particularly those involving debates around network structure and identity. Indeed, such conversations are constitutive: activist networks flourish when there is significant discussion and debate, but they quickly stagnate when communication lags. In this sense, if activist networks are generated by the communication flows that circulate through them, and are thus self-reflexive, organizational debates become important mechanisms for reproducing networks during moments of reduced visibility. Given that contemporary anti–corporate globalization activists are attempting to build political forms that coincide with their emerging political norms, the assemblies and meetings I attended would invariably return to network structure and identity.[13]

Constituting the Movement for Global Resistance

The constitutive nature of such organizational debates was clearly evident in the case of MRG, particularly after Prague, when squatters abandoned the network because of their conflicting political visions, organizational forms, and technological practices. On the one hand, squatters criticized what they viewed as the rapid, unsustainable pace of more computer-savvy activists. Squatters often had limited Internet connection, and many felt that depending on computer networks was a strategic mistake. Moreover, squatters were used to working as tightknit political collectives, as opposed to the more open and diffuse style of network-based movements. Tensions began even before Prague, as Pau recalls: "There were conflicts about the use of the Internet, and whether the space should be more open or closed, what kind of people could take part, if we were organizing buses for everyone or only the people we knew, if it was more of an open campaign, or one based on collectives and more clearly demarcated."

As the fluid networking dynamics continued, many squatters dropped out, while others tired of endless debates about network identity. In particular, a contradiction emerged between a view of MRG as a diffuse space and an approach to the network as a coordinating mechanism for specific collectives. At the same time, there were also ideological differences. MRG positioned itself as grassroots, assembly based, and anticapitalist, but activists were willing to work with reformist sectors and the Marxist Left. On the other hand, militant squatters wanted to maintain a clearly defined political space and thus created an anticapitalist platform during the campaign against the World Bank. Some MRG-based activists later suggested that squatters were simply frustrated that other networks and movements had overtaken their own. As Marta argued, "The squatter movement was extremely important. There were massive struggles, a real boom. Then MRG was born, and after that the World Bank campaign; RCADE was radicalized. There were new realities, and I think some sectors could never accept that."

Even as some activists dropped out, the first MRG assemblies after Prague were designed to forge a minimal structure and identity.[14] Before they could implement a new model, however, MRG-based activists were swept up in a flurry of activity within the Barcelona 2001 campaign. Rather than working together as a unified bloc, participating collectives and individuals acted autonomously, even as they continued to identify with MRG. Nevertheless, as a precondition for participating, activists from MRG laid down a set of guidelines for the campaign: decentralized structure, grassroots assemblies, open participation, and support for nonviolent direct action.

Over the next year, MRG continued to serve as a fluid and open space for communication and coordination through various initiatives and mobilizations, including campaigns against the World Bank and EU in Barcelona, protests in Genoa and Brussels, as well as PGA- and WSF-related gatherings in Barcelona, Leiden, and Porto Alegre. I thus had the opportunity to take part in and observe numerous MRG assemblies and electronic discussions, which provided tools for sharing information, reinforcing political identities, generating ideas, and debating strategies. However, the same questions always returned: What is MRG? Who forms part of the network? Is it a diffuse space or a structured mechanism for coordinating among specific collectives?

The first Catalan-wide MRG gathering after the World Bank campaign was held in early September in a small coastal town just south of Barcelona. The assembly was meant to "reflect on MRG's current situation, its functioning, and political philosophy."[15] In addition to discussing internal structure, activists spent hours talking about MRG's role and identity. Some complained of a lack of coherence and visibility; as Carme suggested, "It seemed like MRG disappeared during the campaign against the World Bank—it was really a phantom!" For others, the main problem was that the balance between local and global struggles had tipped in favor of the global and away from day-to-day organizing. Another group felt that MRG was an open space for coordination and communication. They were more concerned about the lack of time spent defining strategies vis-à-vis other movement sectors. Indeed, for Montse, MRG primarily served as "a bridge between the campaign and more radical anti-capitalists." For their part, activists from outside Barcelona felt the regional network had given way to a small group in the capital. Reflecting the general confusion, Monica asked, "What is MRG? Is it a group of people, a network? I'm totally lost!" Still, everyone agreed that MRG represented a collective philosophy or, as Montse suggested, "a new way of organizing." Building networks was complex work, but despite their differences, everyone was committed to a new kind of politics based on the cultural logic of networking.

Similar issues resurfaced with even greater intensity during the next MRG assembly in Barcelona, when low attendance generated a heated debate regarding the state of the network. As Antoni pointed out, MRG had started out as the only Catalan network focusing on globalization, but the movement had since expanded. For Antoni, it was now more important to stress local activities among participating collectives: "If people want a campaign, now there are broader spaces! What we need is more continuity in terms of our local coordination." Carme quickly retorted, "All we ever do is talk about how MRG should function! We really should be discussing movement autonomy from parties and unions." While some activists wanted to forge priorities based on the interests of local groups, others preferred to discuss broader strategy surrounding MRG as a distinct philosophy. As Nuria argued, "We are falling back into old ways of thinking. MRG is a movement, and we don't need structure!"

Many MRG-based activists were critical of the perceived opportunism, reformism, and lack of democracy on the part of leftist parties and unions, but they often disagreed regarding the alternatives. One group emphasized the need for a clear, albeit decentralized, structure based on coordination among local collectives, while the other expressed a radical networking logic in their support for a fluid space for communication and coordination among diverse movements. The problem for the group promoting a diffuse network model was that the emergence of broader political spaces had threatened to make

MRG redundant, while those who emphasized clearer structures failed to appreciate the difficulty of coordinating around local issues.

At the final MRG assembly I attended in April 2002, the agenda returned once again to network structure and identity. The local organizing group from Terrassa brought a proposal to definitively transform MRG into a network of local collectives that would meet quarterly to share experiences, engage in collective learning, and coordinate around local initiatives. As Marc argued, "We have to move from being an open space of convergence toward functioning as a real network, with an emphasis on local collectives." By this time, many of the Barcelona-based activists had founded their own social center, while others were busy constructing new self-managed communication projects. Meanwhile, a broader movement space had emerged within the campaigns against the World Bank and EU. Some criticized MRG for lacking clear objectives, but others defended the network. "Sometimes we forget everything we've accomplished," insisted Nuria. "We organized Prague and then launched the World Bank campaign in June. We've facilitated a great deal of organizing and brought a lot of people together. That is what it means to build networks and generate collective mobilization."

For Nuria, MRG had served as a critical networking tool. Beyond tangible victories, she saw network building as a concrete political goal in itself. However, MRG was doomed by its own success, as the emergence of larger political spaces would soon render the network obsolete.

Building a Statewide Network against the Foreign Debt

Although RCADE went through similar identity crises, it maintained a solid statewide structure. RCADE had always created a stronger sense of belonging, particularly in regions with less social movement activity. This was in part due to its more clearly defined objectives: abolishing the foreign debt and promoting participatory democracy. Even so, activists spent a great deal of time during local, regional, and statewide assemblies assessing their goals and identity, debating priorities, and evaluating how to relate to other campaigns and political spaces. The statewide gathering in Bilbao in October 2001 provided one such occasion. An impressive three-day affair, the event attracted hundreds of grassroots activists from around the Spanish state. On the first day, participants divided into smaller groups to begin discussing the future of the network. I noticed a divide within my group between the Catalans, who had recently taken part in broader campaign spaces, and activists from the rest of the state, who maintained a clearer identification with RCADE. Miquel characterized the view from Barcelona as follows: "We came from 0.7, then we dealt with the debt as an excuse to critique the entire system, and then all of a sudden we went to Prague. Now we aren't sure who we are! We're kind of schizophrenic, as many of us work closely with MRG and other networks."

On the other hand, in Madrid, MRG and RCADE were seen as completely distinct. As one activist pointed out, "MRG is anarchist. *We* are trying to do something entirely new." An activist from Andalusia further insisted on the need for a discrete, stable identity: "We are RCADE and we have our own identity. Otherwise what sense does the network have? Our point of reference is the foreign debt." Miquel retorted that although RCADE still united many groups in other parts of the state, "In Catalonia we joined the Barcelona 2001 campaign as one group among many." That afternoon the agenda turned to network structure. Activists agreed on the "federal model," involving decentralized coordination based on horizontal flows of information. However, some promoted a stronger version of network identity, emphasizing the need to attract people to the Network, while those from Barcelona remained skeptical. "We don't want to only attract people to the Network," Miquel explained, "but rather also participate in broader networks and campaigns. I don't want an organization that grows. My objective is not to make RCADE grow, but rather to expand the entire movement. Otherwise, we'll become just like the parties and unions who only want more members."

The division once again pitted a classic organizational model against a radical networking ethic that posited RCADE as a more diffuse space for communication and coordination. Catalan activists would discuss these issues again at the regional level during an RCADE assembly in Barcelona the following April. Participants were particularly concerned that many local groups had seemingly disappeared. In this spirit, Pascal asked, "Do we remain a smaller network, or do we try to reactivate the sleeping nodes?" Others, like Joan, were less pessimistic: "There was a 'boom' with the Consulta, then the Network began to deteriorate, but now things are stabilizing. New nodes are getting involved." Moreover, as Enrique pointed out, "There are many groups out there who are using our name and label that we don't even know about." Like

MRG, RCADE was also an important organizational symbol and icon. Although activists disagreed about the continued relevance of the foreign debt as a unifying theme, they were committed to organizing future collective initiatives, including a Europe-wide Consulta.[16]

Digital-age networks such as RCADE and MRG are constructed and reproduced precisely through these kinds of communicative interactions and debates. Given that activists increasingly express their political ideals through concrete technological and organizational practices, it is no accident that such communication often involves conflict over organizational structure and process. In this sense, debates about the network and the maintenance of tools that facilitate such debates are crucial networking activities, which facilitate movement expansion and mobilization during periods of greater public visibility. As Pere, who served on coordinating committees for MRG and PGA, explained, "We are the handymen who clean and maintain the network, making sure it is there when everyone else needs it." Although RCADE proved more sustainable, MRG was thus ultimately dissolved not because the functions it performed were no longer useful but because those functions were now being performed elsewhere.

The Barcelona 2001 Campaign against the World Bank

The anti–corporate globalization movement sectors in Barcelona outlined in chapter 2 involve broad "spaces," a term that Spanish and Catalan activists often use to denote political sectors. During particular mobilizations and campaigns, activists, collectives, and organizations within distinct spaces forge strategic alliances. At any given time, the composition and balance of competing forces represent a momentary snapshot in a volatile movement field as opposed to an enduring portrait of a stable political landscape. In practice, these coalitions are contingent and constantly shifting through a dynamic process driven by concrete networking practices and micropolitical struggles regarding political organization, discourse, strategy, and tactics.

Depending on the context, network-based movements have alternatively forged alliances with militant anticapitalists, assembly-based movements, and institutional sectors. As we shall see, divergent political and organizational logics within specific campaigns have given rise to heated conflicts and debates. The trajectories of alternative activist networks and their evolving patterns of recombination, expansion, and contraction are thus shaped by a complex cultural politics. Given the increasing interpenetration of network technologies, organizational forms, and political norms, these tend to involve struggle over organizational structure and process.

As related earlier, many radical squatters dropped out of MRG soon after Prague because of differences in political style and rhythm. This realignment was further reinforced during the spring 2001 campaign against the World Bank, which developed as a broad convergence space involving more than 350 organizations, including leftist parties, unions, NGOs, ATTAC, and numerous civil society associations, in addition to MRG and RCADE.[17] Grassroots activists had planned to organize against the World Bank under the MRG banner, but the initial coordinating meeting drew participants from a wider array of political sectors. The assembly thus decided to create a unitary campaign, which would include network-based movements such as MRG and RCADE, but also organizations from more institutional spheres and the traditional Left. MRG ultimately decided to join the campaign, but militant anticapitalists opted to forge their own platform called Barcelona Trembles. Fernando explained the reasons for creating a separate platform: "We created Barcelona Trembles because we didn't want to mix with PSOE [the Spanish Socialist Workers' Party], which had been in power for fifteen years. We wanted to bring a different proposal with a clear anticapitalist critique."

Militants also rejected reformists more generally, including political parties, trade unions, and networks such as ATTAC. A Barcelona Trembles document exclaimed:

> Worn-out social democrats, moderate ecologists, co-opted and disoriented unions with their social pacts, and an out-of-place extraparliamentary Left have opted for large antiglobalization media platforms as an infusion of oxygen to legitimate their decaffeinated progressivism. A citizen-oriented current has also emerged (ATTAC, etc.) proposing small reforms to regulate globalization without questioning the structures of capitalist domination. Anticapitalist movements cannot allow reformists to take advantage of and delegitimate our struggles against power. Capitalism cannot be reformed; it must be destroyed—by directly attacking it and building day-to-day alternatives.[18]

MRG-based activists worked with both platforms to establish a bridge between moderate and anticapitalist sectors, but many felt personally attacked by the constant criticism of the larger campaign. Montse recalled, "Many of the people I have worked with for years are now squatting. Barcelona Trembles came out of the squatters' assembly, so it was easy to work with them. But they criticized us constantly, saying the campaign was tarnished. It affected me at a personal level, especially when just a week before the demonstration they put up signs saying, 'Against Parties, Against Unions, Against the Monkeys of Capital, Barcelona Tremble!'"

The rift between MRG and militant squatters widened after a small group of activists, presumably associated with Barcelona Trembles, failed to respect the informal nonviolence pact during the unitary march on June 24, 2001. The Barcelona Trembles assembly had supported the agreement, but there were mutual accusations: MRG criticized militants for not following the pact, while militants retorted that MRG had supported "the system" by publicly condemning the tactics of others. Although MRG never released a public statement regarding the matter, individuals and groups associated with the campaign, mostly from political parties and NGOs, made their own declarations condemning protester violence. Subsequent recriminations contributed to a widening chasm within the campaign between assembly- and network-based sectors and their institutional counterparts. Enric, a political party representative who was at the center of the controversy, recalled the situation: "After the demonstration on June 24, they called me from France Press to ask what I thought. I was confronting activists breaking windows, even if some of them were undercover police. I made some declarations condemning the violence. A previous assembly had decided that we wouldn't condemn violence, but I have the right to do so if it's my personal opinion. At the final two-hundred-person evaluation assembly, people said, 'How can you condemn violence? You are part of the system!' They shut me up; it was terrible."

Moreover, the fluid, consensus-oriented style of many younger activists often conflicted with the representative logic of formal member organizations. "The people from the parties were difficult to work with," explained Montse. "They were all over forty, and it was hard to change their methods. Many have legitimacy in historical terms, and were leaders during previous struggles, and now they want to appropriate this sphere as a space of decision making. They see our newer networks as a form of competition. 'What is a network? What do you mean there are no structures? What do you mean by diffuse?'"

For their part, participants from institutional sectors felt increasingly uncomfortable in the campaign, leading them to found the Barcelona Social Forum (BSF). Although organizers would not make the BSF public until November 2001, they had already initiated discussions before the Barcelona 2001 campaign ended about creating a separate platform based on a more formal representative structure and an emphasis on reforms and alternatives. As Arman told me:

> We already reached the limit during the campaign against the World Bank. I represented my organization, and it was clear that everything was barely holding together. We all knew it. We decided to wait on creating the Barcelona Social Forum because we wanted to support the campaign. It was already called, and we had to give support. But those of us who went to the assemblies felt extremely uncomfortable. An assembly should have some basic standards; I am not even talking about a representative structure. It's okay if everyone participates, but you can't go after people in the middle of an assembly saying, "Your organization isn't worth anything, you should just go home!"

The Barcelona 2001 campaign against the World Bank constituted an extremely tenuous alliance among institutional, assembly-oriented, and network-based movements. Only the militant anticapitalists stayed outside. However, after a great deal of conflict and debate surrounding political discourse, organizational logic, and street-level tactics, participants from the formal organizations decided to split off and form their own platform. By fall 2001 only the critical and network-based sectors remained.

Toward the Statewide Campaign against the Europe of Capital

As soon as the mobilization against the World Bank had concluded, the struggle among the remaining sectors over structure and continuity began. Not surprisingly, militants from the traditional Left emphasized continuity, while activists from MRG, RCADE, and other libertarian currents were reticent. When members of the "red sector" within Izquierda Unida (IU) continued to press the issue, many activists began to suspect overt manipulation. Indeed, conflicts between political parties and grassroots actors have a long history in Spain and Catalonia, including perceived attempts by Communist leaders to shape the direction of the anti-Franco movement. Manipulation is still a sensitive topic for contemporary activists. The issue came up during an evaluation assembly in Barcelona soon after the campaign against the World Bank had concluded, when an IU leader presented a proposal for moving forward. After a brief discussion about the wisdom of creating sustainable structures, she took the floor and explained, "The Barcelona 2001 campaign is over, but you have achieved so much and Barcelona has become central to this movement. I want to continue our work, but not necessarily the campaign. The Genoa Social Forum has become the Italian Social Forum, and we should create something statewide here in Spain."

She went on to propose the formal constitution of a movement with a common name and a calendar of actions, which would be forged during a subsequent statewide meeting. The proposal immediately drew criticism, given the general mistrust of permanent structures, especially those emanating from Madrid. Rather, as one activist responded, "The movement will grow through the network, by the network, and for all those involved in the network!" After the meeting, I sat with several MRG-based activists sipping beers on a terrace outside a bar along the Avenida Paralel in the old working-class neighborhood of Poble Sec. Nuria, who was visibly irritated, denounced the posture of the IU delegate, adding, "I have learned so much over the past year about how to organize from the grassroots, work collectively, and trust each other as activists and friends, but these people only know how to manipulate!" A protracted struggle between two organizational logics had begun: one based on permanent structures and another rooted in flexible, informal, and decentralized formations shaped by a self-generating network ideal.

The Madrid Meeting

Over the next few months, activists organized various assemblies at local and statewide levels to begin planning for a campaign against the Spanish presidency of the EU. In early September 2001, I attended an initial coordinating meeting in Madrid with Catalan activists from MRG and RCADE. After arriving on an overnight bus, we took the metro to a working-class suburb on the outskirts of town and made our way to the civic center. As we approached the building, an older gentleman brusquely asked, "Where are you from? Do you have any contacts?" After we dropped some names, he ushered us inside, where we were greeted by a group of activists from Barcelona Indymedia. It was early in the morning, but a large crowd was already milling about, perusing the bookstands and informational tables.

The assembly finally began an hour later, when the facilitator, who had earlier questioned us at the door, explained, "Our goals are to develop various thematic areas in order to give more content to our work, develop long-term campaigns, and reach out to various sectors." Most of the crowd wanted to talk about anti-EU actions in the spring.[19] Nearly two hundred people attended, including roughly three dozen from Catalonia. After an introductory plenary, we broke into thematic work groups and came back together to discuss our conclusions. We developed concrete proposals the following day. The plenary sessions were chaotic, with little facilitation and a tendency toward long-winded interventions characteristic of the traditional Left. The issue of structure and continuity arose again when the facilitator repeatedly referred to Barcelona 2001 as a statewide campaign. Members of the Catalan contingent began to murmur, and one muttered under her breath, "Barcelona 2001 has ended!" The following morning, the moderator continued referring to Barcelona 2001 as a statewide network, and Meri finally blurted out, "It's not a statewide network because we didn't want to give it a structure; there are no branches!"

The final plenary that afternoon involved a series of interventions regarding campaign names and goals. Some activists stressed the importance of sustained statewide coordination, while others, particularly those from MRG-Catalonia, preferred more fluid, decentralized dynamics. "We want to erase the name Barcelona 2001 forever," Carme explained. "We built the campaign as a unitary space, but many squatters and militants stayed out, so we had to build a bridge between them and the parties and unions. We have to avoid this situation. We still have a network, but we don't need a fixed structure; we have to make sure everyone will participate."

Toward the end of the day, activists finally agreed to create a common statewide name and slogan and to call for decentralized mobilizations in the different cities where the various summits during the Spanish EU presidency would be held. The proposal would be brought back to the various regions and discussed again at the next statewide assembly in Zaragoza in mid-November. However, when someone mentioned the upcoming "constitutive assembly," an activist from MRG quipped, "We don't have to constitute anything; we're already here! We're planning an assembly, not a structure or organization. This has been our new way of working in the antiglobalization movement!" Several Catalans enthusiastically nodded in approval.

Back in Barcelona

Two weeks later in Barcelona, at the final assembly of the campaign against the World Bank, a similar debate pitted Catalan activists from MRG and RCADE against their counterparts from the critical sectors. When the meeting began, roughly forty people were spread out across the hall. After a quick discussion of legal and financial matters, the discussion shifted to the campaign website. Luis from IU's red sector in Barcelona suggested maintaining the website to avoid confusion, adding, "How can we maintain the relations we have built within this movement? Our model has no precedents in terms of magnitude and form of organizing. Perhaps we could keep the name Rose of Fire?[20] We have to do something like the Italian Social Forum, which is a democratic convergence of all movements against globalization. If not, we are just a series of initiatives with nothing in common. We have to maintain this unitary space!"

Albert, a member of CCOO, agreed: "Continuity is important; now we have to organize around the WTO and the European Union." Activists from MRG and RCADE became increasingly uncomfortable, and Miquel finally intervened, indirectly criticizing Luis as he explained, "I'm here to do politics in a different way. There are a lot of people who don't believe in political parties, but who want to be politically active. We have to provide that space. We have to take advantage of what we have—two years of building networks—but with minimal structure!" Carme from MRG went even further:

> We have come from many different sectors to organize things in a different way: assembly based, plural, and diverse. At the end of the twentieth century, political structures are becoming more participatory. We are a movement of movements, where everyone has a space. We can't have a rigid structure or a rigid manifesto. Rather, we have to create a space to bring together the maximum number of people according to some basic common

principles, and each collective should work autonomously. We should not become a homogenizing structure. We have a series of coordinating tools, and we can continue coming together when we have things to discuss. I would sacrifice "unity" to continue building the movement of movements.

This was the classic organizational debate from the First International—expressed in network terms. Traditional leftists emphasized continuity and structure and the need to forge a united movement with clear membership and high visibility. Network-based activists countered that rigid structures discouraged participation and allowed political elites to take advantage of the movement for electoral purposes. Activists from MRG also hoped to bring militant squatters back into the fold, which would not happen if the campaign continued with a representative structure. On the contrary, they argued that subsequent campaigns should be clearly organized along network lines, combining decentralized coordination around common objectives with maximum diversity and autonomy. After several hours of debate, the assembly finally agreed to dissolve the Barcelona 2001 campaign. However, the unitary space would continue under a series of different names: the campaign against the WTO through November, and the campaign against the Europe of Capital and War during the winter and spring.

The Statewide Assembly in Zaragoza

A particularly emblematic struggle took place during the statewide gathering of the anti-EU campaign in Zaragoza in late November. With the contentious Madrid meeting fresh on everyone's minds, more than five hundred activists converged in Zaragoza from diverse networks around Spain. In addition to the workshops and assemblies, the local MRG-based organizers and anti-militarists had prepared an evening of social and cultural events, including music, theater, and a late-night bar crawl. Beyond attending to logistical issues, the meeting was thus also an occasion for generating collective identities and affective attachments. Indeed, all the major anti–corporate globalization networks and sectors were present. The Zaragoza meeting thus provided an excellent forum for observing how broader networking politics would continue to unfold.

During the opening assembly, facilitators announced the goals for the meeting: deciding on a calendar of actions, creating coordinating mechanisms, and establishing a campaign slogan. Most of the subsequent interventions involved updates from the regions and opinions about the relative priority of different mobilizations. Occasionally, political party and union representatives would comment about the need for structure. At one point, a Catalan friend leaned toward me and whispered, "These people want to take advantage of this political space, but they don't know how it works!" When his turn came around, Luis from IU in Barcelona stood up and explained that Barcelona had decided to organize a protest on March 16. Many of the Catalans became extremely upset, and one yelled, "We never decided that, you don't represent Barcelona!" Things settled down for a while, but after the assembly had started to move toward consensus on a series of coordinated actions in Barcelona, Zaragoza, Valencia, Madrid, and Sevilla, the IU delegate who had caused such controversy in Barcelona issued an impassioned plea: "What's this? Where are we going? We're not a travel agency running trips from summit to summit! The total has to be more than the sum of its parts. This has become a caricature. We're fleeing from something we can build together, doing much less than we ought to."

The assembly began to lose patience, but fortunately time had run out for the day. As we left the conference room, a shoving match ensued between Esteban from MRG and Luis over what many viewed as his attempt to "represent" the movement in Barcelona. Luis defended himself during a subsequent meeting among Catalans, suggesting he had done his best to reflect the decisions from the previous meeting, but Marc replied that he should have consulted with everyone before speaking. Carles then snapped, "I thought we were all committed to anticapitalism and assembly-based organizing here, but apparently some of us aren't!" This was tantamount to calling Luis a traitor. Attempting to diffuse the situation, Pere retorted, "I think we advanced sufficiently during Barcelona 2001 not to question our political credentials here." On our way out the door, an Italian friend who was visiting Spain after a year in Amsterdam smiled and noted, "Catalans take their politics so seriously; this kind of thing would never happen in the Netherlands." Indeed, if movements are produced and reproduced by the intensity of the communication flows circulating through them, such intense networking politics go a long way toward explaining the relative strength of social movement networks in Spain and Catalonia.

At the following morning's plenary session, IU delegates continued to press their case, but they were largely ignored. After several hours of debate, the assembly finally approved a calendar of decentralized actions and came up with a campaign slogan integrating an anticapitalist critique with language from more reformist sectors.[21] The crowd broke into a round of cathartic applause when the facilitator proclaimed: "Against the Europe of Capital and the War, Globalize Resistance, Another World Is Possible!" However, Zaragoza would be remembered as the place where Izquierda Unida tried and failed to co-opt the anti–corporate globalization movement.

Building an Autonomous Space in Barcelona

The Barcelona campaign against the Europe of Capital was officially established soon after the statewide assembly in Zaragoza.[22] Meanwhile, MRG-based activists had already begun to talk about the possibility of creating an "autonomous" space beyond the unitary campaign, which would involve network-based movements and their militant counterparts. Autonomous spaces—separate, yet connected to broader campaigns, protests, and events—have allowed more radical anti–corporate globalization activists to organize according to their own organizational dynamics and ideals while remaining connected to larger movement fields (see chapter 7). In this sense, the cultural politics of autonomous space reflect emerging network norms, forms, and practices.

As we casually drank coffee one day, Montse, Sergi, Pau, and I began talking about the anti-EU campaign and the various movement spaces in Barcelona. Montse scribbled a line on her napkin, drawing radical squatters farthest to the right and reformist parties and unions on the left. She placed MRG and RCADE on the center-right, and Marxist and Trotskyist groups toward the center-left, and explained, "During Barcelona 2001, MRG worked with the left side of the spectrum; this time we should move toward the right." Pau took her suggestion to heart and soon after Zaragoza drafted a controversial e-mail proposal arguing for the creation of an autonomous space. The message began:

> The Consulta for the Abolition of the Foreign Debt and the Prague 2000 Campaign began a huge movement that until now—around the state and

in many other places—has worked along open and decentralized lines. In campaigns such as Nice, Barcelona 2001, and the Europe of Capital, militants from parties and unions closer to the "old Left" have joined our mobilizations, with more and more determination, wanting to bring more of a classic centralized structure, which they are legitimately accustomed to, but without paying attention to the development of the movement around new organizational forms.[23]

Pau went on to explain how activists who were not willing to endure endless discussions and power struggles had already abandoned the unitary space. He further pointed out that when such diverse groups converge in a centralized space, there is often a loss of coherence, fluidity, and continuity. Rather, "If we create various spaces, each of them involving groups that have more in common, with a better atmosphere and more discursive coherence, everyone benefits." He concluded:

> We can't force each other to integrate within organizational forms we don't share. The best thing would be to organize within different spaces according to our own traditions, but coordinate in order to complement one another in daily practice. This is how we can apply the lessons learned from Prague and Genoa in our ongoing work. Separating does not mean dividing. On the contrary, it means moving forward in order to take advantage of both newer and older experiences and organizational ideas, learning from the errors of the past, toward a new form of understanding collective action. It's about separating in order to work more effectively together.

Just days before Pau e-mailed his document, another group of MRG-based activists had organized a weekend retreat in the Pyrenees. As pointed out in chapter 2, anti–corporate globalization networks in Catalonia are structured, in part, around strong interpersonal ties within informal friendship networks, which are reinforced during myriad social events and gatherings, including parties, dinners, and collective outings. The MRG retreat in the Pyrenees was meant to further solidify these social relationships while providing an opportunity to discuss important issues related to the network. The first evening's discussion turned to the proposal to create an autonomous space during the anti-EU campaign, continuing a long-standing debate regarding the relationship between social movements, political parties, and unions. MRG-based activists were critical of the institutional sectors, although some expressed a more radical stance. "I felt uncomfortable in the Barcelona 2001 campaign," Joseba confessed, "and will never work with CCOO, UGT, and IU again. They are not our allies." Antoni forcefully added, "Movements like MRG have nothing to do with classic structures. We want to create a new discourse, a new way of doing politics. Participating in unitary campaigns with parties and unions is not consistent: they want to impose their own discourse, while we want to start from zero and build a collective discourse together. We want to generate proposals for discussion, not convince everyone. We can't work with them. We can negotiate and coordinate around concrete issues, but from different spaces."

The discussion ultimately led to a concrete proposal to do just that: create separate platforms. Marçal, from a small anticapitalist collective in Terrassa, a town just outside Barcelona, suggested that we ought to reach out to the militant squatters. Nuria added that perhaps the militants had been right all along, but Marta strongly disagreed, arguing that "the critiques made by Barcelona Trembles were unwarranted and simplistic. We have nothing to be sorry about. During the World Bank campaign, MRG did the right thing, but now it is time to create our own autonomous space."

The group ultimately decided to propose a meeting among grassroots social movements to discuss the possibility of creating an autonomous platform outside the unitary campaign. The gathering took place in early December and involved several dozen people from MRG, RCADE, the Zapatista solidarity collective, squatter groups, and other militant circles. The meeting had a significant impact on the trajectory of social movement networks in Barcelona. Everyone denounced Izquierda Unida (IU) and their perceived attempt to manipulate recent assemblies, but the group was sharply divided over whether to create an autonomous space. The following dialogue is instructive:

Pilar: IU tried to manipulate the assembly in Zaragoza, but the dynamics in Barcelona are different. We should promote our own style of organizing, but within the unitary space.

Joan: But the parties want to create a statewide structure. We have to resist this effort, especially if we are emphasizing grassroots democracy.

Sergi: I agree. We have a different way of working—horizontal, decentralized, self-managed. The solution is easy: organize our own assemblies. We should create our own autonomous space, without the parties and unions.

At the same time, militant anticapitalists were concerned about their political isolation. They suggested that it might be better to join the campaign this time around, particularly since the more reformist political parties and unions, including the dominant sectors within CCOO and IU, had already created their own platform—the Barcelona Social Forum.[24] Militants viewed this as an opportunity to move back toward the broader movement field. The debate thus continued:

Pere: We already have our own space—the unitary campaign. Before creating an autonomous platform, we should think about what that would mean; becoming the Spanish Black Bloc could be dangerous.
Marc: Yeah, we have to find a third way, beyond the parties, but also overcoming the rigidity of the more closed collectives.
Gaizka: Creating two platforms would be extremely dangerous, and would allow the authorities to divide us into the good campaign and the bad campaign. We have to establish some basic principles and work within the broader space. If we leave the campaign to the party leaders, we become politically isolated.

As the consensus seemed to shift definitively against the idea of an autonomous space, I began to understand the subtle complexities of networking in Barcelona.

A subsequent meeting in January 2002 among activists from MRG, RCADE, and militant anticapitalist collectives helped them overcome their differences.[25] At the same time, rather than taking part in the larger assemblies, militant activists focused their efforts on putting together the final concert within a smaller working group. In the end, radical activists ultimately created a separate yet coordinated space, although *within*, rather than outside, the campaign. As I sat with Fernando drinking coffee a few months after the anti-EU campaign had ended, we discussed the complex alliances among diverse anti–corporate globalization networks in Barcelona. As Montse had done several months earlier, Fernando used a napkin to sketch a diagram, this time

June 2001

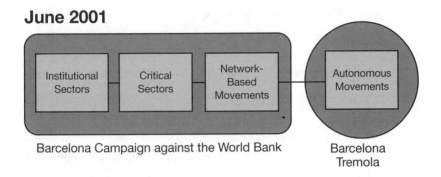

Barcelona Campaign against the World Bank

Barcelona
Tremola

March 2002

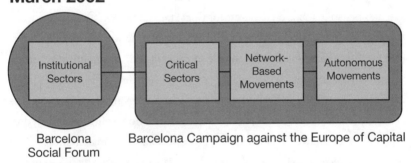

Barcelona
Social Forum

Barcelona Campaign against the Europe of Capital

3. Shifting alliances during anti–corporate globalization campaigns in Barcelona.

to depict how the political terrain had shifted between the campaign against the World Bank and the campaign against the EU. As he explained:

> This time the more autonomous, anticapitalist space was primarily within the campaign against the Europe of Capital, which was based on solid and radical political content. The radical Left moved toward here [he pointed to the unitary campaign space]. The previous separation of the Barcelona Social Forum made everything much easier; it helped us build an alliance between new social movements and grassroots organizations. When the Barcelona Federation of Neighborhood Associations and the Catalan Federation of NGOs position themselves within the campaign [they were also in the BSF]—I mean, when they take that step and support new forms of protest and political participation, with mutual respect, and when you have PSOE, CCOO , UGT, over there [he pointed to the BSF], then we say let's go over here, with the campaign against the Europe of Capital.

The wheel had come full circle. Militant anticapitalists, who left MRG after Prague and created their own platform outside the campaign against the World Bank, decided to rejoin the network-based movements, together with more grassroots civil society organizations, during the campaign against the Europe of Capital. They opted to do this in spite of the presence of groups from the traditional Left largely because the reformist sectors within the major parties and unions had created their own political space—one based on representation rather than grassroots assemblies. In addition, by remaining within the unitary campaign, militant anticapitalists and activists associated with MRG, RCADE, and other collectives would avoid political isolation.

Despite earlier concerns regarding the manipulation of assemblies, once activists began to focus on concrete logistical tasks, different networks worked together more effectively. Still, by primarily organizing within relatively tight-knit groups bound together by shared social, cultural, and political affinities, activists driven by diverse political logics would coordinate around a few concrete objectives through decentralized communication and coordination. The cultural *politics* of networking thus led to the formation, splitting, and recombination of alternative networks through continually shifting alliances, while the cultural *logic* of networking allowed activists from radically different traditions and backgrounds to work together within broad spaces of convergence that constantly evolved according to changing political circumstances.

Conclusion: Networking Democracy

The massive turnout in Barcelona for the mobilizations against the World Bank in June 2001 and against the Europe of Capital the following spring, where the unity march drew a half million people (see chapter 4), should come as no surprise given the intensity of networking politics among Spanish and Catalan anti–corporate globalization movements. Moreover, although MRG ultimately self-dissolved, it helped promote networking logics and practices throughout Spain and Catalonia. MRG's organizational philosophy and vision would thus ultimately outlive the network itself, giving rise to new and constantly shifting political formations.

As pointed out earlier, the differences between Catalan movement sectors reflect a wider struggle between two competing visions of democracy: one based on democratic representation within vertical structures and another rooted in direct participation via decentralized networks. This divide further entails contrasting views about the relationship between social movements and political institutions. In general, larger NGOs, leftist parties, and unions are committed to representative democracy, based on vertical leadership, political representation, majority voting, and electoral politics. According to this tradition, social movements are civil society lobby groups, which apply grassroots pressure to institutional actors, who are ultimately responsible for processing and implementing political proposals. Social movements, parties, and unions should thus work together, filling distinct yet complementary roles within the larger political process. As Arman, the social movement delegate from UGT, explained, "Social movements carry out grassroots work, raising awareness among citizens, but they cannot substitute for political parties. Neither should political parties attempt to direct social movements. Each one has to know what role they play, and in which social and political space they operate. If we don't work together, each one doing what they are supposed to do, we all lose."

According to this view, representative and assembly-oriented forms of organizing are equally legitimate. Each system has different strengths and weaknesses and responds to a distinct political base. As Enric from IC points out, "There are two ways of operating within the antiglobalization movement. Grassroots assemblies and representative structures each have their own deficits, but there is a lack of mutual recognition." Moreover, implicitly criticizing militants on the extreme Left, a delegate from Esquerra Republicana de Catalunya suggested to me, "Sometimes minority actors from within parties and unions attempt to use grassroots assemblies to further their own goals." On the other hand, some institutional actors view social movements as direct competition, a sentiment expressed in the now infamous Barcelona Social Forum press release sent out after the mobilization against the EU in March 2002, which declared, "We hope the situation during the recent Barcelona Summit does not happen again, given the (curiously) good coverage of the 'Campaign' and the confusion on the part of some of the media, which led to more media presence for that other antiglobalization current than the Barcelona Social Forum."[26]

Other members of the Barcelona Social Forum denounced the author, but he was surely not alone in his position. Although some moderate grassroots activists share the view that social movements and political parties are distinct, though complementary, spaces, as pointed out in the previous chapter, radical network-based activists increasingly conceive social movements as an alternative to representative democracy. During the first in a series of debates involving social movement activists and their institutional counterparts, Nuria from MRG strongly criticized the logic of political representation and electoral politics: "I understand how parties work; it's not that I don't recognize them, I simply don't like how they operate." Guillermo from RCADE added that despite their pretensions, parties represent very few people: "We are thus creating a new political culture, a new way of doing politics, based on grassroots citizen participation, and not representation." Indeed, as argued in chapter 2, the critique of institutional democracy has strong roots among Catalan activists. As Santiago, an older member of ATTAC, pointed out during the second debate between movements and parties the following July, "The parties and unions took power between 1977 and 1980 with the idea of transforming society, but I have never forgiven them for abandoning grassroots movements like the neighborhood associations. We prefer to transform society from below."

Traditional anti-party sentiment among Catalan activists has thus recently fused with a growing perception of widespread democratic crisis, given what activists view as the increasing influence of transnational capital and signs of right-wing reaction, as well as the emergence of new digital technologies that facilitate grassroots participation. As Pau from MRG explained, "When the economic system is globalized, a government can't do much to change things in a single place. They can try, but at the cost of losing foreign capital investment. This means governments no longer have the credibility to promote real change. They have created a system in which transformation can no longer come through the state."

When I specifically asked Joan from RCADE what should replace the current system of representative democracy, he was unsure, but he thought it was important to build a more directly democratic system from below. "One of the things that motivates me these days is trying to figure out how we should organize democracy at the beginning of the twenty-first century, given the technological infrastructure at our disposal and new forms of economic integration. How do we deepen our local democratic practices—at work and in our neighborhoods—and transfer that spirit to the global level?"

As della Porta et al. (2006, 197) suggest, new social movements are characterized more generally by their search for alternative models of democratic practice. Indeed, for many activists in Barcelona, learning how to build sustainable but radically decentralized networks, which are locally rooted yet regionally and globally coordinated, suggests a concrete mechanism for generating alternative democratic practices and values. In this sense, at least within more radical anti–corporate globalization sectors, networks are moving beyond the realm of technology and organizational form and are beginning to provide a vision for radically reconstituting politics and society. Whereas directly democratic forms of political participation have historically been restricted to local contexts, digital networking technologies and practices are facilitating new experiments with grassroots democracy, networked at local, regional, and global scales. The most ambitious anti–corporate globalization activists are thus not only promoting grassroots participation within their social movement networks; they are also generating innovative democratic norms, forms, and practices, which they hope might one day transcend representative democracy.

4

PERFORMING NETWORKS AT DIRECT-ACTION PROTESTS

The inherent risk, excitement, and danger of the action creates a magically focused moment, a peak experience, where time suddenly stands still and a certain shift in consciousness can occur. Many of us have felt incredibly empowered and have had our lives fundamentally radicalized and transformed by these feelings. Direct Action is praxis, catharsis and image rolled into one. . . . To engage in direct action you have to feel enough passion to put your values into practice: it is literally embodying your feelings, performing your politics.[1]

After some initial confusion near Náměstí Míru Square, several thousand young anti–corporate globalization activists began their Pink March descent through the narrow, serpentine streets of Prague toward the conference center where the World Bank and IMF meetings were being held. My Barcelona-based affinity group, the Open Veins, took the lead. It was September 26, 2000—the largest mass direct action against corporate globalization outside North America to date. Radical activists had mobilized from around Europe, including large contingents from the Movement for Global Resistance (MRG) in Catalonia, Ya Basta! from northern Italy, and the British-based Reclaim the Streets, while solidarity actions had been organized around the world.

During the months preceding the protest, organizers had worked out an elaborate action plan, dividing the urban terrain of resistance (Routledge 1994) into three color-coded zones. The Blue March would involve high-risk militant action, the Yellow March would entail the lowest risk, and the Pink March would provide an intermediate zone. In practice, the Italian White Overalls transformed the Yellow March into a mass of bodies engaged in spectacular symbolic confrontation, the Blue March became a battlefield pitting Black Bloc swarms hurling stones and Molotov cocktails against riot police armed with water cannons and tear gas, and the Pink March provided a space for creative nonviolent blockades. Additional zones were established for decentralized actions to the south of the congress center, and a mobile blend of festive and militant tactics dubbed Pink and Silver. Alternative social movement networks were embodied through diverse protest performances, inscribing distinct political messages on the urban and mass media landscapes.

Whereas in previous chapters I have explored networking dynamics within "submerged" spheres (Melucci 1989), I now shift to the visible moments of social movement activity. Here I consider how networking practices and politics are physically embodied during anti–corporate globalization protests.[2] During mass actions and mobilizations, the increasing confluence among technology, norm, and form is expressed through human bodies and transposed onto space. In this sense, network norms and forms are reproduced through the division of urban terrains and decentralized coordination among diverse protest blocs. Indeed, this "diversity of tactics" ethic reflects the cultural logic of networking itself. At the same time, mass mobilizations and actions generate powerful emotions, which are particularly important for sustaining commitment within more diffuse, network-based movements. However, when mass mobilizations become routine, their emotional impact may wane, transforming a strategic weapon into a potential weakness.

Mass direct actions are complex performative terrains that produce a dual effect.[3] Externally, they are powerful image events (DeLuca 1999), where diverse activist networks communicate their messages to an audience by "hijacking" the global media space afforded by multilateral summits (Peterson 2001).[4] Internally, they constitute platforms where alternative subjectivities are expressed through distinct bodily and spatial techniques, and emotions are generated through ritual conflict. At the same time, direct-action strategies involving horizontal coordination among autonomous groups and the division of space among distinct protest styles reproduce emerging network norms and forms on the tactical plane. This chapter explores the visceral and performative dimensions of activist networking through a comparative ethnographic analysis of anti–corporate globalization mobilizations in Prague and Barcelona. In what follows, I argue that mass mobilizations are critical networking tools but are difficult to reproduce over time, posing a long-term strategic challenge.

Mass Mobilizations as Performative Terrains

Several months before the June 2001 mobilization against the World Bank in Barcelona, bank leaders announced they would cancel their scheduled conference in the city, fearing major disturbances. The Barcelona 2001 campaign declared victory but faced a major dilemma about whether the mobilization should proceed. Everyone agreed to move forward with the march and counterconference, but the direct action provoked controversy. Institutional actors were worried about the potential for violence, suggesting that direct action was no longer necessary, as the World Bank conference had been canceled. On the contrary, many radicals felt it was important to carry on. As Sergi from MRG explained, "Civil disobedience is not a frivolity; it is a profoundly pedagogic act. Mass nonviolent civil disobedience represents a qualitative advance during the past few years, allowing for the recuperation of an antagonistic space at a moment when traditional demonstrations and counterconferences were being absorbed by the progressive rhetoric of the system."[5]

Sergi viewed direct action as important for two reasons. First, he understood that beyond its practical effects, civil disobedience has an important communicative dimension. In this sense, direct actions are cultural performances, which communicate political messages to an audience.[6] Moreover, direct actions specifically involve conflict, and it is precisely this "antagonism" that distinguishes civil disobedience from traditional marches and rallies. Although mobilizations of all kinds are performative, direct actions are designed to provoke confrontation, thus generating particularly compelling images and emotions. In the end, the campaign decided to go ahead with the action, but ironically, it would be the unity march that generated the most powerful effects. Indeed, following the march, the Spanish police charged crowds of peaceful protesters relaxing in the Plaza de Catalunya, unleashing widespread panic, excitement, and fear.

Mass anti–corporate globalization mobilizations constitute performative terrains where networking practices and politics are physically embodied. This is so in at least three senses. First, mass mobilizations provide spaces where networks are constituted through virtuoso protest performances.[7] As we have seen, activist networks are produced and reproduced through myriad communicative interactions. These are particularly intense and rendered widely visible during public protests. Indeed, mass actions and mobilizations create multiple theatrical spaces where new political subjectivities are forged (Hetherington 1998, 142).[8] As we shall see, the diverse tactics anti–corporate globalization activists perform, including militant confrontation, symbolic conflict, and carnivalesque revelry, thus involve alternative activist "techniques of the body" (Mauss 1973), which generate and embody competing network identities.[9]

Mass anti–corporate globalization mobilizations also provide platforms for experimenting with network norms and forms through the division of urban space among diverse protest tactics. Mass direct actions, in particular, allow activists to challenge the major institutions and symbols of neoliberal capitalism while simultaneously working out emerging network-based models of organization.[10] In this sense, cultural performances are emergent—they make certain aspects of social structure visible and thus amenable to change (Bauman 1977, 43).[11] As performative terrains, mass actions shine a light on hierarchical social relations while providing spaces for working out alternative forms of sociality. At the same time, complex networking politics are also physically mapped and embodied during anti–corporate globalization protests. Competing networks represent themselves through alternative modes of bodily and spatial practice, not only against a common enemy, but also in opposition to one another. Indeed, it is largely through collective praxis, rather than discursive unity, that political alliances are forged.

Finally, anti–corporate globalization mobilizations also generate powerful emotions.[12] As performative rituals, mass mobilizations, and actions in particular, largely operate through affect, amplifying an initiating emotion, such as a sense of injustice, and transforming it into collective solidarity (Collins 2001, 29). The awareness of bodily copresence during mass protests induces particularly strong sensations, which Randall Collins refers to as "emotional energy."[13] My own militant ethnographic experience resonates with this analysis, but I refer to such feelings in less mystical terms as "affective solidarity."[14] Affective solidarity prepares activist bodies for action. However, compared to institutionalized marches and rallies, relatively free-form actions are more emotively potent, in part because activists use their bodies to enact radical confrontation, but also because they introduce elements of danger, uncertainty, and play.

Mass mobilizations thus provide important networking tools, which allow anti–corporate globalization activists to embody their networks and experiment with emerging network norms and forms while generating intense feelings through ritual catharsis. Given their unpredictable, confrontational nature, mass actions produce a great deal of affective solidarity, which is particularly important for diffuse network-based movements that rely on nontraditional modes of political identification and commitment. At the same time, when mass actions and mobilizations become routine, their impact may diminish over time. Indeed, as Sergi pointed out, traditional protests can be "absorbed by the progressive rhetoric of the system." In this sense, whereas the direct action against the World Bank and IMF in Prague was relatively small—yet innovative and emotionally potent—the march against the EU in Barcelona drew masses of participants but failed to produce the same empowering effects.

Prague: Countersummit Action in Europe

After protesters shut down the WTO Summit in Seattle, activists around the world were eager to organize more anti–corporate globalization actions. Europeans had their next chance when the World Bank and IMF fall meetings came to Prague in September 2000. A small group of anarchists, environmentalists, and human rights activists forged a loose coalition called the Initiative against Economic Globalization (INPEG), which began meeting regularly during summer 2000 to prepare for the mobilization.[15] In addition to local Czechs, a small contingent of internationals from the United States, Great Britain, Spain, and Catalonia also began to organize in Prague that summer, while Listservs were established to coordinate at a distance. As with previous actions, decisions were made by consensus, and a "spokescouncil" model was employed based on decentralized coordination among autonomous affinity groups organized into larger clusters and blocs.

Activists hammered out the action framework during an international meeting in Prague in August 2000.[16] Rather than preventing delegates from meeting, activists decided to blockade them inside the congress center. The major sticking point involved strategy. Socialist-oriented activists, particularly from the British Socialist Workers Party (SWP), supported a single march, while those of an anarchist bent preferred autonomous actions. Socialists argued that protesters would arrive late, making it difficult to self-organize, whereas strength in numbers would allow activists to break through police lines. Anarchists felt police would be less prepared to handle autonomous actions, whose discrete movements would surround the congress center from multiple directions. However, the disagreement was not just tactical; it was also expressive.

Terrains of resistance are sites of geographic *and* representational contestation, involving forces of domination and resistance, as well as different values, beliefs, and goals (Routledge 1994, 560–61). Within such terrains, activists carry out diverse movements. For example, "packs" are small and serve as "crowd crystals" (Canetti 1962), enacting scattered motions across space (Routledge 1997a, 76). By contrast, "swarms" openly confront their targets through coordinated actions from all sides. As we shall see, affinity groups move in packs, while the overall blockade strategy produces a swarming effect, where "dispersed units of a network . . . converge on a target from multiple directions" (Arquilla and Ronfeldt 2001, 12). At the same time, these distinct spatial practices embody alternative political visions.

In this sense, for the swp, a single march would exhibit unity, reflecting their underlying Trotskyist goal: fomenting popular uprising from below. For the anarchists, smaller pack actions would express their commitment to diversity, decentralization, and self-management. After nine hours, organizers finally reached a compromise: marchers would start together and then split into separate blocs, swarming the conference center through a diversity of tactics. The agreement physically incorporated a horizontal networking logic, as diverse groups would engage in their own autonomous yet coordinated forms of embodied protest. Moreover, distinct protest styles would also reflect homologous relationships among bodies, styles, and identities. In this sense, protesters would perform their networks through diverse bodily and spatial practices, inscribing symbolic meanings on urban and media landscapes.

My Prague experience began at a workshop in Barcelona where I joined an affinity group called the Open Veins.[17] The morning after arriving in Prague together with several buses from Madrid and Barcelona, we held an assembly downtown. Pau gave us a brief update, describing the three color-coded marches. Our affinity group decided to spend the day getting to know the emerging terrain of resistance. After checking e-mail, we headed to the Infocenter, a modern storefront taken over by INPEG. A Catalan activist met us at a table with event schedules, volunteer sign-up sheets, and information. The walls were covered with posters, schedules, and announcements in Czech, English, German, Spanish, and Italian. Across the hall, the media center was overflowing with Czech and foreign journalists. Finally, we walked over the river to the Vltavska Cultural Center, where the countersummit was taking place.

Over the next few days, the convergence center on the edge of town was transformed into an activist "homeplace" (hooks 1990), a teeming refuge for hippies, students, anarchist punks, squatters, peasants, and aging Marxist intellectuals. There was frenetic activity everywhere, including medical workshops, direct-action trainings, and spokescouncil meetings. Jugglers and fire breathers walked among affinity groups discussing action plans, theories of social change, or the latest protest music. Posters, action updates, activities calendars, volunteer sign-ups, medical and day-care information, and message boards covered the walls. One sign asked affinity groups to appoint a contact person and secure a mobile phone and FM radio to become part of the communication structure.[18] The building next door was used as an art space and vegan kitchen.

The convergence center was like a small, self-managed city, a "heterotopic space" of exchange and innovation (Hetherington 1998; cf. Foucault 1986). Indeed, for many activists, it represented a physical embodiment of the diverse, egalitarian, and self-managed world they hoped to create. This cauldron of sights, sounds, and colors generated powerful feelings of excitement and solidarity, while diverse networks and their complex patterns of interaction were rendered visible. As Pablo from Las Agencias (an art collective allied with MRG) explained, "It's difficult to find words to describe my experience when I arrived at the convergence center. It was fascinating, incredible—color, imagination, desire, work—people never stopped working. At first it was like a beehive, and you didn't understand what was happening, you had no idea where to go. But then you penetrated further and recognized the different movement currents; you began to see how affinity groups came together, combined, transformed, and interacted. There was a mutual learning and exchange."

That evening we went to the convergence center for a spokescouncil meeting involving more than 350 activists from a dozen countries. Public meetings were usually held in English, with simultaneous translation in Spanish

4. German bike caravan arrives at the Convergence Center in Prague. PHOTOGRAPH COURTESY OF JEFFREY S. JURIS.

and other languages, which often provoked criticism of Anglo domination.[19] At the same time, English remained the most widespread lingua franca. An activist from the U.S.-based Direct Action Network facilitated the meeting, which was translated into Czech and Spanish. Organizers went over the battle plan, explaining how the march would begin at Náměstí Míru Square before splitting off into three separate blocs.

The topography would be crucial, as the congress center was located at the edge of a deep ravine. A six-lane access highway ran from the outskirts of the city to the southeastern side of the center. Meanwhile, the high, double-lane Nusle Bridge led directly to the congress center from Náměstí Míru. Finally, narrow cobblestone streets surrounded the center along the western side. The swarming strategy would involve setting up blockades along the primary access road and then surrounding the summit. Two additional blocs would be added during the few days before the action: a Pink and Silver March led by a British-based samba band, and a network of autonomous affinity groups, which would take up decentralized blockades in the south. When the SWP opted to move their 2,500-person contingent from the Pink to the Yellow Bloc, our affinity group decided to reinforce the Pink March, which desperately needed more bodies.

The emerging terrain of resistance was thus divided into various color-coded zones, each providing a space for diverse kinds of political expression enacted through distinct embodied performances.[20] Different styles and forms of direct action reflected divergent political logics, inscribing contrasting political meanings on the urban and mass-media landscapes. Alternative networks were literally embodied through diverse performative styles. While some tactics emphasized violent rejection of the current order, others prefigured utopian alternatives.[21]

The Blue March provided a space for radical youths associated with anarchist networks based in squatted social centers throughout Germany, Poland, the Czech Republic, Greece, Spain, and elsewhere. Masked, black-clad militants would use their bodies to enact rituals of violent confrontation, swarming the western side of the congress center and communicating a radical rejection of the system. The Yellow March involved a classic revolutionary tactic, as a disciplined bloc of massed bodies would approach the congress center across Nusle Bridge from the north, practicing direct, though nonviolent, confrontation. swp and other socialist networks would be identified by traditional sectarian markings, while thousands of young Italian radicals associated with a vibrant circuit of squatted social centers, together with large numbers of anti–corporate globalization activists from around Europe, would perform their emerging network identities during a spectacular White Overalls confrontation.

Meanwhile, the Pink March and southern autonomous actions would practice traditional civil disobedience, using vulnerable bodies to occupy space and communicate political dissent. Finally, the Pink and Silver March would follow a flexible spatial pattern, as activists associated with pga and related networks contrasted a utopian world of creativity, play, and egalitarian relations to the hierarchical universe of states and global capitalism.[22] Competing networks and their distinct styles and visions would thus be performed through alternative bodily and spatial practices. The overall diversity-of-tactics strategy would reproduce a networking logic on the tactical plane as emerging network norms and forms were transposed onto urban space and expressed through horizontal coordination among distinct protest performances.

On the morning of September 26, Náměstí Míru Square was bustling with thousands of activists holding colorful puppets, signs, and props. We lined up

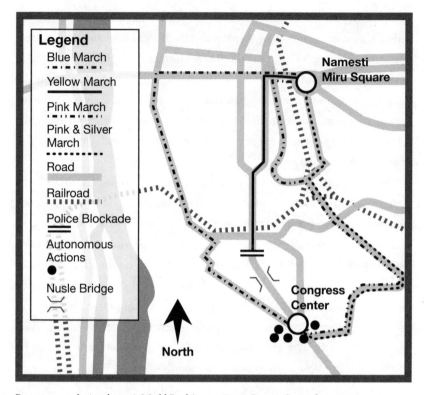

Protest routes during the anti–World Bank/IMF action in Prague, September 26, 2000.

in the street along with the Pink March early that afternoon, and after sending a scout ahead to make sure the route was clear, we moved out, chanting, "Hey, hey, ho, ho, the World Bank has got to go!" Dozens of Czech and international journalists began snapping pictures and recording video footage. Sandra, Miguel, and I exchanged glances as our moral outrage was transformed into feelings of collective power and solidarity. We were literally embodying our networks through a performative "assertion of agency" (E. Wood 2001, 268). Reflecting her sense of historical significance, Nuria from MRG recalled, "There are times when something surges up from inside, as if your body were saying, 'Now you are living something truly important.'" I would experience similar feelings throughout the day as I encountered activists from diverse protest marches around the city.

The Yellow March

After a few minutes, people began shouting at us to slow down. Most of the Pink March had followed the Ya Basta! sound system toward the bridge. The

5. Protesters gather in Náměstí Míru Square. PHOTOGRAPH COURTESY OF JEFFREY S. JURIS.

Blue March successfully navigated its way along the western side of the congress center, but the Pink Bloc was in disarray. Rather than continue with depleted numbers, we decided to turn around and walk back toward the bridge, where thousands of activists from the Pink and Yellow Blocs were standing around a grassy plaza. I made my way through the crowd to get a closer look. Two tanks were blocking the bridge, flanked by an impressive battalion of soldiers and riot cops. Several hundred Italian, Spanish, and Finnish activists dressed from head to toe in white overalls and protective padding were pushing against police lines with huge plastic shields and inner tubes. The Invisibles collective from Madrid describes this strategy as follows: "The white overalls are a collective symbol in order to break out of our individualism, to become part of an idea, to be next to others, close by and far away. It is the corporal base, concrete and enabling, of an important movement of liberation. . . . We believe we have to protect our bodies and organize ourselves to make contact, body to body, to show the conflict to everyone, to create a physical and political problem for our enemy."[23]

As I watched from a safe distance, the performative dimension of the action became clear. Row after row of similarly outfitted yet uniquely adorned bodies were pushing with elbows linked against the multiple lines of riot police protecting the entrance to the bridge. Behind the police stood the two tanks:

6. Militant ethnographer (*center*) at the front of the Pink March in Prague.
PHOTOGRAPH COURTESY OF JEFFREY S. JURIS.

the coercive power of the Czech state on display for everyone to see. Across the line of battle, the multitude of bodies was at once a collective and individualized force. In addition to their white overalls, activists wore multiply colored headgear, including black, silver, white, yellow, blue, and orange helmets. Some also carried shields made from black inner tubes, clear plastic panels, and detached seat cushions. I began to focus on one particular protester, who was wearing goggles and a surgical mask. Covered in protective padding made from yellow industrial foam, he exhibited a defiant yet festive air, inching forward together with his comrades. The mass of assembled bodies continued to push against the police barricade for several hours, communicating resistance to nation-states and their corporate backers in the congress center while creating an emotionally and visually compelling conflict.

The action had practical *and* performative dimensions. For example, the bizarre padded outfits protected activists from powerful baton blows, but they also expressed political messages regarding the importance of frivolity, laughing in the face of power, and uniting across diversity and difference. Moreover, the white overalls represented, in part, the autonomous Marxist ideals promoted by the activist networks who wore them, including making conflicts visible, generating new subjectivities, and the (self-) constitution of

7. Italian White Overalls lead the Yellow March toward the Nusle Bridge. PHOTOGRAPH
COURTESY OF ANDREU BLANCHAR I ARNAVAT.

the multitude (cf. Hardt and Negri 2004). At the same time, diverse bodily
adornments, such as recycled inner tubes, helmets, and foam padding, produced "grotesque" bodies (Young 1993), providing ready-made images for the
mass media.[24] The White Overalls thus not only helped enclose World Bank
and IMF delegates inside the congress center, they also generated a spectacular
image event, as disciplined rows of dystopically decorated bodies conveyed a
powerful message of dissent. Indeed, dramatic photos circulated widely over
the next few days, depicting the massive bloc of protesters pushing against
the police lines high above the streets below. Protesters succeeded in eliciting
widespread media attention while embodying their networks through nonviolent yet highly confrontational performance.

The Pink March

After observing the Tute Bianche, for a few minutes I rejoined my affinity
group, and together with other groups from Britain, Sweden, and Norway, we
began to reorganize the Pink March using our giant flags to lead people down
the narrow streets along the eastern flank of the congress center. As we guided
hundreds of protesters around the corner, Jorge glanced at me and observed,
"This is great; I've never felt so alive!" Indeed, using our bodies to direct such

8. Close-up of the White Overalls in Prague. PHOTOGRAPH COURTESY OF ANDREU
BLANCHAR I ARNAVAT.

a large and determined crowd generated powerful feelings of agency and solidarity. It was largely through these kinds of intense emotional experiences that we began to feel connected, both as an affinity group and as part of a larger convergence of anti–corporate globalization networks.

Eager to begin the blockade, we soon became more purposeful and serious. By the time we approached the access highway, our ranks numbered several thousand. The Swedes and Norwegians marched directly up the ramp, while the rest of us wound our way around the side streets, meeting at a park next to the congress center. A bike messenger gave us an update at a brief spokescouncil meeting: autonomous affinity groups had taken up blockade positions to the south that morning, while the Yellow March was still engaged in a standoff with police at the bridge. Meanwhile, a pitched battle was raging to the west between a few thousand Black Bloc militants from Germany, Poland, Greece, and the Czech Republic and the heavily fortified police lines. Finally, the Pink and Silver march had joined the other Pink Bloc group back along the highway. Although our networks were engaging in distinct protest performances, expressing contrasting political visions and goals, as I listened to the action report, I began to feel connected across our differences as we worked toward a common goal.

9. Swedish activists engage in nonviolent civil disobedience. PHOTOGRAPH COURTESY OF ANDREU BLANCHAR I ARNAVAT.

After the meeting, we took up blockade positions, using our bodies to occupy the space in front of the police lines. The other Pink Bloc group soon came over and joined us as well. Men in business suits occasionally tried to break our blockades, at which point we would all stand up and lock arms to prevent them from passing. The police stood by for the most part, some looking fearful, others mildly amused. Once again, beyond the practical impact of the Pink Bloc action, protesters were communicating messages of determined yet nonviolent opposition, reproducing classic scenes of nonviolent protest. At one intersection, for example, a group of Swedes wearing jeans and colorful T-shirts sat cross-legged across from several dozen riot cops dressed in black. As the police threatened to charge, the young activists quietly held their ground. Just a few feet away, a lone protester with his hair in a bun kneeled quietly in meditation, holding his hands out before him in a classic sign of peaceful intent. Such nonviolent performances symbolically contrasted the vulnerable, morally righteous bodies of the protesters with the menacing bodies of the police, which physically represented the coercive power of the state.

We maintained the blockade for many hours, talking, strategizing, and eating vegan stew. Rumors soon began circulating that most of the delegates had been whisked away via an escape route before the summit had concluded. Our initial euphoria had given way to a period of malaise, but our spirits picked up again when we realized we were having an impact. Moreover, with stories circulating of violent clashes to the east, we began to sense the nervous excitement preceding a "discharging" crowd (Canetti 1962). Shortly after dinner, word began circulating that Blue March reinforcements were on their way. All of a sudden, a long line of police came around the corner. We made a quick decision to sit down, using our bodies to hold the space. Just then, dozens of masked and hooded anarchists appeared, hurling stones and empty bottles at the police lines surrounding us. Several activists were struck with projectiles, and the terrified cops violently broke through our blockade, smashing heads along the way. "Hey, what are you doing, this is a nonviolent zone, people are getting hurt!" we called out, but to no avail, as few militants spoke English or Spanish. The panic, fear, and confusion provoked minutes of chaos before the situation calmed down. Indeed, as Goodwin and Pfaff (2001) point out, managing fear is a critical aspect of high-risk political situations.

After the melee ended, I went around the corner to join my affinity group, which had initiated another blockade. An armored police vehicle soon approached, and we maintained our position. After a brief but intense standoff, the vehicle backed away as a small group of hooded Czech anarchists banged on the windows. The police soon reinforced their lines, and we feared another attack. Our fear transformed into elation, however, when the riot cops backed off again. We had successfully held the space. Miguel, Gerard, and I started to cheer and hug, and then the entire group began celebrating our momentary victory through playful mockery and dancing in front of the stoic, heavily armed riot cops. At one point, we organized a conga line and began to circle, chanting, "The Conga, of Calixto, walks round and round!" We had entered a riveting space of carnivalesque revelry, inducing feelings of collective power and solidarity. Many of us had experienced shifting emotions throughout the day, generating particularly vivid memories. As Gerard from RCADE recalled, "There was a pre-Prague and a post-Prague in my life. I met so many people there and had such an incredible experience. There were moments of happiness, then times when your morale sunk through the floor. There was fear, panic, but also festivity; it was incredible."

Indeed, protesters often remember such rapid shifts from one emotional state to another most clearly (cf. Barker 2001). It was precisely the constantly changing, spontaneous, and open-ended nature of the Pink March, and the Prague action more generally, that generated extremely high levels of affective solidarity. The emotional potency of such free-form actions recalls Don Handelman's (1990) distinction between events that "present the lived-in world" and those "that re-present the lived-in world." The former, which include standard marches and rallies, directly display, declare, and reflect the world as already constituted. On the contrary, the latter enact comparison, contrast, and critique. Events of re-presentation also have an important liminal quality, characterized by strong egalitarian sentiments, or "communitas" (Turner 1969). In this sense, mass actions are shot through with "liminoid" (Turner 1982) outbursts of terror, panic, and play, as well as periodic moments of collective solidarity.[25]

The Pink and Silver March

As we patiently held our Pink March blockades, the Pink and Silver Bloc danced in and out behind the British-based samba band. Dozens of dancers wearing pink skirts, tights, pants, and leotards, and the occasional silver jumpsuit, frolicked to the beat of the drums along with their brightly colored masks and flags. Indeed, drumming, dance, and music help create what Canetti calls the "rhythmic" crowd: "What they lack in numbers, the dancers make up in intensity. . . . As long as they go on dancing, they exert an attraction on all in their neighborhood. . . . They move as though there were more and more of them. Their excitement grows and reaches frenzy" (Canetti 1962, 31–32). Activist bands, including various Samba troupes and the Infernal Noise Brigade from Seattle, provide focal points during anti–corporate globalization mobilizations, producing widespread feelings of embodied agency. In Prague, Samba dancers not only helped generate affective solidarity; their festive and playful performances also represented a stark contrast to both militant protesters and the Czech police.

Meanwhile, Radical Cheerleaders and Pink Fairies would occasionally break away from the group, performing ironic cheers and taunting the police. As we held our intersection, a Pink Fairy approached a nearby police vehicle and began "cleaning" it with her feather duster, much to the delight of the crowd. When the police failed to respond, she was emboldened and approached individual officers, brushing their shoes as they nervously looked

10. Samba band plays during the Pink and Silver March.
PHOTOGRAPH COURTESY OF TIM RUSSO.

on. Chesters and Welsh (2004) later interviewed one of the Pink Fairies, who pointed to the clear performative dimension of her actions: "And this sort of like stage space appears, this performance space seemed to appear between like the rows of policemen and the rows of people blockading, like physically blockading and then there's this little gap in the middle, you know what I mean, and we found ourselves going into this gap and tickling policemen's toes, do you know what I mean, with your feather duster on the side of their face and just like performing" (330).

Such playful provocation represents a form of ritual opposition, a symbolic overturning of hierarchy much like medieval carnival, as Bakhtin suggests: "Carnival celebrated temporary liberation from the prevailing truth and from the established order; it marked the suspension of all hierarchical rank, privileges, norms, and prohibitions" (1984, 10). In this sense, Pink and Silver tactics used burlesque bodies to symbolically contrast a world of creativity, color,

11. Pink Fairy performs for the crowd. PHOTOGRAPH COURTESY OF JEFFREY S. JURIS.

and play to the dark, oppressive forces of law and order. Play, in particular, reveals the possibility of radically reorganizing current social arrangements. It thus exists in the subjunctive mood, "the domain of the 'as-if' " (Turner and Schechner 1986, 169). Ludic critique, including parody, satire, and slapstick, "subverts past legitimacies" while signaling a "store of possible cultural and social structures" (170). Play further involves an intense form of virtuosity, linking bodies, emotions, and lived worlds (Lancaster 1997, 570).

Pink and Silver thus involved the strategic appropriation of carnivalesque performance and aesthetics, including playful mockery, ritualized inversion, gender bending, drumming, dance, outlandish costumes, and wild masks. In addition, Pink and Silver combined militant and playful protest, reproducing network norms and forms within a single tactic dubbed "tactical frivolity." As David from MRG recalled, "There were beautiful people, like the samba band, completely festive, and then there were uniformed militants ready to fight the police." Unlike the other blocs, Pink and Silver actually succeeded in penetrating the congress center, using their creative, mobile blend of tactics to confound the police.[26] Pink and Silver, like the larger action of which it formed a part, thus created a performative terrain that was at once oppositional and subjunctive, a platform for critiquing prevailing social, political,

12. Militants battle the police during the Blue March in Prague. PHOTOGRAPH COURTESY OF
TIM RUSSO.

and economic orders while enacting new forms of sociality and generating
affective solidarity through virtuoso performance.

The Blue March

Meanwhile, as we held our blockades, the Blue March battle raged to the west.
Raul and Paco from MRG-Zaragoza had offered to navigate, assuming the
march would be nonviolent. When they tried to direct the crowd away from
a battalion of riot cops, militants screamed, "Police!" and charged at them
up a hill, pushing a huge blue plastic ball from Náměstí Míru. Activists were
repelled but regrouped at the bottom of the hill and continued to charge again
and again. They were able to move police lines back until riot cops responded
with tear gas and water cannons. Militants then began to dig up cobblestones,
hurling them along with Molotov cocktails. The street battle raged for hours.
Paco from MRG-Zaragoza later recalled: "I had never seen such a violent confrontation, before or after. Genoa was a battlefield, but there wasn't as much
body-to-body contact. There was fire everywhere; cops were burning."

Militant tactics involve the ritual enactment of violent performances
through distinct bodily techniques, political symbols, and protest styles, including black attire, combat boots, and masked faces, which express solidarity

13. Masked Black Bloc protester with riot police in background. PHOTOGRAPH COURTESY OF FLORIAN SCHUH / PIXELFIGHTERS.COM.

while simultaneously portraying archetypical images of rebellion. Peterson (2001, 55) suggests that militant activists generate identities through emotionally powerful embodied ritual performances that construct the militant body as the ground of political agency and produce an "embattled" activist subjectivity. Moreover, the typical image of the Black Bloc activist reflects a masculine ideal of aggressive confrontation. Violent performances thus constitute militant networks by physically expressing a radical rejection of the dominant order, including the major symbols of capitalism and the state. As we shall see, however, militant violence also serves to justify police repression. Indeed, the protest against the G8 in Genoa the following summer would degenerate into a frightening space of terror (see chapter 5).

The Opera House

Later that evening, we headed toward the opera house, where delegates were to reconvene. Nearly a thousand of us marched, danced, and sang our way through the streets, passing shattered bank and McDonald's windows along the way. After arriving, we learned the dinner banquet and opera had been canceled. Before we had a chance to celebrate, however, heavily armed lines of Czech police advanced toward us, using sound grenades and tear gas. My heart began to pound as we were engulfed by smoke. Several hundred of us began playing cat and mouse with the police, who would advance, hurling tear gas canisters, as we ran to the next block and waited for their next charge. The alternating sensations of fear and elation, panic and glee, were at once terrifying and exhilarating.

Meanwhile, Black Blocs continued to smash storefront windows at major transnational banks and car dealerships. A helicopter appeared, shining a spotlight as the police lines advanced. When we realized we were being hunted, a group of us ran toward a large urban park. We had been overtaken by the excitement of the "flight" crowd. As Canetti (1962) explains: "People flee together because it is best to flee that way. They feel the same excitement and the energy of some increases the energy of others" (53). Although a few activists were beaten and arrested, Miguel, Marcela, and I escaped to a bar at the far end of the park. We took off our bandannas, changed shirts, and shared our experiences from the front lines. These stories increased our sense of belonging to a common struggle despite the differences among protest blocs and networks. The emotions sparked by bodily contiguity and collective action had generated intense feelings of affective solidarity throughout the day.

The Morning After

On the following morning, our affinity group met at the Infocenter to attend a series of press conferences, which were largely dominated by the question of violence. Despite the negative attention, however, the action had created a powerful image event, garnering significant press coverage (Juris 2004b, 487–507). Correspondents from Spanish, Catalan, and other international newspapers and television stations covered the protests, creating an anti–corporate globalization media boom throughout the Spanish state. Meanwhile, reports of random beatings and arrests began to circulate, as the Czech police had vowed to take back control of the streets.

In response, activists decided to hold a jail solidarity action that afternoon, congregating at the Watchtower Plaza in the heart of the tourist district. Roughly one hundred protesters began marching over the Charles Bridge, carrying signs that declared, "I'm an antiglobalization activist, arrest me too!" They were met by an intimidating police blockade. After a tense standoff, the group returned to the plaza, where it was announced that the World Bank/IMF meetings had been suspended. The police maintained their distance, and the plaza soon erupted in a wild street party, unleashing an intense outburst of euphoria and communitas. During this "moment of madness" (Zolberg 1972), protesters cheered, hugged, sang, and danced. "There were people from all around the world," Nuria recalled. "It was overwhelming. This was one of the most magical moments in Prague, totally spontaneous. Protesters began to meet up at the Watchtower Plaza, from Asia, Africa, Latin America, Britain, and Spain, all together. We began to talk one by one, everyone applauding. Then there was music, drumming, and we began to realize we had won. When you are so wrapped up in things, you don't have time to enjoy, but we started to realize we had really won!"

Prague was a classic event of re-presentation. Activists performed their networks while generating affective solidarity and oppositional identities by enacting diverse bodily techniques within distinct spaces. These included the use of vulnerable bodies to occupy urban space (Pink Bloc), rhythmic dancing and drumming across space (Pink and Silver Bloc), violent and symbolic confrontation (Blue and Yellow Blocs), and autonomous pack maneuvers (southern actions). The overall action produced a swarming effect characterized by horizontal coordination among diverse autonomous groups. At the same time, through carnivalesque transgression, activists contrasted a utopian world of freedom, creativity, and play to the hierarchical world of states and corporate capitalism. Prague was also a compelling image event, as alternative activist networks physically represented themselves while rendering new conflicts visible. Indeed, many tactics enacted in Prague, such as White Overalls or Pink and Silver, would later circulate through global networks, providing repertoires for activists to appropriate in distant locales. At the same time, the intensely lived emotions in Prague would translate into sustained networking, particularly in Catalonia and the Spanish state.

Victory in the Streets: Barcelona against the Europe of Capital

The Catalan mobilization to Prague mainly involved squatters and radical network-based movements, which have pioneered the use of creative and militant direct action. The subsequent Barcelona campaigns against the World Bank and EU would encompass a wider coalition of actors, including institutional reformists and critical sectors from the Marxist Left. Consequently, the dynamics of mass mobilization would shift from a main focus on direct action toward a greater emphasis on marches and rallies. Such traditional performative terrains provide spaces where complex networking politics are embodied, but they are less emotively potent given the minimal conflict and scripted repertoires.[27]

As we saw in the last chapter, alternative networks in Barcelona are more generally defined by competing political and organizational logics, constituting four distinct sectors within a broader movement field. The first sector involves traditional political and civil society associations, including leftist parties, trade unions, and NGOs. Although many institutional actors took part in the campaign against the World Bank, they created their own platform before the mobilization against the EU called the Barcelona Social Forum. The next three sectors are composed of traditional Marxists, radical grassroots formations such as MRG and RCADE, and an informal network of militant anticapitalists, including squatters, antimilitarists, and Catalan nationalists, all of whom remained with the campaign this time around.

Two rivals, the campaign and the forum, thus dominated the mobilization against the EU in Barcelona. Moreover, less than two weeks before the mobilization, a third bloc appeared: the Catalan Platform against the "Europe of Capital" (the Nationalist Platform), a network of radical nationalist forces including the Basque separatist party, Herri Batasuna (HB).[28] The complex relationships and tensions among these networks would be performed, embodied, and mapped onto urban space during the unitary demonstration on March 16. Although radical activists within the campaign would express their politics in more creative ways during the Day of Decentralized Actions on the previous day, the march would emerge as the main focus of attention.

The Political Context

The mobilization against the EU represented a stark contrast to previous anti–corporate globalization actions. The summer before, protests in Gothenburg, Barcelona, and Genoa had turned increasingly violent, and organizers wanted to avoid another outbreak of repression. The EU was also a complicated political target. Anti–corporate globalization protesters had denounced Europe as an "engine of economic globalization" at summits in Nice, Gothenburg, and Brussels. At the same time, many Spanish and Catalan activists saw the EU as a progressive alternative to the Spanish state. As Guillermo explained, "Everyone was against the World Bank because it was easy to make them out to be the bad guys, but Europe is different; many people feel at home here." While grassroots actors in the campaign were critical of corporate influence and the lack of democratic participation in the EU, institutional sectors remained ambivalent.

The urban terrain also presented a complex challenge, requiring an alternative approach to the swarming strategy implemented in Seattle and Prague. The EU Summit would be held far from the center of town, in a zone resembling a large bunker in the outlying university zone. Activists desperately wanted to avoid the traumatic violence they had experienced the summer before, while the Spanish government had stepped up its antiterrorism efforts after September 11. A contingent of ten thousand riot cops was called in to guard the summit, and the central government constructed a fence around the entire zone. For its part, the convergence center would be housed at the Central University's downtown campus, far removed from the summit area.[29]

Given this context, radicals opted to continue with their plans for direct action, but they called for multiple protests, rather than a single blockade. Instead of attempting a predictable siege, activists felt that a decentralized scenario with multiple events would be a more effective way to enact resistance while avoiding police repression. Moreover, Barcelona-based activists would be able to take advantage of their knowledge of the city streets, as the terrain of resistance was more integrated into their everyday fabric of struggle. At the same time, the action would remain open and participatory, reflecting the networking logics I explore throughout this book. Emerging network norms and forms would be thus transposed onto urban space through decentralized coordination among diverse protest tactics, as the call to action explained: "The proposed scene on March 15 is an armored Juan Carlos Hotel . . . protected by ten thousand riot cops. Given these circumstances, we feel it will be much more productive to leave the predictable script, opting for decentralized actions instead. The Day of Decentralized Actions will provide a space where everyone can coordinate, exchange information, and propose ideas without imposing our criteria on anyone. This has been the political culture of our global movement that has worked so well so far, and we should develop it further."

As in Prague, the day of actions would incorporate a diversity-of-tactics ethic, with an added emphasis on collaborative learning, coordination, and exchange. Indeed, the call reflected a particularly strong commitment to emerging network norms and forms, but the lack of a single target would also make the actions more difficult to follow, reducing their potential visibility. Swarming strategies in Seattle and Prague had been effective, in part, because they combined centralized and decentralized elements. At the same time, however, the security situation around the anti-EU mobilization was *already* drawing intense media scrutiny, so there was perhaps less need for spectacular conflict.

The Mobilization Begins

The Reclaim the Streets (RTS) action on March 9 was widely considered a trial run for the mobilization of the following week. The previous year's RTS had been a huge success, helping to build anticipation before the protests against the World Bank. The police presence had been minimal, allowing protesters to take control of the Passeig de Gracia, an elegant boulevard in the heart of the bourgeois Example district. The rhythmic crowd danced through the streets to the techno beats blasted by a mobile sound system. The action finally ended after a few hours when dozens of activists plunged into a fountain at the intersection with Diagonal Boulevard. A cyclist then climbed a statue rising from the water and lifted his bike in symbolic victory. As Pablo recalled, "It was a moment of incredible personal liberation, fantastic, total corporal liberation; it was amazing!"

This year would be different. When we arrived at the University Plaza, thousands of people were milling about, including squatters, punks, hippies, ravers, and students. Dozens of police vans lined the streets. We began dancing behind the mobile sound system toward the Plaza de Catalunya, following two large banners that read, "Reclaim the Streets" and "Globalize Resistance." Everything remained calm until we cleared the plaza, when two lines of riot cops approached rapidly. Protesters became nervous, but the police took up positions along both sides of the street rather than charging, creating a wedge between the crowd and pedestrians. Instead of repressing the march, police opted to contain us, enclosing and intimidating protesters with their overwhelming physical presence.

As Foucault famously argued, surveillance and control are achieved by regulating bodies in space through the use of disciplinary technologies. Building on this insight, Allen Feldman further explains that power "is contingent on the command of space and the command of those entities that move within politically marked spaces. The body becomes a spatial unit of power, and the distribution of these units in space constructs sites of domination" (1991, 8). Indeed, direct action involves myriad micro-level spatial battles between protesters and police. Specific tactics thus attempt to occupy space, creating forums for political and cultural expression, while the police employ their own bodily and spatial techniques to control, enclose, or disperse protesters (cf. Jansen 2001, 39).[30] By using measured spatial, bodily, and psychological tactics during the RTS action, riot cops projected power, reestablishing control of space and preventing liminoid outbursts. In this sense, violence might be avoided, but at the cost of invisibility.

Despite our concerns, the day of actions generated a great deal of media coverage, providing a theatrical space for radicals to physically inscribe political messages on the urban and mass-media landscapes. On the morning of March 15, I took part in "Lobby Busters," a spoof action where activists "hunted down" transnational corporations involved in European lobby groups. The action began with a moment of tension as riot cops surrounded the crowd at the Sagrada Familia plaza and beat an independent videographer. After a short scuffle, activists sat down and began chanting "No violence!" However, the police ultimately backed down, as dozens of journalists were on hand. The crowd regrouped, and we successfully carried out the action with the help of a mobile sound system.

Carrying vacuum cleaner tubes and dressed in white overalls with the Ghost Busters logo on the back (replete with a euro hat and fistful of euro bills), we enacted playful scenes in front of Spanish transnationals. At one point, we stopped at the Banco Santander, rounded up several international bankers, and "sucked" them into our Lobby Buster tubes. The action concluded with a "die-in" next to a Repsol gas station, where we spilled gallons of red paint to symbolize the blood of indigenous people killed as a result of the oil company's drilling operations in South America. Lobby Busters combined directed symbolic critique with the mobile, festive, and carnivalesque tactics associated with Pink and Silver, suggesting not only the performative dimension of direct action but also the capacity for ongoing experimentation and innovation. Afterward I wandered through the city to observe other actions, including a labor rally against the Spanish telephone giant Telefónica, a Critical Mass bike ride, and a nationalist protest on the Ramblas.[31] Later that evening, thousands of us watched jugglers, acrobats, and fire breathers at the Circus against Capitalism. Whereas activist networks in Prague were embodied through distinct protest styles, the decentralized actions constituted a celebration of performativity itself, as well as emerging network norms and forms among grassroots activists.

The Unity March

The central focus of attention, however, remained the following day's unity march, where the complex relationships among networks were performed, embodied, and mapped through the "war of position" (Gramsci 1971) waged by various protest blocs. As with free-form actions, traditional marches and rallies also involve diverse kinesthetic practices that inscribe alternative political meanings on urban space through the use of diverse bodily techniques and signs within physical territories (cf. Santino 2001). In Prague, this was reflected in the use of color-coded zones, which divided the performance terrain among alternative embodied performances. This time, complex networking politics were physically mapped through heated struggles over position.

The Barcelona Social Forum's initial request to participate in the march had sparked an intense debate inside the campaign. As we saw in the last chapter, many activists saw the forum as an attempt by leftist parties and unions to capitalize on the "antiglobalization movement." Anticapitalists denounced the forum as "reformist," criticizing both its discourse and its hierarchical structure. Given the widespread antipathy, some argued the forum should not be allowed to participate at all, though most felt the forum should be allowed to take part, but at the end of the march. The assembly finally agreed that the forum could participate as a separate block but would go behind the campaign.

The discussion was taken up again at a subsequent coordinating meeting but was further complicated by the Nationalist Bloc's decision to join the march. Position and space had become fiercely contested. Everyone recognized that marching last implied the greatest security risk, since scuffles tend to occur at the end of demonstrations. Participants also felt the government would be most likely to provoke a confrontation near the Nationalist Bloc, which they could blame on Basque terrorists, so it would be more sensible for the forum to march last. As Gaizka from the Zapatista collective pointed out, though, the problem was as much political as strategic: "If HB goes before the forum, there will be a huge outcry." Others insisted it was important for HB to march in the middle for security reasons. Gaizka relented, suggesting that a small contingent from the campaign could march behind the forum as a symbolic gesture, and everyone agreed.

Organizers later produced a diagram depicting the alignment of blocs. The campaign would go first, divided into three sections: open-neutral (whose banner read "Against the Europe of Capital and War"), immigrants ("Another World Is Possible"), and open-sectarian ("The Europe of Alternatives"). The Nationalist Platform would march second ("For the Europe of the Peoples"), followed by the forum ("Another Europe Is Possible), before closing with another small contingent from the campaign. The diagram provided a clear visual depiction of the broader connections among network identities, bodies, and space.

On March 16, I went to the Plaza de Catalunya to help prepare for the march. Shortly before 6:00 p.m., thousands of people poured in, seemingly from nowhere. Suddenly, the large banners and floats that would separate the blocs began moving into place, and before we could figure out who was supposed to go where, a huge crowd swept us along. As we moved toward the street, I saw familiar faces from previous mobilizations. Indeed, mass protests had become important spaces where transnational movement networks were lived and embodied, generating intense emotions. As Nuria recalled, "Seeing Jose Bové, and all the people from Porto Alegre, had a powerful psychological effect. Like, 'Wow, I'm surrounded by *compañeros.*' There was an amazing feeling of internationalism; we were building networks beyond our own countries!"

As the march began, we danced alongside a samba band, chanting "Another world is possible, another world is possible." Other protesters carried colorful banners denouncing the Europe of Capital, depicting greedy businessmen clutching euros and dollar bills, or portraying Presidents Aznar and Bush as war criminals. Meanwhile, packs of euro-fighters darted in and out, and farther along, we passed a drumming troupe dressed as red devils and

Structure of the Unity March

Campaign: Closing Bloc

Barcelona Social Forum **Banner:** *"Another Europe is Possible"*

Nationalist Platform **Banner:** *"For the Europe of the Peoples"*

Campaign: Open Bloc (Sectarian Signs Allowed) **Banner:** *"The Europe of Alternatives"*

Campaign: Immigrant Bloc **Banner:** *"Another World is Possible"*

Campaign: Open Bloc (No Sectarian Signs) **Banner:** *"Against the Europe of Capital and War"*

14. Protest blocs during the anti-EU march in Barcelona, March 16, 2002.

giants. These mobile performances created a festive, carnivalesque atmosphere. As we neared the port, I glanced back and saw hundreds of thousands of protesters. Organizers were ecstatic, suggesting this was the largest demonstration they had ever seen—more than a half-million people. Activists later expressed a sense of catharsis as the accumulated tension was transformed into an explosion of euphoria. "When the march began," explained Mateo of RCADE, "everyone was serious and tense; then all of a sudden, it was like an orgasm. We began walking up and down, and the people just didn't stop! I just couldn't understand how many people there were."

The next morning's headline in *La Vanguardia*, a popular pro-business daily, proclaimed, "Victory in the Streets!" The press hailed the protest as a paragon of "civic virtue," a description that many activists saw as an attempt

15. A half million people take to the streets in Barcelona during the march against the Europe of capital and war. PHOTOGRAPH COURTESY OF JEFFREY S. JURIS.

to subvert the campaign's far-reaching critique. Over the next few days, the campaign thus decided to reiterate its radical stance through an open "Letter to the Citizens," which included the following: "The city and regional governments congratulate us for being civil when we demonstrate. Will they also call their attempts to disrupt our organizing efforts civil? Will they have anything to say about why we demonstrate? Will they recognize that the main protest bloc had a clear message against capitalism and the political class?"

In sum, the unitary march succeeded in reaching masses of supporters, but it was much less confrontational than previous mobilizations and failed to communicate a message of radical confrontation. Still, activists were thrilled that the march had been so large and diverse. Many gloated when they learned the forum had been unable to move forward because of the massive crowds. Pilar from RCADE confessed, "The unity march was for everyone, and it was important to show that so many people agree with us, but deep down, I was glad the forum couldn't march." Some claimed symbolic victory, arguing that the city had expressed its preference for the campaign's anticapitalist message and distaste for the institutional Left. Beyond the political implications, however, many experienced powerful moments of affective solidarity, as Nuria explained:

At the concert, I felt a sensation like, "We have really won!" There was a moment when everyone was onstage that reminded me of the 1930s, with all the people in the streets. You became connected with the past, with your grandparents and great-grandparents. You felt nostalgia for the civil war, the republic, or the collectivizations, things I had always wanted to experience. There was also a sensation of community, like in Genoa, the feeling of solidarity during the march denouncing the death of Carlo Giuliani. I felt that feeling of community during the concert as well, through the songs and videos, with the scenes from the squatter movement I had experienced. It was like, "This was all worth it, so we could all be here, so something important can happen." It was like that moment in Prague, when they told us the World Bank and IMF meetings had been suspended, that intense feeling of community in the Watchtower Plaza.

At the same time, many others expressed contrary feelings of frustration and even defeat, suggesting the movement had been contained and neutralized. Compared to previous mass direct actions, many radical grassroots activists felt the anti-EU mobilization lacked confrontation and was thus less empowering. As Paula from Las Agencias pointed out, "We were afraid to organize confrontational actions, which really make conflicts visible. The actions were great in terms of content—extremely transparent and public. But making sure people weren't afraid to bring their young kids to the actions was excessive."

Indeed, despite occasional moments of communitas, there were relatively few liminoid outbursts of freedom, excitement, and uncertainty. In this sense, the actions and unity march were more akin to events of presentation, as Joan from RCADE pointed out: "The mobilization was a success, but not an epic experience. There were epic moments, but not like in Prague, Genoa, or last year in Barcelona. . . . The demonstration was a numerical success, and it produced an image that makes our critiques acceptable, but it wasn't a life-changing experience where you radically confront the system and live through dangerous situations full of adrenaline, at least not for me."

For many radicals, the anti-EU mobilization felt too controlled, staged, and predictable—the open crowd had been caged. As Pablo suggested, the movement had reached an impasse, involving the "normalization of the new grammar we created." He went on to explain, "The summit was resituated, by the police and the campaign. It was easily appropriated by a traditional political discourse. We are at a moment when our politics are hypercodified: organizing demonstrations that are more and more massive, and decentralized actions that disrupt the demonstration as little as possible to keep us in our place."

In other words, anti–corporate globalization mobilizations were beginning to lose their confrontational edge. Their emotional impact was waning; they were becoming routine. At the same time, the march may well have produced an empowering experience for many protesters, particularly those not accustomed to attending political demonstrations. Indeed, given the intense emotions they produce, mass actions have a certain "addictive" quality to them, and many core anti–corporate globalization organizers, particularly from more radical grassroots networks, such as MRG or PGA, seem to require ever-increasing levels of risk and confrontation. However, such high levels of affective solidarity are often difficult to reproduce over time, particularly given the decreasing novelty of countersummit protests and the growing security around them. This is a particular problem for diffuse network-based movements with informal modes of commitment, as they are particularly dependent on affective solidarity to sustain motivation. In this sense, the same attributes that help make mass mobilizations effective networking tools pose a strategic challenge with respect to long-term participation and movement building.

Conclusion

Mass actions and mobilizations constitute performative terrains where activists embody alternative networks and make their struggles visible while generating affective solidarity and experimenting with new forms of sociality. As we have seen, mass actions in particular create high-profile image events, where competing activist networks physically represent themselves and their struggles through diverse bodily and spatial techniques. Spectacular actions involving Pink Bloc, White Overall, and Black Bloc tactics are thus meant, in part, to capture mass media attention while communicating political messages to an audience. In this regard, anti–corporate globalization mobilizations have largely succeeded. For example, the action in Prague generated a great deal of media attention in Europe and around the world while the march against the EU in Barcelona made front-page headlines in Spain and Catalonia.

Over time, however, the press may come to expect more and more dramatic images and ever-growing numbers of protesters, making it increasingly difficult to break through busy media cycles, let alone convey coherent messages. Indeed, as the novelty of protest wears off, more spectacular actions may be necessary to generate public interest. As Paul Routledge suggests, "As the practice of resistance becomes increasingly dramaturgical, there is a danger that politics may become more about appearance than effect, more about symbolic protest than material change" (1997b, 255).[32] Moreover, although the meaning of actions involving Pink and Silver, Black Bloc, or White Overall tactics may be evident to fellow activists, they are more difficult for an outside audience to interpret. Consequently, impact of mass mobilizations as image events is ambiguous.

At the same time, anti–corporate globalization networks are also embodied during mass mobilizations in an internal sense. As we have seen, diverse networks represent themselves and signal their differences to one another through diverse bodily and spatial practices, reflecting wider links among networks, bodies, space, and performance. The growing confluence among network norms and forms is thus physically expressed not only through emerging organizational architectures but also through the division of space among alternative protest tactics and styles. Whereas activists in Prague divided the terrain of resistance into three color-coded zones, thus reproducing network norms and forms on the tactical plane, alternative networks during the anti-EU march in Barcelona engaged in heated struggles over the distribution of bodies in space.[33]

Moreover, anti–corporate globalization mobilizations and actions also generate intense emotions, which prepare activist bodies for action. As we have seen, mass mobilizations produce their effects by transforming embodied feelings into affective solidarity. In this sense, Prague was a classic event of re-presentation, involving physical struggles over space between protesters and police and the lived experience of prefigured utopian worlds during carnivalesque moments of transgression. The powerful emotions and identities generated by mass actions, in particular, constitute a form of embodied agency, inspiring sustained networking within both public and submerged spheres. In Barcelona, on the other hand, the Day of Decentralized Actions lacked a confrontational spirit, and though the unity march created a significant impact through sheer numbers, for many core activists, it failed to produce a powerful sense of agency.

As I have argued, mass mobilizations are critical networking tools, but they generate diminishing returns over time with respect to visibility and affective solidarity. This presents a particular challenge for network-based movements with diffuse modes of identification and commitment. Whereas formal structures can help sustain political activity within traditional organizations, network-based movements are characterized by grassroots participation and thus depend on greater levels of individual motivation. Indeed, networks such as MRG in Barcelona or DAN in North America were founded as mobilizing and coordinating vehicles for specific actions. Although such networks outlived their initial purpose, they proved unsustainable in the long run without the focus and affective solidarity associated with mass mobilizations.

Many anti–corporate globalization activists have expressed their own doubts regarding the efficacy of countersummit protest. Indeed, a heated debate emerged after Seattle regarding the practice of "summit hopping" (the way activists rapidly move from one protest to another). As a Dutch anticapitalist argued before Prague, "Causing a summit to fail appeals to the imagination and provides the media with pretty pictures, but while a mass protest may have great symbolic value, it does not mean much more. . . . [Moreover] it is very difficult for activists from poorer countries to take part, and this is one of the reasons the protests are predominantly white, even though westerners are the least hit by capitalism."

Social, economic, and racial exclusion is an important and complicated issue. Globally, the critique is somewhat unfair, as anti–corporate globalization mobilizations and actions have been held in Brazil, Bolivia, Ecuador, India, Mexico, Thailand, Ecuador, and elsewhere. Mass mobilizations in Europe and North America, on the other hand, have been largely, though not entirely, white and middle-class.[34] This is a significant weakness. To address it, global networks such as PGA have raised money to cover travel expenses for activists from countries in the global South, who have attended mobilizations in cities such as Seattle and Prague. More of this can be done. Funding and resources might also be provided for working-class activists, immigrants, and people of color *within* Europe and North America.[35] Indeed, many grassroots activists argue that such groups should take on leadership roles.[36] At the same time, these issues will not be resolved quickly or easily, particularly without the long-term structural transformations that anti–corporate globalization activists are struggling to bring about.

Regarding the critique of symbolic protest, other activists have argued that countersummit protests are important strategic weapons, which allow activists to publicly challenge the legitimacy of the contemporary neoliberal order. As the U.S.-based activist Starhawk (2002) argues with respect to multilateral institutions, "Our purpose is to undercut their legitimacy, to point a spotlight at their programs and policies, and to raise the social costs of their existence until they become unsupportable. . . . The big summit meetings are elaborate rituals, ostentatious shows of power that reinforce the entitlement and authority of the bodies they represent. When those bodies are forced to meet behind walls, to fight a pitched battle over every conference, to retreat to isolated locations, the ritual is interrupted and their legitimacy is undercut" (117).

In a world where politics are increasingly waged across global media terrains, mass direct actions, although not always perfectly intelligible, allow activists to communicate beyond their networks, thus rendering conflicts visible. However, the impact of mass mobilizations and actions is more than symbolic. Building a mass movement requires sustained networking, which is facilitated by periodic moments of physical interaction and the generation of new identities and affective solidarity. At their best, mass actions elicit powerful emotions, particularly when they are confrontational and relatively free-form. In all these senses, mass mobilizations remain strategically important. Moreover, direct actions in particular provide spaces for experimenting with new modes of organization and interaction. The network-based forms of communication and coordination used to organize mass actions thus point to a model for reimagining social relations more generally. Indeed, as we have seen, direct actions open up subjunctive spaces, constituting laboratories for developing alternative cultural practices and imaginaries.

But what happens when protests and mobilizations become overly scripted, controlled, or predictable? Can militant ethnography tell us anything that might help activists develop long-term strategy? On the one hand, organizers can attempt to coordinate and reduce the number of mobilizations during a particular period, allowing time for activists to rest and focus on everyday struggles. This would also help maintain the novelty of direct action, allowing time for tactical innovation. On the other hand, moving beyond mass protests, regional and global gatherings of transnational activist networks provide alternative, if less emotively intense, platforms where activists can perform their networks, experiment with network norms and forms, and generate affective solidarity. As the preceding analysis suggests, sustaining a mass movement is a complex art, requiring a delicate balance between periodic outbursts of embodied agency and their controlled management, improvisation, and staged repetition.[37]

The danger is mistaking a specific networking tool for a goal, whether concrete political reforms or more far-reaching economic, social, and cultural transformation. As we have seen, mass mobilizations can help facilitate movement building, but they are not ends in themselves. As Barbara Epstein (1991) points out, the U.S. direct-action movement of the 1970s and 1980s was unsustainable, in part, because it defined itself around a specific tactic. When mass actions began to generate diminishing returns, activists were unable or unwilling to develop new approaches. Although anti–corporate globalization movements are politically more diverse and thus have a wider tactical and strategic repertoire including public education, forums, teach-ins, grassroots organizing, and alternative media, activists today face a similar challenge. Ultimately this points to the need for sustainable organization that can survive the ebbs and flows of mass mobilization. However, as this book suggests, organization need not be traditional or hierarchical.[38] Indeed, anti–corporate globalization activists are attempting to build organizational forms that coincide with their emerging network norms. In this sense, as we shall see, PGA conferences, social forums, and other transnational network gatherings have an important role to play with respect to long-term movement building.

5

SPACES OF TERROR:
VIOLENCE AND
REPRESSION IN GENOA

I remember a battle-torn city with armies at war. We started to run down a street. People began yelling, "No, don't go there!" and I started thinking, "Ah, ah, the police are coming, shit, shit!" There was a place from where we could see the entire city filled with smoke and gas. I am not a violent person. There are many things I can do, but I'm not prepared for such a violent situation. It's one thing to see it on TV, another in person. We weren't raised to handle such violence. I remember feeling a sensation like "Where are we? What happened? How will it end?"[1]

G enoa has become synonymous with protest violence, a metonym evoking images of tear gas, burning cars, and black-clad protesters hurling stones and Molotov cocktails at heavily militarized riot police. Equally evocative are the haunting visions of twenty-two-year-old Carlo Giuliani's hooded corpse lying in a pool of his own blood after being shot twice in the face and then backed over by an armored police jeep. The world was further shocked by pictures of dried blood on the stairs, floors, and walls of the Diaz School, where a special unit of the Italian police carried out a brutal nighttime raid against sleeping protesters after more than three hundred thousand people had taken to the streets earlier that day. Images of street battle cascaded through global mediascapes, helping to construct a mass-mediated image of the Battle of Genoa as an iconic sign of wanton destruction.

As we saw in the last chapter, anti–corporate globalization activists perform their networks during mass direct actions through diverse bodily movements and spatial techniques. At the same time, the increasing confluence among network norms and forms is physically expressed through the division of urban space among diverse action repertoires and styles, a strategy activists refer to as "diversity of tactics." Debates surrounding protest violence are thus resolved in practice by accommodating both nonviolent and militant forms of action. But what happens when certain protest tactics inhibit others? Is it possible to maintain separate action spaces when riot cops treat all protesters alike? As we saw in Seattle and Prague, police repression can help spark the intense emotional outbursts that make direct actions effective networking tools; but what happens when the state refuses to distinguish between "good" and "bad" protesters, quashing dissent altogether within a "zone of indistinction" (Agamben 1998)?[2] Indeed, as we shall see, performative violence can be used to justify the indiscriminate application of low-intensity state terror.

As a protest strategy, diversity of tactics depends on a tacit agreement between protesters and police regarding the latter's willingness to follow democratic rules of engagement and apply force commensurate with protester behavior. However, when authorities refuse to play along, this principle breaks down in practice. In this sense, the injunction to coordinate across tactical differences without regard to context can undermine efforts to establish the necessary ground rules for action. Extreme violence thus constitutes a potential limit, not only in terms of direct-action practice, but also with respect to the network-based organizational forms and political norms I explore throughout this book.

This chapter provides an ethnographic account of the protests against the G8 in Genoa, exploring the interactions among performative violence, state terror, and tactical debates among activists. I argue that the network norms and forms that facilitate anti–corporate globalization activism pose a vexing challenge when it comes to protest violence, making it extremely difficult for activists to challenge the tactical choices of others.

Setting the Stage

Repression against European anti–corporate globalization movements intensified steadily throughout summer 2001. Police used live ammunition for the first time during the June 14–15 mobilization against the European Union in Gothenburg, Sweden, where a protester was shot in the back as he ran, leaving him severely wounded. After Gothenburg, EU leaders such as Tony Blair of Britain and Spanish president Jose María Aznar publicly vowed to crack down on militant protest. On June 24, Spanish police indiscriminately attacked protesters congregated in the Plaza de Catalunya after a peaceful march of

fifty thousand against the World Bank in Barcelona. Hundreds of bystanders, weekend shoppers, and incredulous journalists were caught in the melee,
leaving dozens injured and many psychologically shaken. The following week,
a Milan-based activist from the Italian White Overalls took the microphone
after a march against police brutality and announced the coming siege of the
G8 Summit in Genoa. He exhorted all Catalan and Spanish activists to come
to Italy, proclaiming in the spirit of musician and anti–corporate globalization
favorite Manu Chao, "Next Stop: Genoa!"

Ten days later, two Americans, an Israeli, seven Catalans, and I were discussing our police-evasion strategy on a train we had skipped through southern France. Fearing inspections after crossing the Italian border, we decided
to get off at the first stop in Italy: the beach town of San Remo. The Americans
went on to Turin to visit some of the anarchist social centers there. I next saw
Tom on July 20, following the siege of the G8. He was severely shaken and
wore a bloodied white bandage on his forehead. The rest of us took a dip in
the Mediterranean and then caught a regional train to Genoa. Before board-
ing, two local police officers approached us. "Are you heading to Genoa?" they
asked. "Yeah," Ignaci replied nervously. "We're planning to do some tourism."
One of the officers effected a sinister smile, and we were on our way.

As we pulled into Genoa, the Italian police were out patrolling in force.
Our hearts began to pound as we left the train, although we had done nothing
wrong. The paranoid feeling of being subject to constant surveillance would
remain with us during our entire stay. In fact, the brother of an Israeli friend,
an Indymedia activist who had arrived from Berlin several days earlier, suffered a panic attack and had to leave the city before the protests began. He
was convinced the Italian police had been following him, and he may not
have been entirely off base.[3] Terra di Nessuno (No Man's Land), the squatted
social center where we stayed during our first few days in Genoa, was nestled
in a narrow green valley above the city, around which police had established
several outposts. A rumor circulated that secret agents were patrolling the
entrance road to the squat. Although the police did not stop us along the way,
we had our first taste of the rising tension that would soon transform Genoa
into a space of terror.

After walking through the gate past the international squatters sign, we
made our way up to an abandoned two-story farmhouse renovated by radical

16. Activists share a meal outside the Terra di Nessuno Social Center before the anti-G8 protests in Genoa. PHOTOGRAPH COURTESY OF JEFFREY S. JURIS.

Italian activists. I pitched my tent outside near the makeshift shower, between a young samba band activist from Amsterdam and a fellow traveler from San Francisco. When I had settled in, I joined the Catalans by the entrance to the squat, where they discussed how to get Internet access. As we talked, Ricardo walked over and introduced himself. He was a prominent activist from a well-known squat in Germany and had been extremely active in the European PGA network. He was among the first internationals to arrive in Genoa and was frustrated at how difficult it had been to coordinate with the Genoa Social Forum (GSF). Ricardo was eager to elicit support for a radical "international" contingent. Although we were tired, we wanted to learn more, so we circled around as Ricardo explained, "The Italians have initiated an extremely complex political process. The White Overalls and other groups, both inside and outside the GSF, have been fighting for influence. The major problem for us is finding out how to plug into the action."

Most troubling for Ricardo was that the GSF, given its strict nonviolence policy, had refused to talk with militant anarchist groups. The dominant political forces in the GSF—White Overalls, certain sectors of Cobas (a radical labor union), the Lilliput Network (ecologists, antimilitarists, and solidarity activists), NGOs and ATTAC, and Rifondazione Comunista (Reformed Communist Party)—were characterized by autonomous Marxist, pacifist, social democratic, and socialist ideologies, respectively, as well as the use of non-violent tactics.[4] On the other hand, as I have argued in previous chapters, the guiding ethos among decentralized grassroots networks such as PGA and MRG is broadly anarchist, in the sense of horizontal coordination among autonomous groups.

Networking logics also hold for the question of violence versus nonviolence, as reflected in the diversity-of-tactics ethic. For radicals such as Ricardo, who would never engage in violent actions, it is still important to establish dialogue among all groups, regardless of the tactics they choose. Radicals thus perceived the strict nonviolence stance of the GSF and their unwillingness to communicate with groups not committed to their direct-action guidelines as a major obstacle. This is how violence and nonviolence become enmeshed in the cultural politics of networking. At the same time, an emphasis on coordinating across diversity and difference can discourage internal critique. Indeed, networking logics entail working with as many groups as possible, but this may trump other tactical and strategic considerations, including effectiveness and personal safety. In this sense, the network norms and forms that facilitate anti–corporate globalization activism make it extremely difficult for activists to challenge others with respect to any tactic, let alone denounce violence. The authorities in Genoa would thus be able to exploit both real and imagined protest violence to implement an indiscriminate campaign of terror.

Grasping Protest Violence

Violence involves what Carolyn Nordstrom (1997) refers to as an "essentially defined concept," one whose meaning is generally accepted as given.[5] Indeed, violence is in part a cultural construct generated through social practice. Struggles to define what violence means, what counts as violence, and what constitutes legitimate uses of violence are deeply entangled with questions of power. During mass actions, for example, young militants stage spectacular violent performances in part to gain access to the commercial media, which are in constant search of sensational stories and images. Routine protests go unnoticed, while the iconic images of burning cars and pitched street battles between masked protesters and militarized riot police are instantly broadcast via global mediascapes. At the same time, violent performances can be extracted as texts, removed from their initial setting, and reinserted into new discursive contexts.[6] Indeed, government and police officials can manipulate violent images, framing protesters as dangerous criminals, even terrorists, as a way to divide movements or justify indiscriminate physical repression (Juris 2005b).[7] Meanwhile, activist debates around violence and nonviolence are an important aspect of political identity construction within alternative movement networks.

By performative violence, I mean a mode of meaningful interaction through which actors construct social reality based on available cultural templates. As Anton Blok (2000) points out, "Rather than defining violence *a priori* as senseless and irrational, we should consider it as a changing form of interaction and communication, as a historically developed cultural form of *meaningful* action" (24). Violence has both practical-instrumental and symbolic-expressive dimensions (Riches 1986, 11). The former involves the attempt to directly transform the social environment, while the latter emphasizes communication and the dramatization of key social ideas and values. Performative violence is specifically used here to characterize symbolic ritual enactments of violent interaction with a predominant emphasis on communication and cultural expression.[8] This is in contrast to "direct political violence" (Bourgois 2001) meant to cause death or injury to other human beings, although such differences are often a matter of degree.[9]

In the context of mass direct actions, performative violence is a mode of communication through which activists seek to effect social transformation by staging symbolic confrontation based on "the representation of antagonistic relationships and the enactment of prototypical images of violence" (Schröder and Schmidt 2001, 10). Violent performances operate through spectacular nonverbal forms of iconic display, providing grassroots activists with valuable symbolic resources.[10] For example, as Rhodes (2001) points out in his study of performative protest against the Vietnam War, "For small militant groups with limited resources . . . violent performances against the symbols of the American system proved the most economical and visually arresting way of immediately achieving a symbolic victory over their more powerful adversaries, while concomitantly radicalizing potential support" (3). Since the 1970s, young European radicals have similarly used performative violence to generate public visibility within militant autonomous movements in countries such as Italy, Germany, Spain, and France (della Porta 1995; Katsiaficas 1997). A parallel argument can be made regarding militants today who practice performative violence against the symbols of global capitalism.

Beyond communication, performative violence is also productive in another sense: the forging of political identities. Violence can help define boundaries between different groups. Violent performances, in particular, are often linked to specific oppositional identities, styles, and practices.[11] Moreover, aggressively violent performances often involve the kind of risk taking and bravado traditionally associated with male rites of passage and achievement of masculine political identities in many parts of the world (Gilmore 1990). At the same time, there is a fine line between performative violence as a mode of communication and physical violence against human beings. Indeed, during mass actions, performative violence often gives way to, and helps justify, brutal campaigns of police repression. In this way, performative violence and low-level state terror can feed into each other.

In his account of terror and violence during the rubber boom in the Putumayo region of contemporary Colombia, Michael Taussig (1984) explores the emergence of a "space of death" in which colonial domination of indigenous and black slave populations was achieved through a deeply embedded "culture of terror" based on rumor, silence, paranoid myths of the savage other, and widespread torture and death. Torture not only helped extract information, it also fulfilled the "need to control massive populations through the cultural elaboration of fear" (469).[12] Fantastic stories, rumors, and paranoid fantasies, what Taussig refers to as "epistemic murk," distinguish cultures of terror as "a high-powered tool for domination and a principal medium of political practice" (492). Although characterizing Genoa during the anti-G8 protests as a space of death or as involving a culture of terror might be an exaggeration, similar dynamics did occur there, including the production and dissemination of paranoid stories of violent anarchist "others," the cultivation of rumor and disinformation, and the use of fear-inducing torture, not to mention the murder of an activist.

In what follows, I employ a hybrid concept, referring to Genoa as a "space of terror." As we shall see, performative violence on the part of protesters was used by the police to justify an indiscriminate campaign of low-level state terror that targeted everyone on the streets. The urban terrain was thus transformed into a zone of indistinction, in the sense of both a blurring of the line between the law and violence, order and chaos, and the creation of a generalized area of nondifferentiation.[13] In this way, the attempt to divide the terrain of resistance in Genoa into distinct spaces for competing forms of action broke down in practice. The network norms and forms that influence network interactions among alternative anti–corporate globalization sectors were undermined in the face of extreme political violence.

Planning the Siege

In the summer of 2001, Luca Casarini, a spokesperson for the White Overalls, issued a declaration of war on the G8: "We want to build an army of dreamers to confront the real violent ones, using our bodies and our words as arms. . . . We declare war on the G8 as we declare peace on the city of Genoa and her inhabitants. The G8 is the window of Empire and our goal is to destroy it. . . . We are sending a message: rebellion exists throughout the world, not only where there is poverty; but also where Empire has most consensus."[14] On the heels of Casarini's call to arms, confrontations at recent protests in Barcelona and Gothenburg, and the intransigence of the Berlusconi regime, protest violence was high on everyone's mind before the July 20 siege in Genoa. Moreover, the constant surveillance—including secret police and helicopters—the overwhelming presence of thousands of highly militarized riot cops and *carabinieri* units, the erection of a fence around the no-protest zone, and a spate of purportedly anarchist bomb scares had created a climate of tension and fear. It was in the shadow of this emerging terror campaign that activists made their final "battle plans," involving elaborate negotiations over the use of specific tactics, the division of urban space, and coordination among diverse networks.

On July 14 we packed our bags at the social center and headed to the newly opened GSF media center, a large school building that would serve as our base of operations during the three days of workshops and conferences from July 16 to 18 and the subsequent protests from July 19 to 21. The center housed spaces for commercial and independent media, Internet access, activist meetings, conferences, the legal team, and a temporary infirmary. Whereas the squatted social center was completely self-managed and had already been running for several years, the GSF had rented the media center and other buildings specifically for the mobilization. Still, all the work of opening and closing the facilities, coordinating events and schedules, cleaning, and maintaining security was carried out by volunteers from various organizations and networks. The GSF also secured an open-air convergence center at the Piazza Kennedy along the beach, which housed a stage for the Manu Chao concert, information stands, private food vendors, and many square feet of tarmac for planning, making props and signs, and informal gatherings. Finally, the GSF also reserved several campgrounds and stadiums, where grassroots activists from out of town slept, washed, and prepared their own food.

After another long day of PGA meetings, which had been organized to coincide with the anti-G8 mobilizations, roughly sixty of us gathered in the courtyard for a July 20 action update by two Italian White Overalls. Eva, an activist from Rome, explained that the GSF was a complex experiment, involving more than eight hundred organizations from around Italy. She added that "everyone will be able to express themselves," but laid down clear action guidelines: "(1) the city and its infrastructure will be respected, and (2) do not physically attack any person, even those wearing uniforms." Regarding the siege, the political position of the GSF was the following: "We don't recognize the existence of the red zone, just as we don't recognize the existence of the G8—it is illegitimate and illegal." Finally, Eva went over the physical layout of the urban terrain, which would be very tight and difficult to coordinate among so many groups because of the small area and mountainous terrain. As of that moment, the following actions had been planned:

1. White Overalls March (inside the GSF): involves thousands of young radicals from Italy and beyond who have been influenced by autonomous Marxism; will invade the red zone from the east.

2. Cobas/Network for Global Rights March (inside the GSF): led by Cobas, a radical labor union also influenced by autonomous Marxism; will invade the red zone from the southeast.

3. Gandhian Bloc (inside the GSF): planning not to invade the red zone but to organize nonviolent sit-ins along the hills to the north; led by pacifists, antimilitarists, ecologists, and solidarity activists associated with the Lilliput Network.

4. Western March (outside the GSF): led by an offshoot of Cobas and several anarchist social centers. Plans to invade the red zone from the west but has not confirmed specific tactics.

5. Anarchist Bloc (outside the GSF): involves dozens of anarchist collectives, including the Pinelli Social Center, which have officially stated they will not follow the GSF guidelines.

After the presentation, PGA-based activists posed difficult questions regarding the need to dialogue with militant groups opposed to the GSF action guidelines. As Raul pointed out, "It is extremely unlikely your action will go as planned, because people who don't agree with you will be there. So has anyone discussed what sort of behavior and position you will have if things go differently? There will be people engaging in actions beyond the GSF agreement. It would be wise to communicate with other groups. There are people who will make an important contribution to this day, and who have made a contribution to our movement. There has been a big difference between Genoa and Prague in terms of inclusiveness and openness."

In the end, Raul proposed using the convergence center as a space to coordinate with groups outside the GSF, and the GSF coordinating committee ultimately agreed. Raul and Jordi then went to visit the Pinelli and INMENSA social centers to begin a process of communication between the Italian militants and radical internationals. The battle map was thus beginning to emerge: the action space was divided among diverse networks physically embodied through specific action tactics. Distinct political ideologies, cultural struggles, and interrelationships would quite literally be inscribed into the urban space in the context of a collective attack on the G8—a major symbol and embodiment of capitalist globalization. Broader network norms and forms would thus be physically expressed through the diversity-of-tactics principle, which would create distinct spaces for alternative forms of action, including performative violence.

The remaining unknown factor was where the thousands of international activists would go and what kinds of actions they would organize. Moderate networks, such as ATTAC and Jubilee 2000, together with Globalize Resistance (a British platform linked to the Socialist Workers Party), ultimately decided on a symbolic action: throwing paper airplanes over the fence along the southern edge of the red zone. Radicals associated with PGA would opt for a creative, festive march in the spirit of tactical frivolity from Prague, including a samba band, mobile street parties, and innovative direct-action tactics. The PGA group would thus morph into the Pink and Silver Bloc during subse-

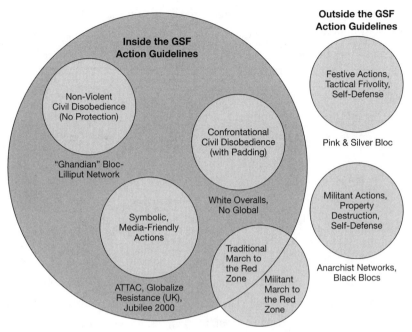

Inside the GSF
Action Guidelines

Outside the GSF
Action Guidelines

Non-Violent
Civil Disobedience
(No Protection)

"Ghandian" Bloc-
Lilliput Network

Confrontational
Civil Disobedience
(with Padding)

Festive Actions,
Tactical Frivolity,
Self-Defense

Pink & Silver Bloc

Symbolic,
Media-Friendly
Actions

White Overalls,
No Global

Militant Actions,
Property
Destruction,
Self-Defense

ATTAC, Globalize
Resistance (UK),
Jubilee 2000

Traditional
March to
the Red
Zone

Militant
March to
the Red
Zone

Anarchist Networks,
Black Blocs

Cobas, Network for Global Rights

17. Protest blocs during the anti-G8 action in Genoa, July 20, 2001. Adapted from Donatella della Porta et al., *Globalization from Below* (Minneapolis: University of Minnesota Press, 2006), 32 and 139.

quent days, planning the action as new activists continued to arrive. These sessions were riven by fierce debates regarding protest tactics and violence.

The first "anarchist" bomb scare took place on July 17. The day's media reports were dominated by the explosion of a letter bomb at a Genoese police station, which severely injured a carabinieri officer, and another bomb outside Carlini Stadium—the White Overalls' home base. For example, the lead headline on the front page of the center-left *La Repubblica* read, "Genoa, a Day of Fear," followed by "Letter bomb injures a carabiniere. Another attempt foiled." Above was written, "The tension around the G8 grows: the anarchists are investigated." The headlines portrayed a situation of chaos and fear, and the accompanying image of an urban crime scene depicted the police as the defenders of order. A front-page story in the center-right *Corriere della Sera* went even further, directly linking the bomb scare to militant protesters, explaining, "The first analysis of the investigation has led to a possible clue that leads to the insurrectionary anarchists."

At a coordinating meeting the next morning, Isabella from the GSF confirmed the bomb reports. She described the struggle within the police and secret service between "democratic" and "radical right" wings, pointing out that "we are sure the bomb was placed by fascist elements within the secret service. They use very small political groups to do this stuff. Everyone knows." She further explained the history of bomb scares in Italy during the 1970s, when Italian police pursued a "strategy of tension," which, as Donatella della Porta explains, combined brutal repression of mass demonstrations with the "covert manipulation of the radical political groups to incite outbursts so as to induce public opinion to favor authoritarian policies" (1995, 60–1).[15] Over the next several days, the bomb scares continued, increasing the tension and fear and raising the specter of violent confrontation.[16]

Later that day, the Pink and Silver Bloc broke into smaller committees to plan the action. As in all our meetings, we used consensus process, and skilled facilitators were often needed to help broker agreements among the diverse viewpoints. I joined a logistics group to hammer out an action proposal. We quickly agreed our goal was to "liberate" as much space as possible and to enter the red zone if possible. The main dispute involved contrasting ideas about what constitutes violence. Raul, who had met with activists from the INMENSA and Pinelli social centers, argued that an aggressive response to police attacks was not violence but a legitimate act of self-defense. He felt we should maintain our festive, nonviolent posture until the "right moment," when some within the march would use alternative means to enter the red zone. Others felt this position was dangerous, and that we had to maintain clear, separate spaces so people could make informed decisions about their level of risk. In the end, we agreed to draft a call to action but left the guidelines and the route to be hashed out during subsequent assemblies.

After much contentious and often acrimonious debate over the next two days, we forged an elaborate compromise. On the tactical level, those who wanted to practice self-defense would mark themselves with silver, while the rest of us would wear only pink. In terms of the route, we decided to gather at the south end of the convergence center, march along the eastern flank of the red zone, next to the Cobas and White Overalls zones, and then hook up with the pacifists in the northern hills, where we would begin our siege. Before reaching the red zone, we would split from the pacifists, and then the Pink and Silvers would separate from the Pinks at the next plaza. It was a seamless plan, tactically and politically, but everything depended on whether the police and militants would cooperate. On the evening before the action, thousands of us gathered under cover at the Piazza Kennedy. As the rain poured down, we sang several rounds of revolutionary songs, including "Bella Ciao," the hymn of the partisans during the Spanish civil war. The next day was shaping up as a major battle indeed.

July 20: Entering the Space of Terror

We arrived at the convergence center at roughly 11:00 a.m. to make final preparations for the siege. The atmosphere of nervous excitement temporarily overwhelmed the mounting tension from the previous days as people finished making costumes, wigs, and props. The samba band headed up an improvised drumming circle by the piazza gate at noon, and the crowd of six hundred Pink Bloc activists filled in behind them. A few minutes later, the march took to the streets; our siege had begun. As we moved down the boulevard to the southeast of the red zone—dancing, drumming, and letting out occasional disco chants—my eyes began to water as I noticed the familiar smell of tear gas. The major confrontation was not supposed to begin until 1:00 p.m., so we already had an inkling of what kind of day this might become. I glanced to the left. Hundreds of protesters had begun a pitched battle near the fence. Riot cops launched tear gas canisters while small groups of hooded, black-clad activists darted about, tossing the canisters back, along with rocks and bottles. "That's the Cobas march," someone pointed out: "It looks like they've gotten mixed up with the Black Bloc." Eager to get to the north side of the city, we hurried past the fray.

After frolicking our way along the eastern flank of the red zone, where thousands of White Overalls decked out in spectacular foam padding would soon begin their march behind massive plastic shields, we approached a tunnel that would take us to Brignole Station and the north side of the city. Just before we entered the tunnel, a group of several hundred young anarchists wearing dark colors, hoods, handkerchiefs, and carrying the occasional stick joined us. "They must be from Pinelli," I thought. Things did not look good. On the other side of the tunnel, we realized that several large containers had sealed off our route. After a brief spokescouncil meeting involving logistical

18. Pink and Silver Bloc marches from the Convergence Center. PHOTOGRAPH COURTESY OF JEFFREY S. JURIS.

coordinators and affinity group delegates, we decided to move into the hills earlier than anticipated. As we moved along parallel to our initial route, we noticed several heavily armed police lines had taken up positions along the side streets. We continued down the other side of the hill before heading to the boulevard leading to Plaza Manin, where the pacifists had assembled. Just before reaching the boulevard, we came to a terrace affording an excellent view of the city below. I recorded the following in my field notes that evening: "It was now unmistakable, the clouds of tear gas had become larger and darker. There were clearly loads of tear gas in the air, as we could feel it in our eyes all the way from the terrace, and the smell was incredible. However, many of the clouds we saw began to appear like real smoke. There were two or three huge clouds of thick, dark smoke rising up in the distance. The city was clearly ablaze."

I later learned that several groups of what appeared to be Black Bloc had begun smashing windows and torching cars and buses in the zone near the White Overalls. We continued moving toward the boulevard. Our plan was to turn left and march toward the red zone fence, where pacifists would later stage their sit-in, and then move to the next plaza. We would then begin our

19. Police fire water cannon at protester during the Cobas march to the Red Zone.
PHOTOGRAPH COURTESY OF FLORIAN SCHUH / PIXELFIGHTERS.COM.

action at the fence, while the Pink and Silver march would separate and move to another section of the red zone. However, when we got to the boulevard, the pacifist march had already begun its descent, and we were trapped at the intersection. By this point, our contingent had grown to over a thousand, and people started to fear a stampede if the police decided to attack. The pacifists took up most of the boulevard from the red zone up to the Plaza Manin, so the logistical group called for another spokescouncil meeting. After sending a scout to further inspect the scene and conferring with various affinity groups, we decided to move alongside the pacifists and head down a small street leading over to the next plaza. This would be the last instance of networking in action before chaos broke out.

When we arrived at the plaza, instead of dividing into separate blocs, however, a large group descended toward the fence while the rest of us milled about the plaza. Several police lines moved toward us from the small street we had just marched from, sealing off the escape route. A police charge seemed imminent, so I moved up the hill to maintain a safe distance and get a better view. Suddenly, a French woman in the crowd below strung a metal cable and then climbed it to the top of the fence. The police fired their water cannons at her, dousing the protesters behind with chemically treated water. The crowd became agitated, and people began throwing bottles and sticks at the police on the other side of the fence. Moments later, the police began a brutal charge with batons and tear gas, unleashing severe panic as protesters frantically scattered toward the top of the plaza. Meanwhile, a small group of us who had taken up a secure position on a nearby stairwell quickly fled uphill to avoid another charge. The morning's tense calm had given way to general panic and fear.

The Pink and Silver Bloc regrouped at the Plaza Manin, which was filled with hundreds of ecologists, pacifists, and feminists. Shortly after I met up with my affinity group, a few dozen Black Bloc activists appeared. A few of us explained that we were in a nonviolent zone and that they would do better to head to another part of the city. After they moved on, the entire Pink Bloc assembled near the plaza, but after just a few moments, a massive police helicopter began hovering directly overhead and firing tear gas canisters at the crowd. Before we had a chance to realize what was happening, the police attacked us from the side streets with more tear gas and batons. I quickly ran up the hill again, and when I turned back to look through the clouds of gas, I saw riot police brutally clubbing peaceful protesters. The Black Bloc was nowhere to be seen. Meanwhile, I heard horrible screams from the midst of the chaos. A group of protesters suddenly came running toward me, followed by charging riot cops. Overcome by panic, I quickly turned around and fled up the hill to escape.

Nuria, an MRG activist from Barcelona who had been caught up in the police attack at the Plaza Manin, later described the events in the following way:

> The police began throwing tear gas, or smoke bombs, I don't know if it was gas or smoke, but there was a moment when I felt three strong impacts on the ground next to me. I began to cry because I couldn't see; I was panicked. Everyone got up quickly and began to run. There were a few of us who didn't, and we were hit with a lot of gas. . . . A friend grabbed me and took me over to a wall. I was saved because the police had come from behind, beating people over the head in such a terrible way. I remember a guy running with his hands on his head, and the police clubbing him from behind. . . . Next to the wall the police were battering people, except for a

few of us with our hands raised. Several officers were totally crazed, while others said, "We don't have to hit them anymore." When the smoke began to clear, the image was grotesque: people on the ground with their heads cracked open and blood all over the ground, blood on people's faces. I was really affected by an image of an older couple, pacifists, I suppose, with white shirts and their hands above their heads and blood all over their faces, and their shirts drenched in blood, begging the police, "Please stop hitting us!"

Meanwhile, I continued running up the hill with a crowd of Italian pacifists until we came to a calm overlook where a half dozen protesters from the Pink Bloc were removing their costumes to avoid police detection. I quickly did the same, also cleaning off the pink lipstick, which was starting to burn my cheek. People were in a state of panic and shock. The nervous excitement that often accompanies mass actions had been transformed into terror and fear. Despite our attempt to maintain separate spaces for distinct forms of action, all the actions had been mixed together within a single zone of indistinction.

To get off the streets, I decided to look for an open bar together with an older man from New York and a young British couple. We found one around the corner, where we watched a live television transmission as we sipped our beer. The screen was divided into four boxes, each showing a different image. There was a street battle in one box, Black Bloc protesters smashing windows in another, burning cars in another, and Berlusconi addressing the nation in the final box. Meanwhile, as we sat inside the bar, the police were ruthlessly attacking the White Overalls march at the other end of the city. Paula, an activist with a political art collective in Barcelona called Las Agencias, later recalled the situation:

I find myself in the midst of a White Overalls mega-demonstration, a march of thousands and thousands and thousands of people, incredible. And in five minutes the police dissolve it. After they have only gone three hundred meters, the police begin firing tear gas, beating people, they didn't even let them demonstrate, dissolving the march with tear gas, breaking their shields, destroying everything. We had to leave the area in order to escape. I didn't have a mask or a helmet; it was terrible. After two hours of gas, I saw a city suddenly at war; there was hardly anyone from Genoa on

20. Police terrorize unarmed protester during the White Overalls march.
PHOTOGRAPH REPRINTED BY PERMISSION OF AP PHOTO / DARKO BANDIC.

the streets. I did come across an old man who was watching, surrounded by the police—the police firing tear gas, containers burning. I looked at the situation and asked, "Where am I? Where am I?"

After resting for a while, we decided to head back out. We walked down the hill and eventually came across a group of Italian reporters. They said the coast was clear, although there were still some intense battles near Carlini. We continued onward, eventually meeting up with the remnants of the Pink Bloc. People were shaken. As we marched back toward the city center, rumors circulated that the police had killed anywhere from two to four protesters, including someone from Barcelona, but we still had no way of knowing what had really happened. The uncertainty only increased our apprehension and fear. Eventually we made it down to a major plaza, but we soon realized that the police had blocked off each of the major exit routes. We were surrounded. Moreover, another major street battle was unfolding between the police and the Black Bloc just a few blocks to the east. Paco from MRG-Zaragoza later described the situation: "The sensation was of tremendous urban disorder. First there were stores that had been assaulted and remains from street battles all around us, and then police were patrolling the streets, showing off, making victory signs, with their armored cars, helicopters flying above. It was a situation of disorder, almost like a war. It was the most similar thing I had ever seen to televised images of a city at war—all that militarization, all that chaos."

Eventually we formed a line across the boulevard that led back to Piazza Kennedy and began marching slowly with our arms linked, creating a powerful sense of solidarity. Back at the convergence center, we met our friends from Barcelona and shared horror stories from the day. People were in shock; many were still missing. As soon as the sun went down, helicopters began flying overhead again. Throughout the day, the sound of helicopters and ambulance sirens had signaled a police attack. It was not until the next morning that we learned about the death of Carlo Giuliani, a twenty-two-year-old activist from Genoa and son of a local labor leader. The killing had a major impact, because of both the shock and horror it caused and the images of his corpse that instantly circulated through global mediascapes. Paula later recounted the scene: "As soon as we left the bar, I come to a corner where people come running, 'Go over there, go over there, a dead person, a dead person!' The intersection where they killed Carlo Giuliani was around the corner from the bar, just around the corner I get there, and Carlo Giuliani was lying on the ground surrounded by police. With what had already happened to me, and then I get there and see this dead kid, I didn't understand it. The police have lost control. I know they are savages, but I never imagined this could happen in Europe."

In addition to the violence and terror experienced by activists on the streets, hundreds of protesters were severely beaten, tortured, and psychologically abused in jail. Paco told me the following story about his experience following the police charge at the Plaza Manin:

They threw us in a police van and rode around with us for four hours. They spit on us, stepped on us, and insulted us. . . . They brought us to a police department in the city and beat us. They ripped a piece of hair out of my friend's head. . . . They put us on our knees against the wall, and if you tried to sit comfortably, they beat you. At the moment you think, "This is horrible," but then you get used to it. And then they took us, put us in a car. We asked, "Where are we going? Where are we going? They didn't answer. Later we found out that we were at the Bolzaneto Detention Center. We were there all night, against the wall; the windows had no glass, it was cold, and there were people with lots of blood. Every once in a while, they would take us for a walk with ten to twelve cops on both sides of us, and they would beat us, always handcuffed. This happened at regular intervals. And all of this, imagine, for hours on end. . . . The worst thing that happened to me was when they tried to make me sign a paper saying they hadn't done anything. I said I wouldn't sign, that I wanted to see a doctor. . . . They made me lift my arms, and when I did, they punched me so hard they broke my rib. Then they took me to the doctor and gave me the worst beating of the night in the doctor's office. There were two doctors; one watched, and the other one hit me. Later . . . I said, "Now it's beginning"; at that moment I was thinking, because they told us that two cops had died, and we were about forty people there, so the first person to fall would have to pay. . . . I thought they were going to begin another torture session, they would kill us . . . but they didn't beat us anymore.

Militant Protest in Genoa

The Italian state unleashed a brutal campaign of indiscriminate police terror in Genoa. But what about violence on the part of protesters? What were militants up to on the streets? More generally, what is the relationship between state terror and performative violence? Like many protesters in Genoa, I had several encounters with what appeared to be the Black Bloc, but it was impossible to say whether they were activists, right-wing infiltrators, or provocateurs. Indeed, the ambiguity and rumor contributed to the epistemic murk that helped characterize Genoa as a zone of indistinction. As we moved through the terrain of resistance, I saw not only devastated bank machines and shattered windows of transnational corporations but also burned-out cars, ransacked storefronts, and broken glass. The city was a war zone, indeed. Black Bloc militancy generally has a specific communicative logic: destruction of the symbols of corporate capitalism and the state. Although there may be tactical disagreements, destructive actions against ordinary cars, homes, and shops fall outside the bounds of accepted militant signification. Black Bloc performative violence tends to be neither random nor senseless.

The Black Bloc is not an organization, or a network, but a specific set of tactics enacted by groups of young militants during protests. Although repertoires vary with each action, they often include destruction of private property, usually banks and transnational storefronts, ritualized confrontation with police, and a series of more specific practices such as "de-arrests," marching in small, compact groups with elbows linked, and jail solidarity. These tactics are connected to a broader militant style, including the use of black pants and jumpers, combat boots, and black masks or bandannas to cover the face, and an aggressive, confrontational attitude. Masks are worn for instrumental reasons—to protect identities for personal security, but also serve certain iconic functions, such as expressing collective solidarity through anonymity or portraying archetypical images of youth rebellion. Black Bloc styles and practices can be seen as the physical embodiment of a political vision based on anticapitalism, physical confrontation, and a total rejection of the market and state. Such values are communicated through particular stylistic codes and signifiers and highly sensational ritualized violent performances.

Militant tactics thus involve the enactment of specific modes of violent performance through distinct bodily techniques, styles of dress, ritual symbols, and communicative practices. The typical image of a Black Bloc activist reflects a masculine ideal of rebellious confrontation. In addition, as Peterson (2001, 55) argues, militant activists construct identities through emotionally powerful embodied ritual performance that constructs the militant body as the ground of agency and produces an "embattled" activist identity. Within anti–corporate globalization movements, performative violence thus provides a mechanism through which militants construct radical anticapitalist subjectivities. At the same time, youth styles and practices have become globalized (Feixa 1999). In this sense, Black Bloc tactics circulate through global communication networks, providing cultural scripts enacted by militant activists in distant locales.

Performative violence—including the accompanying bodily techniques, dress codes, and iconic symbols—helps constitute particular youth subcultural styles. Spectacular subcultures are systems of communication through which diverse forms of discourse and fashion are adapted, subverted, and transformed through bricolage (Clarke 1976). As Dick Hebdige (1979) explains, "The communication of a significant difference, then (and the parallel communication of a group identity), is the 'point' behind the style of all spectacular subcultures" (102). Within many anticapitalist activist networks, squatting and militant protest tactics, styles, and icons thus constitute central elements of a radical youth counterculture. In addition to the production of identity and difference, particular stylized performances can also communicate directed messages, such as rejection of the dominant order or radical confrontation with the symbols of global capitalism and the state. In this sense, Black Bloc tactics can be seen as the active use of specific countercultural practices to engage in spectacular rituals of resistance.

The Pinelli social center served as the base of operations for the Black Bloc in Genoa, while militant internationals slept at the nearby Sciorba Stadium.[17] The first evening planning assembly took place on July 16, where activists decided to separate from the GSF because of the restriction on sticks, rocks, and firearms. The number of participants had doubled to several hundred by the second assembly, including activists from the United States, Italy, France, Germany, Greece, and Spain. The evening before the siege, a large bloc from Pinelli decided to march together with Cobas in the southeast. They moved to Albaro Park that evening to be closer to the start of the action. They were supposed to meet up with another group from Pinelli the next morning, but the police had surrounded the social center. In the end, five hundred Black Bloc militants marched together from the park toward the center of the city to join up with Cobas on July 20. One activist recalled:

> We arrived at the point with other masked comrades and red flags from Cobas. We met and some of us moved toward specific objectives. Our target was a bank, and the police arrived from the right. There was a brief scuffle, and some Molotov cocktails and rocks were thrown. . . . The police stopped their repression briefly, so we took advantage of the opportunity to make barricades with garbage cans, wood, and anything else we could find. We set some of the garbage containers on fire while a part of our bloc, a group of about three hundred, continued attacking the face of capitalism: the banks and gas stations.[18]

Black Blocs carried out similar actions throughout the day against banks, transnational corporations, and gas stations while engaging in pitched street battles replete with barricades, stones, and Molotov cocktails. When it became too dangerous, many activists removed their masks and black clothing to avoid detection. Beyond the directed violent performances, which communicated clear anticapitalist messages, indiscriminate attacks were also carried out against cars, storefronts, and buildings. Because these actions did not fit established patterns of militant performance, many activists, including militants themselves, suspected the Italian police had used provocateurs. Indeed, several Black Bloc activists commented that during the siege on July 20 police had allowed them free rein while selectively repressing peaceful protesters. Others noted that just before the police charges, a Black Bloc group would pass by, escaping repression.

Predictably, media coverage of the siege portrayed the young militants associated with the Black Bloc as the ultimate villains, decontextualizing images and reinserting them within a narrative of the violent anarchist other. The Italian papers on July 21 were thus filled with photos of burning cars, masked protesters in black hurling stones at riot police, armored carabinieri firing tear gas and brandishing shields, as well as the occasional shot of a bludgeoned protester receiving first aid. In the right-leaning Genoese *Il Secolo XIX*, for example, the main front page headline read, "Genoa, blood on the G8," while the text above explained, "City succumbs for hours to the guerrillas. Throwing of Molotovs, incited by the anarchists." A lead article below it, entitled "Everyone Defeated," included the following text: "The images are of a proletarian Genoa in a state of death, devastation, and shaken by violence not seen at other protests. There was the first death of an antiglobalization protester, 180 people injured; it is a depressed and humiliated city, shaken by a day of unending madness. Only the death of this young boy stopped the assault of the terrible Black Bloc, anarchists, and professionals of urban guerrilla warfare. . . . A helpless city, invaded by tens of Black Bloc contingents with only one objective: destroy everything."

July 21: The Day After

After an uncomfortable night in my sleeping bag at Piazza Kennedy, where we spent the night seeking safety in numbers, I went to the media center early the next morning with two Catalan friends to get the latest information. Following the violence of the previous day, Berlusconi announced the protest should be halted, but the GSF decided to continue as planned. Moreover, as

21. Prototypical image of "Black Bloc violence" in the mass media. PHOTOGRAPH REPRINTED BY PERMISSION OF AP PHOTO / MICHEL SPINGLER.

word spread around Italy of Carlo Giuliani's death, people began coming to Genoa in droves. In the end, despite the terror that had been unleashed, more than three hundred thousand people marched against Berlusconi and the G8, constituting the largest anti–corporate globalization protest to date. At the international coordinating meeting that morning, Isabella from the GSF confirmed reports that Carlo Giuliani had been killed: "Yesterday was a tremendous attempt to destroy the movement. We are all shocked, but we believe their attack will not be successful. A few hundred members of the Black Bloc attacked every part of the movement yesterday. They did not attack the G8, just us. Why did the police allow them to do it? We don't know if there will be more trouble today, from either the Black Bloc or the police."

When we got back to the Piazza Kennedy, the Pink Bloc had reassembled to make signs and props for the protest. Just as we finished our report to the Catalans and Spaniards, the march reached the convergence center. We headed over to one of the gates along with the rest of the Pink Bloc, plunging right between ATTAC and a huge bloc of Greek Communists. Minutes after the march began, just before the route turned away from the convergence center, an intense cloud of tear gas came floating our way. A police helicopter flew overhead, and when I turned to look I saw small groups of protesters and riot cops throwing tear gas canisters back and forth. "Shit," I remember thinking, "the police have started again." Sergi, an MRG activist from Barcelona, later recalled:

> I was at the entrance to the Piazza Kennedy, throwing tear gas canisters back at the police, with my gas mask. Two hours throwing back canisters. It was a battle with the police; I don't think it was very useful, but I don't know, at least we did something, helped the people who were fighting. It was really hard, really difficult, because canisters would fall right near my feet, totally burning. Then they arrested two kids, and we took off toward the beach. They followed us with gas, and people were throwing up. All the medical people were hiding in a room at a beach club taking care of people. The police kept chasing us, they almost grabbed us, but we kept running toward the beach, one group throwing stones, us in the middle, the march on one side, the police on the other, we couldn't do anything. The police came toward the beach, it was something, attacking us with a lot of water, no one cannon was so strong, but all of them together . . . man!

Meanwhile, as the battle raged behind us, the front of the demonstration continued toward the city center. We danced to the beat of the samba drums and sang revolutionary hymns with a radical brass band, stopping every few hundred feet as cheering residents dumped buckets of water over our heads to provide some relief from the midday heat. The march ended in a large plaza, where several speakers made presentations about economic globalization, the G8, the debt, and a host of other related issues. We took the opportunity to sit down and rest awhile in the shade. Hordes of people soon began leaving the plaza, heading over to a parking area where they loaded onto buses. Feeling vulnerable, several of us from the logistical group helped round up the Pink Bloc to begin marching back to the convergence center.

After a long discussion, we finally decided to move out along the ravine, continuing to drum, sing, and dance the entire way. We eventually reached the intersection where we had been trapped the day before. After a temporary standoff with police, we walked over to the Brignole Plaza. As a group of us sat on the bench, I noticed that empty ambulances continued to circulate around the plaza every ten minutes or so, while helicopters flew overhead. We soon

22. Protesters resist police attack on the Convergence Center. PHOTOGRAPH COURTESY OF FLORIAN SCHUH / PIXELFIGHTERS.COM.

noticed several young kids tossing stones in the direction of the police behind the large container in front of the hotel. The situation was intensifying again, so after another nervous spokescouncil meeting, we decided to head back to the convergence center.

After winding down, exchanging stories over wine and panini sandwiches, several us walked to the media center for a Pink Bloc meeting to evaluate what had occurred during the last two days. I was still trying to decide whether I wanted to return to Barcelona with the buses later that evening or stay in Genoa to do prison support work, including protests and advocacy to help win the release of activists who had been jailed. The media center was packed with protesters writing e-mails, mainstream journalists conducting inter-views, and Indymedia activists downloading images taken from the day's events. At around 8:00 p.m., we started the Pink Bloc meeting outside, which turned into a collective therapy session as people recounted the violence they had lived through during the past two days.

After the meeting, I went back to the Internet room to let people know I had decided to stay for a few more days. Just then, we heard people yelling in the street outside, followed by several loud bangs on the gates of the me-dia center, and at the Diaz School across the way. Activists charged into the media center, screaming, "Police, police!" Concerned about my pictures and field notes, I grabbed my backpack and went to hide it up on the fourth floor. People were running up and down the stairs frantically, talking about vicious beatings taking place in the school. Apparently, cops outside were chanting, "Long live the Mussolini!" After our experiences during the previous two days, we all assumed we would be arrested and severely beaten, if not killed. There was terrible panic, and many people began crying. Two American direct-action veterans came into the room and told me to grab a sleeping bag, which could be used to soften the blows. We found an empty room, turned out the lights, and hid under a table. As we waited in the dark, we could hear helicopters flying overhead and the sound of police officers smashing computers below. As Feldman (1995) would have it, I had stumbled on an "ethnographic zone of emergency."

We soon heard footsteps approaching. The lights went on; a man with a deep voice mumbled something in Italian. I went out to try to explain that we were peaceful and had done nothing wrong. Instead of a raging group of riot cops, there was just a middle-aged police officer. He accompanied us down to a hallway on the second floor, where about fifty activists were lined up against the walls, and told us to sit down. We were all nervous, and everyone still expected to be beaten and arrested. After about fifteen minutes, however, we heard there were a few important journalists and politicians down below. Although the police had smashed all the Indymedia computers after copying reams of pictures and documents, they soon left the building without doing additional harm. Many people hugged, some cried, while others continued to run around frantically.

After the police left, I went into a nearby room where activists were hanging out of an open window, watching the events below. A huge crowd of activists and journalists had gathered on the media center patio and along the sidewalk, many of them shouting at the police, "Murderers! Murderers!" Ambulances arrived, and paramedics carried people out of the school on stretchers. We could see bloodstains on the sheets, and every once in a while what appeared to be a dead body. As we watched, some people began shouting; others started to cry. As each stretcher was taken out of the building, people hissed and jeered. It seemed as if a riot would break out. After about thirty minutes, a loud helicopter flew overhead, shining a bright spotlight on the street below. When the final ambulance pulled away, the police lines in front of the school retreated.

I rushed downstairs to find the rest of the Catalans. We were all shocked and wanted to get out of Genoa as fast as possible. A journalist from a Catalan newspaper told us he had gone over to the school and had seen bloodstains everywhere, including fresh blood dripping from the banister. Martina contacted the three buses that had been waiting for us at Carlini. The drivers were terrified and anxious to leave, so a group of activists convinced them to wait at a gas station on the outskirts of the city. It was impossible to find a ride, so we called two taxis, joining thousands of other terrified activists that night in a mass exodus from Genoa.

Several months later, I interviewed Ramon, an activist from MRG-Zaragoza, who had been sleeping inside the Diaz School when the police raid occurred. He related the following testimony about what happened inside the school:

> The police began pushing the front doors, and I saw they were going to enter. I said to people that we should get together with our backpacks against the wall, that we should lift our hands above our heads and yell, "No violence!" so it would be clear that we were going to carry out a peaceful resistance. We did this, and began to sit with our hands raised, and I still hadn't yet sat down when the first cop entered. I will never forget that scene for the rest of my life, because he entered like a mad bull, and there were many huge guys with masks. The first thing the guy did was throw a chair at us. . . . Then the rest entered, picked up some wooden school desks and began beating us with them. I had practiced how to do a nonviolent resistance with my body many times, using our bodies collectively, but really just instinctively, I doubled over to protect myself, covering my head and my kidneys and all that, as if I had done it all my life. But I had never had to do it so many times in a situation of such extreme violence. We made a huge wall, everyone with our bodies, some of us in front protecting the rest, and we suffered a tremendous beating. It was the most intense beating I had received in my life. Of all the actions I had done, the clubbings I had received, this was absolutely the worse police violence I had ever experienced. . . . I couldn't see anything in my head except stars, like an impact

of light produced by the blows, as if I were a rubber toy. I received one blow after another, trying to stay firm and suffer through it as much as I could. . . . When we heard the order to stop the beating, I had just about run out of strength to resist. They turned on the lights and we could see what had happened. We saw the hooded police surrounding us; there were pools of blood everywhere. There was a cop, wearing a ribbon like an Italian flag, who seemed to be directing the operation. . . . Then, after a few minutes, I realized that I was really fucked up, my body began to freeze and I started to feel the bruises. I felt like I had a broken arm, a broken leg, which I couldn't move, and I felt cold. I began to shake. . . . Then they took me away in a stretcher, and the rest of us as well. When they took me out in the stretcher, and we saw such amazing press attention at the door, it was a surreal situation. Having lived through this assault at the school, having been in a tunnel of such incredible police violence and then to go out into the light under the attention of the entire world; the whole world knew immediately what was happening.[19]

Silencing Dissent

Why did the Italian police and caribinieri forces carry out such a brutal campaign of terror against antiglobalization demonstrators in Genoa, particularly given the intense global media spotlight? Many commentators, both within and outside of Italy, have accused residual "fascist" elements within the Italian police, laying the blame on specific law enforcement officials. On the other hand, the GSF and leftist parties such as Rifondazione placed the blame squarely on the Berlusconi regime. In a recent analysis of the anti-G8 protests, della Porta et al. (2006, 191) seem to downplay, but not entirely dismiss, the idea that the massive police violence in Genoa resulted from a direct political order.[20] For their part, many anti–corporate globalization activists have suggested that what took place in Genoa was an internationally coordinated campaign of state repression meant to systematically break the will of protesters (cf. Starhawk 2002, 110–15).[21] As Ramon explained, "The moment we start becoming dangerous, they respond with the harshest means at their disposal, no?"

We may never know definitively who was responsible for the repression in Genoa or whether it formed part of an internationally coordinated effort, but what activists experienced during the anti-G8 protests was a campaign of low-intensity state terror.[22] Through the gradual buildup of paranoia and fear, the militarization of the city, and the persistent bomb threats, the Italian state authorities helped create the conditions for an emerging space of terror. During the protests, overwhelming physical force was combined with psychological warfare, including the circulation of rumor, the use of undercover agents, and the production of unnerving somatic cues, such as ambulance sirens and helicopter sounds. In addition, the murder of a protester and the widespread use of torture produced intense psychological and physical effects.

The repeated physical blows against protesters, on the streets and inside detention centers, literally inscribed the memory of violence and terror on activist bodies (see Green 1999, 246–47). As discussed in chapter 4, during mass direct actions, activists use their bodies to occupy physical space and communicate alternative political messages.[23] The symbolic siege of Genoa was thus a ritualized attempt by anti–corporate globalization activists to wrest control of the city's urban space from Italian authorities through diverse color-coded bodily techniques. In this way, activist bodies and urban space are key sites of political struggle. Violence acts as a principal mediator between protesters and riot police as an embodied manifestation of the state. Feldman has characterized the civil war in Northern Ireland in similar terms:

> In Northern Ireland the formation of the political subject takes place within a continuum of spaces consisting of the body, the confessional community, the state and the imagined community of utopian completion. . . . The command of these spaces is practically achieved and sustained through ideology and violence. In each of these spaces, claims of power are made and practices of power are inscribed. The spatial inscription of practices and power involves physical flows, metabolic transactions and transfers-exchanges which connect, separate, distance, and hierarchize one space in relation to another. (1991, 9)

State terror in Genoa thus involved the use of violence not only to spread fear but also to physically crush bodies through the application of repeated and overwhelming physical blows within an urban zone of indistinction, thereby undermining the basis for political agency itself. Indeed, the prolonged uncertainty, tension, violence, and fear experienced by activists produced enduring psychological sequelae. For weeks after returning to Barcelona, many of us flinched at the sight of police vans or the sound of helicopters and ambulances. The political message from the Italian police seemed to be: Stay home, do not engage in confrontational protest, and above all do not mix with militant radicals! Indeed, the experience of indiscriminate repression on the streets of Genoa contributed to an overwhelming sense of physical vulnerability, which many middle-class activists, in particular, are not accustomed to. The attack on what had been considered a "sanctuary"—the GSF media center and dormitory—only reinforced the feeling that there was no safe place and no one was free from repression.[24]

The experience of widespread danger and persecution caused some activists to doubt the wisdom of continued protest, even provoking existential doubts about the security of the world. For example, an activist from the White Overalls explained after Genoa, "We knew we would confront batons; we knew we were risking being detained and arrested. But no one thought it would be a massacre. We were all afraid beforehand, but we hadn't feared death."[25] Ana, a young student activist from Barcelona, offered the following reflection: "Until that point we were all enthusiastic, but Genoa was a difficult blow for everyone. On the one hand, it was really intense, we were extremely afraid, and on the other hand, up to what point are we willing to go? What are we willing to risk on the personal level—that goes for everyone, no? I am extremely political, I am willing to risk my body, but we are a generation of university students, we are not prepared for that kind of violence."

Reflecting Elaine Scarry's (1985) insight that extreme violence makes and unmakes the world, Nuria, another MRG activist, had this to say about the lasting impact of Genoa:

My experience in Genoa undermined the basic fundamentals they had taught me since I was little, the fundamentals of security. It gave me the sense that I had been living a lie until now, that I was living in a world of cotton. In Genoa, I saw the face of terror. Berlusconi acted with such impunity, they did whatever they wanted, and they can, and nothing happens. And then after 9/11 there was the sense that they are going after us. There is also the antiterrorism law in Barcelona, which they are using on our friends. And the next on the list after bin Laden might be the antiglobalization movement. All of this has served to protect me, to make me less ingenuous. Maybe the world is like this; it is difficult to lose my fundamental sense of security, but it makes me less fragile.

Many activists, however, expressed the desire to continue participating in mass actions despite their traumatic experiences in Genoa, as Ramon maintained:

> Genoa didn't take away my desire to continue, but I am a lot more realistic about the risks and the consequences. If tomorrow I am in another one of these protests, in a more complicated part of the world, or if there is more repressive violence, I might never leave. They might kill me. It's a contradictory feeling, because I want to continue participating in this and I am willing to assume all the risks, but I don't want—and I don't think anyone wants—to be jailed, tortured, and beaten. Many people were terrorized by the fear and terror, and they will have succeeded in demobilizing some people, but collectively I think they did not achieve their objective.

Indeed, the brutal Italian police tactics would seem to have backfired in some ways, as the mass participation in the unitary march on July 21 illustrated. Moreover, the Italian and particularly the international press soon began to emphasize activist testimony about police violence. Activists also organized a series of mass mobilizations against Berlusconi following Genoa, including two labor marches in Rome that drew more than a million people. In addition, the World Social Forum brought more than seventy thousand people to Brazil in January 2002, and protests against the European Union the following March in Barcelona drew a half million protesters. The momentum created by the anti-G8 mobilizations in Genoa played an important role in each of these mobilizations. On the other hand, activists were severely affected by the extreme violence they experienced on the streets of Genoa. Indeed, anti–corporate globalization protests have not reached the same level of confrontation since, and activists have generally shied away from mass blockades in recent years.[26]

Conclusion: Reassessing Diversity of Tactics

Hundreds of thousands of activists came to Genoa during the G8 protests to denounce the structural violence associated with capitalist globalization and to undermine the symbolic order from which the legitimacy of multilateral institutions such as the G8 derives. Most sought to achieve this through nonviolent means, while others chose performative violence to achieve the same ends. The overall framework was a symbolic declaration of war on the G8, followed by a ritualized siege of the red zone. The Berlusconi regime had other plans, and the Italian police responded by manipulating fears of anarchist violence to justify the transformation of a symbolic protest into a horrifying space of terror. What was the relationship, then, between performative violence and the space of terror that emerged in Genoa? On the one hand, young militants forged potent oppositional identities and communicated a radical antisystemic critique by enacting prototypical scenes of youth rebellion against the symbols of global capitalism and the state. Performative violence is neither random nor senseless; rather, it responds to a specific economy of signification. The resulting mass-media images helped bring a great deal of public visibility to anti–corporate globalization movements, and to many of their political demands.

On the other hand, once violent performances have been physically enacted, they can be appropriated for other ends. In this sense, media frames decontextualized and reinserted images of militant rebellion into a larger narrative of dreaded criminal, if not terrorist, deviance, threatening to alienate potential supporters and wrest legitimacy from movement demands. Violent images were also used to separate the "reasonable" majority from the radical fringe, thus steering activists in a more reformist direction. As a July 21 story in the *New York Times* explained, "As in previous demonstrations—from Seattle to Gothenburg, where a man was shot and badly wounded by Swedish police—a small number of more radical youths, bent on battling the police, instigated a form of violence that most demonstrators did not condone."

At the same time, local and national authorities in Genoa took advantage of widespread fear of violent anarchist "others" to justify their brutal campaign of state terror. The application of psychological techniques together with overwhelming physical blows inscribed lasting social memories on activist bodies. Indeed, the resulting space of terror threatened to undermine the embodied basis of activist political agency. As we have seen, Genoa did have a stifling impact on the willingness of many, though not all, activists to continue engaging in confrontational action. Performative violence is thus decidedly a double-edged sword. Militant performances in Genoa and the resulting images did generate significant visibility while energizing certain movement sectors, but they also contributed to official efforts to criminalize dissent.

What about the implications of this analysis for ongoing activist debates? As I have argued, violence is a powerful cultural construct, and contests over what violence means and when and where it can legitimately be used help construct alternative political identities, involving what we might call a cultural politics of violence. As maintained throughout this book, anti–corporate globalization movements are characterized by emerging network norms and forms, involving communication and coordination across political, tactical, and organizational differences. Given this broader cultural context, public condemnation of violent tactics have been roundly criticized by many radical activists, even those who would not practice performative violence themselves.

The debate surrounding violence and nonviolence among anti–corporate globalization activists goes back to Seattle (if not before), where small, highly coordinated groups of Black Bloc activists selectively smashed the storefronts of major banks and transnational corporations, including Starbucks, the Gap, and McDonald's. Scuffles between nonviolent protesters and the Black Bloc broke out on the streets, and many NGO-based activists later denounced the violence, arguing that a small marginal group had hijacked their action, taking the focus away from the main issues behind the protest. Militants countered that they have a right to protest, and that denouncing other activists helps police and government authorities divide the movement. Instead, militants and radicals have supported a diversity of tactics, which, as we have seen, places a high value on dialogue, coordination, and mutual solidarity among different sectors and blocs. Radical anticapitalists have specifically criticized networks and groups such as the GSF, which are perceived as shutting down dialogue, and have responded with extreme hostility to public declarations by moderate activists condemning violent tactics.[27]

Predictably, arguments about protest violence continued to rage after Genoa, particularly when Susan George of ATTAC publicly criticized young militants, asking, "Are you content demonstrators? I am not talking about the vast majority within the GSF. I know you were terrorized, and some bloodied, and also not to those among the Black Bloc who were police. Rather, I am talking to the authentic Black Bloc, who didn't take part in the preparatory meetings . . . and who didn't belong to the 700 responsible Italian organizations who decided to practice active non-violence."[28]

George's public declaration unleashed a barrage of criticism.[29] Some radicals continued to support militant tactics while placing blame for violence elsewhere. As one activist argued, "The violence is not provoked by any of the organizations that form part of the antiglobalization movement. It is a natural part of the process of expansion of the capitalist system."[30] Beyond these poles, many protesters disagreed with Black Bloc tactics but recognized that effective critique can only be waged from inside the radical speech community. Indeed, many radicals, particularly those active with PGA and the Pink and Silver Bloc, emphasized a networking logic involving coordination among diverse forms of action across diversity and difference. According to the prevailing diversity-of-tactics principle, the main lesson from Genoa was the broader need for dialogue, coordination, and innovation, as Jordi from MRG-Catalonia argued:

> The "good activists" will have to choose between saving themselves by taking part in an anarchist witch hunt or accepting "diversity of tactics" and trying to criticize within this context, not leaving "outside the movement" those who started it. All this without discounting that police infiltrated the Black Bloc. With more sophistication, they took advantage of the lack of coordination between anarchists and the GSF to attack the Bloc as they passed in front of nonviolent demonstrations. One thing has become clear: we have to coordinate direct action with all other types of protest. Who knows when a sit-in or a Molotov cocktail will be useful? It depends on the moment. And according to Asian wisdom: "Always do what the enemy least expects."[31]

As we have seen, however, the indiscriminate campaign of state terror unleashed in Genoa undermined the prevailing diversity-of-tactics principle, as authorities used the excuse of militant violence to attack violent and nonviolent protesters alike. In many ways, Genoa constitutes a limit to the diversity-of-tactics model, as well as the broader network norms and forms considered throughout this book, particularly as they relate to performative violence. Although authorities may attempt to divide protesters into peaceful and violent

23. New Kids on the Black
Block video cover

camps, in Genoa police did precisely the reverse, creating a generalized zone of indistinction. In this situation, maintaining separate spaces for distinct tactics proved impossible, as performative violence placed others at extreme risk. Paradoxically, tolerance for certain tactics may actually undermine the ability of other protesters to implement more innovative direct-action practices.

In this sense, broader networking logics that promote diversity and creativity may also serve to discourage internal movement critique, particularly when viewed as coming from the "outside." Emerging network norms and forms thus pose a particularly vexing challenge with respect to protest violence, even as they remain a potent source of tactical innovation. Similarly, although network models have provided an alternative blueprint, not just for social movement organizing but also for reorganizing social, cultural, and political relations, the case of protest violence points to a more general weakness. Indeed, coordinating horizontally across diversity and difference may be an effective way to organize protests among widely disparate groups, but when it comes to important long-term political or strategic decisions, mutual tolerance may not be enough. More complex planning, including establishing the basic ground rules for sustained network interactions, requires concrete mechanisms for collective decision making that are highly refined and elaborated. As I explore in the following chapters, radical activists have thus struggled to build decision-making structures that are both effective *and* directly democratic within transnational networks such as PGA and the social forums.

Postscript (The Last Word)

Several months after Genoa, Las Agencias, a political art group in Barcelona, released its new "guerrilla communications" campaign called New Kids on the Black Block. Guided by an emerging networking logic, the project involves postmodern parody, mixing images and codes from two widespread mass-mediated constructions: the Black Bloc and New Kids on the Block, an adolescent pop group that rose to superstardom during the late eighties and early nineties. The main elements of the Las Agencias campaign involved a spoof video—combining scenes from anti–corporate globalization actions with backstage dialogue and images from a New Kids on the Block tour, press conferences, a promotional fanzine, and a poster with the headline "Another World Tour (Is Possible)," which announced the stops on the New Kids Tour: Seattle, Washington, Prague, Quebec, Barcelona, and Genoa. Activists presented the campaign—which uses a pink and black color theme, reflecting the blurring of activist identities and prevailing diversity-of-tactics ethic—at major anti–corporate globalization actions and gatherings after Genoa. The project aimed to criticize the sensationalist media constructions of the Black Bloc, to deconstruct official strategies that seek to criminalize militant activists and divide the movement, and to explore the complexities surrounding the meaning and use of violence more broadly. As Paula explained:

> After Genoa, both within and outside the movement, people began criminalizing the Black Bloc. If the Black Bloc hadn't acted, this wouldn't have happened, the Black Bloc are the bad guys, the assassins—Black Bloc, Black Bloc, Black Bloc. I lived through Genoa, I was brutally attacked, all of our people, but we can't criminalize a group for their tactics. I think the most interesting thing about the antiglobalization movement is its

diversity, and we need the Black Bloc as much as the pacifists, pinks, silvers, and independents. Because this is precisely what we have to do, show our differences. You can't ask us all to be the same. There are many people who want to make the movement uniform, but I want to show our differences, respecting everyone else. The New Kids were born to provoke questions: What is violence? Why does one group accuse another of being violent? Who generates violence? Why do we have to divide ourselves into those who are violent and those who are nonviolent? So we used guerrilla communication tactics, using our mass-mediated society to create a mix, something like a mix between the Spice Girls and bin Laden, between the bad and the famous, and to merchandise a rock group, saying, "Call 'em what you want!"[32]

6

The need has become urgent for concerted action to dismantle the illegitimate world governing system which combines transnational capital, nation-states, international financial institutions and trade agreements. Only a global alliance of peoples' movements . . . can defeat this emerging globalised monster. If impoverishment of populations is the agenda of neo-liberalism, direct empowerment of the peoples through constructive direct action and civil disobedience will be the programme of the Peoples' Global Action.[1]

MAY THE RESISTANCE
BE AS TRANSNATIONAL
AS CAPITAL!

Three months after the anti-G8 protests in Genoa, I was walking through Barcelona's Raval neighborhood with two dozen activists from Catalonia, the Netherlands, Germany, and the United Kingdom. MRG and a Dutch collective called Eurodusnie (Euro, No Way!) had recently taken over the coconvenership of Peoples' Global Action (PGA) in Europe, and we had just finished a three-day meeting together with members of the "support group" to begin talking about how to improve network coordination. As we wandered through the dimly lit streets in search of a place to eat, I realized that several of us had helped organize the Pink and Silver Bloc in Genoa. This was the first time we had seen each other since then, but no one had mentioned the G8 during the previous three days. Indeed, some of us were on opposing sides of the debate over militant tactics in the Pink and Silver Bloc, and perhaps there were still hard feelings. Pablo must have suspected as much. As we sat down to dinner at one of the neighborhood's growing number of Pakistani restaurants, he looked at a group of us from MRG and explained, "I recently saw Nicole in Paris, and she was still really upset about Genoa. I just want you guys to know how terrible I feel about what happened there."

"That's okay," replied Robert, "none of us could have possibly imagined how things would turn out."

The mood lightened considerably after this exchange, and our conversation moved on to more mundane matters, such as where to see live music after dinner. After a few rounds of beer, we began reminiscing about past experiences at mass actions in London, Prague, and Barcelona. Indeed, PGA has not only inspired anti–corporate globalization protests around the world; many activists associated with the network have played key roles planning specific actions, particularly in Europe. The question now was whether PGA could serve as an effective tool for coordination beyond mass actions. During the past three days, we had talked about building an organizational structure in Europe adequate to the task. Much of our continued work over the next year would take place via e-mail exchanges, Listservs, and Web-based forums. At the same time, physical gatherings, including myriad informal conversations such as the one just mentioned, would also provide a critical forum for transnational networking.

Previous chapters have examined the cultural practice and politics of networking among anti–corporate globalization activists in Barcelona, and how alternative networks are embodied through virtuoso protest performance. As we saw in chapter 3, activist networks are created through communicative interaction and struggle, largely involving conflict over organizational process and form. This chapter explores these dynamics at the transnational scale by examining how more radical anti–corporate globalization activists are struggling to build directly democratic network structures. As we shall see, transnational activist networks are generated in practice through ongoing experimentation with emerging organizational forms. Much of this work involves heated debates over network protocols: the concrete mechanisms through which political and cultural ideals are physically inscribed into emerging network architectures.

This chapter explores the growing confluence among network technologies, organizational forms, and political norms within PGA and the No Border Network, and chapter 7 considers the cultural politics surrounding the social forum process. PGA was founded in 1998 as a decentralized space for communication and coordination among grassroots struggles against free trade and corporate globalization. Over the next few years, the network helped to diffuse a new discourse of solidarity, inspiring global days of action against the WTO, World Bank, IMF, and G8.[2] PGA-based activists have also organized conferences, campaigns, and caravans to coordinate and share ideas, resources, and strategies.[3] The No Border Network was created in 1999 to facilitate coordination and exchange around migration and border issues. The World Social Forum (WSF), first held in January 2001, has emerged as a broader space of convergence involving organizations, networks, and movements from diverse political perspectives.

In what follows, I examine the mechanisms through which transnational anti–corporate globalization networks are constructed and how they are physically embodied during periodic meetings and events. Based on ethnographic accounts of PGA and No Border gatherings in Barcelona, Leiden, and Strasbourg, and the organizing surrounding them, I argue that such networks are constituted through ongoing experimentation with digital-age organizational forms, which are shaped by new technologies and reflect emerging political norms.

PGA as a Transnational Counterpublic

Transnational activist networks provide the communicative infrastructure necessary for the rise of transnational social movements, conceived here as "transnational counterpublics" (Olesen 2005), spaces where oppositional identities, discourses, and practices are produced and through which they circulate.[4] Rather than coordinated actions against fixed targets (pace Tarrow 2001; cf. della Porta 1995),[5] transnational social movements are best viewed as arenas where "new cultural and political meanings are produced, dissent is made possible, and direct action can be imagined" (Alvarez 1997, 108). In this sense, anti–corporate globalization movements are oppositional spaces where activists from distant locales create and struggle over political identities, visions, and strategies. At the same time, transnational networks, such as PGA, No Border, and the social forums, allow diverse place-based struggles to reach out across space and articulate around common goals and projects while maintaining their political and geographic specificity (Escobar 2001).[6]

Many theorists of transnational collective action have emphasized the mobilization and diffusion of resources, identities, and ideas within formal organizations (Keck and Sikkink 1998; Khagram, Riker, and Sikkink 2002; J. Smith, Pagnucco, and Chatfield 1997). As we have seen, however, anti–corporate globalization movements largely involve decentralized network formations.[7] In this sense, PGA and No Border are not formal organizations but

TABLE 5. Official PGA meetings and events, February 1998 to September 2006

Event	Date	Place	Significance
1st Global PGA Conference	Feb. 18–27, 1998	Geneva, Switzerland	Network founded, hallmarks drafted, first call for Global Day of Action
1st PGA Global Day of Action	May 16, 1998 (M16)	Decentralized (in conjunction with G8 Summit in Birmingham)	First ever global day of action; thousands mobilize around the world
Intercontinental Caravan	May 22–June 22, 1999	Major European cities	500 Indian peasants tour Europe to promote struggles against free trade
2nd PGA Global Day of Action	June 18, 1999 (J18)	Decentralized (in conjunction with G8 Summit in Cologne)	Tens of thousands protest against global financial and business centers around world
2nd Global PGA Conference	Aug. 23–26, 1999	Bangalore, India	PGA support group formalized; tensions between mass-based Southern movements and European radicals
3rd PGA Global Day of Action	Nov. 30, 1999	Seattle, Washington (PGA West Coast Caravan)	Largest anti–corporate globalization protest in United States; energizes networks around world
1st Latin American PGA Conference	Mar. 26–31, 2000	Nicaragua	First PGA conference in Latin America; aims to strengthen network in region
1st European PGA Conference	Mar. 24–25, 2001	Milan, Italy	First PGA conference in Europe; draws 300 participants from 80 different groups
1st North American PGA Conference	June 1–3, 2001	Amherst, Massachusetts	First PGA conference in North America; hundreds of activists attend from United States and Canada
3rd Global PGA Conference	Sept. 16–23, 2001	Cochabamba, Bolivia	Hallmarks changed to include anticapitalist focus, remove nonviolence clause; decision made to decentralize

TABLE 5. (continued)

Event	Date	Place	Significance
2nd European PGA Conference	Aug. 31–Sept. 4, 2002	Leiden, Netherlands	500 activists attend; clearer regional structure created; call for European infopoints
2nd Latin American PGA Conference	July 7–11, 2003	Comarca Kuna Yala, Panama	Effort to strengthen coordination among grassroots movements in Latin America
PGA Asia and Gender Conference	May 20–25, 2004	Dhaka, Bangladesh	Effort to strengthen coordination among grassroots movements in Asia; gender focus
3rd European PGA Conference	July 23–29, 2004	Belgrade, (post-) Yugoslavia	First PGA conference in Eastern Europe; several hundred attend; renewed efforts to improve structure
PGA Global Consultation Meeting	Oct. 7–10, 2005	Hardiwar, India	Activists attend from Asia, Europe, and North America; attempt to revive global process; proposal for global Internet chats
4th European PGA Conference	Aug. 19–Sept. 3, 2006	Various cities in France	Decentralized structure; smaller thematic meetings and final plenary

arenas where transnational counterpublics can emerge. As Michael Warner (2002) suggests, a public is an autonomous "space of discourse organized by nothing other than discourse itself" (50). This is precisely what activists mean, for example, when they refer to PGA as a flexible tool for communication and coordination. Beyond mobilizing human, financial, and symbolic resources, PGA fosters self-organized transnational communication and exchange regarding tactics, strategies, protests, and campaigns. Much of this activity takes place through e-mail lists, websites, and chat rooms. At the same time, transnational counterpublics are physically embodied during regional and global meetings, gatherings, and conferences. It is largely within and around such events that transnational activist networks, and the counterpublics they generate, are constructed.

PGA's Technological Infrastructure

Much of the communicative interaction through which PGA is constituted occurs within the virtual domain. New digital technologies are crucial to ongoing network communication and coordination, providing the technological infrastructure for the rise of PGA as a transnational counterpublic. Indeed, like other anti–corporate globalization networks explored throughout this book, including MRG or RCADE in Barcelona, PGA reflects the growing confluence among network technologies, organizational forms, and political norms. Among the network's most important communication tools is the global PGA website, www.agp.org,[8] which provides an online archive that documents network history; houses text and video reports from previous actions, meetings, and conferences; and provides information regarding future initiatives and events. The site gives information in ten languages, although English and Spanish are the most prominent. It is hosted by a German server and is maintained by volunteer computer techs in several German cities.[9]

The web team forms part of a larger support group, which has provoked a great deal of controversy. Indeed, the support group is largely composed of northern activists, pointing to the unequal access to information, technology, and resources. Western Europeans, in particular, have enjoyed disproportionate influence within PGA. More generally, the digital divide remains a significant obstacle to the free and open circulation of information. Southern activists are not only less likely to have Internet connection, but those who do, tend to access the Web differently. For example, whereas northern activists usually link up individually, their counterparts in the Global South often depend on organizational staff persons to receive and circulate information. This is a slow and cumbersome process and requires more elaborate structure. Such differences reflect a broader divide between the mass-based peasant and indigenous movements that make up the PGA network in the Global South and the smaller, middle-class collectives in the North.

In addition to the website, much of the network's transnational coordination takes place through Listservs.[10] These include local, regional, and global lists and thematic forums dedicated to specific campaigns and projects, most of which can be accessed through the PGA home page. As we shall see, beyond logistical coordination, PGA Listservs also provide arenas for political and strategic debates. By contrast, grassroots organizations in Latin America and South Asia have tended to use more informal means of communication, including e-mails, phone calls, and face-to-face interactions. Indeed, global coordination has largely taken place through personal exchanges between key network figures. After the unofficial global PGA meeting in Haridwar, India, in October 2005, however, activists organized a series of global chats to plan future network activities, which may suggest the beginning of a concerted effort to make more effective use of the Internet's interactive tools and capabilities.[11]

PGA's technological infrastructure thus constitutes a highly uneven and differentiated field involving electronic networks at multiple geographic scales, which are characterized by varying degrees of participation. In this sense, although European and U.S.-based activists have effectively used e-mail lists, the differential access to new technologies, together with related organizational differences, has consistently hampered the transnational flow of information across the North-South divide (see Bandy and Smith 2005). Indeed, it is important to consider the inclusions *and* exclusions fostered by new digital technologies. As we shall see, PGA-based activists have spent a great deal of time working to address these structural and technological inequities.

PGA's Organizational Architecture

By stressing anticapitalism and direct confrontation with the state, PGA has staked out a more radical terrain within a broader movement field. At the same time, the network remains largely unknown outside anti–corporate globalization circles. Even in Barcelona, where squatters and Zapatista supporters helped organize early PGA-related actions and events, including the Intercontinental Caravan that brought hundreds of southern farmers to Europe, and the second Zapatista Encuentro in Spain, where the idea for PGA was hatched, the network is still relatively enigmatic.[12] As Gaizka from the Zapatista collective pointed out, "PGA is a phantom; it works for some things, but not for others." Ricart, a well-known squatter, had this to say: "PGA is strange; it's extremely diverse, but it's more of a space of encounter." This is largely due to the network's organizational principles, which define it as an open space for communication and coordination rather than an organization. Indeed, PGA has no members, it commands no resources, and no one can speak in its name.

As we have seen, new digital technologies have helped give rise to emerging network-based organizational forms, which increasingly reflect emerging political norms. In this sense, PGA was designed as a flexible, decentralized tool for communication and coordination to inspire "the greatest possible number of persons and organizations to act against corporate domination through civil disobedience and people-oriented constructive actions."[13] The network thus constitutes a broad "convergence space" (Routledge 2003) organized around the following hallmarks:

1. A very clear rejection of capitalism, imperialism, and feudalism; all trade agreements, institutions, and governments that promote destructive globalization.
2. We reject all forms and systems of domination and discrimination including, but not limited to, patriarchy, racism, and religious fundamentalism of all creeds. We embrace the full dignity of all human beings.
3. A confrontational attitude, since we do not think that lobbying can have a major impact in such biased and undemocratic organizations, in which transnational capital is the only real policy-maker.
4. A call to direct action and civil disobedience, support for social movements' struggles, advocating forms of resistance which maximize respect for life and oppressed peoples' rights, as well as the construction of local alternatives to global capitalism.
5. An organizational philosophy based on decentralization and autonomy.[14]

These principles provide the guiding political vision around which diverse movements, organizations, and collectives converge. As a communication and coordination tool, PGA has a minimal structure with no elected leaders, members, or central finances. Instead, participating groups are expected to manage their own affairs and raise their own funds. Rotating continental conveners, who are responsible for planning and coordinating regional and global conferences, and the global secretariat, which provides technical, administrative, and logistical assistance, are the only officially recognized figures within the network.[15] In practice, however, the conveners have not had sufficient time or resources to carry out the necessary coordinating tasks. As a result, an informal support group, largely based in Western Europe, has emerged to fill unmet logistical needs, including fundraising, maintaining network contacts, facilitating meetings, creating newsletters, and managing the central website (see L. Wood 2004, 107). Although the support group has helped sustain global interactions within the network, many activists, particularly in Europe, have criticized the group as an informal hierarchy, which contradicts the network's underlying democratic principles.

As Leslie Wood points out, PGA's nonhierarchical structure was meant in part as an alternative to traditional NGO networks, where southern movements often assume subordinate roles to northern donor organizations (2004, 99–100). In this sense, the insistence on horizontal decision making and the refusal to allow centralized resources were viewed as ways to empower grassroots participants from the Global South. At the same time, PGA's structure resembles other network formations considered in previous chapters, such as MRG and RCADE. Indeed, PGA's emphasis on horizontal coordination, the free and open exchange of information, and directly democratic decision making reflects the inscription of broader networking logics and emerging utopian ideals within its network architecture. Given the increasing confluence among network norms, forms, and technology, the communicative interactions that constitute PGA have been characterized by significant political debate and ideological struggle. As we shall see, these are often coded as conflict over organizational process and form.

More generally, divergent cultural logics have contributed to a series of conflicts within PGA across diverse political, cultural, and technological divides. With respect to technical and monetary resources, for example, many activists and observers have criticized the unequal access to technology and finances within the network. As Paul Routledge suggests, this has contributed to the rise of an elite group of mobile, Europe-based activists who have regular Internet access and resources to travel (2003, 340–41). In response, conveners here raised money to subsidize airfare for southern participants and have limited the slots for northerners during global conferences, but the support group remains controversial, given their significant role in shaping network activities. To overcome these obstacles, southern movements have emphasized building shared understanding and commitment, while northern groups often seek structural solutions (L. Wood 2004, 107–8). This reflects an emerging political culture within more radical European and North American circles where organizational, political, and technological values increasingly coincide.

Moreover, diverse movements and groups within PGA have also clashed over competing organizational models. For example, as pointed out earlier, northern activists tend to come from small, direct-action-oriented networks and collectives, including MRG, Ya Basta! in northern Italy, and the British-based Reclaim the Streets, while their southern counterparts often belong to larger and more centralized formations, such as the Brazilian Landless Workers Movement (MST) or the Karnataka State Farmers Association (KRRS) in India. Global conferences have proved particularly contentious. For example, during the second PGA conference in Bangalore in 1999, southern activists complained that northerners representing very few people dominated the discussions at the expense of grassroots movements that claimed hundreds of thousands of participants (L. Wood 2004, 107). In contrast to political parties and trade unions in Barcelona, southern movements have not called for a more representative structure, but they did make the case for limiting the number of northern delegates at future conferences.

The third conference, held in Cochabamba, Bolivia, in 2001, was again rife with intense organizational debates.[16] Notably, the Europeans emphasized consensus process and strict meeting facilitation, while Latin Americans preferred longer, programmatic interventions. Indigenous participants also spent significant time in caucus, reporting common positions back to the assembly. Many Latin Americans complained that Europeans were trying to impose their own style. Indeed, Quechua delegates reported that they felt silenced by northern facilitators, who attempted to restrict lengthy, repetitious declarations (L. Wood 2004, 107). In general, southern participants were more likely to stress common political positions and collective solidarity, while northerners tended to express their politics through organizational praxis. Partly in response to these cultural and political chasms, conference delegates decided to promote greater regional autonomy.[17] The stage was thus set for building a stronger, more directly democratic PGA network in Europe.

TABLE 6. Present and past PGA network conveners, February 1998 to September 2006

Organization/Network/Movement	Location	PGA region
Zapatista National Liberation Front (FZLN)	Chiapas	Latin America
National Confederation of Farmers' Security Affiliates–National Farmers' Council (CONFEUNASSC-CNC)	Ecuador	Latin America
Kuna Youth Movement	Panama	Latin America
Sandinista Union Federation (FNT)	Nicaragua	Latin America
Landless Workers Movement (MST)	Brazil	Latin America
Process of Black Communities (PCN)	Colombia	Latin America
Central American Network of African Peoples (ONECA/ODECO)	Central America	Latin America
Aoteoroa Educators (branch of intertribal Maori independence movement)	New Zealand	Pacifika
Krishok Federation (federation of peasant and agricultural workers)	Bangladesh	Asia
Movement for National Land and Agricultural Reform (MONLAR)	Sri Lanka	Asia
Karnataka State Farmers Association (KRRS)	India	Asia
Nationwide Federation of Landless Peasants (KMP)	Philippines	Asia
National Alliance of Peoples Movements (NAPM)	India	Asia
Ya Basta!	Italy	Europe
Reclaim the Streets	United Kingdom	Europe
Movement for Global Resistance (MRG)	Catalonia	Europe
Eurodusnie	Leiden, Netherlands	Europe
Drugaciji Svet je Moguc! (DSM)	(Post-)Yugoslavia	Europe
Sans-Titre Network	France	Europe
Tampa Bay Action Group (TBAG)	Tampa, Florida	North America
Anti-Capitalist Convergence (CLAC)	Montreal, Quebec	North America

Convening PGA in Europe

As we have seen, PGA is not a traditional organization but a digital-age network formation, a transnational counterpublic organized around a series of electronic tools, calls to action, and conferences. PGA has no fixed structure or stable membership. Given this situation, when I began fieldwork in Barcelona, I realized that conducting an ethnographic study of such a diffuse network would pose a greater challenge than I had anticipated. However, I soon realized that instead of approaching PGA as already constituted, I would do better—as I had also done with MRG—to study the specific communicative mechanisms through which the network was constructed in practice. Fortunately, my time in the field coincided with MRG's tenure as a European PGA co-convener along with the Dutch collective Eurodusnie.[18] As an active member of MRG's international work group, I had an excellent opportunity to observe and engage in transnational networking firsthand.

I first met several key PGA-based figures during an informal meeting in Genoa before the protests against the G8 began. Roughly ten of us had gathered in a cozy room on the second floor of an Italian squat to discuss key issues, such as the upcoming global conference in Cochabamba. Except for two Catalans, a Dutch activist, and a German of Latin American descent, the rest of us were expats, either by choice or by political necessity, including a Spaniard who lived in Amsterdam and several Colombians and a Bolivian who resided in Geneva. Most of the participants were middle-class activists in their late twenties and early thirties, except for the Geneva group, which included several older participants with ties to grassroots movements in Colombia and Bolivia. Indeed, PGA was more than a global communication network; many organizers were thoroughly globalized themselves.

After a few minutes, it became clear that a few activists, who I later learned were active in the PGA support group, were privy to much of the information, while the rest mostly listened. Despite PGA's expressed goal of providing an open space for communication and coordination, certain contradictions were already apparent. Why did some activists have more information than others? Why did a small group of mobile Europeans play such prominent roles? Why were the conveners from Asia and Latin America not more actively involved? As European co-conveners, MRG and Eurodusnie would spend much of their time over the next year and a half addressing these issues. It was largely through these discussions and debates that a more solid foundation for the European PGA network would begin to emerge.

Although many observers view transnational networks as always already formed, or, alternatively, as lacking concrete substance altogether, the reality is more fluid and complex. As mentioned earlier, transnational networks provide the communicative infrastructure necessary for the emergence of self-organized discursive production. However, for self-organization to take place, someone has to create the required tools, facilitate network contacts, and "give discussions an initial push," as one support group member suggested. These processes are always uneven and incomplete, which is why networks can be so confusing. Moreover, determining who has the authority to carry out specific network tasks is often politically charged, particularly in a network committed to flat hierarchies, grassroots participation, and direct democracy.

Much as in our MRG assemblies, discussions within European PGA convener and support group meetings often revolved around network structure and process. Beyond logistics, structure and process constitute network protocols, which shape the ways in which diverse network actors interact. They represent the "rules of the game," the mechanisms through which political visions are physically inscribed into emerging organizational architectures. Discussions *about* networks are thus not only constitutive; they allow activists to express their utopian political imaginaries directly through organizational and technological practice. At the same time, such debates can be extremely conflictual, involving contrasting ideas about democracy, legitimacy, and power.[19]

Jo Freeman raised similar issues with respect to the women's movement many years ago (cf. Polletta 2002, 164). Her influential article "The Tyranny of Structurelessness" (1972) is still widely read by grassroots activists within European PGA circles. Freeman argued that there is no such thing as a structureless group, and that the absence of formal structures will necessarily give rise to informal ones, which are less transparent, less democratic, and more difficult to control. Promoting structurelessness thus represents a subtle way of "masking power" by those who control information and resources.[20] Jamie King (2004) has more recently adapted this reasoning to criticize the widespread ideology of "openness" within contemporary network-based movements. He points to the emergence of open source as a broader model of social and political organization, noting that "structures like PGA and those being experimented with more widely are part of the social movement's general rejection of organizational models based on representation, verticality, and hierarchy" (5). Many activists believe it is the "open, networked, horizontal form of the movement that produces its radical potential for social change" (6). However, much like the open-source process, decision making within networked movements often revolves around a small number of influential people who act as " 'supernodes,' not only routing more than their 'fair share' of traffic, but actively determining the 'content' that traverses them" (7).

Activists from Eurodusnie, and others throughout the network, have specifically leveled such critiques against members of the PGA support group (cf. Routledge 2003). Although PGA was intended to be, and has often served as, a self-organizing counterpublic where diverse struggles around the world can share ideas and experiences and plan concrete actions against corporate globalization, information has not always flowed fluidly or democratically. There has often been a marked contradiction between the expressed ideals incorporated within PGA's network architecture and the actual practices enacted by key network participants. At the same time, these ideals have provided an important framework for interaction, and activists have spent many hours trying to address perceived inconsistencies. Given the growing confluence among network norms, forms, and technologies, these efforts have largely revolved around ongoing experimentation with organizational and technological architectures.

The Barcelona Meeting

When members of Eurodusnie contacted MRG about organizing an initial meeting among conveners, their goal was to start building a more clearly organized, democratic, and transparent network. Would the answer be more or less formal structure? If more structure was called for, what kind of structure would it be? MRG and Eurodusnie agreed that clearer and more effective structures were needed, and moreover that they should be directly democratic, but there was a significant difference in emphasis. Whereas MRG stressed what we might call "structured openness," reflecting the horizontal networking logic characteristic of grassroots movements in Barcelona, Eurodusnie was more concerned with "transparency." MRG saw its role as primarily to facilitate global and European networking and thus wanted to focus on communication tools; Eurodusnie emphasized leadership roles and responsibilities.

After a long negotiation, we agreed to hold the first conveners' meeting in Barcelona in November 2001, the first day restricted to new conveners, the second involving new and former conveners, Reclaim the Streets and Ya Basta!, and the third also including the support group. The three-day affair would involve a series of discussions around various aspects of the PGA network, interspersed with informal gatherings over beer, wine, and cigarettes within the dense urban network of activist bars, squats, and apartments that make up the social movement landscape in Barcelona. Although there would be a great deal of conflict and misunderstanding, the evening discussions, parties, and dance sessions within the Barrio Gótico, Raval, and other neighborhoods around the city provided an opportunity to reinforce personal ties, which helped provide a more solid base for an emerging European network. These intense personal interactions represented the human dimension to a transnational activist network that otherwise depended on disembodied technologies. Indeed, it was precisely through the mutual interplay between physical and virtual realms that the network would be constituted in practice.

Members of Eurodusnie's PGA working group arrived in Barcelona on November 16. I picked up Andries and Janneke at the Sants train station in the afternoon and met the rest of the Dutch contingent that evening at an activist social center in the nearby town of Terrassa, where local MRG-based activists had organized an informal discussion. Seven activists made the trip from the Netherlands, while a similar number also took part from MRG, although many more participated in the informal gatherings. This uneven and shifting participation infuriated Ruud from Eurodusnie, who was eager to create a more stable group of core organizers. Indeed, the differences between MRG as a diffuse network and Eurodusnie as a tightly organized collective fueled many of the political differences that would soon emerge.

The conveners' meeting started the next day with a brief introduction and brainstorm regarding the challenges faced by the network. The following terms and phrases kept arising: "ambiguous," "chaotic," "needs structure," "lacks clarity," "needs better communication tools," "different cultures and styles of organization." Our work was cut out for us. Former convener and support group members soon arrived from Germany, Switzerland, the Netherlands, Italy, and the United Kingdom, swelling the number of participants to twenty-five. Most were young, direct-action-oriented activists from grassroots networks and collectives. Over the next two days, we discussed the issue of conveners and how to improve network coordination, but the support group sparked particular controversy.

During one intense debate, Rodrigo, a German-born son of South American refugees, suggested that a support group member ought to "have fluency in two or more languages and cultural flexibility." His comment was particularly revealing, reflecting the multicultural nature of transnational networks, which requires activists to draw on unique skills and experiences to negotiate linguistic and cultural differences. For this reason, many activists have criticized support group members for using their cultural capital and insider positions to hoard information, albeit sometimes inadvertently.[21] In response, we spent many hours debating alternative ways to prevent or manage the emergence of such informal hierarchies. The debate reflected two very different approaches to power. Ruud from Eurodusnie argued that authority should remain exclusively with the conveners, while Pau from MRG argued that we should identify specific needs and tasks and invite people to participate. "Let's create technical working groups which are clear and open," said Pau. "We should widen the support group, not get rid of it." As with MRG in Barcelona, activists thus held distinctly different views of PGA. Was it a fluid space for communication and coordination or a more rigidly structured organizational network?

At the same time, there was widespread agreement about the lack of fixed parameters. As Rodrigo explained, "[The conveners] have a certain weight within the network; you can start a political dynamic by calling people together. How this happens is largely due to your political culture." Although he agreed with Eurodusnie that conveners play an important role in generating network dynamics, ultimately "the network should become organic and self-run." Building on Pau's earlier comments, Patrice suggested, "There are concrete ways of doing this—Listservs, web pages, finances—it's no accident we have been talking about these things." When the meeting ended, an uneasy balance prevailed. Eurodusnie's insistence on transparency had initiated an important discussion regarding democracy and power. On the other hand, MRG's emphasis on openness led to a series of concrete proposals, including the creation of technical work groups surrounding network tasks. These issues would be taken up again at the next convener and support group meeting the following December.

The Winter Meeting

Debates continued electronically before the winter meeting in Leiden. As pointed out earlier, much of the sustained communicative interaction within the European PGA network has taken place through Listserv and e-mail exchanges. Much like real-world discussions, these debates often revolve around network structure and process. When Eurodusnie sent out an agenda for the winter meeting that included discussions of proposed campaign areas—militarization, autonomous zones, privatization, North-South links, and migration—MRG objected, not because they opposed the particular topics, but because they wanted to discuss technical coordination, leaving the thematic discussions for the European conference in September. In response, Ruud, a Eurodusnie member, sent the following reply:

> The MRG suggestion to start the workgroups (or campaigns) at the next PGA conference sounds [like it's] from another planet. . . . You do not . . . start a workgroup or campaign during an open conference. It is naive to think that 300 people . . . [who] do not even know each other . . . [can] start a serious and lasting workgroup/campaign. . . . I believe networks, workgroups, or campaigns are gradually built, step by step. I believe PGA Europe can be built best by starting some workgroups which are close to the reality of those involved in the network.[22]

Ruud felt the conveners should play a more active role in shaping network content, largely owing to practical concerns. For MRG-based activists, on the other hand, facilitating self-organized discursive production was more important than content or political efficacy. Indeed, this self-generated network ideal reflected a concrete expression of their broader political vision. MRG's reply was thus particularly instructive:

> We do not think the role of the European PGA conveners includes deciding on issue areas. . . . Ideally, the "network" should decide. . . . Of course, this is complicated by the fact that we don't exactly know who the network is, the communications tools we have to reach the network are not perfect, and we have different views of what networks are and how they should operate. . . . So, there is no perfect way to do this, and the conveners have to find some way to facilitate this process . . . but the initial proposal went too far in that it . . . determined what the issue working areas would be [without] any feedback at all from the rest of the network.[23]

MRG went on to suggest that conveners might issue a proposal regarding campaign content, but the principal focus should remain creating an open space for dialogue and exchange, that is, building the infrastructure necessary for the emergence of a self-organized counterpublic. Within that space, specific activist groups, movements, and collectives would determine for themselves which issues to address. Whereas Eurodusnie wanted to create a clear structure based on identifiable campaign areas, MRG was more concerned with facilitating the process of self-organization itself.

The winter meeting began on December 17, following a mass mobilization against the EU in Brussels. Since an open invitation had been sent via the PGA Listservs, activists from London, Oxford, Düsseldorf, Thessaloníki, New York, and Chicago also attended, joining participants from MRG, Eurodusnie, and the support group. There were about thirty attendees in all, mostly but not entirely middle-class activists in their mid-twenties to early thirties from small, direct-action-oriented collectives, many of whom had taken part in the Brussels protest. Two leaders from a larger immigrant rights organization also participated on the first day, but they had to return to Germany. Indeed, the length of such coordinating meetings often makes it difficult for activists with stable jobs and families to take part, while travel costs constitute a significant obstacle for those without resources. Ironically, despite its commitment to openness and grassroots participation, the PGA network thus generated its own exclusions.

As in Barcelona, we spent much of our time getting to know the local activist scene. Eurodusnie itself involved various self-managed projects distributed among two buildings: a large office and meeting space in a former school near the train station, and a squatted social center downtown, which housed a vegan cafe, bar, infoshop, swap meet, and communal meeting rooms. Whereas the squats in Barcelona always felt slightly dingy and were constantly under threat of eviction, the Eurodusnie spaces were clean, well attended, and well integrated into the local urban context. Eurodusnie volunteers organized the logistical aspects of the meeting, including scheduling and food preparation. Moreover, all the meeting spaces were free, representing a sharp contrast to more institutional processes. Beyond daily sessions regarding PGA, we also got to know local activists, listened to live music, and drank copious amounts of beer.

On the first day of the official meeting, we continued discussing various technical issues carried over from Barcelona and the subsequent e-mail discussions, including the European PGA conference, finances, communication tools, and global contacts. These formed the basis for a series of open working groups, which would be formally proposed at the European conference in September 2001. How participatory they would be, and whether they would prevent informal hierarchies, remained to be seen, but the influence of an open network ideal was apparent. The following day's agenda was more complicated. The major debate revolved around whether the network should have thematic areas at all. For Ruud, the answer was clear: thematic areas would "create clear formal structures within which people can operate." Others disagreed. Rodrigo pointed out, "This sounds like the perfect way to create a top-down, hierarchical organization. . . . Thematic political spaces need to be based on actually existing dynamics!"

Siding with MRG's position from the Listserv discussions, most participants agreed that the role of conveners and work groups was to facilitate an open space for communication and coordination, rather than establish campaign areas. It was precisely through such debates about structure and process, as well as the associated organizational and technological experimentation, that the PGA network in Europe would be constituted in practice. As the meeting concluded, the work groups agreed to continue their efforts electronically, while Eurodusnie agreed to oversee the logistical aspects of the conference. The results of this submerged networking would become visible at the European conference next fall.

Border Camping in Strasbourg

Mirroring a pattern we saw in Barcelona, radical anti–corporate globalization activists tend to move fluidly among several competing transnational networks. For example, many radicals have also been active in the No Border Network, which overlaps with PGA but tends to attract greater numbers of militant activists. No Border specifically provides a decentralized space for communication and coordination among grassroots groups working in support of migrants, refugees, and the freedom of movement. Its main activities include anti-deportation actions and self-organized border camps each summer in Europe and along the U.S.-Mexico border.[24] These camps provide an opportunity for activists to challenge specific policies regarding immigration and the border while organizing forums and workshops around related issues. Like mass actions and mobilizations, border camps also provide alternative, albeit less emotionally intense, platforms where transnational counterpublics are performed and embodied.

The July 2002 camp in Strasbourg drew two thousand people, the largest border camp ever. The Strasbourg camp was specifically conceived as a challenge to the nearby Schengen Information System (SIS), which tracks movements within and across EU space. Activists also attempted to incorporate migration issues into a broader anticapitalist framework. At the same time, there were major disagreements about whether the camp should emphasize direct action or collective living and discussion, reflecting a divide between militants and network-based movements. In this regard, the camp provided a transnational convergence space for both Black Bloc and Pink Bloc circles. Moreover, the cultural politics dividing these sectors would be physically played out through numerous micropolitical conflicts.

The most innovative aspect of the camp was the physical division of the space itself into a series of autonomous, self-managed sectors coordinated by a system of decentralized collaboration and directly democratic decision making. The broader idea of a self-managed counterpublic, or a series of interlinked counterpublics, was thus literally inscribed into the territorial landscape. More generally, Kevin Hetherington (1998) has referred to the way activists project their political ideals onto geographic territory as the practice of "utopics," where ideas about how society ought to be organized are mapped onto physical space. In this sense, the increasing confluence among network technologies, organizational forms, and political norms explored throughout this book was physically expressed in Strasbourg through the organization and division of the camp into a network of autonomous, self-managed territories. This spatial and organizational arrangement further reflected an emphasis on process and lived experience among many younger activists (cf. McDonald).[25] The Strasbourg camp thus embodied the utopian worlds that more radical anti–corporate globalization activists are struggling to create.

After my train pulled into Strasbourg on July 19, I headed over to the campsite with a Swiss activist I had met at the station. A few hundred people had already pitched their tents, including several Catalans who had been touring France to promote various activist projects. The camp was only partially constructed when we arrived, but over the next day and a half, a vast and empty swath of parkland next to the Rhine River was transformed into a bustling tent city, with mobile kitchens, dining areas, tactical media labs, wireless Internet zones, information tables, makeshift showers, video projection squares, action spaces, electronic dance floors, latrines, and domes for medical attention, legal aid, and security. The campers themselves were mostly younger activists from countries around Europe, including large contingents from France, Germany, the Netherlands, the United Kingdom, Spain, and Italy, as well as smaller groups from Eastern Europe and other parts of the world. Moreover, there was a combination of activists from radical network-based movements, such as MRG and PGA, and militant squatters, many of whom had a distinctly punk aesthetic. Several local immigrant groups also participated in the camp, including the Mouvement de l'Immigratión et des Banlieues (MIB).

Inspired by the Argentine popular rebellion, organizers had devised a directly democratic structure based on a network of self-managed barrios. Each neighborhood staked out its territorial space surrounding one of the mobile kitchens and managed its affairs through a local assembly. Decisions affecting the entire camp, including matters related to infrastructure, security, media, and collective actions, were made through larger spokescouncil meetings, or *inter-barriales*, including delegates from each local barrio. The scheme was extremely complex and often broke down in practice, particularly during crisis situations, yet it represented an attempt to actually manifest a horizontal networking logic in the design and management of social space. In this sense, the camp provided a terrain for the spatial practice of "utopics." As the introduction to the camp handbook, "The Manual of Inter-barrio Geopolitics," explained:

> The experience of this camp will be a challenge to put our ideas into practice. Its success will lie in everyone getting involved in the collective activities and tasks needed for the self-management of a camp of around 2,000 people. One of our objectives is to implement a complete vision of the world(s) we're fighting for in the here and now, and right down to the smallest details of daily life. . . . The individuals and collectives involved in the preparation of the camp have decided upon a philosophy of organization based on an on-going search for self-management, decentralization, autonomy, and . . . equality.

We spent much of the next ten days attending workshops related to migration, refugees, capitalism, states, and the border regime while continuing to plan for the European PGA conference together with a few dozen activists from the Netherlands, Germany, France, Italy, Spain, Finland, and Sweden. We also explored different barrios, had informal discussions during meals, wandered through town, and danced long into the night. Much of the conflict within the camp revolved around the daily autonomous actions. For example, after organizers publicly presented the camp in the central plaza, several dozen black-clad activists began smashing windows and spray painting walls at a hotel owned by Accor, which protesters accused of profiting from immigrant deportations. On the fourth day, militants blocked a bridge connecting France and Germany in response to police detentions earlier that day. Two days later, police used tear gas to disperse a march to the city center after skirmishes broke out between protesters and police.

For many longtime No Border and PGA-based activists, militant actions—while perhaps justified during countersummit actions—brought negative publicity and jeopardized the safety of the camp. The situation was compounded by the militants' refusal to engage the corporate media. However, not all the actions were confrontational. MIB organized daily caravans to marginal neighborhoods around Strasbourg to highlight issues related to police violence, education, and discrimination. At the same time, a Dutch samba band led ludic actions in the tradition of the Pink and Silver Bloc. On the evening of July 25, for example, after another day of tense interaction, the samba band led a spontaneous fire march around the camp, which involved hundreds of musicians and dancers dressed in pink and silver. The crowd danced and howled its way across the camp as fire breathers sent huge flames into the sky, heightening the hypnotic effect. The march culminated in a wild cathartic release, sparking hours of collective drumming and dancing.

More than a space for dialogue and exchange, the Strasbourg No Border camp provided a physical terrain beyond countersummit actions where alternative networks were able to come together and perform their politics. The communicative interactions through which transnational counterpublics are generated thus take place not only in cyberspace; as mass actions and mobilizations become more and more difficult to organize, activist gatherings provide alternative spaces where transnational activist networks can represent themselves and make their conflicts visible. At the same time, the camp provided an opportunity for activists to further experiment with innovative organizational architectures while projecting their emerging network norms and forms onto physical territories.

The European PGA Conference in Leiden

The European PGA conference began two months after the Strasbourg No Border camp, providing another chance for radicals to continue their transnational networking activities.[26] On my second night in Leiden, I ran into Ricart, who was drinking beer outside a neighborhood bar run by Eurodusnie. Activists were milling about out front while a local band played inside. We had just finished another long day of discussions about the future of the network, and I was happy to see a familiar face who had not been involved. Ricart was a Catalan squatter and anticapitalist who had taken part in many early PGA-related actions and events but had since become less active in the network. When I had interviewed him several months earlier, he had expressed doubts about PGA, so I was surprised to see him in Leiden.

> *Jeff:* Hey, Ricart, how are you?
> *Ricart:* Great, man, it's good to see you here.
> *Jeff:* Yeah, I didn't think you'd be coming; you didn't sound too enthusiastic last time we spoke.
> *Ricart:* That's true. I wasn't planning to come, but then some friends of mine said they wanted to take a ride up, so I figured it'd be a good party. That's the best thing about these events. You know, during the last conference a whole group of us from Barcelona and Madrid piled in a van and drove all the way to Milan. The meetings were totally chaotic, but it was great hanging out and seeing everyone.
> *Jeff:* So you're just planning to hang out here in the bar the whole time?
> *Ricart:* Well, no, I actually came to make some connections around Latin America and present some stuff on Repsol [the Spanish oil company]. This is a great place to meet up with folks working on these things, but it should also be another great bash!

Ricart liked to play it cool, but he was a committed activist. In fact, he had just finished writing a book about the impact of Repsol on indigenous communities in Bolivia, where he had spent a year conducting research and doing solidarity work. Ricart thus reflected an interesting contradiction. As a militant squatter, he emphasized local self-organization and was skeptical of transnational networks. However, those same ideals also led him to support various struggles for autonomy around the world, including indigenous movements in Latin America. He was critical of PGA but relied on the network as an outreach tool. Like many of the hundreds of activists at the European conference, he had not been involved in the ongoing networking around PGA, but he did take advantage of the network's Listservs, conferences, and other events to forward his own projects. At the same time, Ricart pointed to the dual role of transnational activist conferences. On the one hand, they allow activists to cultivate and reinforce personal ties and connections, particularly during more informal gatherings. On the other hand, they also provide spaces for planning and coordinating concrete actions, campaigns, and initiatives.

Establishing Ground Rules

Several weeks before the conference began, Eurodusnie and MRG initiated an electronic exchange regarding the decision-making process during the final plenary. The Dutch proposed a three-fourths majority vote. Although Eurodusnie operated internally by consensus, they argued that such a model would be unwieldy among five hundred people from diverse political backgrounds. On the other hand, MRG viewed consensus as an integral part of their assembly tradition, a defining feature that distinguished them from political parties and unions. MRG-based activists practiced a less-technical form of consensus than their North American counterparts, but they categorically rejected majority voting.[27] The dispute intensified when Toni sent a message to the new Listserv created to plan the conference, indicating that MRG would refuse to take part in any process not run by consensus.[28] Ruud from Eurodusnie forcefully responded, "The way consensus decision-making has been presented as 'the only direct democratic' decision-making mode has made clear for me one of the biggest difficulties PGA has to overcome, which is to understand there is not just one right way. . . . You can have a voting system and still a democratic process."[29]

The following week, Pau sent a reply from MRG, which summarized the Catalan position with respect to consensus:

> [We] felt VERY strongly about sticking to consensus process, which is one of our most basic and important organizational principles. In fact, for us

it is what characterizes the PGA space, as opposed to more traditional political spaces based on representation. Some people said that they simply would not be able to vote, and might even feel discouraged about coming to the meeting. MRG has always emphasized the *"sin qua non"* condition of decision-making by consensus when we have worked with other organizations. Now, we simply cannot vote in Leiden.[30]

This exchange unleashed a barrage of e-mails from activists around Europe, and as far away as the United States and Israel, regarding voting, consensus, and direct democracy.[31] MRG ultimately proposed breaking the final plenary into affinity group discussions, which would coordinate through a larger spokescouncil. Activists from the French Sans-Titre (No Name) network supported this position but complicated matters by rejecting large assemblies entirely: "We need to put into practice some of our ideas about decentralization and direct democracy, encourage exchange and reflection at the lowest organizational level, and think about breaking our meetings into several steps."[32] A final decision would not be reached until the final evening of the conference, but it was already clear that such "technical" debates would generate a great deal of passion. Indeed, more than logistical matters, structure and process represent the network protocols through which political visions are physically inscribed.

The Conference Begins

When I arrived in Leiden on August 31, most of the conference participants had already left for a demonstration in Amsterdam to protest the Earth Summit taking place in Johannesburg, so I walked to the campsite and pitched my tent. After settling in, I made my way to the Eurodusnie squat downtown, where meals and cultural events would be held. The conference itself was spread around the city, taking place in both Eurodusnie locations and several buildings around Leiden. In December, during the winter meeting, the air had been cold and dank, and the streets quiet. Summer brought with it a more casual feel, and beyond the hours of meetings, we would also spend a great deal of time talking informally and strolling along the picturesque medieval streets beside the canals.

The three-day conference involved more than five hundred delegates from thirty countries in roughly eighty workshops, which included thematic sessions, strategic and tactical debates, cultural events, and a series of structure and process debates meant to generate proposals for the network. The hosts took care of the logistical arrangements: securing meeting spaces, scheduling events, preparing vegetarian meals, and providing camping facilities. With respect to content, MRG and Eurodusnie had designed the overall framework, but participants were expected to organize their own workshops, discussions, and activities. The co-conveners had thus provided the necessary infrastructure for the emergence of a self-organized counterpublic. As the call for the conference declared, "We are counting on you, the participants, to provide the contents of the program. We, the conveners and conference support people, will be mostly concerned with providing good facilitating support."[33] Listservs were created for this purpose around the following themes: migration and racism; autonomy and self-organization; economy; ecology and conservation; militarization and repression; structure and process; and strategy and tactics.

Participants came from around Europe, including large contingents from the Netherlands, Germany, France, Spain, the United Kingdom, and Italy, as well as a small number from the Americas, Asia, and the Middle East. Moreover, as in Strasbourg and previous European PGA meetings, most participants were young middle-class activists from direct-action-oriented collectives and decentralized networks such as MRG. Delegates from larger immigrant rights organizations and southern movements also attended. The final schedule included workshops related to the WTO, free trade in Latin America, globalization and Africa, gender, water, immigration, biopiracy, food autonomy, computer privacy, media democracy, and strategy and tactics. In addition, grassroots media activists organized an Indymedia Center, pirate radio, and daily conference newspaper. Finally, there were nightly films, music, and theater, providing a much-needed respite from the intense sessions during the day.

After registering for the conference, I ran into Pau, who gave me an update from MRG. The long-standing debate concerning decision making from the conference Listservs had still not been resolved, but everything else was set. The crowd arrived from the demonstration soon thereafter, and I caught up with other friends from Barcelona. Over dinner, I spoke to many other activists whom I had met during the past few years in places like Prague, Genoa,

Brussels, Barcelona, and Leiden. Many of us had developed a strong sense of familiarity and trust, providing a solid human foundation to our otherwise virtual networking activities. The evening ended with a dance party featuring local bands from the Dutch music scene, and we finally stumbled back to camp along with the Catalan contingent hours after midnight. As I knew well by now, the conference would involve days of hectic activity and very little sleep.

Debating Structure and Process

Together with activists from MRG-International, Eurodusnie, Sans-Titre, and the PGA support group, I spent much of the next few days hammering out a series of concrete proposals during the structure and process discussions. The workshop had the following goal: "PGA has served to inspire numerous and diverse actions and campaigns in places in Europe and around the world, but it has not always been able to carry out its most basic network functions: fluid, open, and transparent communication and coordination. . . . We hope to address these issues and begin to create some clear, horizontal, and directly democratic structures for the PGA network in Europe."

The task sounded particularly daunting. Indeed, network building is difficult, complex, and messy work, but it can also be extremely exciting, as an activist from Sans-Titre recalled: "We all found that imagining transparent, non-hierarchical, and decentralized structures for a network of this type was as thrilling as it was difficult."[34] As I have been arguing, much of the work of transnational movement building involves precisely this kind of experimentation with emerging network-based norms and forms, although the most contentious debates would come back to the process of decision making itself.

Roughly forty activists took part in the structure and process sessions, which began with recommendations from the co-conveners. Eurodusnie suggested maintaining dual conveners, each staying on for two years, but rotating so that a new group would always serve with a more experienced one. They also proposed condensing the four technical support groups into one as a way to ensure greater transparency. MRG proposed two conveners as well, one to organize the European conference and another to facilitate global contacts, but preferred to maintain the four technical work groups to enhance efficiency. MRG further suggested dividing the network into subregions and creating zonal contacts to encourage grassroots participation. The proposals set off a round of intense debate. Most participants agreed with the suggestion to decentralize, which would increase PGA's visibility. As Lora suggested, "The reason so many groups join ATTAC is because we are invisible. How do we become more visible without reproducing a corporate identity?" Meanwhile, others worried about too much structure. Hannah from Indymedia-Berlin pointed out, "We should avoid a top-down approach, improve the structures we have; not create more bureaucracy!" The tension between increasing local participation while maintaining minimal structure would continually resurface throughout the conference.

The main issue involved how to multiply the number of access points to the European network while maintaining the focus on local self-management. The following day, we agreed to an innovative solution involving the creation of "Infopoints," local groups that would do PGA-related work without becoming official members, which is prohibited by the network hallmarks. Infopoints could thus call for regional meetings and projects, but without fixed representative structures.[35] These initiatives might be "inspired by" PGA, but they would not be organized in its name. Moreover, Infopoints would also circulate information regarding participating movements and collectives, publicize actions and conferences, explain how PGA operates, and publicize the network's history. They would become the basic units or nodes of the network, relay points that would generate, process, and circulate information, thus increasing the flow of discourse within a self-managed transnational counterpublic. As Alain from Sans-Titre reminded us, "PGA is not a network of groups, but rather a space where different groups interact."

The next day in the afternoon, we turned our attention to the convener and support group. We had already identified three necessary tasks: organizing the European conference, maintaining and extending the network in Europe, and facilitating global contacts. The main question was who would carry out which roles. Some, including MRG, wanted to further empower the open working groups, while others felt the support groups should remain responsible to the conveners, the only officially recognized figures in the network. This ultimately brought us back to the issue of power and authority. At one point, Rodrigo suggested that the Infopoints might take over the work of the conveners and support groups entirely, generating a "self-convened" network.

However, most felt we still lacked sufficient participation and adequate tools to make such an autopoietic network feasible, meaning that the conveners and support groups would continue to play key roles.

The Denouement

The final structure and process session took place that evening. We were a smaller group this time, perhaps around fifteen, but all the key figures from Eurodusnie, MRG, Sans-Titre, and the support group were on hand. Ironically, we had ended up reproducing the kind of "inner circle" we were trying to abolish, despite our best intentions. Indeed, informal hierarchies, and contradictions with respect to power and authority, are endemic to all networks. Our main task was to create mechanisms for managing them. When the discussion began, Eurodusnie repeated its proposal to establish two conveners: one old and one new. Moreover, since MRG had already declined to serve, Eurodusnie offered to stay on, provoking a loud grumble. Amador from the MRG contingent turned to me and whispered, "Sneaking this in at the last minute is the oldest trick in the book!" Pere responded, "MRG has already said there should be convener rotation to bring new ideas, contacts, and practices!" The French waved their hands in enthusiastic approval. Although the proposal was sensible, everyone wanted to avoid further disputes, agreeing that the current conveners would carry on until a new candidate emerged.

It was getting late, so we finally took up the much-anticipated decision-making debate. The facilitators presented the Eurodusnie proposal for a three-fourths majority vote during the final plenary and the MRG counterproposal for strict consensus. We all felt it was important to strive for consensus but disagreed about what to do if a small group or an individual decided to block. Eurodusnie and several others argued that voting was a reasonable solution. As we have seen, however, the Catalans and Spaniards consider voting taboo. "Consensus is not just about decision making," explained Raul. "It's an entire philosophy and politics. If this space is not run by consensus, the people who I work with won't participate." Indeed, more than merely a technical matter, consensus formed part of a wider networking politics involving autonomy, horizontal coordination, and direct democracy. In this sense, political ideals were expressed directly through concrete organizational practice.

Despite the seeming impasse, a British activist proposed a compromise: the plenary would be run by consensus, but if the assembly bogged down, the facilitators could use a series of creative techniques if necessary, including a vote. Finally we all agreed, although afterward, an older activist who had remained silent began shouting, "You see what your friends did; they applied social pressure to shut me up!" Strictly speaking, he could have chosen to "stand aside" to express his dissent without blocking, but his point was well taken. Consensus may be designed to prevent the majority from imposing its will, but the same thing often occurs in more subtle ways (cf. Polletta 2002, 213). Indeed, there are no easy paths to direct democracy.

That night I went for a late dinner and round of beers with the dozen or so Catalans who had taken part in the meeting. Although we were exhausted, the conversation was animated as we exchanged views about what had happened earlier in the evening. Amador was incensed about the perceived manipulation and the refusal of many activists to support consensus process. "I thought this was a space of grassroots assemblies and direct democracy, but perhaps I was wrong! It was just like an assembly of Izquierda Unida" (a leftist electoral coalition, which includes the Spanish Communist Party). Nearly everyone nodded in agreement. Amador and the others had interpreted the meeting through the lens of networking politics in Barcelona. I tried to interject, suggesting there had been widespread support for consensus in principle, but that the Dutch were taking a pragmatic approach. Moreover, where the Catalans saw manipulation, one could also see a good-faith effort to ensure that at least one convener would be in place at the end of the conference. Amador would hear nothing of it, although several others saw my point, without necessarily agreeing.

In this sense, even minor differences in political culture were expressed through heated debates regarding network protocols. In the end, the final plenary unanimously agreed to most of the proposals we had generated, rendering a vote unnecessary. The specific agreements included a call for Infopoints, the formalization of the dual-convener model, and the creation of new Listservs.[36] However, a new convener failed to emerge, so Eurodusnie and MRG agreed to stay on until the next winter meeting.[37] The only concerns were voiced by two longtime support group members who complained about the "growing bureaucracy." Indeed, as Freeman recognized, informal elites often oppose structure precisely because they fear losing power. In this regard, the hours of discussion and debate toward creating a more transparent and directly democratic structure had clearly paid off.

Conclusion

Transnational activist networks such as PGA and No Border provide the organizational infrastructures necessary for the emergence of transnational counterpublics, in this case, global fields of meaning and action against corporate globalization. By providing concrete tools for communication and coordination, transnational activist networks allow geographically dispersed actors to reach across space and forge broader ties and connections. This chapter has explored the communicative interactions through which transnational activist networks are constructed in practice. As we have seen, this partly takes place in cyberspace, where activists have used new digital technologies, including websites, Listservs, and Internet chat rooms, to share information, ideas, and resources while engaging in heated political debates. Such conflicts largely revolve around network structure and process: the concrete protocols through which broader political ideals are physically inscribed into emerging network architectures. Moreover, these struggles are constitutive, producing and reproducing transnational networks themselves.

At the same time, transnational activist networking also takes place within physical domains. Periodic meetings, conferences, and events, and the ongoing organizing that surrounds them, facilitate sustained communicative interaction on regional and global scales. For example, as we have seen, PGA events and No Border camps constitute concrete physical spaces where activists develop personal ties while expressing their broader utopian ideals. Beyond creating spaces for reflection and debate, these gatherings provide platforms where activists generate ideas, exchange information, and physically perform their alternative social movement networks. Indeed, as mass direct actions become increasingly difficult to carry out, transnational gatherings provide alternative means for generating movement identities and affective attachments.

I have argued here that transnational activist network architectures are constructed in practice through ongoing experimentation with digital-age network forms, which are facilitated by new technologies and reflect emerging political norms. In this sense, PGA and No Border organizational structures incorporate a horizontal networking logic, but at the same time, myriad micro-level struggles over network protocols determine their particular shape and trajectory. In other words, transnational activist networks, and the counterpublics they generate, are never fully formed but are always produced, reproduced, and transformed through concrete networking practices and politics. These often involve conflicts over power and authority, as well as competing views regarding the way networks operate.

Given the increasing confluence among network norms, forms, and technologies, such complex networking politics are rendered particularly visible during discussions about structure and process. Within the European PGA network, for example, activists committed to building diffuse digital-age networks have engaged in heated debates with those accustomed to more traditional organizational forms, whether based on representative or direct democracy. On the other hand, even where a self-organizing network ideal prevails, concrete mechanisms are needed to prevent the rise of informal hierarchies or manage those that already exist. Much of the sustained work of transnational networking involves precisely this kind of experimentation with technological practices and organizational forms, which increasingly reflect emerging political norms.

As this chapter suggests, debates about organization and leadership are moving beyond the familiar controversies over the tyranny of structurelessness. In this sense, activists associated with the European PGA network largely agreed about the need to combat informal hierarchies. However, this did not mean the answer was more representative structure, which would simply replace one kind of hierarchy with another. At the same time, most activists also recognized that it would be impossible to get rid of hierarchy altogether. Instead the focus shifted to developing decentralized structures that would be as open, transparent, and directly democratic as possible, thus more effectively controlling the hierarchies that inevitably emerge. The goal was not to eliminate, but to decentralize and effectively manage, power. The debate was thus no longer about structure versus nonstructure but about what *kind* of structure activists should create, particularly given the new digital technologies at their disposal.[38]

Meanwhile there was also an implicit recognition of the importance of leadership within the network, whether in terms of logistical coordination, contributing expertise or enthusiasm in a particular area, or even providing inspiration. The proposals to create a rotating convenership and series of open working groups were thus not meant to create a "leaderless" democracy but rather to identify, empower, and *multiply* the number of leaders within the network. In this sense, like the multiple generations of U.S.-based participatory democrats studied by Polletta (2002), PGA activists "sought not to dispense with authority but to base it on more sensible criteria" (8). At the same time, the concern among many activists regarding the need to reach concrete decisions and build lasting structures reflected a concern for practical results. Their organizational and technological experimentation thus reflected an effort to develop innovative structures that not only reflected emerging network ideals but would also prove sustainable and effective. As we shall see, similar dynamics are also at work within the social forum process.

7

SOCIAL FORUMS AND THE CULTURAL POLITICS OF AUTONOMOUS SPACE

There were two different worlds in Porto Alegre, one slow moving, totally grassroots and self-managed, and another organized along completely different lines, two worlds coming together at different velocities.[1]

It was the morning of January 4, 2002, the next-to-last day of the second edition of the World Social Forum (WSF) in Porto Alegre. I sat together with several hundred young anti–corporate globalization activists, mainly from Europe and Latin America, in a large circle tucked away in a hidden corner of the youth camp called the Intergaláctika Laboratory of Disobedience. While high-profile panels at the Pontifical Catholic University (PUC) explored issues such as international organizations, sovereignty and the nation-state, and the links between globalization and militarism, we shared our own stories of resistance from the front lines in Barcelona, London, Buenos Aires, and Milan. We listened intently as an Italian militant explained how the repression in Genoa had produced such a traumatic effect that Ya Basta! had decided to turn to everyday forms of "social disobedience." As he argued, "Countersummits no longer make sense when conflicts are already visible." With typical rhetorical flair, he captured the prevailing mood. Although mass actions would continue beyond Genoa, ever-larger world and regional forums would soon displace them as the primary public expressions of an evolving anti–corporate globalization movement field.

Before the Italian could finish his characteristically long-winded explanation, one of the facilitators reminded us of the direct action set for that morning. Rather than focus on a corporate target, we decided to challenge the forum itself, together with a group of Brazilian anarchists associated with PGA. The idea was not to question the legitimacy of the forum but to criticize the perceived top-down way it had been organized. Indeed, the forum was a chance to reach out to masses of potential supporters, but for many radicals, its institutional and reformist character contradicted their own self-organizing networking logic. Shortly thereafter, dozens of us took the bus to the PUC for a guided tour of the VIP room. As Joan from RCADE pointed out, "What better symbol of how the forum reproduces the oppressive structures we're fighting!"

Soon after arriving, we joined the anarchist samba band from São Paulo (dressed in black, rather than the pink we were accustomed to) and danced our way up to the second floor, past a large procession of indigenous youths. We continued marching through crowds of surprised yet delighted onlookers. When we finally burst into the VIP room, a heavyset Brazilian with long dreadlocks jumped onto the counter, tossed plastic bottles of water to the crowd, and led us in an enthusiastic chant: "We are all VIPs! We are all VIPs!" We then gave ourselves, and a group of nervously amused NGO delegates, an impromptu bath. The WSF organizers were livid. Only the intervention of well-connected allies spared us from a direct confrontation with the police. However, as a Brazilian organizer confided to me in Barcelona later that spring, there would be no VIP room the following year.

Since the WSF was first held in Porto Alegre, Brazil, in January 2001, the forum process has emerged as a broad space of convergence involving organizations, movements, and networks from diverse political traditions. While radical grassroots activists continue to organize around decentralized networks, such as PGA or No Border, the forums involve newer *and* traditional formations, including NGOs, unions, and the Marxist Left. Meanwhile, as the story of the VIP room suggests, radicals have criticized the forums for their perceived "reformist" orientation and hierarchical practices, but many continue to engage the process in various ways. The forums have thus largely eclipsed mass actions and mobilizations as the main vehicles where activists from diverse anti–corporate globalization networks converge and make their struggles visible.

In this chapter I explore how network norms and forms are reproduced within and around the forums through alternative conceptions of space. Like PGA and

No Border, the social forums provide the organizational infrastructure necessary for the rise of self-organizing counterpublics, incorporating a network ideal through the discourse and practice of "open space."[2] The forum is specifically defined as an open meeting place for individuals, groups, and networks opposed to corporate globalization; no one can represent the forum or speak in its name. However, although many organizers support the model of open space, others have argued for the need to develop common strategies and demands, pointing to an ongoing struggle between networking and command logics at the heart of the forum process. As we shall see, given that activists increasingly inscribe their ideals directly into emerging organizational architectures, such tensions are largely coded as conflicts over organizational process and form.

Complex networking politics also shape the margins of the forum, as more radical activists alternatively take part in, abandon, or create their own autonomous spaces with respect to official events. The constantly shifting alliances explored in chapter 3 thus also operate at the transnational scale. Whereas *open* space suggests a singular sphere encompassing diverse actors, *autonomous* spaces imply a multiplicity of horizontally networked spaces. In this sense, the cultural politics of autonomous space reproduce a networking logic along the terrain of the forum. Mirroring the recent diffusion of autonomous spaces, the WSF itself has increasingly moved toward a similar model of horizontally coordinated, self-organizing spaces.

Through ethnographic analyses of world and regional social forums in Porto Alegre and London, and the organizing surrounding them, this chapter examines the micro-level conflicts through which the social forums are built in practice. I argue that networking politics within and around the forums involve ongoing struggles over emerging organizational architectures, which are specifically expressed through alternative spatial discourses and practices.

The World Social Forum: An Ethnographic Account

A handful of activists from Barcelona attended the first WSF in Porto Alegre in 2001; given the event's overwhelming success, many more made the trip for the second edition the following year. I traveled to Brazil with a dozen Catalan activists, mostly from MRG and RCADE. Radicals were critical of the forum, but everyone wanted to see what the hype was about. We spent our first few days in Brazil living with poor families from the Landless Workers

Movement (MST) at a squatter camp in a vast expanse of rolling green hills on the border of São Paulo and Paraná states. Together with Sandinista communities, MST camps have long been popular destinations for Catalan solidarity activists. As Joan explained, "I went to Porto Alegre to learn about the WSF, but more to watch, because of the reformists, but I really wanted to get to know the landless workers." Many activists from MRG and RCADE felt the same way, but institutionalized actors from Barcelona would become more deeply involved in the forums.[3]

Arriving at the Youth Camp

After a twenty-four-hour bus ride, we pulled into Porto Alegre in the early morning of January 31. Eager to pitch our tents, we quickly made our way to the International Youth Camp (IYC), where over the next six days we would join nearly fifteen thousand young people from around the world. Located in a large urban park far removed from the main activities at the PUC, the IYC was part Woodstock, part political rally. The camp was filled with locals itching for a party, but also with young people from political parties as well as grassroots collectives. Enthusiastic chanting during the day gave way to loud music and dancing long into the night. Most campers were in their late teens and early twenties, and the majority came from Latin America's Southern Cone. There were also visible numbers of Europeans and North Americans, but fewer from Asia and Africa, and most were notably middle-class.

Beyond the official food stands, concert stages, information booths, handicraft sellers, bathrooms, and shower stalls, radicals also organized a series of self-managed spaces, including an alternative media tent housing an Indymedia Center, a computer lab running free software, and a pirate radio, as well as the Intergaláctika Laboratory of Disobedience, a participatory forum for sharing and exchange that MRG-based activists helped organize. Moreover, unlike the official forum, the youth camp was built using environmentally sustainable techniques and food was provided by local organic producers, movements, and cooperatives.[4]

After claiming an available patch of grass next to a group of Argentines near the far end of camp, we discussed our strategy for the day. We were eager to get to the university, but I also wanted to attend an assembly to plan autonomous actions at the media tent that morning. Most of the group set off for the

24. International youth camp at the 2002 WSF in Port Alegre. PHOTOGRAPH COURTESY OF
JEFFREY S. JURIS.

official forum, but I stayed behind with a Catalan friend who had just arrived
from Bogotá. Shortly before noon, Marta and I walked through the rain to the
central plaza, passing various groups of socialist youth—identifiable by their
large red banners and Che Guevara T-shirts. When we got to the Indymedia
tent, I recognized familiar faces from Genoa. After an enthusiastic embrace,
Antonia explained that a group of Brazilian anarchists were planning to squat
a building during the opening march against the war. José and Daniela, from a
PGA-inspired group in São Paulo, announced that the assembly would begin
as soon as the samba band called everyone to attention.

A few minutes later, drumbeats sounded, and the Brazilian samba band appeared. They were dressed in Black Bloc gear, carried White Overalls shields,
and moved through the urban space like the Pink Bloc from Prague or Genoa.
Echoing the punk- and reggae-inspired rap blaring from the radio, their style
represented a complex fusion of sounds and images creatively downloaded
and reworked from global communication networks. The assembly began
with a declaration of intent: "This is not an action against the WSF. We agree
it should take place, but want to show another way of operating: more horizontal, democratic, and assembly based." Indeed, political divisions were expressed through differences over organizational process and form. We wanted

to stay, but time was running short, so we took off for the PUC before the European meeting got under way.

I would feel a continual rush of stimulation and excitement throughout the week. Simply deciding which of the myriad conferences, workshops, seminars, assemblies, marches, actions, and autonomous events to attend posed a challenge. Among the official events alone, there were 27 conferences, 96 seminars, and 652 workshops.[5] Academic-style panels were held each morning, divided into four thematic areas: production of wealth and social reproduction, access to wealth and sustainability, civil society and the public arena, and political power and ethics in the new society. Afternoons were reserved for self-organized workshops, and evenings were typically filled with speakers, assemblies, and cultural events. Numerous informal networking activities also took place in the streets, plazas, and cafes surrounding the university. Moreover, the forum was as massive as it was diverse. Participation had ballooned from 25,000 in 2001 to 70,000 this year (increasing to 100,000 in 2003, 125,000 in 2004 in Mumbai, 150,000 in 2005, and nearly as many at three decentralized forums in 2006).[6] As Michael Hardt (2002) put it, "The Forum was unknowable, chaotic, and dispersive. And that overabundance created an exhilaration in everyone, at being lost in a sea of people from so many parts of the world who are working similarly against the present form of capitalist globalization" (113).

Despite the insistence by many organizers that the forum primarily constitutes a space for debating alternatives, perhaps more importantly, it provides an opportunity, beyond mass actions, for anti–corporate globalization activists to perform their networks, create affective solidarity, and communicate oppositional messages. More than a Habermasian arena for rational discourse, the forum is also a ritual where anti–corporate globalization networks are embodied.[7] In this sense, the WSF provides a vehicle through which alternative transnational counterpublics are generated. As Meri from MRG later explained, "The debates weren't great, and I didn't learn anything new, but it was an amazing experience. I felt part of a huge global movement!" Even anarchists would have a hard time resisting this magnetic attraction.

As explored in chapter 4, mass actions and mobilizations provide physical terrains where activists perform their politics for the mass media and with respect to one another. In this sense, like the 1992 Rio Earth Summit analyzed by Paul Little (1995), the WSF can be understood as a performative ritual, where speech acts are meant less to communicate specific messages than to "'create' an event of importance regardless of what [is said]" (275). The forum thus derives its importance, for activists and observers alike, less from what is publicly discussed—hence the widespread sentiment that "I didn't learn anything new"—than from myriad informal networking activities and the fact that certain people are speaking to certain others, and in particular ways. Indeed, the WSF can be interpreted both externally as a symbolic manifestation of the strength and diversity of the anti–corporate globalization movement, and internally as a terrain where diverse activist networks constitute themselves and symbolically map their relationship to one another through verbal and embodied communicative interaction.

Opening Activities

Thousands of people were milling about the university when we arrived, just as colorful as, but somewhat better dressed than, the young people at the IYC. The PUC had a distinct feel, institutionalized and involving a relatively mainstream but more diverse crowd. After registering, we negotiated our way through the main door and up to the auditorium on the second floor, where the European Assembly of Social Movements had begun. I noticed Ignaci and Meri from MRG and joined them. Two activists, one from the Trotskyist Revolutionary Communist League and ATTAC-France, the other from the Italian Social Forum, were facilitating a discussion about the antiwar and anti-globalization movements, but the debate quickly drifted to the most anticipated topic: where to hold the first European Social Forum (ESF).[8] As Ignaci, Meri, and I looked on, the moderators presented proposals from Italy and Barcelona to host the regional event, while a delegate from the Greek Social Forum nominated Athens. Meanwhile, Bernard Cassen, a political rival of the facilitator from ATTAC-France, surprised everyone by forwarding Paris as an alternative. Ignaci leaned over and whispered, "The Italians are planning a more radical forum, and Cassen wants to block their bid!" Time was running short, so the assembly appointed a smaller working group to decide during an open meeting the following day.

When the assembly let out, we quickly made our way downtown for the beginning of the march against the war in Iraq. There was always someplace

25. Brazilian samba band plays in the WSF opening march in 2002. PHOTOGRAPH COURTESY
OF JEFFREY S. JURIS.

to rush off to, and not a second to lose. Thousands of people were crowded
into a small plaza when we arrived, including large contingents from the
World March of Women, ATTAC, MST, and the ever-present Brazilian PT
(Workers Party). Soon after the march began, we passed a building that had
been illegally squatted by militants from the *sin techo* (homeless) movement,
who were hanging out of the windows and waving to the crowd. Although the
PT-controlled city government appeared to tolerate their actions, a very different response awaited the young anarchists.

A few minutes later the samba band marched by, waving rubber shields
decorated with slogans such as "Occupy and Resist!" or "Dance and Revolution." Marta and I followed them around the corner, where a group of activists
entered a deserted building and appeared on a second-floor balcony waving
a black anarchist flag. Riot police were on the scene in minutes, however, and
the action was quickly abandoned. We then rejoined the main demonstration
and marched to the amphitheater for the opening ceremony, where local government officials welcomed the crowd. Although political parties are techni-
cally excluded from the forum, PT banners were everywhere. Longtime PT
leader Luis Inácio Lula da Silva would be elected Brazilian president later that
year, further increasing the party's influence.

26. Opening ceremony at the 2002 WSF. PHOTOGRAPH COURTESY OF JEFFREY S. JURIS.

Living the Forum

After a sleepless night in the youth camp—the concerts, discussions, and mayhem lasted till sunrise—we rolled out of our tents and headed to the university for a panel on global trade with prominent movement intellectuals, including Martin Khor from the Third World Network, Bernard Cassen from ATTAC-France, and Lori Wallach from Public Citizen. The panel was held in a large ballroom seating several thousand spectators. The presenters analyzed various aspects of the global trading system as the audience listened intently. Regarding the academic-style conferences, Carme from MRG later said, "I would have liked to have heard someone from the indigenous movement in Ecuador, or the women's movement in Indonesia; real social movement voices . . . not the intellectuals who have everything figured out." Indeed, many radicals criticize the forum precisely because of its institutional character, but as we shall see, subsequent forums would move toward a more grassroots model.

In any event, the real drama was occurring elsewhere. After the conference, I rushed off to the Catalan meeting to prepare a strategy for the regional forum. We finally agreed to support the Italian candidacy, which was better prepared and also led by more radical-movement-oriented sectors, thus holding off on the Barcelona bid. A few of us went to the European working group meeting, where the Italians, Greeks, and French each presented their case.

Susan George, vice president of ATTAC-France, made a strong plea for Paris: "We have the necessary infrastructure and financial backing to organize this kind of huge event." Ignaci from MRG quickly replied, "We want a militant European Social Forum led by movements, not the institutions. We should do it in Italy where the movement is strong and unified." The debate largely pitted institutional reformists against Trotskyists for control of the European process. The radical forces from Italy ultimately prevailed, although Paris would be chosen the following year.

After the meeting, we escaped to the courtyard for some fresh air and found ourselves in a different world. The carnival atmosphere was electric: thousands of people milling about; T-shirts, books, and crafts for sale, capoeira and African drumming performances; as well as the ubiquitous and passionate political debates. Despite the micro-level conflicts beyond public view, there were also numerous moments of intense interaction and collective solidarity. Later that afternoon, we saw Noam Chomsky speak about war, globalization, and imperialism. A riot nearly broke out when organizers decided to switch venues, but we decided to stay and watch the presentation on a video screen, which only reinforced the sense of enormous proportions. When the talk ended, I rushed over to another building where the first international "social movement assembly" had begun. The lecture hall was packed with hundreds of grassroots activists, mostly from Asia, Europe, and the Americas. Individuals came up to the stage one by one to share their experiences, involving the kind of participatory process my Catalan friends had hoped for.

Over the next few days, we followed a similar routine, shuffling back and forth between conferences, assemblies, workshops, actions, and gatherings each evening at the Intergaláctika space in the IYC. Highlights included a roundtable discussion with radical youth movements from Barcelona, Seattle, Quebec, and Buenos Aires; a panel on the antiglobalization movement with anticapitalist intellectuals, including the Egyptian-born sociologist Samir Amin, Vittorio Agnoletto from the Italian Social Forum, and Walden Bello, a Filipino sociologist from Focus on the Global South; and a conference on global civil society with well-known figures such as Naomi Klein, author of *No Logo*, and, yet again, Vittorio Agnoletto. This last event was held in an old gymnasium, where rope netting separated the panel from the audience in the bleachers. Klein stole the show when she lambasted WSF organizers for failing to appreciate the symbolism of such barriers, when "our movement should be about tearing them down." Agnoletto drew a more critical response when he affirmed the time had not come to create a political party, "at least not yet." Irritated by the suggestion that a civil society movement would even consider entering the political arena, Joan from RCADE whispered to me, "These guys just don't get it!"

Alternative Spaces, Competing Logics

The next-to-last day of the forum was particularly instructive. The morning began with a discussion of strategies and tactics at Intergaláctika. After looking through action photos from various struggles around the world displayed on flimsy wooden structures around the meeting area, I joined a semicircle around an activist formerly with Reclaim the Streets. He gave an inspirational talk about diversity, decentralization, and interdependence. "Our movements are like an ecosystem," he told us, "very fluid, always changing, and working toward their own survival." Later, reflecting the networking logic that had been muted in the forum, he exclaimed, "I hate the slogan 'Another World Is Possible'—many other worlds are possible!" As we shall see, Intergaláctika would prefigure the strategy of creating autonomous yet connected spaces around the official forums, reflecting a networking strategy MRG had already employed in Barcelona and would promote leading up to the ESF in Florence.[9]

The final social movements assembly had an entirely different feel. As soon as we had dried ourselves following the action in the VIP room, we rushed to a large pavilion at the other end of the city to see the presentation of the manifesto. As we arrived, dozens of volunteers were handing out flyers promoting the new "World Social Network," whose goal was "to transform the World Social Forum into a movement that produces concrete alternatives to neoliberalism." Who these organizers were and what kind of process they had in mind were as yet unclear. Banners of socialist parties and NGO networks, including Jubilee 2000 and the World March of Women, lined the walls. We took our seats near the front.

Roughly a half hour later, a musician appeared and began playing Latin American leftist folk songs. When he concluded with a version of "Guantanamera," everyone was enthusiastically clapping, swaying, and singing. Meanwhile,

organizers had recruited two Catalans to go onstage for the opening ceremony. As soon as the singing stopped, volunteers unfurled five long ribbons
representing the five continents. At the end of each, the recruits onstage held
large banners with images of typical scenes from the social and economic life
in each region. Suddenly a man ran down the center aisle with a burning torch
and placed it in the middle of the stage. The MC then announced we would
burn the evils of capitalism and proceeded to toss pieces of paper into the
fire while calling out a litany of sins, including greed and exploitation. Meanwhile, Mercedes Sosa's "Everything Changes" was playing in the background.
Finally, when all the papers had burned, activists unfurled an even larger banner: "Another World Is Possible: With Socialism!" Organizers then led the
volunteers in an enthusiastic round of the *Internationale*.

When the anthem concluded, my Catalan friends were indignant. The start
of the ceremony, though overdone, had been quite moving, but the references
to socialism had gone too far. The attempt to impose an ideological cast on the
assembly violated the horizontal networking logic expressed within the forum's
organizational architecture, which generated an angry response. Montse, who
had been called onstage, later recalled, "I can't believe they made me sing the
Internationale! I can understand the MST, but in a forum that accepts everyone from anarchists to socialists, you can't do that. There was a specific strategy, and I felt manipulated." Joan added, "I am closer to anarchism, and felt
excluded. People like me simply won't go to the next forum!"

The assembly continued along similar lines. In contrast to Jordan's analysis
that morning, the first speaker proclaimed, "Seattle was our first strike against
empire, then Prague and Genoa, but only unity will bring us victory, we have
to remain united!" At one point the crowd became restless, prompting a Via
Campesina delegate to utter a memorable command: "Silence! Without discipline there will never be socialism!" The Catalans looked at one another in
disbelief. Other presenters were careful to emphasize diversity and grassroots
participation, but the tone had been set. The event finally concluded with a
presentation of the social movements manifesto, which included a long list
of actions for the coming year. Nuria later recalled the scene: "It was like we
were building a new international, the styles of dress, demanding silence. I
was excited to be part of a huge movement, but discipline? That word has so
many contradictions. And socialism? I am closer to the anarchists, so what
are we doing here?"

The WSF provided a physical terrain where alternative transnational counterpublics were embodied. At the same time, it also housed multiple forums for interactive debate and exchange, particularly in grassroots spaces such as Intergaláctika or the many self-organized workshops. As we shall see, the forum's organizational architecture is specifically conceived as an open space. However, radicals also criticized the process for its lack of internal democracy, pointing to a potential contradiction with respect to theory and practice. In this sense, as the controversy surrounding the ESF suggests, the process is marked by struggles for power, and decisions are often less than transparent. Still, given the event's high profile, many grassroots activists chose to participate along the margins or criticize the process from within. By contrast, as the final social movements assembly demonstrates, traditional actors reject the open-space model. Such conflicts between networking and command logics are constitutive of the forum itself.

The Emergence of an Open-Space Architecture

According to official accounts, the Brazilian NGO leader Oded Grajew and his compatriot Francisco Whitaker proposed the idea of a forum for constructing and debating alternatives to corporate globalization to Bernard Cassen, director of *Le Monde Diplomatique* and president of ATTAC-France, in February 2000. Cassen liked the idea and suggested the event be held in Porto Alegre given its location in the South, its celebrated model of participatory budgeting, and the resources commanded by the leftist PT-controlled state government. Moreover, this World Social Forum would coincide with the annual World Economic Forum in Davos. The Brazilian Organizing Committee (OC) was soon formed, involving the main Brazilian Labor Federation (CUT), MST, and six smaller organizations.[10] The OC organized the first WSF in January 2001 and subsequent forums every year until 2004, when it moved to Mumbai. The WSF now rotates between Porto Alegre and other cities around the world, shifting to a biannual format following the 2007 WSF in Nairobi.[11]

The International Committee (IC) was convened after the first WSF as a way to enhance the forum's international legitimacy, in part by promoting regional and thematic forums. The IC now includes several hundred members drawn from prominent transnational NGO, trade union, and social movement networks. Slots have also been established for permanent and temporary observers, who can attend, but not participate in, periodic IC meetings.

Although the process for becoming an ic member was initially confusing and opaque, organizers have since introduced formal guidelines (Patomäki and Teivainen 2004, 3).[12] Steps have also been taken to promote diversity, although certain regions, such as sub-Saharan Africa, remain underrepresented.[13]

Since their inception, the forums have blossomed into a global process involving diverse events at multiple geographic scales. First, the wsf has been held annually (biannually after 2007), shifting between Porto Alegre and other cities around the world. Second, the ic sponsors regional events, including Asian, European, and Pan-Amazonian Social Forums, as well as the Social Forum of the Americas. European Social Forums, in particular, have drawn tens of thousands of participants.[14] Third, the ic sponsors thematic events that address priority issues, including a forum on the Argentine financial crisis in 2002, and another on democracy, human rights, war, and drug trafficking in Colombia the following year. Finally, activists have also organized hundreds of national and local forums not formally tied to the wsf process.[15]

As I have been arguing, anti–corporate globalization movements involve an increasing confluence among organizational forms, political norms, and new digital technologies. In the case of the forums, network norms and forms are expressed through organizational architectures conceived in spatial terms. Organizers thus view the forum as an "open space," a model that incorporates a horizontal networking logic within its network architecture. As pointed out in chapter 6, structure and process represent network protocols, the rules of the game, which shape how diverse participants and organizers interact. The discourse and practice of open space thus reflect a wider networking logic characterized by decentralized coordination across diversity and difference. In this sense, the wsf Charter of Principles specifically defines the forum as "an open meeting place for reflective thinking, democratic debate of ideas, formulation of proposals, free exchange of experiences, and interlinking for effective action."[16] Because the forum is conceived as a civil society initiative, "neither party representations nor military organizations shall participate." Moreover, like the pga hallmarks discussed in chapter 6, the wsf charter declares that no one shall speak in the forum's name: "The meetings of the World Social Forum do not deliberate on behalf of the World Social Forum as a body. No-one . . . will be authorized . . . to express positions claiming to be those of all its participants. . . . It does not constitute a locus of power to

TABLE 7. Official world, regional, and thematic social forums, January 2001 to July 2007

Event	Place	Date	Participation (if available)
World Social Forum	Porto Alegre, Brazil	Jan. 25–30, 2001	20,000
Pan-Amazon Social Forum	Belém, Brazil	Jan. 25–27, 2002	
World Social Forum	Porto Alegre, Brazil	Jan. 31–Feb. 4, 2002	70,000
Argentina Thematic Social Forum	Buenos Aires, Argentina	Aug. 22–24, 2002	
European Social Forum	Florence, Italy	Nov. 6–10, 2002	60,000 (1 million in antiwar march)
Palestine Thematic Social Forum	Ramallah, Palestine	Dec. 27–30, 2002	
Asian Social Forum	Hyderabad, India	Jan. 2–7, 2003	
African Social Forum	Addis Ababa, Ethiopia	Jan. 5–9, 2003	
Pan-Amazon Social Forum	Belém, Brazil	Jan. 16–19, 2003	
World Social Forum	Porto Alegre, Brazil	Jan. 23–27, 2003	100,000
Thematic Social Forum: Democracy, Human Rights, War, and Drug Trafficking	Cartagena de Indias, Colombia	June 16–20, 2003	
European Social Forum	Paris, France	Nov. 12–15, 2003	50,000 (150,000 in final march)
World Social Forum	Mumbai, India	Jan. 16–21, 2004	125,000
Pan-Amazon Social Forum	Ciudad Guayana, Venezuela	Feb. 4–8, 2004	
Social Forum of the Americas	Quito, Ecuador	July 25–30, 2004	10,000
European Social Forum	London, England	Oct. 15–17, 2004	25,000 (100,000 in final march)
Pan-Amazon Social Forum	Manaus, Amazonas	Jan. 18–22, 2005	
World Social Forum	Porto Alegre, Brazil	Jan. 26–31, 2005	150,000
Mediterranean Social Forum	Barcelona, Catalonia (Spain)	June 16–19, 2005	
World Social Forum (Polycentric)	Bamako, Mali Caracas, Venezuela Karachi, Pakistan	Jan. 19–23, 2006 Jan. 24–29, 2006 Mar. 24–29, 2006	100,000 in march 53,000 delegates 30,000 delegates

continued on next page

TABLE 7. (continued)

Event	Place	Date	Participation (if available)
European Social Forum	Athens, Greece	May 4–9, 2006	35,000 (100,000 in final march)
Caribbean Social Forum	Martinique	July 5–9, 2006	
World Social Forum	Nairobi, Kenya	Jan. 20–25, 2007	50,000
United States Social Forum	Atlanta, Georgia	June 27–July 1, 2007	15,000

be disputed by the participants in its meetings, nor does it constitute the only option for interrelation and action by the organizations and movements that participate in it."

As the charter suggests, the forum was not conceived as a traditional organization or unified actor, but rather, like PGA, as a tool for communication and coordination, which the Indian activist and researcher Jai Sen has consistently referred to as an "open space": "The Forum . . . is not an organization or a movement, or a world federation, but a *space*—a non-directed space, from and within which movements and other civil initiatives . . . can meet, exchange views, and . . . take forward their work, locally, nationally, and globally."[17]

At the same time, open space should be viewed as a guiding vision, not an empirical depiction. In principle, the forum was designed as a sphere of open participation and horizontal exchange. But as we have seen, the process involves numerous struggles for power and authority while differently situated actors, including network-based movements and their more traditional counterparts, hold contrasting views of the forum.[18] At the same time, the discourse and practice of open space generate their own exclusions based on axes of race, class, gender, religious faith, and political views.[19] However, although it is often undermined in practice, the open-space ideal represents the inscription of a networking logic within the forum's organizational architecture. Like other transnational activist networks, examined in this book, the forum's network design thus facilitates the rise of a self-organizing counterpublic opposed to corporate globalization.

Technology, Organization, and the Forum

The discourse and practice of open space reproduce the networking logics associated with anti–corporate globalization movements more generally, involving a growing confluence among network norms, forms, and technologies. Compared to more radical networks, however, such as MRG and PGA, the social forums have been less *directly* shaped by new technologies.[20] This partly reflects the forums' institutional character. As Pippa Norris (2001) suggests, traditional organizations often adapt new technologies to their ongoing communication routines, while informal actors are more likely to reorganize themselves around such technologies, using their interactive capacities to overcome disadvantages with respect to size and resources. At the same time, the forums are beginning to use technologies more creatively. Organizers have used electronic tools such as websites and e-mail lists for their internal communication and outreach, while specific projects and workshops constitute platforms for experimenting with digital media and debating issues related to their use within grassroots movements for social change. Moreover, such technological innovation mirrors a process of organizational and political experimentation within and around the forums.

Official Technological Infrastructure

The WSF website (www.forumsocialmundial.org.br) constitutes the forum's most visible communications tool.[21] Hosted on a Brazilian server and managed by the Secretariat, the site operates as an administrative facilitator and archive, housing information about the history and structure of the forums, logistical and program details, and analyses and archival materials, as well as registration forms for individuals, organizations, and journalists. The site provides content in four languages—Portuguese, English, French, and Spanish.[22] Significantly, there are no forum-wide Listservs, although users can sign up for periodic electronic bulletins. Some IC committees have created their own e-mail lists and are experimenting with new digital tools, including chats and wikis, but these have not been well publicized (Waterman 2005). More recently, however, the IC Communications Commission has built new interactive Web tools and has also developed a communications plan proposing a more innovative use of digital technology.[23] At the regional level, the dynamic

ESF website (www.fse-esf.org) and open Listserv reflect the relatively more participatory nature of the European process, while across the Atlantic the United States Social Forum website (https://www.ussf2007.org) features innovative tools that facilitate coordination and participation, including an open blog, Listservs, and an online registration system.[24]

Alternative Technology

Until recently the official forums have made relatively limited use of new media. However, alternative projects within and around the forums have been more technologically oriented. For example, when members of the London ESF organizing committee objected to the creation of open Listservs and restricted the free flow of information, grassroots activists established their own website (http://esf2004.net) and distribution list.[25] The former was wiki based, allowing users to edit and update content, reflecting an emphasis on open access, decentralized coordination, and horizontal collaboration among grassroots activists. Moreover, diverse autonomous spaces, including Beyond ESF in London in 2004 or the Caracol at the 2005 WSF in Porto Alegre (discussed hereafter), have created their own interactive websites and tools.[26] In this sense, the cultural politics of networking are also expressed through alternative technological practices.

Free and Open Source Software (FOSS)

Since the WSF in Mumbai, organizers have made a concerted effort to use FOSS, including GNU/Linux operating systems, on all forum-related computer networks.[27] FOSS is nonproprietary and based on open-source development principles, where programmers improve and distribute new versions of software code through collaborative networks. FOSS thus requires the right to distribute and access source code, posing a major challenge to corporate software monopolies, such as Microsoft. Despite differing views of the value of FOSS and whether it was inherently democratizing, the Indian Organizing Committee ultimately ran FOSS as another "way to support people's struggle against marginalization and uneven and unfair distribution of resources (Caruso 2005, 174)." The 2005 WSF in Porto Alegre installed FOSS on all one thousand computers and shifted the official website to an open source language.[28] The European and United States social forums have also employed

FOSS,[29] which brings together technical, organizational, and political domains, inscribing network ideals within the forum's technological architecture.

Babels and Nomad

Among the most politically and technologically innovative forum-based projects, Babels is a network of interpreters and translators founded before the 2002 ESF in Florence. From an initial pool of 350 names, the Babels database now includes more than seven thousand volunteers who speak sixty-three languages.[30] Babels organizers see themselves as political actors and are committed to financial and technical autonomy. In this sense, using amateur interpreters is understood as an expressly political act affirming the links among technical, organizational, and political domains. Moreover, in line with their politics, Babels volunteers have developed an alternative computer-based translation system called Nomad, which combines free software for recording and streaming live audio between speakers and interpreters with various audience transmission formats, including FM radios (Reyes et al. 2005). First implemented during the 2004 WSF in Mumbai, Nomad is cheaper and more efficient than available commercial systems while reflecting a commitment to self-management and horizontal collaboration.

Technology and Media Projects

The social forums have also provided sites for numerous technology and media projects. Since the first WSF, the International Independent Information Exchange has provided a Web-based forum for posting and distributing news stories related to the WSF (www.ciranda.net).[31] The 2005 WSF also featured the Radio Forum, involving community stations from around the world and webcast twenty-four hours a day, as well as the TV Forum, which coordinated video recordings and created a one-hour television show.[32] In addition, radicals have organized their own projects, including Indymedia Centers, the European Forum on Communication Rights during the 2004 ESF, and the Laboratory of Free Knowledge at the IYC in 2005, a space for creating and sharing audio, video, and software. Social forums have also featured panels, workshops, and activities around themes including social change and the Internet, media democracy, independent media, free software, and intellectual property rights. In 2005 the WSF dedicated an entire "territory" to "autonomous thought, reappropriation, and socialization of knowledge and technologies," which included dozens of self-organized workshops related to new digital media.

The Forum as Contested Terrain

The technological and organizational architectures of the forum thus reflect emerging network norms and forms, expressed through the discourse and practice of open space. At the same time, although the open-space model has been passionately defended by many organizers and participants, others would like the forum to become a unified political actor.[33] Indeed, as "a hotly contested political space" (Ponniah and Fisher 2003), the forum is constituted in practice through ongoing conflicts over organizational process and form. Nowhere have these struggles been more intense than within the International Council. As we shall see, the cultural politics of networking, which are performed at the WSF as a "transnational mega-event" (Little 1995), are further played out within submerged spheres.

Several months after returning from Porto Alegre, I attended the April 2002 IC meeting in Barcelona as a member of MRG's International Working Group. Many local organizations had been invited to attend as guest observers, but MRG was asked to become an official IC member, presumably based on its reputation as an exemplar of the new network-based political culture. As its organizational principles precluded taking part in a representative structure, MRG decided to offer its delegate status to a coalition of grassroots social movements in Barcelona, which drafted a statement criticizing the IC for its lack of transparency. Given my command of English, I was entrusted with helping to translate and read the statement aloud. Although I was uncomfortable at first with this role because of my dual status as activist and researcher, the opportunity to practice what I now call militant ethnography allowed me to learn a great deal more about the forums than I would have otherwise.

The IC meeting began the following day in Nou Barris, a working-class neighborhood on the outskirts of Barcelona. The meeting hall was set up like a mini-UN conference room: tables organized in two large rectangles, one inside the other, including two additional rows set aside for observers. Official delegates were given an identity tag, microphone, and a bottle of water.

Organizers had arranged a translation system, and speakers communicated in Spanish, Portuguese, and English. The number of participants numbered roughly two hundred; most were middle-aged or older (in their forties to seventies) and represented NGO networks and unions. A member of the Brazilian OC facilitated each session, which began with a presentation and continued with an open round of discussion. Each speaker was given five minutes, and presentations usually lasted the entire allotted time, so there was little direct interaction. Moreover, there was no voting, and, indeed, no real decision making at all. Instead, before starting each new section, the OC would summarize the previous discussion and outline their tentative conclusions.

When the meeting began, Fernando from CUT reminded participants, "We are heirs to the Seattle protests, where we learned that unity is based on pluralism. The WSF does not intend to be the only instance of the movement or its leadership. We want to stimulate convergence and articulation. The forum is not a space of power but is rather trying to create a different political culture." However, the ensuing discussion featured radically contrasting assertions. For example, some wanted to amend the charter and allow for the creation of collective strategies through the IC's political leadership. "We are against neoliberalism and war," an Italian delegate argued. "We are a radical movement, part of the revolution. There has been an objective radicalization, and we should not only be a forum for debate; we should also become a forum for struggle." Others steadfastly opposed this view. An Argentine thus pointed out, "We have already tried the path of revolution. In response to the radicalization of the Right, we have to radicalize our process of diversity and participation. We are not a central committee!"

The following day's debate was even more contentious. Some delegates saw the forum as a "trademark," with the IC ensuring that regional processes conform to the WSF charter. As Bernard Cassen himself argued, "We need a strong, clear International Council. If the center is not strong, the peripheries will do what they want." Alternatively, others viewed the forum as a "public domain," emphasizing a decentralized process where regions could adapt the model according to local conditions. "We should make the recipe available so everyone can use it," argued another delegate, "but we aren't responsible for the success or failure of the experiments." The Brazilian OC ultimately approved a compromise, establishing official and nonofficial forum tracks.

The debate then turned to democracy and openness within the IC. Sensing the moment had arrived, I raised my hand, and when my turn came around, I read the declaration we had completed the previous evening, which included the following statement regarding MRG:

> We would like to thank the Council for the membership invitation, although we are not sure how it happened. MRG is part of a new political culture involving network-based organizational forms, direct democracy, open participation, and direct action. A top-down process, involving a closed, nontransparent, nondemocratic, and highly institutional central committee will never attract collectives and networks searching for a new way of doing politics. This should be a space of participation, not representation.

The declaration was meant as a provocation, a communicative direct action from within the heart of the IC. We expected a cold, if not downright hostile, reception. Much to our surprise, however, many council members were supportive. A prominent European-based Trotskyist said, for example, "We have to figure out a way to include this new political culture despite their unique organizational form." Others, like a delegate from CUT, reacted negatively: "We have to clarify who wants to be a member and who does not!" Most members recognized the validity of our critique and expressed support for a process based on openness, transparency, and diversity. In this sense, the IC was internally divided. Much like the broader forum, the IC was a contested space, not in terms of formal quotas of power but over the underlying vision of the forum itself. Indeed, such conflicts among networking and command logics involved contrasting views of the forum's organizational architecture among organizers espousing distinct political visions.

The Cultural Politics of Autonomous Space

Whereas networking politics inside the forums involve heated debates with respect to the discourse and practice of *open* space, similar conflicts characterize the relationship between the social forums and more radical transnational activist networks, resulting in constantly shifting boundaries and alliances driven by a cultural politics of *autonomous* space. Open space implies a singular discursive arena, similar to an ideal Habermasian public sphere, where diverse networks and groups converge to share ideas and develop proposals. Autonomous spaces, on the other hand, imply a multiplicity of smaller, networked spaces, loosely coordinated but retaining their political autonomy and specificity. Whereas open space involves the inscription of a horizontal networking logic within the forum's organizational architecture, autonomous spaces reproduce a horizontal networking logic through the relationship among distinct, self-organizing spheres. Autonomous spaces have thus allowed radicals to express their differences with respect to the official forums while remaining connected to the larger anti–corporate globalization movement field.

During spring 2002, activists associated with radical transnational activist networks such as PGA and No Border began discussing how to interact with the social forums. The experiences of MRG-based activists during the recent WSF and IC meeting in Barcelona had been revealing. On the one hand, it was clear the forums could bring together tens of thousands of participants from diverse networks, organizations, and movements, constituting a unique space of encounter and exchange. On the other hand, although the WSF charter reproduces a horizontal networking logic, the forum was rife with contradictions with respect to access, grassroots participation, and hierarchical relations. At the same time, critically engaging the forum had proved useful in terms of moving projects forward while promoting constructive change from within. As preparations began for the 2002 ESF in November, MRG initiated a series of critical debates among colleagues in Barcelona and elsewhere about how best to engage the process.

Defining Autonomous Space

The Strasbourg No Border camp in July 2002 provided an initial opportunity to discuss the idea of building an autonomous space at the ESF in Florence. A workshop around the ESF drew significant interest, as dozens of radicals from the Italian Disobedientes and Cobas, as well as PGA-based activists from around Europe, came together to share their ideas and strategies with respect to the forums. An activist from Berlin characterized the dilemma as follows: "People say everything is open, but a small group makes all the decisions. There are mostly Trotskyists, trade unionists, political parties, and ATTAC, but very few from networks like PGA or the larger movement. How do we bring radical ideas and proposals without becoming part of the power structure?"

In response, some argued that radicals should participate but organize things in a different way, highlighting a vision of self-managed change from below. Others felt it was better to remain outside. As one activist said, "Participating is a way of legitimating their attempt to make the ESF *the* space of the antiglobalization movement." At one point, a woman from Berlin proposed a compromise: "In Porto Alegre many people never saw the youth camp; there was not enough interaction. We should have one foot outside, but also another inside." Her position elicited enthusiastic support, and a squatter from southern Spain added, "We should organize a different space, beyond, but not against, the ESF." After a long discussion, the group decided to release the following statement:

> We agreed to launch the idea of constituting a concrete space for those of us who traditionally work with structures that are decentralized, horizontal, assembly-based, and anti-authoritarian; a space that would maintain its autonomy with respect to the "official" space of the ESF, but at the same time remain connected. . . . This would mean . . . having one foot outside and another inside the ESF. . . . This autonomous space should visibilize the diversity of the movement of movements, but also our irreconcilable differences with respect to models attempting to reform capitalism. The space should not only incorporate differences with the program of the ESF in terms of "contents," but also in terms of the organizational model and forms of political action.[34]

The "one foot outside and another inside" formulation would reproduce a networking logic along the terrain of the ESF, allowing radicals to express their differences but remain linked to the wider forum. Organizers further elaborated the autonomous space at a workshop during the European PGA conference in Leiden that September. Some were still reticent about participating, but as one activist suggested, "The ESF is a perfect moment of visibility. We are a ghetto here in Leiden; there is very little media coverage." At the same time, support was growing for a space completely outside the forum. Others were concerned about being integrated into a social democratic project, which led to a consensus around the need to organize "legible" actions to communicate the underlying political distinctions.[35] Such complex networking politics involved a delicate balance, as a workshop report later explained: "The challenge . . . consists of making sure, on the one hand, the initiatives are not co-opted; and, on the other hand, avoiding . . . isolation."[36] The space was ultimately recast completely outside the forum, allowing individuals and groups to make their own decision about whether to participate in the official event.

The Proliferation of Autonomous Spaces

What began as a single project ultimately broke down into parallel autonomous initiatives in Florence, including Cobas Thematic Squares, the Disobedientes "No Work, No Shop" space, and Eur@ction Hub. The official ESF surpassed all expectations, involving sixty thousand participants (della Porta et al. 2006, 6) and drawing nearly one million to the demonstration against the war in Iraq on November 9, 2002. Hundreds of activists also passed through the autonomous events, as well as a feminist space called Next Genderation.[37] Although small, the Eur@ction Hub, in particular, provided a forum for sharing skills, ideas, and resources; exploring issues related to information, migration, and self-management; and experimenting with new digital technologies. Above all, the Hub was meant to facilitate interconnections, representing a concrete example of networked space, as the flyer explained: "Hub is . . . a connector. It is not a space already marked by pre-established content. Anyone can contribute proposals designed specifically for the Hub, but 'also connect' to this space others that might take place in other places or moments in Florence. Hub is also an interconnection tool: for bringing together proposals or ideas that have been dispersed or undeveloped until now, which might acquire greater complexity."[38]

After Florence, the autonomous-space model caught on. During the 2003 WSF in Porto Alegre, for example, grassroots activists organized several parallel spaces, including a follow-up Hub project, the second edition of Intergaláctika, and a forum organized by Z Magazine called Life after Capitalism. Moreover, Brazilian activists hosted a PGA-inspired gathering involving activists from Europe and the Americas. Although emerging from distinct political contexts and histories, autonomous spaces at the 2004 WSF in Mumbai were even larger, including Mumbai Resistance (a gathering of Maoist and Gandhian peasant movements), the Peoples Movements Encounter II (led by the Federation of Agricultural Workers and Marginal

Farmers Unions), and the International Youth Camp.[39] PGA also held a parallel session, involving Asian and European movements.[40] Finally, activists organized various autonomous initiatives at the second ESF in Paris in 2003, including a grassroots media center, Metallo Medialab, and a direct-action space called GLAD (Space toward the Globalization of Disobedient Struggles and Actions).

Despite this proliferation of autonomous spaces, many radicals have refused to take part in the forums entirely. Paul Treanor (2002), a Dutch anarchist, argued with respect to the ESF, "The organizers want to establish themselves as 'the leaders of the European social movements.' They want to become a negotiating partner of the EU." At the same time, many anticapitalists recognize the strategic importance of the forums. As Pablo Ortellado (2003), a Brazilian media activist, suggested, "The social forums are attracting a wide range of people, many of whom we really want to bring to our part of the movement. It's not enough to sit and criticize the forum. . . . We should somehow set our own events and attract those people." Linden Farrer (2002) issued a widely influential call for a strategy of "contamination," which he explained in the following way: "The best way of working with the ESF [is] being constructive in criticism, attempting to change the organization from inside and outside, preventing liberals from tending towards their self-destructive habits of strengthening existing structures of government. Rather than abolishing the ESF because it had a shaky—but ultimately successful—start, we should work to make the ESF a truly revolutionary force."

Many radicals agree, and in ever-increasing numbers. Indeed, the cultural politics of autonomous space perhaps reached their fullest expression at the London ESF in November 2004. Once again, given the growing confluence among norm, form, and technology, debates within and around the ESF largely revolved around organizational structure and process.

The European Social Forum, London 2004

The organizing process leading up to the London ESF had been characterized by a deep divide between a group of self-described "horizontals," who supported open, participatory forms of organization, and their institutional counterparts, whom they dubbed the "verticals" (Juris 2005c). Contrasting organizational logics also corresponded to alternative strategies and visions for social change. Whereas the horizontals were committed to autonomous self-organization beyond the market and state, the verticals wanted to exercise political power within formal democratic institutions and influence them from outside. Although particularly pronounced in London, as we have seen, such conflicts among networking and command logics have long characterized the social forum process and anti–corporate globalization movements more generally.

As conflict escalated before the forum, grassroots groups decided to organize their own self-managed spaces. Despite numerous differences in ideology and position with respect to the official forum, these projects were united in their commitment to horizontal, directly democratic practices and forms, expressing their values through concrete organizational and technological practice. During an orientation for the "autonomous spaces" in London, an organizer recalled, "We have spent six months defining ourselves in opposition to the ESF, but our way of showing opposition is by organizing ourselves in a different way." Another added, "To fight the top-down, vertical culture, we created the horizontals based on our own culture of openness." The autonomous spaces would thus reflect a clear networking logic, as the following declaration suggests: "We want to create open spaces for networking, exchanges, celebration, thinking, and action. We believe our ways of organizing and acting should reflect our political visions, and are united in standing for grassroots self-organization, horizontality, for diversity and inclusion, for direct democracy, collective decision making based upon consensus."[41]

Ironically, by creating autonomous spaces—separate, yet connected to the official ESF—radicals would reaffirm the open-space ideal inscribed within the forum charter. Thousands of grassroots activists ultimately took part in an array of alternative projects, actions, and initiatives during the London Forum, including Beyond ESF (a gathering of antiauthoritarian, anticapitalist struggles), Radical Theory Forum (a workshop exploring the links between theory and practice), Indymedia Center (a space for grassroots multimedia production, including a bar, computer lab, and cultural events), Laboratory of Insurrectionary Imagination (a forum for creative interventions and exchange, involving workshops, discussions, and actions around the city), Mobile Carnival Forum (a project using theater and music aboard a double-decker bus to address issues such as peace, democracy, and neoliberalism), Solidarity Village (vendors and stalls focusing on fair trade and alternative economics), Women's Open Day (talks and films about women's survival work), and Life Despite Capitalism (a two-day forum around the idea of the "commons").

TABLE 8. Autonomous spaces at European Social Forum in London, October 14–17, 2004

Event	Description
Radical Theory Forum (October 14)	Workshops and discussions exploring how theory can inform practice. Specific themes include feminism, post-Marxism, popular education, complexity theory, as well as politics and organization of the European Social Forum.
Indymedia Center (October 14–17)	Space for independent reporting and multimedia production around the ESF and autonomous spaces, including protests and creative interventions. Also housed bar, public access.
Laboratory of Insurrectionary Imagination (October 14–17)	Self-organized space for tactical intervention and exchange, including workshops, discussions, and direct actions around the city. Actions include Corporate Olympics, 5th biannual March for Capitalism, Yomango shoplifts and Tube parties, and Clandestine Insurgent Rebel Clown Army trainings.
Mobile Carnival Forum	London-to-Baghdad bio-diesel double-decker bus circulated around the forum and city. Used political theater and music to generate discussions and workshops around peace, democracy, and neoliberalism.
Solidarity Village (October 13–17)	Projects and initiatives involving alternative economics, such as Land Café, Well Being Space, Art Space for Kids, Local Social Forums Area, Commons Internet Café, and SUSTAIN! space, which featured presentations and information stalls.
Women's Open Day (October 14)	Speak-outs, food, video screenings, child care, and information stalls focusing on unremunerated survival work of women: breast-feeding, subsistence farming, caring, volunteering, and fighting for justice.
Life Despite Capitalism (October 16–17)	Two-day forum around issues and struggles surrounding the idea of the "commons" in diverse spheres: cyberspace, the workplace, public services, free movement, and autonomous spaces, and several crosscutting themes: power, networks, democracies, creative excesses, and the commons generally.

Throughout the London Forum, activists thus moved fluidly across the urban terrain from one autonomous space to another, and between autonomous and official events. A networking logic was reproduced through the division of space, allowing diverse projects and initiatives to converge while maintaining their autonomy and specificity. Meanwhile, radicals also carried out direct actions against the ESF. On the second day of the forum, for example, two hundred activists from the autonomous spaces stormed a plenary stage where London mayor Ken Livingstone had been scheduled to speak. Their intention was not to stop the discussion but to publicly denounce what they saw as the nondemocratic, exclusionary practices of many ESF organizers, including the mayor's Socialist Action faction. Such conflicts were productive: making tensions visible, generating collective debates, and pressing the forum to live up to its expressed ideals. Networking politics within and around the London Forum thus revolved around organizational process and form, expressed through alternative spatial discourses and practices.

From Open to Networked Space

As we have seen, the cultural politics of autonomous space allow radicals to engage in their own self-managed forms of political and cultural production while tactically intervening along the terrain of the official forum. Partly in response to such pressure, the WSF itself has increasingly moved toward a decentralized model of networked, self-organizing spaces. The 2005 WSF in Porto Alegre shifted from a single site at the Catholic University to a decentralized area around the International Youth Camp along Guayba Lake. In spatial terms, the forum was reconceived as a "World Social Territory," divided into eleven thematic zones, each with open-air tents housing conference rooms, cultural stages, food courts, craft markets, and information stalls. Moreover, the youth camp and the diverse projects housed there, including a new version of Intergaláctika called the Caracol, were located at the center of the forum rather than along its margins. The WSF as a singular transnational counterpublic thus gave way to separate yet horizontally linked counterpublics, physically embodied in the forum's networked terrain. The 2006 "polycentric" WSF moved even further in this direction, distributed among three remote geographic sites—Caracas (Venezuela), Bamako (Mali), and Karachi (Pakistan).[42]

At the same time, the forum is approximating a self-organizing network ideal in another sense. Whereas previous editions relied on organizing committees to plan and coordinate major events, the 2005 WSF was entirely self-managed. Delegates thus proposed themes and submitted proposals for their own workshops through an electronic consultation process. The Brazilian OC collected and consolidated the proposals, rejecting only those that violated the WSF Charter of Principles. When the forum concluded, organizers col-

27. Scene from the Caracol Intergaláctika at the 2005 WSF in Porto Alegre.
PHOTOGRAPH COURTESY OF JEFFREY S. JURIS.

lated the results from various workshops and posted them virtually on the
"Mural of Proposals."[43] The Polycentric WSF in 2006 implemented a similar
methodology. The collaborative forms of interaction and exchange that characterize the open-source process are thus increasingly reflected in the forum
as a network of self-organizing counterpublics. In this sense, the forum has
moved closer to its expressed open-space ideal through ongoing organizational and technological innovation.[44]

Conclusion: Open Space Revisited

As mass direct actions become more and more difficult to organize, world and
regional forums have emerged as the main public expressions of an evolving
anti–corporate globalization movement field. As we have seen, the forums
are high-profile image events where activists come together to perform their
politics and make struggles visible, constituting a series of overlapping transnational counterpublics where global activist identities and affective ties are
generated. As Meri from MRG pointed out, "I got to know the global movement
in Porto Alegre; that's where I felt connected." Moreover, like other transnational activist networks explored in this book, the forums reflect an increasing confluence among organizational forms, political norms, and new digital

technologies. In particular, forum *events* are critical sites for technological and organizational experimentation, while forum *architectures* incorporate a horizontal networking logic within their organizational designs expressed through the discourse and practice of open space.

At the same time, given that contemporary activists inscribe their political ideals directly into emerging network architectures, the cultural politics within and around the forums largely involve struggles over organizational process and form. As I have argued, such conflicts are specifically expressed through alternative spatial discourses and practices. On the one hand, the forum process involves heated debates among those committed to an open-space ideal and their traditional counterparts, while, on the other hand, the forums make up part of a wider series of struggles among competing transnational activist networks. Indeed, the cultural politics of autonomous space reproduce emerging network norms and forms, as radicals maintain their autonomy and specificity while staying connected to broader movement fields. Meanwhile, the forum itself is moving toward a model of horizontally connected, self-organizing spaces, which suggests an ongoing process of organizational, technological, and political innovation.

The social forums have brought together tens of thousands of participants from around the world to share ideas, strategies, and resources and to discuss concrete alternatives to corporate globalization. At the same time, they have also provided physical platforms for experimenting with innovative organizational and technological practices. But what about practical impacts? Have the forums produced any tangible results? On one level, the forums have elicited a great deal of media coverage, although more so outside the United States. During the second WSF, for example, an article in the Spanish newspaper *El País* observed, "The global communications media . . . has gone from disdain to sending thousands of reporters. . . . In the past they opted for the Economic Forum in Davos . . . and now had to cover Porto Alegre as the required story" (February 3, 2002).[45]

The forum's high public profile has translated into few concrete victories, however, as activists and organizers readily admit. For some, this is beside the point, as the forum's most important contribution has been to raise global awareness and develop new forms of organization inspired by the discourse and practice of open space. As WSF cofounder Francisco (Chico) Whitaker has observed, the expansion of the process "is bringing something new, a qualitative change in the kind of unity that has been forged . . . a unity that respects diversity and in which everyone plays a leading role."[46] For others, this is insufficient, as Walden Bello argued at the 2005 WSF: "Being an open space is no longer enough. We must de-romanticize ourselves and professionalize this movement so that it remains relevant."[47]

Indeed, traditional actors have long maintained that the forum should speak and act as a unified force, but such calls have become more pronounced in recent years. During the opening ceremony at the 2004 WSF in Mumbai, for example, the noted Indian activist and author Arundhati Roy called on participants to develop a coordinated plan of action against the war in Iraq, which would specifically target corporations benefiting from the war. Also in Mumbai, cofounder Bernard Cassen suggested the current forum model had run its course and the WSF should now take common positions and actions (J. Smith 2004, 418). The following year, a group of prominent intellectuals including Cassen, the so-called Group of 19, drafted a series of proposals during the WSF in Porto Alegre and presented them publicly as the "Consensus of Porto Alegre."[48] In response, many organizers downplayed the initiative as simply one declaration among many. The spirit of the document had contradicted the Charter of Principles, which stipulates that no one can speak in the forum's name. As Candido Grzybowski, a member of the Brazilian OC, pointed out, "Here all proposals are equally important and not only that of a group of intellectuals, even when they are very significant persons."[49]

A larger group of intellectuals made a second attempt to forge a common set of principles and strategies at a meeting in Bamako on January 18, 2006, the day before the Polycentric WSF began. Unlike the G19 intervention or past social movement assemblies, the event was clearly set apart from official activities, although the resulting Bamako Appeal was still widely perceived as coming from the forum.[50] The statement itself included a collection of themes, principles, and proposals meant to promote "radical transformation of the capitalist system" while contributing to the rise of a "new popular and historical subject." Predictably, many grassroots organizers and activists criticized the appeal's universalizing thrust and the closed process by which it had been organized. As Antonio Martins pointedly asked, "Why should we rush into a 'choice' of campaigns supposedly capable of 'unifying' the Social Forums?

Why should we propose them from small groups, re-establishing the barrier between those who think and those who fight and violating the simultaneous commitment to equality and diversity?"[51]

At the same time, the document seems to have struck a chord with many activists, with respect to both its content and the broader goal of forging a common agenda among anti–corporate globalization activists. Indeed, the appeal has elicited dozens of endorsements and significant debate, even among those who have been most intensely committed to an open-space ideal. For their part, Jai Sen and his colleagues at CACIM (Critical Action: Center in Movement) have initiated a Web-based discussion of the appeal, which they present with the following text: "We at CACIM believe that while the Bamako Appeal has the quality of a dramatically important world intervention . . . it has [the] potential . . . of some . . . negative [outcomes] . . . both because of . . . its content . . . and also the process by which it seems to have been finalized. Precisely because it addresses so many important dimensions of life, society, and struggle . . . and also because of the high pedigree of its authorship, it needs, we believe, the most attentive reading and a careful, critical debate."[52]

The discussion of the Bamako Appeal suggests two critical points with respect to the forums. First, although grassroots organizers and activists increasingly express a desire to forge collective strategies, they remain committed to an open-space ideal. This contradictory impulse points to both the strengths and the weaknesses of the process. The horizontal networking logic inscribed within the forum's architecture promotes egalitarian relations and diversity but may also present an obstacle to the development of coordinated positions and action plans. At the same time, however, it is largely the open-space model that has allowed the forums to attract so many diverse participants without succumbing to sectarian divisions. Moreover, the forum's open-space architecture was designed precisely to promote the formation of common strategies, but these are meant to be developed by actors *within* the forum. In this sense, the best way to develop the kind of long-term, focused struggles required to achieve concrete goals is to *use* the forum process, but not attempt to *unify* or *represent* the political will of the entire forum.

Second, and related to this point, any proposal for a common set of strategies and action plans that does not reflect emerging network norms and forms is likely to generate widespread criticism, even among those who agree with its contents. As we have seen, anti–corporate globalization movements, and more radical, grassroots sectors in particular, are characterized by a deep commitment to collaborative process and a refusal to distinguish between means and ends. The critical question is whether activists can strike a balance between prefigurative politics and their more instrumental goals.[53] The challenge in coming years will thus be to build an open, grassroots, and interactive process that allows activists to develop collective strategies, demands, and proposals while remaining consistent with their directly democratic ideals. As we shall see, however, activists have been experimenting with such emerging modes of collaborative practice most intensively in other domains.

8

THE RISE OF
INFORMATIONAL UTOPICS

> We need to invent a new utopianism, rooted
> in contemporary social forces, for which . . . it
> will be necessary to create new kinds of move-
> ment.[1]

On the afternoon of December 13, 2001, after the opening labor march and rally during the anti-EU mobilization in Brussels had ended, Sandra and I walked over to the Independent Media Center (IMC) to meet up with colleagues from MRG. Located in an old squatted theater in the center of town, the IMC was a teeming center of activity for radicals. While the official convergence center was situated in a large open-air tent and primarily housed NGO information tables, the IMC had a much more countercultural feel. After slipping through the plastic curtains protecting the doorway from the cold wind and rain, we found ourselves in a dark foyer covered with protest signs, schedules, and posters. The former concession stand had been converted into an information desk, and two young Belgian activists were sitting behind the bar distributing flyers and fielding questions from newcomers.

Manuel and Paula from Las Agencias, a Barcelona-based political art group, were sitting on top of the bar at the far end of the room. They had just finished presenting their new project, "New Kids on the Black Block," which, as we saw in chapter 5, fuses mass-mediated images of militant protesters and a teen pop band to challenge our taken-for-granted notions of violence. Paula was ecstatic that the event had gone so well: "The punks and squatters loved us, but the official art space thought we were too controversial!" After discussing our plans for the evening with Manuel and Paula, Sandra and I went through a red silk curtain into a large auditorium, which housed the main IMC workstations. Most of the seating toward the front had been cleared out and replaced with computer-topped tables where people were busy at work. Terminals on the left were set up for public access; those on the right were reserved for Indymedia reporters working on news stories and advanced editing projects. The auditorium was buzzing with activity as grassroots media activists uploaded images and audio files, swapped reports and information online, and edited video files.

The basement below was dedicated to a project called Radio Bruxxel, a coalition of community and pirate radio stations airing twenty-four-hour programming about the EU and related issues, such as immigration, economic exclusion, autonomy, and war. Transmissions were sent out through the local airwaves and simultaneously webcast worldwide via the Internet. After checking e-mail, I went downstairs to see the studio, where four activists wearing bulky headsets were producing a show about squatting in Brussels. Just outside the production area, half a dozen squatters were lounging around a collection of dusty couches, drinking beer and exchanging stories. The contrast between the gritty, decaying infrastructure of the theater and the high-tech wires, cables, and computer systems was particularly striking. Indeed, there seemed to be a resonance between the alternative lifestyles of many radicals and the egalitarian values they projected onto the surrounding networked terrain.

I visited dozens of IMCs throughout Spain, Europe, and other parts of the world during the course of my fieldwork. As in Brussels, Indymedia Centers are often exciting and innovative spaces where anti–corporate globalization activists come together to practice grassroots media activism, socialize informally, and exchange ideas, information, and resources. At the same time, IMCs also provide important sites for using and experimenting with new digital technologies. Activists thus not only employ new technologies as tools; they use them to engage in horizontal collaboration, expressing their utopian ideals through technological practice. Digital technologies have also given rise to new media activist tactics, such as electronic civil disobedience, culture jamming, and "guerrilla communications," including the New Kids on the Black Block project discussed in chapter 5.

Throughout this book, I have explored the increasing confluence among network norms, forms, and technologies, mediated by concrete activist practice. Some chapters have emphasized the relationship between organizational architectures and political values; others have explored how networking logics are embodied during direct-action protests and inscribed onto urban space. This chapter emphasizes the domain of technology, examining how utopian ideals are expressed through innovative technological practices. Over the past few years, Indymedia and other digital networks have mobilized hundreds of thousands of protesters around the world, generating transnational counterpublics for the circulation of alternative news and information. At the same time, they have also provided forums for experimenting with new modes of political and social interaction. Have these technological practices contributed to new political visions? What is the relationship between new digital technologies and emerging utopian imaginaries?

Samuel Wilson and Leighton Peterson (2002) have recently called on anthropologists to explore the "link between historically constituted sociocultural practices within and outside of mediated communication and the language practices, social interactions, and ideologies" they give rise to (453). In this chapter, I take up this task by exploring the utopian visions, political idioms, and new forms of sociality emerging among grassroots anti–corporate globalization activists as they increasingly interact with digital technologies. As we saw in chapter 6, radicals project their political ideals onto physical territories during activist camps and gatherings, a practice Kevin Hetherington (1998) refers to as "utopics." Building on this idea, I introduce the concept "informational utopics" to characterize the way activists express their political imaginaries by experimenting with new digital technologies, projecting their utopian values onto networked terrains and emerging technological architectures. In what follows, I examine the rise of informational utopics within various domains of anti–corporate globalization activism. I specifically argue that as activists increasingly use digital technologies, they are developing new political visions, cultural grammars, and collaborative practices that point to utopian models for reorganizing social, political, and economic life.

The New Digital Media Activism

Perhaps nowhere is the growing confluence among network technologies, organizational forms, and political norms more apparent than within the new digital media activism that has emerged over the past several years in connection with anti–corporate globalization movements. New digital media include alternative and tactical varieties (Meikle 2002), the former involving independent sources of news and information that operate beyond the corporate logic of the mainstream press. Alternative media, or "radical media" in John Downing's terms, are diverse, small-scale outlets that "express an alternative vision to hegemonic policies, priorities, and perspectives" (Downing 2000, v). Alternative media also tend to be independently operated and self-managed through horizontal collaboration. Tactical media, on the other hand, intervene along mass-mediated terrains, either facilitated by the Internet or within the sphere of cyberspace itself. At the same time, both tactical and alternative media incorporate a horizontal networking logic within their organizational and technological architectures.[2]

Alternative Media

As we saw in chapter 4, mass anti–corporate globalization actions and mobilizations are powerful image events where activists perform their networks and make conflicts visible. However, many radicals view the corporate media as agents of domination, preferring to build their own autonomous media projects instead. In this light, Indymedia (www.indymedia.org) was organized as a grassroots communications network involving digital technologies, including the Internet, and multimedia platforms such as electronic print, video, audio, and photography.[3] As we shall see, Indymedia also represents an example of informational utopics, as values related to direct democracy, egalitarianism, and horizontal collaboration are directly inscribed into the network's technological and organizational architectures.[4]

Using open publishing software developed by the Australian programmer Matthew Arnison, the first IMC was established during the anti-WTO protests in Seattle. IMC journalists reported directly from the streets as activists in Seattle and beyond uploaded their own text, audio, and video files. Indymedia sites were soon up and running in Philadelphia, Portland, Vancouver, Boston, and Washington, D.C., while the network quickly expanded on a global scale to cities such as Prague, Barcelona, Amsterdam, São Paulo, and Buenos Aires. The global network now includes nearly 160 local sites and receives up to two million page views per day.[5] Previously, activists had to rely on experts and the commercial media to circulate their messages, but digital technologies now allow them to take on much of this work themselves, assuming greater control over the media production process and enhancing the speed of information flow.

During mass mobilizations, hundreds of media activists take to the streets to record video footage, snap digital photos, and conduct interviews. As Meri from MRG exclaimed during the anti-EU protest in Barcelona, "Everyone is filming everyone else!" Indeed, contemporary social movements are uniquely self-reflexive. At the same time, as we saw in Brussels, IMCs become dynamic communication hubs, providing physical terrains where protesters carry out several concrete tasks. First, activists send e-mails to each other as well as to their friends and families, facilitating action coordination while rapidly circulating information about events on the ground. Second, activists produce formal updates, which are instantly posted and sent out via global distribution lists. Third, protesters immediately upload and disseminate video and image files. Fourth, IMCs feature workshops for more complex operations, including live video and audio streaming and documentary film editing. Finally, IMCs also provide forums for exchanging ideas, information, and resources, facilitating the practice of informational utopics as activists experiment with digital technologies and inscribe their political ideals onto networked space.

Local IMC collectives are organized in a decentralized, nonhierarchical fashion, involving consensus decision making and horizontal coordination among autonomous groups. For example, Barcelona Indymedia is divided into volunteer technical, editorial, and video commissions, which coordinate through biweekly assemblies and e-mail lists. Barcelona-based activists have also participated in the global Indymedia process, which manages the main portal site. Although the network holds periodic regional and global gatherings, transnational editorial, technical, and logistical working groups primarily communicate through transnational e-mail lists and Web forums. In this sense, the global network involves a sustained process of transnational collaboration supported by new digital technologies. A Barcelona-based Indymedia activist recalled his experience with a global editorial group:

> I learned how a group of people, some in the U.S., others in London, and others, who knows where, coordinated through a global Listserv. Suddenly someone would send an e-mail saying, "I think this story is important, what do you think?" In less than a week, ten people had answered, one

or two saying it wasn't clear; but most feeling it was important, so we distributed the tasks: "I'll reduce it to so many characters," "I'll translate it into German," and "I'll do Italian." The next day we started working, and the messages began arriving: "Spanish translation done," "Italian done," "French done." Then someone sent a photo, "What do you think about this picture?" The comments went around, and then someone sent another picture, and suddenly we had created an article![6]

Reflecting the horizontal collaboration through which the global network is organized, open publishing software facilitates collaborative practice among Indymedia's grassroots users, inscribing a network ideal into the project's technological architecture. Open publishing allows activists to develop and distribute their own news stories by autonomously posting multimedia files. Users simply fill out an electronic form provided on the site, click "publish," and the story instantly appears in the right-hand column. Readers can also post comments, which appear below the original posts, generating an open forum for debate. Editorial groups then choose the most relevant posts to include within the featured stories in the central column. Most local sites continue to run a version of the original Active software, which was developed according to open-source principles and can thus be continually improved and adapted. Other sites have created their own programs, but regardless of the software format, all use some form of open publishing technology, as Matthew Arnison explains:

> The process of creating news is transparent to readers. They can contribute a story and see it instantly appear in the pool of stories publicly available. Those stories are filtered as little as possible to help the readers find the stories they want. Readers can see editorial decisions made by others. They can see how to get involved and help make editorial decisions. If they can think of a better way for the software to help shape editorial decisions, they can copy the software because it is free, change it, and start their own site. If they want to redistribute news, they can, preferably on an open publishing site.[7]

Open publishing is not simply an innovative model of decentralized news production and distribution; it constitutes an end in itself, reflecting the values associated with the network as an emerging political and cultural ideal. By offering concrete networking technologies, Indymedia provides a laboratory for building innovative forms of collaborative practice. In this sense, open publishing reverses the implicit hierarchy dividing author and consumer, empowering grassroots users to participate in the production process. As the programmer Evan Henshaw-Plath points out, "It's all about using technology to dis-intermediate the authority and power structure of the editor."[8] Moreover, says Henshaw-Plath, the system promotes nonhierarchical interactions and infrastructures: "I see my task as building technological systems where people can exert power through egalitarian systems that will reproduce . . . cooperative social relations and institutions."[9] Open publishing thus allows activists to physically inscribe their emerging utopian values directly into Indymedia's network architecture.

At the same time, as Indymedia expands and along with it the number and diversity of posts, many activists see an increasing need to develop additional mechanisms for controlling content. In this regard there is sometimes a contradiction between the network's utopian values and the demand for quality. For example, Indymedia sites have had to contend with occasional instances of hate speech, sparking heated debates over censorship.[10] In addition, news wires are often saturated with duplicate, irrelevant, or inaccurate posts. In some cases, individual users have tried to sabotage particular sites by posting disruptive messages under a variety of names.[11] At the same time, given the open nature of the system, all stories are knocked off the front page at the same rate, regardless of content. As a result, many activists now support a proactive editorial approach, as Mar from Barcelona Indymedia explained: "The page has to change; we have to provide more editing. If we want to reach the next level, we have to stress quality." Although many collectives maintain a completely open site, some remove commercial or technologically faulty posts; others screen for content. Still others, such as Indymedia-Madrid, have introduced an automated ratings system using software such as Slashdot, where the highest-ranking posts are transferred automatically to the central column, striking a balance between quality and open collaboration.

Indeed, many activists argue that Indymedia can offer more relevant content while taking advantage of new software tools to ensure that the network remains committed to its self-directed and participatory production process.

For his part, Matthew Arnison has proposed the creation of an "automated open-editing" system similar to the one employed by wikipedia.[12] Users would post their own "subediting" stories to correct facts and sources; edit spelling, grammar, and content; translate the story to another language; or nominate features for the central column. Grassroots users might also produce highlights pages featuring high-quality posts and subedits, which the editorial collectives would periodically survey and draw from to build front pages. An alternative solution would allow people to link their own weblogs into an automated system for front-page decision making reviewed by local editorial groups. In the highest spirit of informational utopics, open editing would do more than facilitate effective web page editing and design; it would foster technological and structural mechanisms for expanding grassroots participation, decentralized coordination, and horizontal decision making. Indymedia activists are thus experimenting with new technologies and forms of interaction as they strive to balance their utopian ideals and instrumental goals. In this sense, Indymedia provides a laboratory for generating new modes of collaboration, reproducing network norms and forms through concrete technological practice.

Tactical Media

Anti–corporate globalization activists have also expressed their emerging network ideals by experimenting with digital technologies in the tactical media domain. Whereas alternative media facilitate autonomous media production and the development of grassroots counterpublics, tactical media creatively intervene *within* dominant media circuits to confront hegemonic forces directly through projects such as culture jamming, guerrilla communications, and electronic civil disobedience. First theorized and put into practice at a series of "Next 5 Minutes" festivals in the Netherlands during the early 1990s,[13] tactical media thus reproduce horizontal networking logics within mass-media terrains, bringing together new technologies, mobility, and flexibility. As Geert Lovink (2002) suggests, "It is above all mobility that most characterizes the tactical practitioner ... [the ability] to cross borders, connecting and re-wiring a variety of disciplines and always taking full advantage of the free spaces in the media that are continually appearing because of the pace of technological change and regulatory uncertainty" (265).

Tactical media interventions do not necessarily take place in cyberspace, but they almost always make extensive use of the Internet. For example, the Canadian-based Adbusters provides online commentary and multimedia resources to support "culture jamming": the parodying of corporate ads and logos to create and disseminate critical messages through diverse tactics such as billboard pirating, physical and virtual graffiti, and website alterations.[14] With respect to website alterations, anti–corporate globalization movements have specifically used ®™ark software to develop clone websites, such as the "World Trade Organization/GATT Home Page," which features mock stories and quotes from WTO officials.[15] Guerrilla communication involves a related practice using the strategic juxtaposition of incommensurate elements to generate subversive meanings (Grupo Autónomo A.f.r.i.k.a et al. 2000). As with New Kids on the Black Block, such projects employ paradox to shatter our tacitly accepted notions, opening spaces for alternative formulations.[16]

In addition to New Kids, the Barcelona-based Las Agencias has carried out numerous tactical media projects in the context of anti–corporate globalization actions and mobilizations, employing digital technologies to create and distribute posters, flyers, stickers, videos, and Web-based content. Their latest project, "Yomango," combines guerrilla communication, culture jamming, civil disobedience, and corporate sabotage. Mango is a Spanish-owned multinational clothing chain, and "Yo mango" is slang for "I steal." The Las Agencias campaign provides materials and information encouraging people to steal clothing and other items from transnational corporations. Yomango also features public events such as collective shoplifts and banquets with stolen food. During one action, for example, activists shoplifted a dress from the clothing chain Bershka and marched it through the streets of Barcelona, later exhibiting it as an installation in a downtown art museum.[17] Reflecting a horizontal networking logic, Yomango aims to provide concrete "tools and dynamics that flow, proliferate, and are re-appropriated,"[18] to facilitate, as activists ironically point out, "the free circulation of goods!"[19]

Electronic civil disobedience (ECD), or direct action in cyberspace, constitutes a final tactical media domain.[20] Initially conceived by Critical Art Ensemble (CAE) as a way for small groups of highly skilled digital artists, activists, and programmers to intervene politically through the strategic use of the Internet, ECD has since become more popular and mass based.[21] Whereas

28. "The value of resistance is on the rise." Postcard from the Las Agencias "La Borsa o La Vida" (Stock Exchange or Life) guerrilla communications campaign.

CAE insisted that ECD remain underground, Electronic Disturbance Theater (EDT), and its principal theorist Stefan Wray (1998), have promoted a public approach to digital protest. Using FloodNet software, which made it possible for large numbers of Web surfers to participate in electronic actions by simply clicking their browsers, EDT organized the first "virtual sit-ins" in 1998 as part of a series of coordinated actions against the Mexican government's war on the Zapatistas.[22] The "Digital Storm" in August was the largest of these, mobilizing twenty-four thousand virtual protesters around the world (Meikle 2002, 143–44). The "Electrohippies" used similar tactics to flood the WTO website during the Seattle protests in November 1999. Since that time, radical media activists have practiced ECD during mass anti–corporate globalization mobilizations in cities such as Prague (October 2000), Quebec City (April 2001), and New York (January 2002).

Other ECD tactics include bombarding target servers and website servers with e-mails, leaving ironic messages or "electronic graffiti," and "hijacking," or redirecting surfers to mock websites. During the September 2000 protests against the World Economic Forum in Melbourne, for example, the Nike domain name was rerouted to the main protest site (Meikle 2002, 163). Virtual actions rarely succeed in shutting their targets down, but they often generate significant media attention through a process of "micro-to-mass media crossover" (Bennett 2003, 161). Perhaps most importantly, ECD and other tactical media involve ongoing technological experimentation, forming part of an emerging digital activist culture. The tactical media theorists and practitioners Geert Lovink and Florian Schneider (2002) refer to such practices as the "new actonomy": "Equipped with pies and laptops . . . [it] consists of thousands of bigger and smaller activities. For this we do not need a General Plan, a singular portal website, or let alone a Party. . . . Create and disseminate your message with all available logics, tools, and media. The new actonomy involves a rigorous application of networking methods. Its diversity challenges the development of non-hierarchical, decentralized, and deterritorialized applets and applications" (317).

The new actonomy combines horizontal collaboration, new technologies, and a flexible approach to political intervention. Tactical media thus reproduce emerging network norms and forms specifically within a media and technological milieu. Like their alternative media counterparts, tactical media practitioners express their utopian political ideals through concrete technological practice. At the same time, alternative and tactical media have contributed to an emerging digital activist culture around the practice of informational utopics. As we shall see, media hubs and hacklabs provide concrete networked spaces where radical media activists experiment with new digital technologies and collaborative practices.

Temporary Media Hubs and Hacklabs

Beyond providing forums for political protest and debate, anti–corporate globalization mobilizations and gatherings have become key sites for technological practice and innovation. As we have seen, Indymedia Centers are bustling centers of activity where activists create news reports, upload data files, share information, surf the Web, send e-mails, and chat with each other through global communication networks in real time. Activists have also built temporary media hubs and hacklabs featuring digital audio, video, and live streaming, providing critical spaces for experimenting with new technologies and practicing horizontal forms of collaboration. Digital networking projects are thus no longer limited to reporting about, or providing technical support for, other activities; they have become critical events in their own right, particularly during anti–corporate globalization events, including social forums, PGA gatherings, and No Border camps.

As discussed in chapter 6, the No Border camp in Strasbourg was both a space of encounter and an ambitious experiment in collective living and grassroots self-management. Mirroring the inscription of utopian ideals into the park's physical terrain, media activists also projected their political values onto multiple physical and virtual spaces as they experimented with new digital technologies. The alternative media zone, ironically called "Silicon Valley," was among the most innovative and lively spaces in the camp, housing an IMC, Internet cafe, radio tent, Web-based news and radio, and a double-decker tactical media bus from Vienna called Publix Theater Caravan. When Pau and I first visited the media zone, a friend from Indymedia-Berlin, who was using his laptop outside the Internet cafe, explained that he was sending e-mail and surfing the Web, as the entire zone was outfitted with WiFi (wireless) connection. He later took us to the radio tent, which was equipped with a fifty-watt transmitter generating simultaneous webcasts and broadcasts. Throughout the week, grassroots media activists moved back and forth between the media zone and the rest of the camp, and among the different experimental projects within the media space itself.

Among the most interesting of these experimental projects was a series of workshops and discussions called d.sec—database systems to enforce control—which explored the links between freedom of movement and freedom of communication, as well as physical and virtual struggles against increasing mechanisms of control. Specific themes included open source, guerrilla communication, technology and the body, hacktivism, and media activism. More generally, d.sec was conceived as an open space for experimentation with digital networking, self-organization, and horizontal collaboration. The d.sec program flyer explained:

> People move across physical and virtual borders [and] push electronic frontiers through digital and physical communication. . . . Information technology is part of the free-flowing culture of resistance. . . . d.sec is meant to reflect about mechanisms of repression/control . . . over free movement and free communication, the experience of electronic and physical border crossing, an attempt to integrate cyber-activism and taking the streets, and

find the relation between social and technical skills . . . to give momentum to an ongoing exploration of technical potentials in resistance.

D.sec constituted a platform for generating ideas and practices that physically embodied an emerging network ideal. Along with the wider media zone, which featured live Web access, audio and video streaming, and interactive p2p file sharing, activists had created an innovative digitally networked space. To characterize such high-tech terrains, Andalusian activists have developed the term "hackitecture," which refers to new "forms of spatial production that connect social networks, information and communication technology (ICT) networks, and territories."[23] José Pérez de Lama (2004) has similarly written about the "geographies of the [connected] multitude," where media activists experiment with "digital tools that facilitate the appropriation and resignification of space." As they interact with digital technologies, radical media activists are thus creating new political ideals, cultural grammars, and collaborative practices. Moreover, the practice of informational utopics allows them to imagine and experiment with alternative digital-age geographies, fusing the "space of places" and the "space of flows" (Castells 1997).

These digitized autonomous zones were modeled after, and inspired by, the experimental media labs of the late 1990s and the Italian tradition of hackmeetings: self-organized gatherings within squatted social centers where media activists and hackers come together to exchange ideas, resources, and practices while extending virtual connections into the physical domain.[24] Hackmeetings involve social events; workshops related to technology, communication politics, and open source; and informal chill zones; but they principally revolve around the *networked space*, "an area where everyone can bring their computer and wire it to the net to communicate with everyone else, experimenting, playing, and sharing freely."[25] Since the first hackmeeting in Florence in 1998, radical media activists have organized yearly hacktivist gatherings throughout northern and central Italy. Meanwhile, beginning in 2000, annual hackmeetings have also been held in cities around the Spanish state.[26]

Beyond occasional gatherings, Italian and Spanish squatters have also built permanent "hacklabs." Equipped with recycled computers and free software, hacklabs provide open Internet access, spaces for digital experimentation, and public workshops. As Blicero, an Italian activist, explains, "We try to combine the hacker attitude . . . the act of understanding the functioning of complex machines in order to deconstruct them and reconstruct them in a non-conventional manner, with the ambition of analyzing the real."[27] In this sense, "Reality hacking" involves the extension of networking logics to the social realm as a way to deconstruct dominant ideas and practices and reconstruct them as concrete alternatives, creating an affinity between technological and nontechnological spheres. Blicero continues, "If we transpose these characteristics into the 'non technical milieu,' it's easy to identify occupied social centers and self-managed social spaces as clear and obvious attempts at reality hacking."[28]

A parallel argument can be made regarding d.sec or No Border camps more generally, which many digital media activists refer to as "hacking the border." The Kernel Panic lab in Barcelona similarly organizes periodic events called "hacking-in-the-streets," combining music, workshops, and public computer installations.[29] Contrary to the Critical Art Ensemble's (1996) claim that the streets have become dead space, reality hackers are attempting to reclaim public space *and* cyberspace from the logics of market commodification and state control, expressing their utopian values through both physical and virtual practice.

Radicals have also built temporary media labs during regional and world social forums. As we saw in chapter 7, for example, the Eur@ction Hub project at the ESF in Florence in 2002 provided an open space for sharing ideas and experiences, experimenting with new digital technologies, carrying out actions, and organizing in a horizontal and participatory fashion. The Hub housed a temporary computer lab and workshops around themes such as hacking the borders and corporate Europe, digital media activism, and culture jamming. The project combined diverse strands of a digital activist culture within a wider anti–corporate globalization context, bringing together digital and social networking practices and ideals. At the same time, the Hub was viewed as an alternative to the hierarchical practices within the official ESF, even as it reflected the forum's own expressed network ideal through its emphasis on "opening spaces as a political element in itself, and as a catalyst to the multiplication of spaces and relationships among networks and movements."[30] Similar projects would be held at the 2003 WSF in Porto Alegre and the subsequent ESF in Paris that fall. As Ulrich, a German-based media activist, explained, "Hub seems to fit perfectly into the network of networks we are creating. PGA as a network of social movements, Indymedia (and others) as a network of alternative media, hub as a laboratory for media and communication experiments and for social alternatives, and as a base for interventions into its environment (such as the social forum)."[31]

At the same time, radical digital media activists harbor no illusions about the extent to which new technologies represent a terrain of struggle. If they express utopian visions, it is not because they believe the Internet *necessarily* induces a more democratic and egalitarian society (pace Rheingold 1993). Rather, these are values to be fought for and defended, particularly against increasing government surveillance and corporate control. It was in this spirit that radical media activists organized an alternative We Seize! project during the World Summit on the Information Society in Geneva in December 2003, aiming to contrast their own technological practices and ideals with those of the government and civil society elites at the official forum. As the We Seize! call proclaimed, "While the representatives of governments and non-governmental organizations only talk about networking, we are going there to actually practice it. When the leaders of the nation-states negotiate about the digital divide, we are struggling for free and unfettered access. As they shiver with piracy, we are sharing our skills and capacities, resources, and experiences. Though the corporations desperately try to control the flow of material and immaterial goods, we reclaim the world as the invention and creation of the multitudes."[32]

Indeed, during temporary hacklabs and media hubs, radicals are simultaneously putting into practice and struggling to defend their utopian visions based on open access, horizontal collaboration, self-managed coordination, and the free circulation of information. Moreover, such projects are prefigurative, allowing activists to express their emerging political ideals through technological and organizational practice, which points to the growing confluence among network norms and forms as activists increasingly interact with new technologies.

Diffusing Informational Utopics

Informational utopics have largely been restricted to small circles of grassroots media practitioners and more radical anti–corporate globalization activists. The question remains as to whether such innovative networking logics and practices can be incorporated into everyday forms of political, social, and economic life. With precisely that goal in mind, a group of activists formerly associated with MRG went on to build a new grassroots collective called the Infoespai in the Barcelona neighborhood of Gracia. The project was designed to provide concrete digital networking tools for local groups and organizations while promoting a broader "horizontal network culture."[33] As Pau suggested, the Infoespai was intended to go "beyond periodic mobilizations in order to generate more sustainable movements and networks."

The project combines virtual tools, including a Web server, wireless access, and activist database, with physical tools, such as a solidarity economy project; publishing, editing, and research services; and a storefront office housing reception, meeting, and computing spaces. Beyond providing free resources for grassroots movements, Infoespai organizers are working to build economic autonomy by offering services for hire and organizing cooperatives. Their ultimate goal is to create an alternative network of self-managed institutions, and, further, to provide the necessary tools, practices, and resources to help others do the same. With respect to their long-term vision for social change, Pau had this to say: "We are building autonomous counterpower . . . by networking movements . . . and creating our own alternatives without waiting for the government . . . and helping others to achieve them as well."

Radical anti–corporate globalization activists are thus not only resisting neoliberalism; they are challenging representative democracy itself. But what would such an alternative democratic system look like? The European Social Consulta (ESC) represented one ambitious attempt to use digital networking to construct a directly democratic political process at a regional level based on grassroots participation and horizontal collaboration.[34] Developed by activists from MRG and RCADE, as well as PGA-based radicals from around Europe, the project was initially envisioned as a global Internet-based Consulta. However, organizers realized the scale was too broad and decided to focus on the European sphere instead. Moreover, as radicals became more involved in spring 2002, the focus began to shift from a referendum to a more sustained process of critical reflection and debate around issues related to corporate globalization and democracy. As Pilar explained, "I'm excited about the European Social Consulta because it's an ongoing process that allows us to talk about everyday problems and reach local communities. Working from local spaces that are interconnected is better than a central campaign."

In terms of structure, the ESC incorporated a networking logic within its organizational architecture, as one document explained: "The European Social Consulta [is] a network-based organizing system, shaped by the grassroots and operating in a participatory, horizontal, and decentralized manner."[35] At the same time, the ESC was ambiguous—indeed, indeterminacy was built into the process itself—and activists held divergent views about the nature of the project. Some viewed the ESC as a regional referendum around issues to be determined by the local groups involved. For others, it constituted a system for building direct democracy through a Europe-wide network of neighborhood assemblies, which would discuss relevant issues, develop action proposals, and generate agreements via e-mail lists and websites.[36] The most far-reaching visions viewed the project as a directly democratic alternative to the elite-driven process of political convergence within the European Union.

The first step in the ESC process involved an internal consultation (IC) to decide which issues to address and how to address them. To facilitate the IC, activists created a guide, which outlined specific proposals regarding objectives, themes, and methods. Decentralized European promoter groups would then distribute the guide and coordinate the collection of data. Responses would be collated and archived on an interactive website, allowing for further debate and elaboration. The IC was an innovative experiment in collaborative development, as the IC guide explained: "Everything still has to be decided and constructed among everyone. . . . The concept of the ESC means that it has to be a process developed collectively, from beginning to end."[37] For many activists, the European Consulta provided a way to extend their network-based organizing practices outward. As a project flyer explained, "We have to take the way we organize ourselves, our movements, not only as a way to organize protests, but also as a way to organize society, especially in the political realm." This would entail promoting practices designed to generate grassroots "counterpower," including "municipalism, bio-regionalism, consultas and referendums, community neighborhood plans, and neighborhood assemblies."[38]

In the end, the project proved overly ambitious, and the IC failed to elicit the anticipated response. Perhaps it was too abstract, divorced from everyday life in the neighborhoods activists sought to mobilize.[39] On the other hand, the ESC led to the formation of a regional network of promoter groups in cities around Spain, Catalonia, Portugal, Britain, Germany, Sweden, Norway, and the former Yugoslavia, many of which continue to promote participatory democracy at the local level. At the same time, the Consulta model has influenced other anti–corporate globalization projects, including the world and regional social forums. Indeed, as we saw in the last chapter, the forums now regularly use Internet-based Consultas to facilitate collective decision making around thematic proposals for upcoming events. Whether such practices can transform wider social, economic, and political relations remains to be seen. Meanwhile, the ESC's most far-reaching goal—using new digital technologies to build an alternative, directly democratic political system—stands as a testament to the ongoing search for new political norms, organizational forms, and technological practices in an era of rapid social and cultural change.

Conclusion

I have explored in this chapter some of the concrete technological practices through which anti–corporate globalization activists express their emerging utopian ideals. Alternative and tactical media, including Indymedia, culture jamming, guerrilla communication, and electronic civil disobedience, have facilitated the rise of a global network of alternative counterpublics while providing mechanisms for intervening within dominant media terrains. As we have seen, both alternative and tactical media reproduce emerging network norms and forms within their technological architectures. At the same time, radicals are building a digital activist culture as they practice informational utopics within and around mass anti–corporate globalization actions and mobilizations. Media hubs and hacklabs allow activists to experiment with new digital technologies while expressing their commitment to open participation and horizontal collaboration. Finally, more far-reaching initiatives such as the ESC and Infospace in Barcelona suggest that activists are beginning to envision how digital networking might transform social, political, and economic relations more generally.

As I have argued, more radical anti–corporate globalization activists are generating new political visions, cultural grammars, and collaborative practices as they increasingly use new digital technologies, pointing to utopian models for reorganizing social, economic, and political relations. Indeed, as suggested in the book's introduction, many activists specifically view the Free and Open Source Software (FOSS) development process—where programmers collaborate within horizontal networks to create and distribute new versions of software code—as a model for postcapitalist forms of social and economic organization. Such technological paradigms reflect the values associated with the network as an emerging political and cultural ideal: open access, free and open circulation of information, self-management, and decentralized coordination through diversity and difference.

In this sense, theorists associated with the German-based Oekonux project look to open source as the germ of a new directly democratic society.[40] Oekonux (a fusion of "oekonomy" and "Linux") is an e-mail list involving leftist intellectuals, Marxists, programmers, and others committed to exploring how FOSS principles might eventually migrate into wider social domains, leading to postcapitalist forms of economic production and social organization. For his part, project cofounder Stefan Merten believes that FOSS represents "an early form of the new society embedded in the old," which is "no longer based on ... exchange value," but "the individual self-unfolding ... combined with self-organization and global cooperation."[41]

Oekonux focuses on collaborative forms of *economic* production, but the networking logics embedded within open-source principles have also inspired utopian *political* projects, such as the European Consulta. More generally, electronic democracy advocates are interested in how "the technical possibilities of cyberspace make innovative forms of large-scale direct democracy practical," not only through the Internet but also through the "collective and continuous elaboration of problems and their cooperative, concrete resolution by those affected" (Lévy 2001, 176). Although the ESC failed to capture widespread public support, the project represented an innovative proposal for building a directly democratic political system based on the values associated with the network as an emerging political and cultural ideal. As we have seen, such emerging forms of collaborative practice have already transformed how the social forums are organized, and may suggest a model for building collective strategies and proposals in ways that facilitate action while reinforcing more far-reaching, directly democratic ideals.

Projects such as the Infoespai, Oekonux, and the ESC thus reflect the growing confluence among network technologies, organizational forms, and political norms explored throughout this book. At the same time, they are attempting to diffuse network norms, forms, and technologies outward to transform wider social, political, and economic relations. Such radical cultural transformation is a long-term process, however, and is likely to produce few immediate results. Indeed, although particular networking projects may come and go, this should not be taken as their measure of success. As Steve Weber (2004) has pointed out, "What is potentially durable and possibly deserving of the term 'revolutionary' [is] not a particular manifestation of the process, but the process itself" (14). In this sense, the rise of informational utopics suggests the (re)emergence of a postmodern utopianism, not of the traditional sort, involving totalizing visions of a far-off, perfectly harmonious world. Rather, contemporary utopian ideals are increasingly expressed directly, here and now, through concrete political, organizational, and technological practice.

POLITICAL CHANGE
AND CULTURAL
TRANSFORMATION
IN A DIGITAL AGE

We have lost all certainty, but the openness of uncertainty is central to revolution. "Asking we walk," say the Zapatistas. We ask not only because we do not know the way (we do not), but also because asking the way is part of the revolutionary process itself.[1]

I walked through the doors of the Infoespai on October 19, 2004, after spending the previous week at the European Social Forum in London. It had been more than a year and a half since the Movement for Global Resistance (MRG) had self-dissolved. Some former MRG-based activists had teamed up with former colleagues from the campaigns against the World Bank and European Union to create a new unitary space called the Network for Global Mobilization. This new network was primarily designed to mobilize activists around the social forum process, and indeed, I had met up with a group of several hundred Catalans in London. At the same time, many key figures formerly associated with MRG, including Pau, remained skeptical of the social forums, shifting their attention to local projects instead. As we saw in chapter 8, the Infoespai represented one such initiative, squarely situated in the neighborhood of Gracia, yet designed to promote networking technologies and practices within wider social domains.

As I left the bustle of the Plaza de Sol and made my way past the small bookshop toward the computer lab at the back of the building, Pau came out to greet me. It had been some time since we last met, and I was eager to share my experiences from the London forum. However, Pau was more concerned with other matters. "We're working on a new project with the city of Barcelona to provide wireless Internet in Gracia," he explained. "The signal will come from the top of Tibidabo, and we'll be able to provide free access to local cooperatives and collectives!"

"That's great," I replied, "but don't you want to hear about the European Social Forum?"

"The forums can't produce real social transformation," he shot back. "We have to reach out to ordinary people and work in our local neighborhoods. It's more important to build self-sustaining projects."

"But don't you think it's also important to work on multiple levels?" I protested.

"You know, there was a time when no one was talking about globalization. We had to spend our time introducing a global discourse, and making connections with other movements. Counter-summit protests and forums had an important role to play. We did that. Everyone knows about globalization today, but now we have to become more grounded."

As I thought about my conversation with Pau later that afternoon, I realized his insistence on the importance of local organizing reflected a much larger shift within Catalan anti–corporate globalization networks. The cycle of protest that started in Barcelona with the actions against the World Bank and IMF in Prague began to lose steam after the spring 2002 mobilization against the EU. Similar dynamics have occurred elsewhere. Despite occasional forums, gatherings, and protests, mass mobilizations have largely given way to less-visible forms of organizing. As we saw in chapter 4, mass actions and mobilizations generate a great deal of affective solidarity but are difficult to sustain over time. Meanwhile the global "war on terror" has also had a profound impact on movements around the world, largely eclipsing corporate globalization as a principle focus of activist attention. But what have anti–corporate globalization movements accomplished? More generally, how should we think about movement success?

Practicing Dual Politics

I have argued that anti–corporate globalization movements involve an increasing confluence among network technologies, organizational forms, and political norms, mediated by concrete activist practice. Beyond technology and organization, the network has also emerged as a widespread cultural ideal, a model of—and model for—new forms of radical, directly democratic politics. In this sense, previous chapters have examined the rise of horizontal networking logics within decentralized formations such as MRG, RCADE, and PGA. However, as we have seen, networking logics are often challenged by vertical command logics, particularly within "broad convergence" (Routledge 2003) spaces including the "unitary" campaigns in Barcelona or the world and regional social forums. Moreover, given that political values are increasingly inscribed directly into emerging network architectures, ideological debates among competing networks are often coded as conflict over organizational process and form. Indeed, networking politics are constitutive of alternative networks and the relationships among them within broader movement fields.

At the same time, anti–corporate globalization networks are physically embodied during mass actions and gatherings through virtuoso protest performances. Activists have thus used diverse bodily and spatial techniques to generate affective solidarity, make hidden conflicts visible, and challenge dominant meanings. By hijacking the mass-mediated terrains surrounding high-profile summits, anti–corporate globalization activists have challenged the legitimacy of the major symbols of corporate capitalism. Meanwhile, action strategies involving decentralized coordination among autonomous affinity groups reflect a horizontal networking logic on the tactical plane, prefiguring the directly democratic worlds activists are struggling to create. As discussed in chapter 5, however, violence and repression suggest a potential limit to network models with respect to their ability to achieve higher levels of strategic coordination (particularly during times of crisis), a point to which I return later. Moreover, beyond actions and mobilizations, anti–corporate globalization activists continue to express their utopian political imaginaries through ongoing organizational and technological experimentation. In this sense, network norms and forms point to new models for reorganizing social, economic, and political relations.

Anti–corporate globalization activists have thus spent a great deal of time debating and experimenting with new organizational and technological practices. At the same time, they have also carried out spectacular actions, challenging dominant cultural codes regarding globalization, development, and democratic participation. In this sense, anti–corporate globalization activists enact a "dual politics." As Cohen and Arato (1992) suggest, new social movements target both political *and* civil society, constructing self-managed associations, identities, and publics while simultaneously targeting institutional spheres.[2] Wini Breines (1989, 5) makes a similar argument regarding the American "New Left," which sought to build alternative organizational forms reflecting the communal, participatory, and nonhierarchical values of the movement while strategically intervening within the formal political arena. Breines contends that the New Left ultimately failed to synthesize its prefigurative and strategic dimensions, but this was not a necessary outcome: "The effort to build a grassroots movement, a community that foreshadowed the future society, in which manipulation and hierarchy would be absent and participation universal, meant that strong and instrumental organization was weakened. At the same time, the two goals are not irreconcilable: an instrument of social change can be a microcosm of new relationships and a new culture" (144).[3]

To what extent have anti–corporate globalization movements integrated their prefigurative and strategic goals? As I have argued, the rise of flexible, distributed networks powered by new digital technologies has allowed activists to communicate and coordinate at a distance without strong central organization. In this sense, new digital technologies have helped contemporary activists develop organizational forms that more closely reflect their emerging political norms, while overcoming the problem of scale.[4] Although sustainability remains an important concern, the historical tension between directly democratic organization and political effectiveness, while not obsolete, can now be more readily overcome. Indeed, the search for new organizational forms in an area of rapid technological change represents one of the most important contributions of anti–corporate globalization movements. To assess their impact, we thus have to consider two distinct yet mutually reinforcing modes of activist networking: tactical and strategic. The former involves the construction of short-term networks to facilitate interventions within dominant public spheres; the latter entails the creation of autonomous, self-managed networks. Whereas tactical networking aims to achieve political change, strategic networking is oriented toward long-term social transformation.[5]

Tactical Networking

Perhaps the most obvious way to evaluate whether movements succeed is to assess their impact on the state—or within transnational political and financial institutions, as the case may be—that is, whether they generate concrete policy outcomes within institutional domains.[6] The impact of social movements, however, is likely to be mediated, not direct (Tarrow 1998, 174). In other words, political change may be institutionalized, but only after a long-term process of discursive change. In this sense, social movements—both old *and* new—operate on the terrain of culture, generating new ideas, frames, values, and identities. Indeed, as Alberto Melucci (1989) suggests, social movements are "prophetic": they announce the existence of a conflict and render power visible. Although it may be too soon to detect shifts in neoliberal policies and practices, anti–corporate globalization movements have influenced public debates. In this context, tactical networking specifically involves the creation of networks to plan and coordinate mobilizations targeting dominant media spheres.[7] Although a detailed analysis of media framing is beyond the scope of this book, a few observations regarding the media impact of anti–corporate globalization movements can help illuminate their repercussions, particularly in Spain and Catalonia.[8]

As in many parts of the world, the anti-WTO protests in Seattle marked the beginning of a highly visible public debate around globalization, free trade, and democracy within the Spanish and Catalan press. In particular, Seattle pointed to the emergence of a new political actor, even if depicted as confused, chaotic, inchoate, and violent. For example, as the center-left daily *El País* reported, there was "an absurd coalition of young and old, North Americans, French people, and Asians, ecologists, and labor activists, anarchists and nationalists" (December 1, 1999, 69). In some cases, activists were able to communicate a clear message, as the conservative *La Vanguardia* succinctly explained: "Demonstrators are united under the common banner that the WTO favors corporate profit, while damaging human rights and the environment" (December 2, 1999, 96).

The anti–World Bank/IMF protests in Prague sparked an "antiglobalization" boom in Spain and Catalonia, facilitating the expansion of grassroots social movement networks and a significant increase in public dialogue. On the one hand, media accounts began to distinguish between "good" and "bad" protesters, disparaging radical youths while providing more positive coverage of moderate NGOs. As *El País* reported on September 23, 2000, "[World Bank president] Wolfensohn met with 350 moderate NGOs requesting dialogue . . . but radicals are not interested in building bridges and will play revolution in the streets" (73). On the other hand, the World Bank and IMF were depicted as increasingly embattled; as another *El País* story explained, Wolfensohn "did not hide the fact that protests in Washington, D.C., last April and those upcoming in Prague have weakened the institution's spirit" (September 25, 2000, 76).

If Seattle and Prague signaled the emergence of a new, if somewhat ambiguous, global actor, the World Social Forum in Porto Alegre represented its consolidation as a positive force for change. For example, during the 2002 edition of the forum, which was given equal billing to the World Economic Forum in New York City,[9] *El País* characterized WSF participants as "non-governmental organizations, unions, human rights associations, ecologists, farmers, and all kinds of movements struggling for another globalization" (January 31, 2002, 8). Finally, despite repeated attempts to divide moderates and radicals, associating the latter with senseless violence, Spanish and Catalan media increasingly emphasized "peaceful protesters" following the mass demonstration against the EU in Barcelona on March 16, 2002. As a headline in *La Vanguardia* proclaimed: "Huge anti-globalization march, hundreds of thousands march peacefully in Barcelona" (March 17, 2002, 1). An *El País* editorial further explained: "It was said they had no clear ideology, that they are tolerant of or given to violence. . . . After all this, the movement in favor of an alternative globalization . . . broke out of its isolation after September 11, demonstrated its mobilizing potential, and made those who criticize it from ignorance or ideological blinders look ridiculous" (March 17, 2002, 3).

Thus not only have Spanish and Catalan anti–corporate globalization movements elicited favorable press coverage, their arguments have entered mainstream political discourse. On the other hand, the situation in the United States has been far different. Even before September 11, when anti–corporate globalization mobilizations drew significant press coverage, they rarely dominated U.S. headlines. Moreover, most opinion columns, even in the *New York Times*, have staunchly defended globalization. Indeed, as I mentioned in the introduction, Thomas Friedman famously characterized Seattle protesters as a "Noah's ark of flat earth advocates" (December 2, 1999, 51), while his counterpart Paul Krugman argued during the anti-FTAA protests in Quebec City that protesters are "doing their best to make the poor even poorer" (April 22, 2001, sec. 4, p. 17). These comments reflect a media climate in the United

States that has generally been favorable to economic globalization and widely dismissive of alternative views.[10]

To what extent, then, have anti-corporate globalization movements made new conflicts visible? As we have seen, at their peak they have generated a great deal of press coverage, both within Spain and Catalonia and to a lesser extent in the United States. Following mobilizations in Seattle, Prague, Barcelona, Genoa, Porto Alegre, and other cities, institutions such as the WTO, World Bank, IMF, and G8—and globalization processes more generally—have been subject to critical public debate, even when dominant media frames criminalize or marginalize protesters. Despite persistent efforts to divide militants and reformists, an uneasy balance thus obtains during periodic mobilizations between the threat (and periodic outbreak) of violence, which generates intense media interest, and the participation of a majority of nonviolent protesters, who provide legitimacy.[11] At the same time, when institutional actors become involved and moderates emphasize concrete alternatives, press coverage becomes correspondingly more favorable, leading to a self-generating dynamic with respect to participation and movement legitimacy.

In this sense, although they have generated few significant policy changes, anti-corporate globalization movements have introduced new ideas into the public domain. For example, global political and financial elites at the WEF increasingly talk about the need to give globalization a "human face," while debt relief has been thrust onto the agenda of G8 countries. Moreover, the former World Bank chief economist Joseph Stiglitz has publicly supported anti-corporate globalization movement critiques, suggesting in the *New York Times* that "the IMF's prescriptions in times of economic crisis . . . have caused far more human suffering than they have resolved economic problems" (June 9, 2002, sec. 3, p. 6). During the lead-up to the anti–World Bank/IMF protests in Washington, D.C., in April 2000, the Harvard economist Jeffrey Sachs similarly declared his support for protesters, contending that "the tradition that allows the U.S. to create any mission it wants for these institutions is being questioned—and it should be" (*New York Times*, April 9, 2000, sec. 1, p. 6).

Finally, beyond sympathetic intellectuals, leftist political parties have also taken up anti-corporate globalization movement demands, particularly in Europe and Latin America. Although they ultimately failed at the polls, the French Socialists under Lionel Jospin endorsed the Tobin Tax in the context of a wider call for global market regulation. Meanwhile, political parties in Spain, Catalonia, France, Italy, Brazil, Venezuela, and elsewhere have embraced the rhetoric of Porto Alegre and have taken part directly or indirectly in various forum-related activities.[12] Moreover, leftist allies supportive of movement ideas have assumed power in countries such as Brazil and Bolivia, joining a growing challenge to free trade agendas in many parts of the world, particularly in Latin America. Indeed, the Brazilian president Luis Inácio Lula da Silva is a former labor chief and vocal critic of globalization, and the Bolivian president Evo Morales was a longtime leader of the indigenous Cocalero movement, which has been an active participant in PGA. In addition, Manuel Lopes Obrador, the leftist former mayor of Mexico City, nearly won the Mexican presidency running on a solidly anti-neoliberal platform, and in Ecuador, the left-wing economist Rafael Correra was sworn in as president in January 2007.

The situation is less optimistic in the United States, where anti–corporate globalization movements have had a much more limited impact on public discourse and the two-party electoral system, which restricts the influence of alternative ideas. At the same time, there is often a significant disjuncture between the U.S. public and the rest of the world. Indeed, the anti-WTO protests in Seattle produced such a dramatic impact, both inside and outside the United States, not only because U.S. political and economic elites were viewed as major architects of globalization, but also because Americans in general had previously shown little interest in the topic. Moreover, U.S. audiences have had little exposure to the growing discontent with corporate globalization in other regions and are thus often confused by events such as the rise of populist leaders in Latin America. This disjuncture also manifests itself *within* grassroots movements. For example, while anti–corporate globalization activists in Asia, Africa, Europe, and Latin America have largely shifted their focus from mass actions to the social forums, U.S.-based movements have been less involved in the forum process and have thus not been as visible in recent years. However, this may change following the first-ever U.S. Social Forum, which took place in Atlanta in summer 2007.[13] Meanwhile, although the forums have helped integrate antiwar and anti–corporate globalization movements in many parts of the world, these currents remain separate in the United States, at least in terms of public perception.

With respect to their tactical interventions, anti–corporate globalization movements have thus generated widespread visibility while contributing to shifting political terrains, particularly in Europe and Latin America. Indeed, activists have sparked heated public debates around values and ideas that just a few years ago were ignored, tacitly accepted, or widely taken for granted: the supremacy of unfettered markets, unrestricted free trade and foreign investment, production for export over domestic consumption, and other neoliberal tenets. As Philip Stevens admitted in the *Financial Times* following Genoa, "The protesters are winning . . . on the streets. Before too long they will be winning the argument. Globalization is fast becoming a cause without credible champions" (August 17, 2001, 15). For his part, the former World Bank president James Wolfensohn flatly declared, "The Washington Consensus is dead" (*El País*, November 25, 2002, 71).[14] Although such commentaries may be overstated—indeed, the World Bank and IMF continue to impose structural adjustment, while governments have canceled little foreign debt and market reforms continue unabated—neoliberal hegemonies are increasingly contested.

Strategic Networking

At the same time, more radical anti–corporate globalization activists are not only seeking to intervene within dominant public spheres; they are also challenging representative democracy, in part by developing their own directly democratic forms of organizing and decision making. Even as they generate alternative discourses and practices, activists are thus working to build grassroots "counterpower" (Negri 2001) through long-term strategic networking. The anti–corporate globalization networks considered in this book—MRG, PGA, the Barcelona campaigns, and the social forums—thus constitute a shifting web of alternative infrastructures, which not only provide platforms for mounting mobilizations and actions but also reflect new models and ideas for (re)organizing social, economic, and political life around values such as open access, direct democracy, and ecological sustainability.

To some extent, activists have had more success organizing provisional tactical coalitions than longer-term strategic networks. Radically decentralized formations, such as MRG or PGA, have thus mobilized and inspired thousands of activists around common discourses, actions, and identities, yet they have proved relatively unstable. By contrast, although the world and regional social forums involve more hierarchical actors, they have also been more sustainable. However, more radical activists have criticized the forums for reproducing many of the vices—hierarchy, exclusion, and lack of participation—they are struggling to overcome. For their part, radicals have emphasized decentralized, directly democratic organizational forms while, as we saw in chapter 8, they are also experimenting with new modes of horizontal collaboration, using new digital technologies to physically express their emerging utopian ideals. In this sense, technology and organization are much more than instrumental tools. Rather, they constitute political ends in themselves, reflecting the wider egalitarian worlds that activists are struggling to create.

As I have argued, emerging technological and organizational practices reflect a powerful dialectic among technology, norm, and form, mediated by concrete activist practice. Innovative projects such as the Infoespai in Barcelona or the European Social Consulta thus form part of an expanding web of counterinstitutions that are attempting to diffuse network norms, forms, and technologies outward. In many ways, this is a classic anarchist strategy: building a new society "in the shell of the old" by developing prefigurative organizations that can incubate alternative sets of values (Lakey 1973; cf. Epstein 1991, 268).[15] Among radical anti–corporate globalization activists in Barcelona and elsewhere, strategic networking aims precisely to create autonomous networks of globally coordinated yet locally rooted institutions, which can serve as platforms for launching tactical interventions while fostering emerging network ideals.

In this sense, anti–corporate globalization movements should not only be evaluated in terms of their instrumental effects. Instead, as I have argued, contemporary social movements involve a dual politics, constituting tactical infrastructures for intervening within dominant political spheres while simultaneously prefiguring alternative, directly democratic worlds. As Alberto Melucci (1989) has argued, social movements are cultural innovators, challenging dominant cultural codes while simultaneously developing new "models of behavior and social relationships that enter into everyday life" (75). Beyond the production of alternative values, discourses, and identities, however, anti–corporate globalization movements are perhaps best understood as social laboratories, generating new cultural practices and political imaginaries for a digital age.[16]

Theoretical Implications

In addition to the social, cultural, and political impact of contemporary anti–corporate globalization movements, they also have significant implications for anthropological and social theory, particularly with respect to three related themes I have explored throughout this book: globalization, networking, and social movements. First, the movements considered here lend support to a multidimensional and pluridirectional approach to globalization. Although anti–corporate globalization activists are contesting a specific mode of global economic and political integration, their networking practices represent an alternative form of grassroots globalization encompassing social, cultural, and political domains. In this sense, activists are using the tools and mechanisms of global capitalism to challenge a particular globalizing project while turning globalization discourse on its head. At the same time, the novel forms of activism considered in this book reveal the critical role that social actors play in constructing globalization from the ground up. In this sense, globalization is not simply imposed from above; it is generated through a dynamic interaction among multiple practices, flows, and processes at varying scales.

Related to this point, anti–corporate globalization movements largely transcend the local-global divide, as activists follow diverse geographic trajectories. In this sense, regional forums and gatherings point to the rise of alternative grassroots "scale making projects" (Tsing 2005, 57). Meanwhile, studying networks that are locally situated yet globally connected has a critical methodological corollary with respect to ethnographic research. As Arturo Escobar (2001) has suggested, network ethnographies should "relate place-based, yet transnationalized struggles to transnational networks" and "investigate the ways in which . . . actors relate to both places and spaces as they 'travel' back and forth" (163).[16] In this light, as pointed out in the introduction, my own research was multisited, as I followed activists to diverse mobilizations, gatherings, and meetings while observing discussions and debates via electronic networks. At the same time, I also conducted long-term fieldwork within a specific network locale. It was only by remaining situated within a concrete node that I was able to appreciate the complex imbrications of local, regional, and global scales. Studying transnational networking ethnographically thus requires a combination of mobile and place-based research.

Second, throughout this book I have argued for a practice-based approach to the study of networks. Although as observers have noted, anti–corporate globalization movements are indeed decentered and rhizomatic, we need to account for the concrete practices through which such patterns are generated. Guided by an emerging networking logic, activists have woven together intersecting local, regional, and global networks by reaching out across diversity and difference, exchanging information, and communicating and coordinating through both online and face-to-face encounters. However, as we have seen, discursive flows do not merely circulate through transnational networks; they actually constitute them through diverse forms of communicative interaction. Given the increasing interpenetration of network norms, forms, and technologies as activists directly inscribe their political ideals into emerging organizational architectures, it should come as no surprise that much of the network communication explored throughout this book has revolved around network structure and process. In this sense, debates *about* social movement networks largely *constitute* social movement networks themselves.

Finally, the heated internal debates considered in previous chapters suggest the need for a theoretical approach to social movements that takes into account the heterogeneity of movement actors and discourses. Traditional sociological accounts often treat social movements as bounded and undifferentiated. As Kay Warren (1998) points out, "It is not uncommon for scholars of new social movements to treat their goals and organizations as self-evident and, thus, to focus on the formal ideologies and established collectivities that people embrace" (210). This is precisely where contemporary anthropological views of culture and power have the most to offer. As John Burdick (1995) suggests, "Rather than a seamless whole . . . [culture] is best understood as an arena in which multiple, differently empowered actors and groups generate and employ discourses that compete with each other for dominance" (362). In this light, I have specifically examined the relationship between social movement networking and complex micropolitical struggles for power, both within and among alternative movement networks.

As we have seen, networking logics are often challenged by traditional command logics, particularly within broad convergence spaces, such as the campaigns against the World Bank and EU in Barcelona or the social forum process more generally. The rhizomatic structure of contemporary social movement networks is thus generated in practice through evolving patterns of shifting alliances driven by a complex cultural politics of networking at multiple scales. Such politics involve struggles over ideology, strategy, tactics, organizational process, and form as competing networks position themselves vis-à-vis one another within broader movement fields. Although this activity largely takes place within submerged spheres, conflicts are also physically expressed through alternative protest performances during public gatherings and forums. In this sense, the intense networking politics explored throughout this book do not necessarily constitute a weakness. Rather, the high levels of communicative interaction associated with such politics actually point to the relative *strength* of transnational networking processes.

Militant Ethnography Revisited

As pointed out in the introduction, I also hope this book will prove useful for activists. To grasp the concrete logic of activist practice, I have employed a methodological practice I call militant ethnography. Militant ethnography suggests a mode of politically engaged fieldwork carried out together with, rather than apart from, grassroots social movements. In this sense, I have argued that to fully understand activist practice, it is necessary to overcome the divide between researcher and practitioner. In my case, this has meant taking advantage of my dual role as activist and observer, which allowed me to take an active role in networking and protest activities. Moreover, I have also employed an embodied approach to fieldwork, using my body as a research tool to grasp the affective dynamics of mass actions, mobilizations, and gatherings. At the same time, militant ethnography also involves a particular way of relating to movements *after* the moment of research, seeking to contribute to ongoing strategic and tactical debates. This happens on at least three levels: (1) collective reflection and visioning regarding movement practices and emerging cultural models; (2) collective analysis of social processes and power relations that affect strategic and tactical decision making; and (3) collective ethnographic reflection regarding diverse movement networks, how they interact, and how they can more effectively reach out to wider constituencies. I briefly conclude with some reflections about the implications of this study within each of these domains.

First, with respect to emerging cultural practices and models, as I have argued throughout this book, one of the most important contributions of contemporary anti–corporate globalization movements is their development of innovative network norms, forms, and practices. Horizontal networking provides an effective model of political organizing, particularly in a world characterized by increasing global connectedness, transnational communication, and technological innovation. Effectively challenging corporate globalization requires the formation of broad coalitions involving actors from a variety of social, cultural, and political backgrounds. In this context, organizational strategies based on autonomy, diversity, horizontal coordination, and the use of new digital technologies are often more successful than traditional organizations based on top-down structures, singular identities, and ideological conformity. However, the most radically decentralized formations have proved unstable. In this sense, building broad-based movements that are effective *and* sustainable may require a combination of horizontal and more centralized organizational models.

At the same time, decentralized networks are also prefigurative, pointing to a wider model for reorganizing society based on open access, direct democracy, and grassroots participation. Horizontal networking can thus be seen as a wider utopian experiment in building new forms of sociality. Indeed, as Wini Breines points out with respect to the New Left, there is no necessary contradiction between an instrument of social change and a microcosm of new social relations (see also Polletta 2002). The crucial point here is the need for balance. Emphasizing instrumentality at the expense of egalitarian values can undermine the utopian ideals activists are struggling to promote and defend. However, a stubborn insistence on ideological purity can often complicate efforts to accomplish concrete objectives. In this sense, emerging networking logics ultimately imply an open, flexible approach to both organizational and technological practice.[17]

In terms of social processes and power relations that shape strategic and tactical debates, I wish to make two points specifically regarding direct action. First, as we saw in chapter 4, mass actions allow activists to generate affective solidarity while constituting spectacular image events that make struggles visible. At the same time, such actions generate diminishing returns over time. Meanwhile, as Pau's comments at the beginning of this conclusion suggest, many grassroots activists increasingly emphasize the importance of reaching out to local communities and addressing their everyday concerns. Once again, the preceding analysis suggests the need for balance. Although strategic networking is crucial to longer-term social transformation, movement building requires periodic moments of intense physical interaction. Mass direct actions thus continue to provide critical tools for generating visibility and affective solidarity. However, they should be used judiciously and as part of a larger strategic repertoire. Second, regarding specific tactics, violence has long dominated movement debates among anti–corporate globalization activists. As my analysis of the protests in Genoa suggests, violent tactics produce spectacular images but also alienate potential supporters and facilitate repression. At the same time, the diversity-of-tactics ethic, which reflects a horizontal networking logic on the tactical plane, makes it difficult to criticize the tactical choices of others. Consequently, activists will have to find creative ways to critically evaluate protest violence while continuing to respect diversity and difference.

Finally, militant ethnography can also help activists negotiate broader movement fields by analyzing diverse sectors, how they are structured, and how they interact. Anti–corporate globalization movements are extremely complex, involving multiple networks from diverse social, cultural, and political backgrounds. For heuristic purposes, I have identified four movement sectors: institutional reformists, critical sectors, including Marxists and Trotskyists, radical network-based movements, and militant anticapitalists. Organizing within broad convergence spaces, such as the campaigns against the World Bank and EU in Barcelona or the world and regional social forums, requires learning how to work effectively across such political divides. I hope that my ethnographic analysis can facilitate this process by helping activists grasp the competing organizational logics and political visions that characterize alternative movement networks.

Anti–corporate globalization movements have largely entered a submerged phase. Despite occasional actions and mobilizations, world and regional social forums now represent the main vehicles for public expression and interaction among diverse movement networks. At the same time, in a globalized world increasingly dominated by threats of ecological collapse, terrorism, war, and rival fundamentalisms, the need has never been greater for a powerful and broad-based movement in support of peace, democracy, environmental sustainability, and global justice. In this context, as discussed in chapter 7, recent forums have generated increasing calls for a common set of movement goals, agendas, and demands, culminating in the Bamako Appeal, released by a group of high-profile intellectuals before the January 2006 polycentric forum in Mali. Many grassroots activists denounced the appeal as a violation of the WSF Charter of Principles. However, subsequent discussions on forum-related Listervs revealed widespread interest in the document, even among the most ardent supporters of the forum's open-space ideal. Perhaps anti–corporate globalization activists are beginning to see the need for more coordinated planning and decision making. Indeed, one of the most important challenges over the coming years will be to achieve a productive balance: improving long-term strategic coordination while continuing to emphasize more far-reaching utopian goals.

APPENDIX 1.
ELECTRONIC RESOURCES

The websites listed here were accessed on January 26, 2007.

Adbusters	http://www.adbusters.org
ATTAC	http://www.attac.org
Delete the Border Network	http://deletetheborder.org
Euromovements	http://www.euromovements.info
European Social Forum	http://www.fse-esf.org
Fifty Years Is Enough Network	http://www.50years.org
Focus on the Global South	http://www.focusweb.org
Grassroots Global Justice	http://www.ggjalliance.org
The Hacktivist	http://www.thehacktivist.com
Indymedia	http://www.indymedia.org
Infoshop.Org	http://www.infoshop.org
International Forum on Globalization	http://www.ifg.org
Jubilee Debt Campaign	http://www.jubileedebtcampaign.org.uk
Jubilee South	http://www.jubileesouth.org
Jubilee USA Network	http://www.jubileeusa.org
Mobilized Investigation	http://manifestor.org/mi/en
No Border Network	http://www.noborder.org
Open Space Forum	http://www.openspaceforum.net
People's Global Action	http://www.agp.org
Sociologists without Borders	http://www.sociologistswithoutborders.org
Third World Network	http://www.twnside.org.sg
United for Peace and Justice	http://www.unitedforpeace.org
United States Social Forum	http://www.ussf2007.org
Via Campesina	http://viacampesina.org
World March of Women	http://www.marchemondiale.org
World Social Forum	http://www.forumsocialmundial.org.br
Yo Mango	http://www.yomango.net
Zapatista Sixth International	http://www.zeztainternazional.org

APPENDIX 2.
PINK AND SILVER CALL,
GENOA, JULY 20, 2001

The following text is reproduced from the archive of global protests at http://www.nadir
.org/nadir/initiativ/agp/free/genova/leaflet.htm (accessed January 26, 2007).

Dance Down the G8!!

Pink Silver March—Tactical Frivolity

We are a colorful party in the street, a carnival with theatre, pink fairies and radical
cheerleaders, clowns and music, a creative, magical and confrontational dance that takes
decisions in a horizontal manner through affinity groups. We want to reduce aggressive-
ness to the minimum with imagination, samba, art, playing with space (and with the
police), to create a relaxed atmosphere with good vibes. While we dance we denounce
the brutality of capitalism, patriarchy, racism and all the forms of oppression and domination, denying any legitimacy to those 8 men who meet as if the world belonged to
them and they could exploit and destroy at their will.

We want to enter the red zone, if possible get to the palace where the summit takes
place and stop it with our dances, but we don't want to initiate any kind of violence
against the police. Among us there are people who will not respond to police violence, no
matter how brutal it is, but there are also people who are not willing to take high levels of
aggression without offering resistance. We respect all these options and will try to create
spaces for all of them to express themselves without interfering with each other. But
we clearly do NOT want heroes, machos or martyrs: we want to act in a collective and
consensus-based manner at all times, especially while we are all together, so we ask people who want to have total autonomy in their actions and reactions to look for other
groups which are closer to their vision of total autonomy. We also don't want anyone to
bring into the pink silver any logos or organizational labels in order to avoid having the
feeling that we are being instrumentalized for aims that are not shared by everyone.

On the 20th we will meet at 9:00 in the convergence centre (Martin Luther King
square) to make the last preparations and give IMPORTANT INFORMATION (legal, medical, communications, etc.). We will leave all together at 10:30 (NOT LATER) towards the
Manin square, where we will meet women's groups and pacifist affinity groups. What
happens after that moment will depend on all of us, we will take decisions on the day

through affinity groups, and we might split in different groups after reaching the Manin square. While we are with pacifist groups, it is very important that everybody respects their forms of action and reaction towards police provocations.

Our strategy: Tactical Frivolity

Our identification: Pink Silver

Our meeting point: 9:00 at Convergence centre (Martin Luther King Sq.)

Bring with you: An affinity group (if possible), pink and silver stuff, things to make noise, water and food, a good map, protective things if you want, and a good and vibrant party mood!!

APPENDIX 3.
PEOPLES' GLOBAL ACTION ORGANISATIONAL PRINCIPLES

The following text is reproduced from http://www.nadir.org/nadir/initiativ/agp/cocha/principles.htm (accessed January 26, 2007).

1. The PGA is an instrument for co-ordination, not an organisation. Its main objectives are:

    i. Inspiring the greatest possible number of persons and organisations to act against corporate domination through civil disobedience and people-oriented constructive actions.

    ii. Offering an instrument for co-ordination and mutual support at global level for those resisting corporate rule and the capitalist development paradigm.

    iii. Giving more international projection to the struggles against economic liberalisation and global capitalism, as well as to the struggles of indigenous people and original cultures.

2. The organisational philosophy of the PGA is based on decentralisation and autonomy. Hence, central structures are minimal. Following the same idea, each region's participating organisations and movements will decide how to organise locally. Nevertheless, there needs to be a point of contact and coordination for each of these regions, decided at regional level and known to all the participating organisations and movements of the network.

3. The PGA has no membership.

4. The PGA does not have and will not have a juridical personality. It will not be legalised or registered in any country. No organisation or person represents the PGA, nor does the PGA represent any organisation or person.

5. There will be conferences of the PGA when judged necessary by the participating organisations and movements. The functions of these conferences will be:

    i. Updating the manifesto (if necessary).

    ii. Advancing in the process of coordination at global level of the resistance against "free" trade.

    iii. Coordinating decentralised actions according to the global days of action and the sustained campaigns of the PGA.

There will be an equal participation of women and men in the international and regional conferences. The gender issue will be discussed at all of the PGA conferences, both at the international and regional levels.

6. The conferences of the PGA will be convened by a committee conformed by representative organisations and movements of each region, including the points of contact named for each of these regions. The composition of this committee must show a regional balance, and a balance regarding the areas of work of the organisations and movements that conform to it. The local organisers will be part of the committee.

This committee will fulfill the following tasks:

i. Coordinating the program of the conference according to the proposals for themes, actions and issues emerging from the regional conferences.

ii. Coordinating the selection of the delegates, in respect with the principle of decentralisation and autonomy of each region as well as in accordance with the decisions taken on this matter at the regional conferences.

iii. Deciding about the use of resources; especially, deciding which organisations will receive help to pay the travel expenses to attend the conference.

iv. Advising the local organisers in technical and organisational questions.

v. Interpreting the manifesto if this would be necessary (the whole part on publications and info to be taken out).

The committee, just like any other participating organisation or movement, cannot speak in the name of the PGA.

Each conference of the PGA will be coordinated by a committee conformed of different organisations and movements. Also, the points of contact named for each region will change in each regional conference (used to be in each international conference but it is now a problem to leave it like that if we're going to have international conferences only when judged necessary . . .). The old committee will choose a small group that will act as advisers of the new committee. It will also provide technical support at the regional level. This advisory group will not have decision-making power.

7. In keeping with PGA's philosophy, all communication processes will be diverse, decentralised and coordinated. There will be at least one point of contact in each region to be decided at regional level.

Whilst recognising there are limits to the Internet, the PGA website will comprise of PGA documents including conference notes and contact lists. All documents will be translated into as many diverse languages as possible. For all this communication to work effectively, responsibility must be taken at the regional level by as many groups as possible.

8. The PGA will not have any resources. The funds needed to pay the conferences and the information tools will have to be raised in a decentralised way. All the funds raised for the conference will be administered by the committee. The publications will have to be self-financed.

9. The PGA has a rotational secretariat, which changes every year. Each committee, during its term, will decide where the secretariats will be.

10. The conferences of the PGA will not include the discussion of these organisational principles in the programme. If there is a concrete request, a discussion group on organisational questions will be formed. This discussion group will meet parallel to the programme of the conference, to elaborate concrete modification proposals which shall be voted upon in the plenary.

The PGA hopes that it will inspire the creation of different platforms (both regional and issue-based) against "free" trade and the different institutions that promote it. There will not be, however, a relationship of pertinence between these platforms and the PGA. The platforms will hence be completely autonomous.

The PGA also aims to initiate discussions at the regional level through various means, emphasizing on the organisation of caravans, as well as the exchange of people, products and experiences between regions. The results of these debates will then be shared at the global level with the whole network.

APPENDIX 4.
WORLD SOCIAL FORUM
CHARTER OF PRINCIPLES

The following text is reproduced from the World Social Forum website, http://www
.forumsocialmundial.org.br/ (accessed January 26, 2007).

The committee of Brazilian organizations that conceived of, and organized, the first
World Social Forum, held in Porto Alegre from January 25th to 30th, 2001, after evaluating the results of that Forum and the expectations it raised, consider it necessary
and legitimate to draw up a Charter of Principles to guide the continued pursuit of that
initiative. While the principles contained in this Charter—to be respected by all those
who wish to take part in the process and to organize new editions of the World Social
Forum—are a consolidation of the decisions that presided over the holding of the Porto
Alegre Forum and ensured its success, they extend the reach of those decisions and define orientations that flow from their logic.

1. The World Social Forum is an open meeting place for reflective thinking, democratic debate of ideas, formulation of proposals, free exchange of experiences and
   interlinking for effective action, by groups and movements of civil society that are
   opposed to neoliberalism and to domination of the world by capital and any form
   of imperialism, and are committed to building a planetary society directed towards
   fruitful relationships among Humankind and between it and the Earth.

2. The World Social Forum at Porto Alegre was an event localized in time and place.
   From now on, in the certainty proclaimed at Porto Alegre that "another world is possible," it becomes a permanent process of seeking and building alternatives, which
   cannot be reduced to the events supporting it.

3. The World Social Forum is a world process. All the meetings that are held as part of
   this process have an international dimension.

4. The alternatives proposed at the World Social Forum stand in opposition to a process of globalization commanded by the large multinational corporations and by
   the governments and international institutions at the service of those corporations'
   interests, with the complicity of national governments. They are designed to ensure
   that globalization in solidarity will prevail as a new stage in world history. This will
   respect universal human rights and those of all citizens—men and women—of all

nations and the environment and will rest on democratic international systems and institutions at the service of social justice, equality and the sovereignty of peoples.

5. The World Social Forum brings together and interlinks only organizations and movements of civil society from all the countries in the world, but it does not intend to be a body representing world civil society.

6. The meetings of the World Social Forum do not deliberate on behalf of the World Social Forum as a body. No-one, therefore, will be authorized, on behalf of any of the editions of the Forum, to express positions claiming to be those of all its participants. The participants in the Forum shall not be called on to take decisions as a body, whether by vote or acclamation, on declarations or proposals for action that would commit all, or the majority, of them and that propose to be taken as establishing positions of the Forum as a body. It thus does not constitute a locus of power to be disputed by the participants in its meetings, nor does it intend to constitute the only option for interrelation and action by the organizations and movements that participate in it.

7. Nonetheless, organizations or groups of organizations that participate in the Forum's meetings must be assured the right, during such meetings, to deliberate on declarations or actions they may decide on, whether singly or in coordination with other participants. The World Social Forum undertakes to circulate such decisions widely by the means at its disposal, without directing, hierarchizing, censuring or restricting them, but as deliberations of the organizations or groups of organizations that made the decisions.

8. The World Social Forum is a plural, diversified, non-confessional, non-governmental and non-party context that, in a decentralized fashion, interrelates organizations and movements engaged in concrete action at levels from the local to the international to build another world.

9. The World Social Forum will always be a forum open to pluralism and to the diversity of activities and ways of engaging of the organizations and movements that decide to participate in it, as well as the diversity of genders, ethnicities, cultures, generations and physical capacities, providing they abide by this Charter of Principles. Neither party representations nor military organizations shall participate in the Forum. Government leaders and members of legislatures who accept the commitments of this Charter may be invited to participate in a personal capacity.

10. The World Social Forum is opposed to all totalitarian and reductionist views of economy, development and history and to the use of violence as a means of social control by the State. It upholds respect for Human Rights, the practices of real democracy, participatory democracy, peaceful relations, in equality and solidarity, among people, ethnicities, genders and peoples, and condemns all forms of domination and all subjection of one person by another.

11. As a forum for debate, the World Social Forum is a movement of ideas that prompts reflection, and the transparent circulation of the results of that reflection, on the

mechanisms and instruments of domination by capital, on means and actions to resist and overcome that domination, and on the alternatives proposed to solve the problems of exclusion and social inequality that the process of capitalist globalization with its racist, sexist and environmentally destructive dimensions is creating internationally and within countries.

12. As a framework for the exchange of experiences, the World Social Forum encourages understanding and mutual recognition among its participant organizations and movements, and places special value on the exchange among them, particularly on all that society is building to centre economic activity and political action on meeting the needs of people and respecting nature, in the present and for future generations.

13. As a context for interrelations, the World Social Forum seeks to strengthen and create new national and international links among organizations and movements of society, that—in both public and private life—will increase the capacity for non-violent social resistance to the process of dehumanization the world is undergoing and to the violence used by the State, and reinforce the humanizing measures being taken by the action of these movements and organizations.

14. The World Social Forum is a process that encourages its participant organizations and movements to situate their actions, from the local level to the national level and seeking active participation in international contexts, as issues of planetary citizenship, and to introduce onto the global agenda the change-inducing practices that they are experimenting in building a new world in solidarity.

NOTES

Introduction

1. Bruno Latour (1993, 116).
2. Squatted social centers are abandoned buildings that have been squatted, or occupied, by young activists and converted into spaces for social movement activities and community events. These "squats" sometimes also provide free housing for activists and represent a challenge to speculation in real estate. As communal spaces they are entirely self-managed.
3. Marc Edelman (1999, 36) describes a similar experience involving the "death" of the peasant organization he was studying after sending them his completed manuscript about a 1988 peasant strike. MRG-Catalonia actually proved relatively sustainable, coordinating activities, meetings, and actions from shortly before the Prague mobilization through January 2003, when activists finally "self-dissolved" the network as a response to declining participation and as a political statement against the reproduction of rigid structures.
4. This and similar dialogues throughout the text were recorded in my field notes. Unless otherwise indicated, subsequent individual quotations are cited from personal interviews. The kind of fluid, shifting mode of participation reflected in my exchange with Laurent suggests that the networking logics and practices explored in this book may reflect an intensification of the "personalized" (Lichterman 1996) or "individualized" (Furlong and Cartmel 1997) patterns of commitment and belonging observers have identified among younger, middle-class activists in the West (see chapter 2; see also Pleyers 2005a). Regarding multiple belongings and "tolerant" identities among Italian anti–corporate globalization activists, see della Porta (2005).
5. Although the corporate media helped diffuse the "antiglobalization" label after Seattle, the term had already been in use for several years. As far as I can tell, the term "antiglobalization" first appeared in a 1996 article of the same title by Doug Henwood in the *Left Business Review*.
6. For example, see Klein 2002; Graeber 2002; and Starhawk 2002.
7. See Friedman's op-ed "Senseless in Seattle," *New York Times*, December 1, 1999.
8. Regarding the multidimensional aspects of globalization, see Appadurai 1996 and Held et al. 1999. For more on changing perceptions of time and space with regard to globalization, see Giddens 1990 and Harvey 1989.

9. This discussion of economic globalization is derived from the following sources: Castells 1996; Dicken 2003; Comaroff and Comaroff 2000; Nash 2001; and Trouillot 2003.

10. Regarding the significance of space, place, and locality in the context of globalization, see Appadurai 1996; Prazniak and Dirlik 2001; Escobar 2001; and Gupta and Ferguson 1997.

11. For an analysis of globalization as discourse, see Kalb 2000, 4.

12. Stiglitz 2002, 5.

13. Brecher, Costello, and Smith 2000, 6.

14. *New York Times*, February 24, 2004, C5.

15. Brecher, Costello, and Smith 2000, 8.

16. For more on prefigurative politics, see Epstein 1991; Graeber 2002; and Polletta 2002.

17. In her study of participatory democracy within U.S. movements, Francesca Polletta (2002) similarly argues that participatory forms of organization can be both expressive and strategic, emphasizing their solidary, innovatory, and developmental benefits (see also Lichterman 1996). Whereas Polletta tends to focus on leadership and decision making, this book is more concerned with the relationship between new technologies and emerging forms of organization and with the way broader political values are inscribed directly into organizational structures themselves.

18. Regarding protest cycles, see Tarrow 1998.

19. Quoted in Guérin 1970, 43.

20. Networks have (re)emerged over the past few years as an important topic of study in anthropology, sociology, and related fields. Whereas recent theories have tended to obscure human action, an older tradition of network analysis primarily emphasized rational actors (cf. Barnes 1954; Boissevain 1974; Bott 1971; Kapferer 1973). However, at least one early theorist, J. Clyde Mitchell (1974), pointed to the importance of communication flows within networks, including information, ideas, and rumors. With respect to activism, Mario Diani (1995, 8) has more recently suggested that social movement networks provide arenas for the circulation of cultural codes, including identities and political discourses. Keck and Sikkink (1998) make a similar point specifically with respect to "transnational advocacy networks."

21. I adapt this term from Jameson (1991), who refers to postmodernism as "the cultural logic of late capitalism," and Ong (1999), who explores a specific type of late capitalist cultural logic—transnationality (cf. Juris 2004a). Like Pierre Bourdieu's *habitus*, cultural logic implies a set of internalized dispositions, shaped by social, economic, and political conditions, which generate concrete practices. Unlike habitus, however, they are not so deeply embedded and can thus be contested and transformed.

22. Andrew Barry has criticized the network metaphor, suggesting that it "may convey an illusory sense of rigidity, order and of structure; and it may give little sense of unevenness of the fabric and the fissures, fractures and gaps that it contains and forms" (2001, 15). However, by shifting the emphasis from network structure to practice, involving myriad microlevel struggles, this book specifically elucidates the fluid, uneven, and contradic-

tory nature of network formations. Kevin McDonald (2006) has criticized the concept of the "network" as implying a disembodied form of relationality. In contrast, my approach explores the discursive *and* embodied dimensions of networking practice.

23. For analyses of transnational social movements from traditional social movement theory perspectives, see Smith, Chatfield, and Pagnucco 1997; Smith and Johnston 2002; Bandy and Smith 2005; della Porta and Tarrow 2005; and Tarrow 2005. For more on the transnational dimension of social movements, see chapter 6.

24. As Anne Mische (2003) has argued, networks are not merely conduits for cultural forms; rather, "we should look at how both of these are generated in social practices, that is, by the dynamics of communicative interaction" (262).

25. Rabinow's analysis of competing norms in the development of modern architectural and urban forms in France and its Moroccan colonial satellite builds, in part, on Canguilem's 1989 study of the role of the normal and the normative in the definition of health and disease.

26. Regarding Internet use and everyday life, see Miller and Slater 2000; Wellman 2001; and Wellman and Haythornthwaite 2002.

27. On the Internet and free trade campaigns, see Ayres 1999 and Smith and Smythe 2001.

28. In their survey of participants at the European Social Forum in Florence in November 2002, for example, della Porta et al. (2006) found that online and offline activism are strongly related. My own ethnographic work among Barcelona-based activists further supports this contention.

29. See www.agp.org and www.forumsocialmundial.org.br (accessed January 26, 2007). For analyses of anti–corporate globalization–related websites, see della Porta et al. 2006, 96–7; and Van Aelst and Walgrave 2002.

30. See www.indymedia.org (accessed January 26, 2007).

31. For example, see Cohen 1985 and Offe 1985.

32. Diverse network patterns include the "wheel," which involves all direct linkages emanating from a central ego; the "circle," encompassing linkages that connect actors to each other without passing through a central node; and the "all-channel" network, where every node is connected to every other (Kapferer 1973).

33. Diane Nelson (1999) specifically employs the term "Maya-Hacker" to characterize Mayan activists engaged in cultural activism and transnational networking.

34. Here I follow recent trends in the anthropology of social movements, including Alvarez, Dagnino, and Escobar 1998; Burdick 1998; Edelman 1999; Starn 1999; and Warren 1998. Melucci (1989) has long maintained that social movements are not unified characters moving along a historical stage. Rather, the construction of movement identities is precisely what needs to be explained.

35. This brand of left-wing "libertarianism" should be distinguished from the variety prevalent in the United States. Libertarianism in Barcelona, and in much of Europe and Latin America, involve a radical critique of both the market *and* the state, while the U.S. variety is oriented toward limiting the role of the state to unleash the potential of the free market.

36. Initially developed in the field of experimental biology, complexity theory posits the recursive nature of living systems organized as self-generating networks (see Varela, Maturana, and Uribe 1974). In this view, living systems are produced through the complex interactions among their constituent parts (Maturana 1981, 21). Luhmann (1990) later elaborated a theory of autopoietic *social* systems, which are forged through the recursive flow of communication. By importing a neofunctionalist paradigm from biology to the social realm, however, Luhmann obscures human interaction, while portraying autopoietic systems as closed and self-referential. A similar dynamic occurs when complexity theory is applied to social movements without considering concrete activist practice. For an analysis of anti–corporate globalization movements through the lens of complexity theory, but from a more open and processual Deleuzian perspective, see Chesters and Welsh 2006.

37. The main difference here involves the level of analytic abstraction. Whereas complexity theory assumes a distant view, a practice-based approach delves into the complex interactions, revealing underlying struggles, tensions, and micropolitical dynamics that generate the resulting patterns. Other recent network approaches in anthropology obscure human action even more profoundly. For example, Annelise Riles (2000) provides a rich analysis of the formal properties of matrix and network designs in the documents crafted by Fijian NGO workers, but neglects the practices through which social and organizational networks are generated. Whereas early network analysts privileged rational actors, Riles subsumes agency within the specificities of form. Actor-network theory provides another model, exploring the production of scientific "facts" through translation, alliance building, and the alignment of interests within sociotechnical networks. Such processes link scattered resources into singular "black boxes" that can be unpacked to reveal the histories and controversies through which scientific knowledge is generated. Here networks are conceived as actors in their own right, involving complex chains of people, machines, and other nonhuman elements (cf. Latour 1987, 1993; see also Callon 1991). Actor-network theorists thus attempt to move beyond modernist paradigms, employing networks to draw connections and commonalities without making totalizing claims (Riles 2000, 64). Perhaps for this reason, the links between networks, practice, and broader social, economic, and political contexts remain unexamined.

38. Steve Weber (2004) has suggested a narrow definition of open source, which he restricts to processes that specifically entail a new conception of property as the right to distribute, not the right to exclude. However, many activists view open source as a broader metaphor, inspiring emerging postcapitalist imaginaries (see Lovink 2003, 195).

39. Regarding networks of capital, state, and terror, see Arquilla and Ronfeldt 2001; Castells 1996; and Hardt and Negri 2000.

40. Anti–corporate globalization activists thus appropriate the logics and practices employed by capital and the state, but subvert them for other ends, while infusing them with alternative values. Torin Monahan (2005) similarly posits a theory of "structural

flexibility" to characterize how people might employ the logic of flexibility demanded by late capitalism in empowering ways.

41. For more on "grounding globalization" through ethnographic practice, see Conway 2006, 13–15; and Thayer 2001.

42. Sidney Tarrow (2005) refers to the upward or downward spread of contentious action across geographic scales as "scale shift." Here I am more concerned with the processual, uneven, and contested patterns of communication and coordination among actors at multiple scales, which Paul Routledge (2003) refers to as "multi-scalar" politics (see also Escobar 2001 and Tsing 2005).

43. For an analysis of discourses surrounding privilege and antiracism within North American anti–corporate globalization movements, see Starr 2004.

44. By working with those who are in many ways my social counterparts in Barcelona, I decided to study not "up" or "down" (see Nader 1972) but rather "horizontally," in networking parlance.

45. For a related argument in the context of ethnographic research among community-based organizations in Chile, see Paley 2001, 18.

46. Nancy Scheper-Hughes (1995) similarly refers to ethically grounded and politically committed ethnographic research as "militant anthropology." However, her emphasis on witnessing differs from the kind of proactive solidarity outlined here. I thus refer to ethnographic research that is politically engaged *and* collaborative in nature as "militant *ethnography*," recognizing the influence of Scheper-Hughes while distinguishing my approach from her somewhat different conception. The emphasis on ethnography also moves it beyond the exclusive realm of anthropology.

47. As Loïc Wacquant (2004) puts it, this kind of research requires not only a "sociology *of* the body . . . but also a sociology *from* the body" (viii). For more on the body as a research tool, see Parr 2001.

48. As Conway (2006, 21) suggests, knowledge production—a process of ongoing communication and interpretation—is a critical aspect of contemporary social movement practice.

49. Charles Hale (2006) has outlined a similar practice, which he also calls "activist research" (see also Speed 2006). This involves a method similar to participatory action research (cf. Greenwood and Levin 1998), where the anthropologist establishes a clear political alignment with an organized group in struggle and allows dialogue with them to shape each phase of the research process. Although politically engaged and action oriented, Hale's conception still relies on the kind of clear distinction between researcher and object that militant ethnography seeks to overcome.

1. The Seattle Effect

1. Zapatista Declaration from the 1996 Intergalactic Gathering in Chiapas against Neoliberalism and for Humanity, cited in Halleck 2002.

2. The sea turtles represented the way WTO policies undermine government regulations protecting sea turtle populations. They also came to be seen as a symbol of the radical environmental movement.

3. For an analysis of the transnational organizations, linkages, and mobilizing structures behind the anti-WTO protests in Seattle, see Smith 2002.

4. In addition to the anti-WTO protests in Seattle, activists organized solidarity actions across the world, in cities such as Atlanta, Austin, Philadelphia, Toronto, London, Lisbon, Paris, Geneva, Amsterdam, Berlin, Milan, Prague, Turkey, Tel Aviv, Muzafer Ghar (Pakistan), Bangalore, Seoul, Manila, and Melbourne.

5. DAN was specifically organized on the basis of PGA organizing principles. See http://www.nadir.org/nadir/initiativ/agp/cocha/principles.htm (accessed January 26, 2007). Information regarding the history of the Direct Action Network was gathered from a personal conversation with a key activist on October 21, 2002.

6. For more on this organizing model, see Graeber 2002; and Hardt and Negri 2004, 288.

7. Activists founded Jubilee 2000 in England in 1997, inspired by the biblical tradition that marks every fiftieth year as a jubilee year, when all slaves are set free and debts canceled. After 2000, the network was reconstituted under a variety of names in different countries.

8. See http://www.ffq.qc.ca/marche2000/en/bref.html (accessed January 26, 2007).

9. Bové became famous in 1999 after attacking a McDonalds in Millau in southwestern France as a protest against U.S.-imposed trade barriers on Roquefort cheese (Bové and Dufour 2001, ix).

10. See http://www.indymedia.org (accessed January 26, 2007) for a listing of Independent Media Centers around the world.

11. For additional historical overviews of anti–corporate globalization movements, see Notes from Nowhere 2003; and Starr 2005, 19–42.

12. For examples of indigenous and peasant struggles against corporate globalization, see Notes from Nowhere 2003.

13. Regarding movements against mining and oil drilling, see Gedicks 2001. For an analysis of struggles against World Bank projects in the Brazilian Amazon, see Moog Rodrigues 2004.

14. "Gathering Food" 2001, 456–61.

15. The MAI would have limited the ability of governments to regulate transnational corporations for the purpose of environmental, consumer, and labor protection. Regarding activist use of the Internet to defeat the MAI, see Ayres 1999; Cleaver 1999; and Smith and Smythe 2001.

16. Art and Revolution was itself inspired by projects such as Bread and Puppet Theater, which has a long history of working with giant puppets and guerrilla theater. These tactics were widely used in the United States during the mobilization against the first Gulf War in 1991.

17. At the third RTS street party in 1996, nearly ten thousand protesters occupied a roadway in west London for several hours; the following April, twenty thousand people took to the streets in support of London dockworkers (Jordan 1998, 145–46; Wall 1999, 87). Previous groups had organized under the banner of Reclaim the Streets during the 1970s and then again in 1992.

18. The theory of Autonomia, which emerged among factory workers in northern Italy, held that class struggle could become autonomous from capital and that workers should organize outside formal organizations such as trade unions and political parties (Katsiaficas 1997, 7).

19. Ya Basta! was founded in 1996 by Zapatista solidarity activists who had recently returned from the first Intergalactic Zapatista Encounter in Chiapas. The group later became the second PGA convener in Europe.

20. After Prague, activists began using White Overall tactics during anti–corporate globalization actions and more localized protests in diverse cities around the world, including London, New York, Madrid, Barcelona, and São Paulo.

21. German autonomen mobilized thousands of militant activists from Germany, Italy, Holland, Denmark, and the United States during the September 1988 protests against the World Bank and IMF in Berlin, where they met severe police repression (Katsiaficas 2001, 69).

22. For more on Zapatista support networks, see Khasnabish 2005 and Olesen 2005.

23. See Olesen 2005 for an analysis of transnational framing within Zapatista support networks.

24. Subsequent global meetings were held in Bangalore, India, in 1999, and Cochabamba, Bolivia, in 2001 (cf. Routledge 2003; L. Wood 2004). PGA's original name was Peoples' Global Action against Free Trade and the WTO. The latter part of the name was dropped a year later, reflecting a broader focus on corporate globalization.

25. See also http://www.nadir.org/nadir/initiativ/agp/en/pgainfos/index.htm (accessed January 26, 2007).

26. John Jordan, "The Sound and the Fury: The Invisible Icons of Anti-Capitalism," an early draft of the article published subsequently as Jordan 2004.

27. "Edition" here refers to the forum as an event and should not be confused with its more common usage to refer to editions of books and other publications.

28. The No Border Network was founded by antiracist and immigrant rights activists in 1998 to challenge the emerging border regime of "Fortress Europe." No Border camps, temporary self-managed zones organized in cities near major international boundaries, have been organized in Europe and along the U.S.-Mexico border. Such camps provide spaces for debates, workshops, and direct actions.

29. The Nairobi forum attracted fewer participants than anticipated (50,000), but many organizers considered holding the forum in sub-Saharan Africa a success in and of itself. It should be noted that, given the forum's capacity for continual learning and self-reform (see Santos 2006), plans for and visions of the WSF are constantly changing.

30. These movements are generally anticapitalist but may include reformists who organize according to directly democratic principles.

31. See Starr and Adams 2004 for a similar breakdown of anti–corporate globalization sectors. Such frameworks are useful for heuristic purposes, but they tend to portray a static picture of a fluid, evolving movement field and often miss subtle distinctions.

2. Anti–Corporate Globalization in Barcelona

1. Mar, from the Barcelona 2001 campaign against the World Bank. As stated in the introduction, all individual quotations are cited from personal interviews unless otherwise specified.

2. For more on the importance of friendship in Spain and Southern Europe generally, see Brandes 1973 and Gilmore 1980. Regarding the role of informal social networks, such as friendship and family, within Spanish civil society, see Pérez Díaz 2002. For a critical view of the dynamics of friendship within informal social movement collectives, see Polletta 2002.

3. Many Spanish and Catalan organizations from the traditional Left had previously taken part in the December 2000 mobilization against the European Union in Nice.

4. The brief history of Spanish and Catalan movements that follows roughly coincides with Alvarez-Junco's 1994 classificatory scheme, which divides collective action in modern Spain into three periods: the classic stage from the late nineteenth century until the end of the civil war, a modern stage of opposition during the Franco regime and the transition to democracy, and a postmodern stage beginning after the consolidation of democracy.

5. Alvarez-Junco (1977) identifies two forms of anarchism based on distinct ways of conceiving liberty: individualist and communitarian. Whereas Spanish anarchists before the civil war were communitarian, working-class, and morally austere, the resurgence of anarchism during the 1960s and 1970s corresponded to the individualist type and was prevalent among young middle-class rebels reacting against traditional forms of authority. However, more recent anarchist-inspired movements may be moving back toward a communitarian model. Squatters and antimilitarists, for example, while not morally ascetic, emphasize self-management, communal autonomy, and collective decision making. These values have diffused more widely among radical anti–corporate globalization sectors. For more on Spanish and Catalan anarchism, see Bookchin 1998; Brenan 1943; Esenwein and Shubert 1995; and Kaplan 1977.

6. In Barcelona, students helped launch a mass movement against Franco during the Capuchin affair, when police attacked five hundred student delegates, professors, and intellectuals gathered in the Capuchin convent in March 1966 to found the Democratic Student Union of the University of Barcelona (Conversi 1997, 132).

7. The working class in Catalonia is largely composed of first- and second-generation Spanish-speaking immigrants from elsewhere in Spain (Woolard 1989, 30–34). In the process of building a unified movement, activists underwent a complex transforma-

tion whereby middle-class and Catholic nationalists increasingly moved to the left, while working-class immigrants and leftist militants took up nationalist demands for political and cultural autonomy (Johnston 1991, xii).

8. For more on Catalonia's civil society tradition, see Brandes 1990; Linz and De Miguel 1966, 308; and Pi-Sunyer 1974, 123.

9. Scholars have argued that party-driven elite bargaining led to an anemic form of democracy lacking channels for popular participation (Subirats 1999, 23; Tarrow 1995, 229). For more on the transition, see Edles 1998; Fishman 1990; Linz and Stepan 1996; and Pérez-Díaz 1993.

10. More generally, party affiliation in Spain dropped from 6 percent of the adult population in 1980 to between 2 and 3.4 percent by 1993 (Pérez-Díaz 2002, 271), and political parties generate lower levels of public sympathy than other Spanish institutions (Orizo 1999, 76; Wert 1996, 15).

11. The new social movements that remained following the transition were more autonomous, but relatively weak and small-scale (Alvarez-Junco 1994, 320). Stronger independent movements emerged during the 1980s. For example, the student movement against selectivity exams rejected manipulation by unions and parties (Pastor 1998, 212–228), as autonomy and assembly-based organization became important identity markers (362). The anti-NATO movement was the largest and most diverse mobilization in Catalonia during this period, involving a broad-based alliance among civil society organizations, religious institutions, and the radical Left (Laraña 1999, 321–27; Pastor 1998, 76–9).

12. Alternatives to military service were created in 1984 with the Law of Conscientious Objection.

13. Together with Zapatista supporters, Barcelona squatters helped organize the second Zapatista Gathering in 1997 and later hosted the Spanish leg of the PGA Intercontinental Caravan. Squatters in Barcelona also organized local protests as part of the first three PGA Global Days of Action, including a Reclaim the Streets protest on June 18, 1999, and a blockade against the Barcelona Stock Exchange during the anti-WTO protests in Seattle. Squatters later played a crucial role within MRG during the Catalan mobilization to Prague.

14. Martínez López (2002, 39–40) identifies three factors that contribute to, and provide a context for, squatting among contemporary Spanish youths: (1) the difficulty of economic emancipation and finding a stable job, (2) the construction of countercultural forms and practices (stimulated in part by the lack of programs for young people that allow for active participation and decision making [Assens 1999, 65]), and (3) a major housing crisis exacerbated by urban speculation.

15. Most social centers also organize diverse cultural activities, including talks, discussions, communal meals, parties, and concerts, while many squatters carry out grassroots neighborhood work, including developing relationships with local neighborhood associations.

16. Although international solidarity activism has been viewed in terms of the post-material values (Inglehart 1977) associated with new social movements (Díaz-Salazar 1996, 72), solidarity activists have also carried out a systemic critique of the political economy. The same can be said of squatters and antimilitarists, suggesting that the divide between economic and cultural activism has become increasingly blurred.

17. Regarding the relationship between new technologies and emerging political languages, ideologies, and visions, see Wilson and Peterson 2002, 453.

18. Cited from an early proposal for RCADE working groups and commissions.

19. Ibid.

20. Cited from a document created by MRG activists regarding network identity, structure, and process sent to the global@ldist.ct.upc.es Listserv on October 18, 2000.

21. I developed this classificatory scheme together with Pau during a Social Movement Gathering on April 26–28, 2001, which involved dozens of activists from MRG, RCADE, ATTAC, student groups, squatted social centers, and other related movements.

22. These include Iniciativa per Catalunya, Izquierda Unida, Esquerra Republicana, and at times El Partit Socialista de Catalunya, the Socialist Unión General de Trabajo and the Communist-leaning CCOO, the Catalan Federation of NGOs, the Barcelona Federation of Neighborhood Associations, and certain sectors of ATTAC.

23. Between 1951 and 1970 alone, 1.16 million immigrants entered Catalonia (Johnston 1991, 104; Conversi 1997, 191). Bilingualism has since become the norm given the widespread success of Catalan language policy (Woolard 1989).

24. Spanish speakers would often complain when meetings were held in Catalan, to which Catalan speakers would invariably reply that they have a right to speak in their native tongue.

25. For more on the benefits and drawbacks of consensus, see Epstein 1991; Lichterman 1996; and Polletta 2002.

26. Trotskyists differ from traditional Marxists in their call for a "permanent revolution," which would be led by grassroots workers at the global scale. Critical sectors specifically include radical currents within CCOO and Izquierda Unida; alternative unions such as the anarcho-syndicalist Confederación General de Trabajo (CGT), which split off from the reformulated CNT following the transition, and the Alternative Inter-Syndicate of Catalonia; as well as autonomous movements such as En Lluita, which is associated with the British Socialist Workers Party.

27. Paul Lichterman (1996) notes a similarly fluid, shifting mode of participation and a preference for horizontal structures among Green activists in California in the 1980s and early 1990s. The current emphasis on diffuse, decentralized networks thus resonates with a wider phenomenon Lichterman calls "personalized politics" and others, building on the work of Ulrich Beck (1992), refer to as "individualized commitment" (Furlong and Cartmel 1997). I argue that these new modes of participation among many younger, middle-class activists have been reinforced by their interaction with new digital technologies, constituting an example of what Barry Wellman (2001) re-

fers to as "networked individualism." However, the individualized, shifting, and diffuse nature of late modern sociality should be viewed in light of a contrasting trend toward embodied, communal interaction among many younger activists (Maffesoli 1996; cf. Hetherington 1998; McDonald 2006). For more on multiple patterns of belonging among anti–corporate globalization activists, see della Porta 2005 and Pleyers 2005a.

28. Unemployment among people aged twenty-five to twenty-nine in Spain was 30.4 percent in 1992 and reached 35 percent by 1998 (Martínez López 2002, 45).

29. The Platform for Peace involved two hundred Catalan civil society groups, including neighborhood associations, organizational federations, squatters, antimilitarists, autonomous collectives, leftist parties, and unions, providing a model for subsequent anti–corporate globalization campaigns.

30. Ward 1973, 52.

31. Cited from a proposal presented at the Fifth RCADE Encounter (October 12–14, 2001).

32. Only a third of Spanish citizens participate in civil society organizations (Díaz-Salazar 1996, 56), far below the European average (Linz and Montero 1999, 80). However, Pérez-Díaz (2002) downplays the importance of formal associations, suggesting that loose-knit kin and friendship networks are more important among Spaniards. Given the decline in traditional associational forms since the transition, together with a strong anarchist tradition, it should come as no surprise that Spanish and Catalan activists gravitate toward informal political activity.

33. Della Porta et al. (2006, 200–216) found widespread mistrust of representative democratic institutions and political parties in their surveys of participants at the July 2001 anti-G8 protests in Genoa and November 2002 European Social Forum in Florence (see also della Porta 2005). Indeed, scholars have noted a general loss of confidence in traditional forms of political participation throughout the West (cf. Beck 1992; Castells 1997, 342–49; Linz 2002, 291). New social movements can thus be seen as a response to growing alienation from mainstream politics (Escobar and Alvarez 1992, 10; Laraña 1999, 364). In this sense, against claims that young people are disengaged and apathetic, others have suggested that contemporary youths are simply more likely to take part in alternative modes of political action (Pleyers 2005a; Youniss et al. 2002).

3. Grassroots Mobilization and Alliances

1. Manifesto of the Movement for Global Resistance.

2. "L'MRG ha mort . . . comença la festa!" communiqué sent by MRG to the bcn2001@yahoogroups.com Listserv, January 26, 2003.

3. A similar dynamic unfolded following the Consulta the previous year, giving rise to new projects, campaigns, and rapidly proliferating spaces. As Joan from RCADE confessed, "After each mobilization, people think they've created 'the network to end all networks,' only to realize later they are just another group among many."

4. Moreover, many RCADE activists had come out of the more reformist-oriented world of international solidarity activism, while MRG activists were more influenced by the libertarian vision of the squatter movement. Such broad depictions fail to account for the complex reality, however, and in practice there was significant overlap. Miguel once quipped, "Choosing between MRG and RCADE is like choosing a cup of coffee!"

5. As Manuel Castells (2000, 16) suggests, the most important network nodes are not centers but rather "switchers," which receive, interpret, and circulate information. Mario Diani (2003) has referred to activists who take on this role as "network bridgers." I further distinguish between "relayers," who process and distribute information within a single network, and "switchers," who occupy key nodal positions within multiple movement networks. Network relayers and switchers occupy key positions of power, shaping the flow, direction, and intensity of network activity.

6. Activist-hackers are often widely admired for their highly refined networking skills—physical and virtual—and their crucial role in terms of movement building, yet they are often mistrusted and even feared because of their position of relative power within the network, given their ability to control, manipulate, and distribute information, contacts, and social relations.

7. The numbers have grown steadily since then. To negotiate this constant bombardment of information, Pau relied on one key attribute: speed. For example, I once approached him while he was reviewing messages at the convergence center during the World Bank campaign, and noticed dozens of files on the screen of his laptop, which he brought with him everywhere (direct actions, meetings, international trips). I asked him why he kept so many documents on his desktop, and he responded, "It's all a matter of velocity!"

8. Anti–corporate globalization Listservs, in particular, provide a forum for three types of communication. First, activists post logistical information regarding network meetings, protests, and activities. Second, participants engage in debates about the present state and future direction of particular networks. Finally, activists exchange information about political mobilizations and events in Spain, Catalonia, Europe, and around the world.

9. Similarly, Christopher Pound (1995) has pointed out regarding the Internet that "networkers write endlessly about access, anarchy, censorship, privacy, and property. . . . As reproductive processes, these never-ending simulated dialogues, on and about the NET, network the Net" (535). Indeed, the boundaries of communication networks are largely generated through communication and the observation of communication, as Luhman (1990) explains: "Self-observing communication refers to the system that is produced and reproduced by the communication itself" (7). As pointed out in chapter 1, anti–corporate globalization movements are thus uniquely "self-reflexive," as activists circulate their own reflections and analyses via transnational activist networks.

10. The twinkling sign was initially derived from American Sign Language.

11. For more on "consensus process" among U.S. activists, see Epstein 1991; Graeber 2002; Sturgeon 1995; and Polletta 2002. In Spain and Catalonia, this technical system

merged with the informal tradition of decision making characteristic of Spanish and Catalan assemblies. In either case, consensus process reflects a commitment to flat hierarchies and collaborative practice.

12. See Schwartzman 1989 and Myers 1986 for more on the ethnography of meetings.

13. Lichterman (1996) and Polletta (2002) similarly describe how U.S. activists, including Greens, feminists, New Leftists, and anti–corporate globalization activists, have spent a great deal of time discussing organizational structure and decision making. This has sometimes involved a search for more effective, egalitarian structures, and, at other times, heated debates among promoters of flexible, participatory forms and supporters of clearer structures and hierarchies. Moreover, as we shall see, similar discussions have characterized debates among anti–corporate globalization activists in Barcelona, within both decentralized networks, such as MRG or RCADE, and wider campaigns. I specifically argue that debates over structure and process reflect the way activists inscribe their political ideals directly into organizational architectures. At the same time, new digital technologies have largely shifted the balance in favor of diffuse, decentralized models. Chapters 6 and 7 discuss related dynamics at the transnational scale.

14. MRG's structure ultimately consisted of periodic assemblies, permanent commissions, and thematic areas. Assemblies provided a space for coordination and decision making, while smaller groups carried out ongoing tasks as part of permanent commissions involving coordination, finances, media, and outreach.

15. Cited from a document accompanying the agenda for the MRG assembly in Castelldefels on September 15, 2001, "Bloc VII—questions generals sobre continguts," sent out in a message to the mrgcatalunya@yahoogroups.com Listserv, August 30, 2001.

16. The European Social Consulta was a project developed by RCADE- and MRG-based activists in Spain and Catalonia as well as PGA at the European scale. The idea was to organize a Europe-wide process around a series of issues that would emerge through collaborative discussion. The first step would involve a series of consultations around what issues to address, and the second would consist of the Consulta itself. A more ambitious version of the project sought to create a continental network of grassroots assemblies to discuss common issues and generate collective action proposals, reflecting a self-generating network ideal.

17. The complete list of networks and organizations that signed on to the Barcelona 2001 campaign manifesto is archived at http://www.nodo50.org/bcn2001/lista5.htm (accessed January 26, 2007).

18. http://www.nodo50.org/barcelonatremola/labora12.htm (accessed July 15, 2003).

19. As my Catalan friends explained, the facilitator was from a radical left-wing research project, and it was a small miracle they had organized the meeting together with the IU "red sector" at all, as they were sworn enemies.

20. "Rose of Fire" was the name of the website for the campaign against the World Bank. Regarding the historical relevance of this name, see chapter 2 and A. Smith 2002, 3.

21. The assembly agreed the statewide campaign would prioritize the mobilization against the Summit of the European Heads of State in Barcelona on March 15–16 and the

final Summit of the European Commission in Seville on June 21–22. The following decentralized actions would also be organized: March 22–23 (Meeting of the European Ministers of Defense in Zaragoza), April 12–14 (Meeting of the Commission of Economic and Finance Ministers in Oviedo), April 23–24 (Euro-Mediterranean Conference in Valencia), and May 17–18 (Meeting of the European, Latin American, and Caribbean Heads of State in Madrid).

22. As with Barcelona 2001, the anti-EU campaign was organized around a general assembly and a series of autonomous work groups. The campaign manifesto emphasized the lack of genuine democracy in the process of European construction and the predominant role of transnational corporate interests: "Participation in the European Union has been marked by an overwhelming democratic deficit. Spanish citizens have never been consulted, via referendum, about entry into the Union, or about the draconian conditions imposed. We have also never been consulted about the decisions that directly affect us: the Euro, independence of the Central Banks, the Schengen Treaty."

23. The message, "Opening the Debate after the Statewide Meeting in Zaragoza: Separating in order to Work Together More Effectively," was sent to bcn2001@yahoogroups .com and other Listservs on December 4, 2001.

24. Rather than directly opposing the European Union, or the capitalist logic behind European construction, the Barcelona Social Forum (BSF) manifesto, "For a Social Europe of the Citizens," emphasized deepening the construction process to include greater democracy and social rights. As further discussed in the next chapter, an additional space was subsequently created: the nationalist "Catalan Platform against the Europe of Capital."

25. The call for an autonomous assembly, sent to the mrgcatalunya@yahoogroups.com Listserv on January 6, 2002, included the following explanation: "Our intention is to bring together people who we haven't seen since the Prague assemblies. . . . We start from the idea that the sphere of autonomous struggles, or at least horizontal and anti-hierarchical struggles has broadened over the past few years, and although it might not be the moment to create large convergence spaces, neither is it the moment to retreat to our own tribes. We also think we still have things to discuss regarding the Campaign against the World Bank, about different political visions and misunderstandings."

26. The press release was sent to the mrgcatalunya@yahoogroups.com Listserv on April 16, 2002, leading to widespread criticism on the part of grassroots activists.

4. Direct-Action Protests

1. John Jordan. Cited in Jordan 1998.

2. In this sense, networks should not be viewed as disembodied (pace McDonald 2006). Rather, the activist networks explored here are produced and reproduced through both online *and* embodied interactions, the latter including protests, meetings, conferences, forums, and other gatherings.

3. Pulido (2003) similarly refers to the "exterior" and "interior" dimensions of social movements. The exterior involve social, cultural, economic, and political structures, while the interior include "emotions, psychological development, souls, and passions" (47).

4. Anti–corporate globalization activists thus engage in what John Thompson (1995) refers to as "struggles for visibility." For more on media logics and the increasing demand for spectacular images, see Altheide and Snow 1991 and Castells 1996, 333.

5. Cited from a message sent to the bcn2001@yahoogroups.com Listserv on May 21, 2001.

6. Performances involve a "heightened intensity of communicative interaction" (Bauman 1977, 43) and are associated with meaningful repetitive behavior (Schechner 1985; Turner 1982, 1986). Performances thus allow participants to experience symbolic meanings through ritual interaction (Schieffelin 1985). With respect to "cultural performances," see Singer 1972.

7. As Paolo Virno (2004) suggests, virtuosity involves an activity that has no extrinsic end product and makes sense only if seen or heard. Protest virtuosity thus points to the performative dimension of mass mobilizations, involving the continual (re)production of its own effects. Virtuosity increasingly characterizes all spheres of social and economic reproduction under post-Fordism (61). For more on performance and contemporary anti–corporate globalization protest, see Hardt and Negri 2004, 211.

8. As Kapchan suggests, "To perform is to carry something into effect" (1995, 479). See also Butler 1993; Diamond 1996; and Schein 1999.

9. I use the idea of embodiment in two ways. On the one hand, "embodiment" refers to the way meanings and identities are expressed through the body, conceived as a text or canvas through which cultural and political signifiers are inscribed (Douglas 1970; Strathern and Stewart 1998). On the other hand, "embodiment" refers to the body as lived subject and agent (Csordas 1990; Lyon and Barbalet 1994), the source of multiple forms of bodily praxis (Scheper-Hughes 1992, 184–85). Here I combine these approaches, exploring how activists employ distinctive bodily techniques and styles to occupy space while expressing political messages, visions, and identities.

10. Multilateral political and financial institutions, such as the World Trade Organization (WTO), World Bank, International Monetary Fund (IMF), and G8, primarily operate during mass actions as "summarizing symbols" (Ortner 1973, 1339), representing a broader set of ideas regarding the nature of the global economic and political order.

11. Victor Turner (1986) eloquently captures this idea with the term "performative reflexivity." Also regarding the emergent aspect of performance, see Conquergood 1992 and Pagliai 2002.

12. For more on social movements and emotion, see Goodwin, Jasper, and Polletta 2001; Jasper 1998; and Taylor 1995. While much of this work emphasizes the reasons why activists take part in social movements, here I consider the emotional dynamics associated with moments of *public* protest (cf. Berezin 2001; Barker 2001; Collins 2001; Routledge and Simons 1995).

13. Abu-Lughod and Lutz (1990, 3) have rightly cautioned against "essentializing" emotions by presuming a false universality. At the same time, as Kapchan (1995) points out, discursive and performative approaches overlook how emotions are lived and embodied. I thus stake out what Jasper (1998, 400) refers to as a "weaker constructionist model," recognizing that emotions are characterized and experienced in culturally specific ways, but that there may be certain universal sensations tied to bodily states. The notion of affective solidarity tries to capture this embodied dimension of emotion.

14. Grasping the emotional dynamics of protest performances requires careful attention to the ethnographer's own body (cf. Kapchan 1995, 502), an important aspect of militant ethnography.

15. According to Chesters and Welsh (2004, 32), INPEG was created before Seattle—in September 1999—but it did not start meeting until much later. For a detailed discussion of the Czech actors on the ground during the Prague mobilization, see Welsh 2004.

16. This discussion is based on conversations with activists, an account provided by Starhawk (2002, 49–55), and minutes sent to the s26-traducciones-esp@egroups.com Listserv on September 1, 2000.

17. We took the name of our affinity group from Eduardo Galeano's well-known 1973 book about colonialist exploitation in Latin America, *Open Veins of Latin America*.

18. The communication, command, and control center, called "Centrum," was located in a nearby hotel room (Chesters and Welsh 2004, 325). Unfortunately, the Prague police disrupted the mobile phone airwaves on the day of the action, which rendered the phone system inoperable.

19. Although many non-Anglos were impressed by the organizational and direct-action practices American and British activists introduced, others were critical. In particular, many Indymedia activists complained of a condescending attitude on the part of their American counterparts.

20. See Chesters and Welsh 2004 for an analysis of color codes in Prague from the perspective of framing, where colors serve as "sense-making devices." Here I am more interested in the embodied and spatial performances enacted within each geographic zone.

21. For more on the prefigurative aspect of direct action, see Epstein 1991 and Graeber 2002.

22. Pink and Silver was introduced by RTS, Earth First!, and samba band activists from the United Kingdom, but the tactic emerged as a favored mode of performance among activists associated with grassroots anticapitalist networks.

23. Cited from http://www.nod050.org/invisibles/propuesta.htm (accessed May 15, 2003).

24. In this sense, clothing and bodily decorations express political and cultural identities (Scheper-Hughes and Locke 1987, 25), helping to produce subcultural styles via assemblage and bricolage (Clarke 1976). Tute Bianche and other protest tactics thus appropriate and recombine diverse commodity signs, including white overalls, industrial tubing, black boots, masks, wigs, and pink dresses, as styles that express dis-

tinct subjectivities and visions. For more on the dynamics of liminality and carnival during mass protests, see Auyero 2002, 175–78.

25. For Turner (1982, 52–55), the "liminal" is a functional requirement of premodern societies, which compensates for the rigidity of social structure. The "liminoid" corresponds to dynamic industrial societies and is often associated with social, even revolutionary, critique.

26. For more on tactical frivolity, see Chesters and Welsh 2004, 328–31.

27. According to Charles Tilly (1978), a "repertoire" of contention refers to the tactical choices that are available to a social movement in a given historical period (see Tarrow 1998).

28. Herri Batsuna was widely linked to the Basque terror organization ETA, and many grassroots activists were thus extremely reluctant to associate with HB.

29. Although relatively institutional compared to the convergence center in Prague, the Central University provided a safe space for painting banners, building puppets, and creating artwork. Media activists created a separate space that would serve as an Independent Media Center and workplace for the campaign's communication commission.

30. These include negotiations, ritualized displays of strength and aggression, and various forms of crowd control, such as water cannons, tear gas, and baton charges (Fillieulle and Jobard 1997).

31. During Critical Mass actions, bicyclists ride en masse through city streets to reclaim public space and denounce the hegemony of car culture.

32. Mass anti–corporate globalization actions are thus examples of what Routledge (1997b) calls "imagineered resistance," struggles that exist in embodied and mass-mediated forms.

33. Although particular activists will engage in diverse forms of action, which vary over time, protesters from specific networks often coalesce around certain tactics during a given action. For example, in Prague, militant squatters enacted Black Bloc tactics during the Blue March, while activists from Ya Basta! and their allies took part in the White Overalls contingent during the Yellow March. Meanwhile, organizers associated with PGA helped coordinate Pink and Silver.

34. The first ever U.S. Social Forum (USSF) in Atlanta in June-July 2007 was a notable exception in this regard, as many grassroots groups and people of color not only attended the forum, but also took on leadership roles within the National Planning Committee.

35. Examples of lower-income and people-of-color groups that have participated in anti–corporate globalization mobilizations include the Mouvement de l'Immigration et des Banlieues (MIB) in France, the Anarchist People of Color Network in the United States, and the Root Cause march during the November 2003 anti-FTAA protests in Miami.

36. This is precisely what happened at the USSF. For an influential version of this position, see http://cwsworkshop.org (accessed January 26, 2007). Regarding the debates around race within U.S.-based movements, see Martínez 2000 and Starr 2004.

37. This discussion harkens back to an old anthropological debate about the political effects of carnival. Many scholars have argued that incidents of public license, liminality, and ritual inversion, including carnival or what Max Gluckman more generally calls "rituals of rebellion," operate as safety valves, allowing people to release pent-up frustrations, reproducing established hierarchies (Brandes 1980; Gluckman 1954; Turner 1969). Alternatively, others have maintained that such events are indeed subversive, providing opportunities for people to question systems of domination and imagine possible alternatives (Lancaster 1997), potentially leading to overt class conflict and open rebellion (Mintz 1997). However, when activists appropriate the carnivalesque as a political tool, the outcome is more contingent, depending on their ability to create affective solidarity through virtuoso performance while transferring emotions into sustained networking.

38. Following George Lakey (1973), Epstein similarly suggests, "Although massive nonviolent direct action can be an important tactic, it is the process of building democratic and revolutionary organizations and institutions as an alternative basis of power (as well as for alternative social relations and values) that is crucial to social transformation" (1991, 276).

5. Spaces of Terror

1. Ana, from the Movement for Global Resistance.

2. The trope of "good" and "bad" protesters is common within radical anti–corporate globalization discourse, where militant activists often criticize the media and the state for trying to divide "the movement." Indeed, given their rebel styles, imagery, and tactics, militants lend themselves to media frames that construct them as political deviants (see Hall 1974, 267). In Genoa, however, police and government officials blurred this distinction. Indeed, following a police raid on sleeping protesters at the Diaz School (discussed later in the chapter), Prime Minister Berlusconi remarked that it was impossible to tell the difference between peaceful protesters and militants (della Porta et al. 2006, 163).

3. As it turns out, the Italian police employed an information strategy involving numerous undercover agents, which was specifically based on the "indiscriminate, widespread collection of information" (della Porta et al. 2006, 172).

4. For an extended discussion of the key networks and sectors that took part in the protest against the G8 in Genoa, both inside and outside the GSF, see della Porta et al. 2006, 31–43.

5. David Riches defines violence as "an act of physical hurt deemed legitimate by the performer and illegitimate by (some) witnesses" (1986, 8). Jon Abbink (1990, xi) builds on this definition but strictly limits his discussion to violence against people. Others also consider attacks against property as violence (Graham and Gurr 1969, xxvii). These definitions raise important questions: Who is authorized to deem certain acts legitimate? What constitutes "damaging physical force"? Should property destruction count as violence? Indeed, these issues are crucial to tactical debates among activists and wider battles of political signification.

6. Regarding the production, appropriation, and manipulation of performances as texts, see Bauman and Briggs 1990.

7. See Gitlin 1980 for an analysis of protest violence and the media during the U.S. anti-war movement in the 1960s.

8. Some activists and observers characterize what I refer to as performative violence as "symbolic violence." However, to avoid confusion with Pierre Bourdieu's (2001) more restricted use of the latter term, I use "performative violence" here.

9. At the same time, militant anti–corporate globalization activists often justify their actions by citing the "structural violence" caused by global capitalism. See Bourgois 2001 for a discussion of four interrelated classes of violence—direct political, structural, symbolic, and everyday.

10. For an analysis of the symbolic uses of iconic violence among Basque terrorists, see Zulaika and Douglass 1996.

11. For more on the links between violent performances, styles, and identities, see Bowman 2001; Feldman 1991; Peteet 2002; and Peterson 2001.

12. See Feldman 1991; Scarry 1985; and Suárez-Orozco 1987 regarding the instrumental and symbolic aspects of torture.

13. For Agamben (1998, 35), sovereign power is specifically constituted through the creation of a state or zone of indistinction between violence and the law. As Diken and Laustsen (2002, 302) suggest, terror similarly operates by establishing a zone of indistinction, a "battlefield without demarcations." In this sense, state terror in Genoa can be understood as an act of reestablishing sovereign power through the indiscriminate (and illegal) application of violence. Diken and Laustsen further argue that terror constitutes one of three modes through which contemporary power operates. The other two are discipline, which works by regulating bodies in space, and control, which functions along the terrain of mobility and difference.

14. Movement-related document from Genoa.

15. The strategy of tension was implemented during the 1970s in response to the rise of radical left-libertarian terrorist organizations, including the Red Brigades. Collective memories of this period were stirred by media hysteria surrounding anarchist violence and bomb scares before the mobilizations and during the protests, as participants accused the police of infiltrating activist groups and instigating violence in order to criminalize activists and justify a brutal crackdown.

16. The potential for violence was exacerbated by the negative views of the different protest blocs held by the police forces deployed in Genoa (della Porta et al. 2006, 173), as well as their lack of trust in negotiations (159).

17. For more on Black Bloc actions in Genoa, see Riera 2001, 191–222.

18. Anonymous testimony from Riera 2001, 202.

19. Of the 93 activists detained at the Diaz School, 62 were hospitalized (della Porta et al. 2006, 162), and 72 suffered injuries; all but one were quickly released without being charged (5). Altogether more than one thousand protesters were injured during the Genoa protests (Gubitosa 2003, 177; cited in della Porta et al. 2006, 161).

20. Della Porta et al. (2006, 163–95) propose a variety of reasons to explain the massively violent response on the part of the Italian police in Genoa, including negative views toward, and a general lack of understanding of, the movement, a legacy of coercive tactics, partial militarization and politicization, low accountability and professionalism, a lack of coordination, and a political climate conducive to repression, including a refusal to recognize movement actors as legitimate political subjects. However, none of these explanations necessarily contradict the claim that the police violence in Genoa was the result of a politically coordinated campaign (taken together, in fact, they help explain how such a campaign might succeed), nor do they contradict the terror activists actually experienced on the streets.

21. Many of the police tactics employed in Genoa had already been used during previous mass mobilizations. Indeed, it was widely reported that the special unit responsible for the raid on the Diaz School was trained by the Los Angeles Police Department, which had implemented special intimidation techniques during the July 2000 protest against the Democratic National Convention (DNC) in Los Angeles. See, for example, "Genoa Police Unit Trained by LAPD," Reuters, August 7, 2001, http://italy. indymedia.org/news/2001 (accessed March 15, 2003). For more on the transnational dimension of protest policing in Genoa, see della Porta et al. 2006, 187–91. Moreover, special units trained to fight the Mafia and control soccer hooliganism were also deployed in Genoa, suggesting an anticipation of violent confrontation (179).

22. As more and more reports of police abuse surfaced over the next few weeks, many European governments and members of the EU parliament began calling for a complete investigation of the incidents, including the death of Carlo Giuliani and the raid on the Diaz School. A November 2001 Amnesty International report called "Italy: G8 Genoa Policing Operations of July 2001, a Summary of Concerns," noted the following allegations: (1) peaceful protesters were denied entry into Italy; (2) law enforcement officials used excessive force during street demonstrations on July 20 and 21 against nonviolent protesters, journalists, doctors, nurses, and bystanders; (3) law enforcement officers subjected individuals to "deliberate and gratuitous beatings, resulting in numerous injuries, some of them requiring urgent hospitalization and in some cases surgical operations," during a police raid on buildings legally occupied by the GSF in the early morning of July 22; (4) dozens of activists were subjected to "arbitrary and illegal arrest, detention and subsequently expulsion from the country"; (5) during police vehicle transfers as well as inside detention centers, law enforcement officials "subjected individuals to beatings and other cruel, inhuman and degrading treatment"; (6) people were deprived of their internationally recognized rights when arrested. Cited from http://web.amnesty.org/ (accessed March 15, 2003). The Berlusconi government initially resisted calls for an investigation, blaming protesters for the violence, but eventually agreed to an inquiry by the Ministry of the Interior, resulting in the transfer of three police chiefs to other administrative duties. "Genoa Police Admit Fabrication," BBC, January 7, 2003, http://news.bbc.co.uk (accessed

March 15, 2003). On October 14, 2005, officials announced that twenty-eight police officers accused of beating anti–corporate globalization protesters would be tried, while an additional forty-five officers, prison staff, and medical workers charged with abusing activists at the Bolzaneto detention center also awaited court proceedings. Moreover, senior police officials admitted to planting evidence at the Diaz School, including two Molotov cocktails. "G8 Summit Police Lied, Says Report," BBC, http://news.bbc.co.uk (accessed January 26, 2007). On January 19, 2007, however, it was announced that the Molotov cocktails had "disappeared," placing the entire case at risk. "Genoa Riot Evidence 'Disappears,' " BBC, http://news.bbc.co.uk (accessed January 26, 2007).

23. In this sense, Foucault's (1979) conception of the body as a passive site for the inscription of political messages is inadequate. Rather, the body should also be conceived as an active producer of political and cultural signs (Peteet 2002; Peterson 2001).

24. For more on the concept of the sanctuary, see Franco 1985 and Feldman 1991, 36–39.

25. "Un movimiento pacifista y revolucionario," http://www.sindominio.net/fiambrera/web-agencias/ (accessed March 15, 2003).

26. The White Overalls, for example, declared their protest tactics dead and have since turned their energy toward building a European network of everyday "social disobedience." However, the June 2007 protests against the G8 in Heiligendamm, Germany, constitute an exception in this regard, in terms of the level of militancy as well as the overall blockade strategy.

27. For useful overviews of the debates around violence and nonviolence among anti–corporate globalization activists, see Starhawk 2002, 93–100; and Starr 2005, 127–38. For an analysis of activist debates regarding violence in the wake of Genoa involving Italian focus groups, see della Porta et al. 2006, 142–47.

28. Message sent to the bcn2001@yahoogroups.com Listserv, July 29, 2001.

29. The debate between Susan George and radical anticapitalists began after the anti-EU protests in Gothenburg the previous May, when George specifically condemned activist violence in her public declarations. Radicals viewed this as a violation of the diversity-of-tactics ethic and the movement's widespread emphasis on tolerance and diversity.

30. "Manifiesto en favor de la acción direct violenta," http://www.sindominio.net/fiambrera/web-agencias/ (accessed March 15, 2003).

31. "Infos para un puzzle," http://www.sindominio.net/fiambrera/web-agencias/ (accessed March 15, 2003).

32. For more on New Kids on the Black Bloc, see http://sindominio.net/lasagencias/ (accessed January 26, 2007).

6. Resistance as Transnational as Capital!

1. "Peoples' Global Action Manifesto," http://www.nadir.org/nadir/initiativ/agp/en/pgainfos/manifest.htm (accessed October 15, 2003).

2. Leslie Wood (2004, 99) calculates that between 1998 and 2001, roughly 1,500 movements, organizations, and collectives took part in regional and global PGA conferences and participated in five global days of action. At the same time, as Wood admits, some of these groups may not have realized they were taking part in globally coordinated actions. For a detailed breakdown and timeline of PGA-related events, see L. Wood 2004, 103.

3. PGA caravans include the 1999 Intercontinental Caravan in Europe, the U.S. West Coast Caravan before the WTO protests in Seattle later that year, and caravans before and after global conferences in Bangalore (1999) and Cochabamba (2001). The network also initiated several campaigns in Cochabamba, including (1) militarism and paramilitarism, (2) self-determination and land sovereignty, (3) privatization, and (4) alternative models to the capitalist system, but these have largely struggled to get off the ground.

4. Invoking Habermas, Guidry, Kennedy, and Zald (2000) have referred to transnational social movements as "transnational public spheres." However, as Nancy Fraser points out, the bourgeois public sphere was based on systematic exclusions, including women, peasants, workers, minorities, gays, and lesbians. These groups have created their own "subaltern counterpublics," involving "parallel discursive arenas where members of subordinated social groups invent and circulate counter-discourses to formulate oppositional interpretations of their identities, interests, and needs" (1992, 123). I thus follow Alvarez, Dagnino, and Escobar (1998), who view social movements as alternative publics that generate oppositional discourses and identities vis-à-vis dominant public spheres (see also Conway 2004). For additional analyses that examine meaning and identity within transnational social movements, see Cohen and Rai 2000; Cunningham 2000; and Seidman 2000.

5. For example, Sidney Tarrow (2001, 11) has defined transnational social movements as "socially mobilized groups with constituents in at least two states, engaged in sustained contentious interactions with power-holders in at least one state other than their own, or against an international institution, or a multinational economic actor" (della Porta 2005, 177).

6. See also Routledge 2003. Sidney Tarrow (2005) refers to the way protests and forums spread from the local to the global and vice versa as "scale shift." However, rather than focusing on discrete events, I am more concerned with ongoing communication and coordination, including the micropolitical struggles through which transnational activist networks are generated.

7. W. Lance Bennett (2005) characterizes the difference between formal, NGO-led transnational activist coalitions and more fluid, shifting, and technologically oriented direct action networks in generational terms as a distinction between first- and second-generation transnational activism.

8. Last accessed January 26, 2007.

9. North American activists have also developed a new PGA website to address network activities in that region, www.agpna.revolt.org (last accessed January 26, 2007).

10. The PGA website and Listservs are housed on various social change servers, including www.nadir.org, www.riseup.net, and www.squat.net.

11. The "consultation" meeting in Haridwar was organized instead of the planned global PGA conference in Nepal, which was canceled because of political instability in the region.

12. See chapter 1 for a discussion of PGA network history.

13. "Organisational Principles," http://www.nadir.org/nadir/initiativ/agp/cocha/principles .htm (accessed October 15, 2003).

14. These were updated at the third global conference in Cochabamba, Bolivia, September 16–23, 2000. Cited from "Hallmarks of Peoples' Global Action," http://www.nadir .org/nadir/initiativ/agp/free/pga/hallm.htm (accessed October 15, 2003).

15. See table 6.

16. This discussion is based on personal correspondence. For more on the conference, see L. Wood 2004 and Routledge 2003.

17. In the end, delegates initiated several campaigns and agreed to change the hallmarks to reflect a clear rejection of capitalism. Participants also agreed to replace the phrase "nonviolent" with "respect for life" to express support for a diversity of tactics, including property damage, while respecting the sanctity of human life.

18 Eurodusnie was established during a 1997 anti-EU mobilization in Amsterdam and sponsors several projects, including a free shop, bookstore, and vegetarian cafe.

19. See Lichterman 1996 and Polletta 2002 for analyses of debates regarding similar issues among Greens, feminists, New Leftists, and anti–corporate globalization activists in the United States. Greens and feminists, in particular, spent a great deal of time discussing the distribution of power and trying to find a new basis for legitimate authority. As I argue here, debates about organizational process and form, which are an important dimension of the cultural practice and politics of transnational activist networking, reflect the growing confluence among organizational forms, political norms, and new digital technologies within contemporary anti–corporate globalization movements.

20. In her study of the U.S. direct-action movement in the 1970s and 1980s, Barbara Epstein (1991) similarly notes, "The absolute equality to which the movement aspires can never exist, and attempts to achieve it easily take on repressive overtones" (271).

21. Despite formal assertions to the contrary, some activists possess more desired skills than others. For example, as an anthropologist who speaks English and Spanish, I have used my linguistic and cultural skills, particularly the ability to translate, to gain network access.

22. Message sent to the mrginternacional@gmx.net Listserv, December 6, 2001.

23. Message sent to the eurodusnie@squat.net Listserv, December 7, 2001.

24. Founded during the mobilization against the EU summit on migration and asylum in Tampere in October 1999, the No Border Network emerged from the Europe-wide

campaigns in support of the autonomous actions waged by the Sans-Papiers (un-documented residents).

25. Such temporary camps reflect the individualized, shifting, and ephemeral nature of late modern sociality, as well as a resurgent communalism involving collaborative, embodied, and affective interaction within the intimate spheres of daily life (Maffesoli 1996).

26. Ya Basta! hosted the first European PGA conference in Milan the year before. Many activists criticized the Milan conference for its lack of a structured agenda and its unwieldy plenary sessions. Eurodusnie was thus determined to have a more organized conference this time.

27. For more on consensus process in North America, see Epstein 1991, 3; and Graeber 2002, 71; and Polletta 2002: 194–96. For critical views, see Epstein 1991, 94–5; and Bookchin, "What Is Communalism?" http://dwardmac.pitzer.edu/anarchist_archives/bookchin/ (accessed July 19, 2006).

28. Message sent to the pga2002_process@aseed.antenna.nl Listserv, August 9, 2002.

29. Message sent to the pga2002_strategy@aseed.antenna.nl Listserv, August 13, 2002.

30. MRG response to Eurodusnie sent to the pga2002_process@aseed.antenna.nl Listserv, August 21, 2002. Consensus was an important part of the political identity of MRG-based activists, whereas it was more of a practical matter for their counterparts with Eurodusnie. This debate reflected a contrast between a "normative" and "practical" basis for consensus (Polletta 2002, 197–98).

31. For a discussion of hierarchy, leadership, and power among U.S.-based anarcha-feminists who have been influential within North American direct-action circles, see Epstein 1991, 167–69. For an analysis of similar issues among Direct Action Network (DAN) activists in New York City, see Polletta 2002, 194–99.

32. Message sent to the pga2002_process@aseed.antenna.nl Listserv, August 20, 2002. When Sans-Titre became European conveners, they decided to organize the August 2006 European PGA Conference as a series of decentralized meetings in various cities throughout France. See http://pgaconference.org/en/2006/decentralised (accessed January 26, 2007).

33. Call for the Second European Peoples' Global Action (PGA) Conference, http://www.nadir.org/nadir/initiativ/agp/pgaeurope/leiden/call.htm (accessed October 15, 2003).

34. "Short Report from Leiden PGA Conference," http://www.nadir.org/nadir/initiativ/agp/pgaeurope/leiden/ (accessed October 15, 2003).

35. In terms of who could become an Infopoint, everyone supported "openness" in principle, but some were concerned that sectarian groups might take on the role to advance their own interests. We finally agreed to a process of "self-selection," while establishing a special recall provision.

36. These included a single Listserv for all support group activities and separate European lists for announcements, political debates, and network process.

37. A new convener finally emerged at the March 2003 winter meeting in Dijon: DSM!, a network of autonomous collectives from (post-)Yugoslavia.

38. For an interesting approach to dealing with formal and informal hierarchies using new digital technologies, see http://www.open-organizations.org (accessed January 26, 2007).

7. Social Forums and Autonomous Space

1. Nuria, from the Movement for Global Resistance.
2. I follow Manuel Castells (1997) here in viewing space as "the material support of time-sharing social practices" (411). In this sense, the social forums and other transnational activist networks provide the organizational infrastructures that facilitate time-sharing practices among activists.
3. Two Catalan organizations, the Fons Català de Cooperació al Desenvolupament (Fons) and the Associació per a l'Estudi i la Promoció del Desenvolupament Comunitari (AEPD), were past members of the WSF International Council.
4. Although the camp's national coordinating body was dominated by institutional movements, the local organizing group also involved grassroots actors such as the Free Metropolitan Council of Architecture Students, who contributed their horizontal practices and vision of the camp as a city divided into self-managed zones (Nunes 2005a).
5. For statistical information regarding the various editions of the WSF, see the WSF Memorial, http://www.forumsocialmundial.org.br/ (accessed January 26, 2007).
6. However, participation in the 2007 WSF in Nairobi dropped to fifty thousand, owing in large part to the logistical obstacles associated with organizing the forum in Africa.
7. Habermas (1989) specifically refers to the "bourgeois public sphere" as a space where private actors come together to form political positions through rational-critical debate.
8. After the first WSF, the International Council (IC) decided to promote regional forums as a way to globalize the process. The Fons and AEPD spearheaded an effort in fall 2001 to bring a Euro-Mediterranean Forum to Barcelona. The Italian bid for the regional forum ultimately won out, although the Euro-Mediterranean Forum was finally held in Barcelona in June 2005.
9. For an interesting ethnographic account of Intergaláctika and its relation to the official forum during the third edition of the WSF in 2003, see Osterweil 2004.
10. These included the Brazilian Association of Nongovernmental Organizations (ABONG), ATTAC-Brazil, Brazilian Justice and Peace Commission (CBJP), Brazilian Business Association for Citizenship (CIVES), the Brazilian Institute for Social and Economic Studies (IBASE), and the Center for Global Justice (CJG). The Brazilian OC later expanded to twenty-three organizations.
11. A Day of Decentralized Actions was planned for January 2008 instead of a centralized WSF.
12. Guidelines were approved at the June 2003 IC meeting in Miami and are archived at http://www.forumsocialmundial.org.br/ (accessed January 26, 2007). In 2004 Indian organizers joined the OC, which was renamed the International Secretariat (IS). The IS

became the Facilitation Group the following year, and now plays a coordinating role with respect to the IC (Santos 2006, 48–51). Meanwhile, local organizing committees are responsible for the logistics on the ground wherever the WSF is held.

13. See "Composition of the International Council," http://www.forumsocialmundial.org .br/ (accessed January 26, 2007). For more on the geographic composition of the IC, see Santos 2006, 100–107.

14. European Social Forums have drawn 40,000 in Florence (2002), 70,000 in Paris (2003), and 50,000 in London (2004).

15. For example, U.S. activists have organized local and regional forums such as the New York Social Forum (2002, 2003), Boston Social Forum (2004), Chicago Social Forum (2005, 2006), Midwest Social Forum (2004–6), and, along with Mexican activists, the Border Social Forum (2006). Moreover, the first-ever U.S. Social Forum took place June 27 to July 1, 2007. For a list of forums around the world, see http://www .forumsocialmundial.org.br/ (accessed January 26, 2007).

16. "WSF Charter of Principles," http://www.forumsocialmundial.org.br/ (accessed December 15, 2003).

17. Jai Sen, "The Long March to Another World, http://www.choike.org/PDFs/introduc .pdf (accessed December 15, 2003).

18. Although the process has changed (see later section), the hierarchical format of the official panels and role of the organizing committees in shaping program content initially contradicted the idea of a nondirected space. Moreover, the injunction against political parties is often contradicted by the close ties between specific forums and political parties, such as the PT in Brazil (see Baiocchi 2004), Rifondazione in Italy, or Labour Party in London. For more on the contrast between the forum as an "ideal model" and the forum in practice, see Pleyers 2005b.

19. In a survey conducted at the 2005 WSF in Porto Alegre, Reese et al. (forthcoming) found that WSF participants tend to be young, mostly white, and highly educated, while the periphery is significantly underrepresented. Indeed, traveling to the WSF costs a great deal of money, which is beyond the reach of many grassroots actors, particularly from Africa and South Asia. For more on the social characteristics of forum participants, see Santos 2006, 85–94. The polycentric forum and the decision to hold the WSF in Mumbai in 2004 and Nairobi in 2007 were meant to address this issue. Although reports from Nairobi suggest there was a preponderance of northern activists and NGOs, partly owing to the forum's distance from the city center and high admission fees (Trevor Ngwane, "What Happened in Nairobi," http://germany.indymedia .org/2007/ [accessed January 26, 2007]), Mumbai featured a larger proportion of grassroots actors, including indigenous and poor people's movements such as the Dalits (Conway 2004, 371). In addition to factors such as race, ethnicity, region, and class, Muslims and activists of faith more generally have been excluded from what has been constructed as a largely secular, modernist project (cf. Caruso 2004; Daulatzai 2004; Khan 2004). Meanwhile, feminist scholars have criticized the uneven participation of

women, particularly on high-profile panels, and the marginalization of women's issues within the forum (Desai 2005; Eschle 2005; Karides forthcoming). On a more theoretical level, as Nunes (2005b, 316) points out, open spaces are always defined by what lies outside their margins—that is, by what they exclude—while those who open the space determine its shape and contents, thus excluding other possibilities. Organizers of the U.S. Social Forum made a conscious and largely successful effort to reach out to and involve more grassroots activists and people of color.

20. For more on technology and the forum, see Waterman 2005.

21. Accessed January 26, 2007.

22. Separate websites were created for the 2004 WSF in Mumbai (www. wsfindia.org, accessed January 26, 2007) and the 2007 WSF in Nairobi (www.wsf2007.org, accessed January 26, 2007).

23. For example, the global portal designed to coordinate around the Day of Decentralized Actions planned for January 26, 2008, allows organizations to sign on the initiative as well as upload and share information regarding their project activities (http://www.wsf2008.net, accessed on September 15, 2007). Plans are also in the works for a World Social Clock, which would provide daily audio, radio, and video reports from actions around the world. In addition, the new WSF process site provides collaborative tools allowing groups to network, plan, and develop collective proposals, thus promoting greater decentralization, self-organization, and internal transparency (http://www.wsfprocess.net, accessed on September 15, 2007).

24. The ESF site was last accessed on January 26, 2007, and the United States Social Forum site on September 15, 2007.

25. The http://esf2004.net website was last accessed on January 3, 2006.

26. Regarding Beyond ESF and the Caracol, see http://www.wombles.org.uk/auto/ and http://www.a114all.org/2004/, respectively (accessed January 26, 2007).

27. GNU stands for "GNU's Not Unix" (Caruso 2005, 173).

28. Stefania Milan, "Communication: Open Systems for Open Politics," www.ipsterraviva .net/tv/wsf2005 (accessed January 3, 2006). See also Byrd 2005, 156.

29. The ESF website runs on an FS platform called Système de Publication Pour L'Internet (SPIP) the United States Social Forum websites uses an FS package called Drupal, and the new ESF and WSF process sites run an alternative FS content management system called Plone.

30. Juli Boéri and Stuart Hodkinson, "Babels and the Politics of Language at the Heart of Social Forum," http://www.euromovements.info/newsletter/babel.htm (accessed January 3, 2006).

31. Last accessed January 26, 2007.

32. See http://www.forumderadios.fm (accessed January 26, 2007).

33. A survey conducted at the 2005 WSF in Porto Alegre found that participants were evenly split on the question of whether the forum should articulate common positions as opposed to remaining an open space (Reese et al. 2007).

34. Cited from "Proposal for Discussion about the Creation of an Autonomous Space in Relation to the European Social Forum (ESF) in Florence," http://www.nadir.org/nadir/initiativ/agp/space/index.html (accessed December 15, 2003).

35. Forum participants may actually hold more radical views than many grassroots anti-capitalists believe. For example, a survey of participants at the 2005 WSF in Porto Alegre found that 58 percent of respondents favored abolishing and replacing capitalism, while 42 percent preferred reforms. Moreover, 87 percent of respondents favored abolishing multilateral financial institutions such as the World Bank, IMF, and WTO, while only 13 percent wanted to reform them (Reese et al. 2007).

36. "Towards an Autonomous Space at the European Social Forum in Florence, November 2002," http://www.nadir.org/nadir/initiativ/agp/pgaeurope/leiden/autonomous_space.htm (accessed December 15, 2003).

37. For more on the 2002 ESF, see Waterman 2002.

38. See http://www.nadir.org/nadir/initiativ/agp/space/hubproject.htm (accessed January 26, 2007).

39. The social composition of the autonomous spaces in Mumbai, which included large numbers of peasants and workers, differed from the young, middle-class urban activists behind previous autonomous spaces, which were also more inspired by libertarian visions and a commitment to the politics of autonomy in the strict ideological sense (I want to thank Michal Osterweil for reminding me of this point). However, I continue to use the term "autonomous space" with respect to Mumbai to signal such spaces' structural relationship to the main forum. For more on Mumbai Resistance and the Mumbai Forum more generally, see J. Smith 2004.

40. Olivier de Marcellus, "Divisions and Missed Opportunities in Bombay," posted to the pga@lists.riseup.net Listserv, February 12, 2004.

41. "Autonomous Spaces," a free paper distributed at the London ESF. For additional information, see http://www.altspaces.net (accessed January 26, 2007).

42. Although skeptics argued that the polycentric model represents a loss of focus, taken together, the three forums mobilized more than 100,000 participants.

43. The "Mural of Proposals" is archived on the WSF website (www.forumsocialmundial .org.br). Boaventura de Sousa Santos (2006) suggests that the WSF has shown an enormous capacity for learning, self-reform, and reinvention. For an analysis of the changes that took place in the WSF from 2003 to 2006, see Santos 2006, 72–81.

44. The 2007 forum in Nairobi, however, which was held in a football stadium on the outskirts of town, moved back toward a centralized model. This was no doubt due to logistical considerations and the local context in Nairobi. Marc Becker, "The World Social Forum Comes to Africa," http://www.yachana.org/reports/wsf7/report.html (accessed January 26, 2007). At the same time, it also suggests that the shift toward more participatory processes and decentralized forms within the forum is not unidirectional but rather highly uneven, contingent, and always subject to ongoing political struggles at specific moments and within concrete places. Still, the push toward

decentralization accelerated again following Nairobi with the announcement of a globally coordinated "Day of Mobilization" for 2008 instead of a single wsf.

45. In a 2007 report the ic Communications Commission notes that press coverage has declined in recent years and others a strategy for enhancing the public profile of the forum.

46. Chico Whitaker, "Towards Kenya in 2007," http://www.forumsocialmundial.org.br/ (accessed July 25, 2006).

47. Walden Bello, "Being an Open Space Is Not Enough," *Terraviva*, January 30, 2005, 12, http://www.ipsterraviva.net/tv/wsf2005/pdf/30.pdf (accessed July 25, 2006).

48. The text is archived at http://www.zmag.org/sustainers/content/2005-02/20group_of_nineteen.cfm (accessed January 26, 2007).

49. Terraviva Team, "A Divisive Consensus," *Terraviva*, January 31, 2005, 3, http://www.ipsterraviva.net/tv/wsf2005/pdf/31.pdf (accessed July 25, 2006).

50. For more on the appeal, see Waterman 2006. The Bamako appeal and other materials are archived at http://www.openspaceforum.net/ (accessed January 26, 2007).

51. Antonio Martins, "That Another World Is Possible," http://www.openspaceforum.net/ (accessed July 25, 2006).

52. "The Bamako Appeal—cacim's Initiatives," http://www.openspaceforum.net/ (accessed July 25, 2006). For a collection of essays critically assessing the Bamako Appeal from a variety of perspectives, see http://www.cacim.net/bareader/home.html (accessed January 26, 2007). This discussion was taken up again during a special workshop at the 2007 wsf in Nairobi.

53. Given the diversity of actors involved, achieving this balance may require a long-term process of translation, through which, as Boaventura de Sousa Santos (2006) has theorized, the wsf would serve as a contact zone where diverse movements establish a plane of mutual intelligibility with respect to their varying knowledges and practices. Anna Tsing (2005) has similarly referred to the importance of translation within transnational environmental networks, specifically with respect to local Indonesian activists and their global counterparts.

8. The Rise of Informational Utopics

1. Pierre Bourdieu, in Grass and Bourdieu 2002, 66, 76.

2. Tactical media theorists draw on the work of Michel de Certeau (1984), who distinguishes between *strategies*, which require a "proper" place from which to interact with opponents, and *tactics*, which are enacted in the territory of the enemy. Tactics are opportunistic and flexible, combining disparate elements to gain a momentary advantage.

3. Commercial media networks are increasingly concentrated in the hands of seven large corporate owners: Disney, aol Time Warner, Sony, News Corporation, Viacom, Vivendi, and Bertelsmann (McChesney 2001). The www.indymedia.org website was last accessed on January 26, 2007.

4. For more on Indymedia, see Downing 2003; Halleck 2002; Kidd 2003; Meikle 2002; and Nogueira 2002.

5. Indymedia faq page, http://process.indymedia.org/faq.php3 (accessed March 14, 2004).

6. Personal interview, June 4, 2002.

7. "Open Publishing Is the Same as Free Software," http://www.cat.org.au/maffew/cat/openpub.html (accessed March 14, 2004).

8. "Interview with Evan Henshaw-Plath," http://lists.indymedia.org/mailman/public/mediapolitics/2001-November/ (accessed March 14, 2004).

9. Ibid.

10. European Indymedia activists, and Germans in particular, have been more likely to support censoring hate speech than have their U.S.-based counterparts, who have been more committed to the principle of free speech.

11. Regarding sabotage of Indymedia sites, see the "Case of Biodun Iginla," http://www.anarchogeek.com/archives/ (accessed January 26, 2007).

12. See http://www.wikipedia.org (accessed January 26, 2007).

13. See http://www.next5minutes.org (accessed January 26, 2007). For more on tactical media, see Lovink 2002, 254–75; and Meikle 2002, 113–72.

14. See www.adbusters.org (accessed January 26, 2007). For more on culture jamming, see Klein 2000, 279–310; and Lasn 1999.

15. See www.gatt.org (accessed January 26, 2007). ®™ark (pronounced "artmark") provides funding and technical assistance for corporate sabotage projects.

16. Culture jamming and guerrilla communications tactics employ the Situationist strategy of détournement: taking well-known phrases, images, and ideas from mass culture and giving them an unexpected twist or detour to create surprising and playful combinations (see Richardson 2003, 124–25).

17. Yomango, "Presentación de la Marca Yomango," http://www.sindominio.net/lasagencias/yomango/ (accessed March 15, 2004). The text is now archived at http://www.yomango.net/ (accessed January 26, 2007).

18. Yomango, "10 Sugerencias para un Estilo Yo Mango," http://www.sindominio.net/lasagencias/yomango/ (accessed March 15, 2004). The text is now archived at http://www.yomango.net/ (accessed January 26, 2007).

19. Yomango, "Presentación de la Marco Yo Mango."

20. For more on electronic civil disobedience, see Jordan and Taylor 2004; and Meikle 2002, 140–72. For many activists and observers, ECD is largely synonymous with "hacktivism." However, many self-described hacktivists oppose the kind of "denial of service" attacks associated with ECD as a violation of the basic hacker tenet: all information should be free (Jordan and Taylor 2004, 98). Hacktivism can thus be defined more generally as "hacking for a political cause" (MetacOm 2003, 1), which includes experimenting with computer systems or software code for a political purpose. Building on an even broader definition of a hacker as "an expert or enthusiast of any kind" (Himanen 2001, viii), I consider hacktivism as any political practice inspired by a hacker ethic, including the collaborative networking explored in this book.

21. The term "ECD" was coined by Critical Art Ensemble in a 1996 work of the same title, which argued that as capital becomes increasingly dispersed, mobile, and electronic, resistance should take a similar form. Given that power today operates via global information flows within virtual networks, effective civil disobedience ought to block these flows.

22. The first virtual sit-in in February drew 18,000 participants over a two-hour period. The next protest in April drew more than 8,000 protesters around the world (Meikle 2002, 143–44).

23. Call for the Multitude Connected Conference organized by hackitectura.net in Huelva, Spain, September 2–4, 2003, sent to the prep-1@geneva03.org Listserv, August 23, 2002.

24. For more on experimental media labs, see Lovink 2002, 240–53.

25. "Call for Hackmeeting 2002 in Bologna from June 21 to 23," http://www.ecn.org/hackit02/index.en.html (accessed March 19, 2004).

26. Regarding Italian hackmeetings, see http://www.hackmeeting.org (accessed January 26, 2007).

27. "Hacklabs—a Space of Construction and Deconstruction," http://www.hubproject.org/ (accessed March 19, 2004).

28. Ibid.

29. See http://www.sindominio.net/ (accessed January 26, 2007).

30. Call to Eur@ction Hub project.

31. Ibid.

32. Early version of the project call posted to the prep-1@geneva03.org Listserv, August 24, 2003. For more information, see http://www.geneva03.org (accessed January 26, 2007).

33. Infospace project flyer.

34. The ESC was modeled after the March 1999 Spanish Consulta for the Abolition of the Foreign Debt and the Zapatista National Consulta for Peace and Democracy in August 1995.

35. "European Social Consulta Presentation Document," http://www.nadir.org/nadir/initiativ/agp/free/leiden/consulta.htm (accessed April 24, 2004).

36. ESC Internal Consultation Guide.

37. Ibid.

38. Flyer titled "This Is What Democracy Looks Like."

39. Spanish and Catalan groups ultimately carried out a statewide referendum during the European parliamentary elections in June 2004 around war, the economy, democracy, civil rights, and the environment. See http://www.consultaeuropea.org/consultafisica.htm (accessed April 24, 2004).

40. See www.oekonux.org (accessed January 26, 2007). For more on Oekonux, see Lovink 2003, 195. As we saw in the last chapter, this emphasis on openness is reflected in the social forum process through the discourse of "open space."

41. "Interview with Stefan Merten by Geert Lovink," http://amsterdam.nettime.org/Lists-Archives/ (accessed April 23, 2004).

Conclusion

1. Holloway 2002, 215.

2. Although Cohen and Arato contend that new social movements are "self-limiting," operating alongside but not seeking to replace formal democratic institutions, more radical anti–corporate globalization activists are attempting to do just that. Radicals are thus building what Trotsky (1930) called "dual power," the parallel network of alternative institutions that exist alongside the official governing apparatus, ultimately giving rise to revolutionary situations. However, rather than seizing state power, contemporary radicals are building autonomous "counter-power" (cf. Holloway 2002; Negri 2001), constituting noncapitalist spaces within the capitalist order, potentially leading to "new emerging forms of sociability and justice, a cumulative effect that ultimately shifts the prevailing balance" (Benasayag 2001, 69).

3. In her study of the U.S.-based direct-action movement of the 1970s and 1980s, Barbara Epstein (1991) makes a similar argument regarding that movement's inability to "solve the problem of how to build a movement that prefigures a better society and is at the same time sustained and effective over time" (266). Francesca Polletta (2002) has argued that participatory democratic organizations *have* proven strategic with respect to solidarity, innovation, and leadership development, but this says little about their sustainability, scale, or ability to intervene within institutional political spheres, while remaining consistent with activists' directly democratic ideals. This is precisely the challenge for all grassroots movements seeking long-term social transformation as well as more immediate political change.

4. In this sense, with respect to the historical tension between Marx and Bakunin, new digital technologies have reinforced anarchist ideas regarding decentralized coordination and directly democratic decision making. Indeed, horizontal forms of organization are diffusing rapidly, even among many forces of the traditional Left.

5. "Tactical networking" is adapted here from the analogous "tactical media" concept discussed in chapter 8 with respect to activist tactics that creatively intervene along mass media terrains. Likewise, whereas "alternative media" are grassroots sources of news and information, "strategic networking" involves the construction of autonomous social, political, and economic institutions. This formulation ultimately derives from Michel de Certeau (1984), for whom strategies involve frontal attacks launched from one's sovereign territory, while tactics are conducted along enemy terrain. See chapter 8, note 2.

6. William Gamson (1990) provides one of the best-known models for evaluating movement impact with respect to the state, involving a classification scheme based on whether challengers receive new advantages or gain acceptance. For a recent edited volume regarding the impact of social movements, with a particular emphasis on the institutional sphere, see Giugny, McAdam, and Tilly 1999. More influenced by New Social Movement theorists, anthropological accounts of social movement impact have tended to focus on broader cultural change and shifts in consciousness (cf. Edelman 1999; Warren 1998).

7. As argued in chapter 4, the contemporary world is characterized by a pervasive media logic. In this context, anti–corporate globalization movements stage spectacular image events as a way to gain visibility in a media environment dominated by "informational politics" (Castells 1996). Although radical critiques are often blunted by trivialization and disparagement and an emphasis on violence and internal divisions (Gitlin 1980, 27–28), reformist actors are more likely to elicit positive press coverage and thus have an indirect effect on electoral agendas by shaping public discourse (cf. McCarthy, Smith, and Zald 1996).

8. Regarding "media framing" and competing "media packages," see Gitlin 1980 and Gamson and Modigliani 1989, respectively. For an analysis of media framing with respect to anti–corporate globalization movements in Spain and Catalonia, see Juris 2004b, 487–507.

9. For example, in *El País* from January 29 to February 5, 2002, the World Social Forum and World Economic Forum were covered together under the following headings: "Davos and Porto Alegre Summits" or "The Globalization Debate."

10. In recent years, however, commentators such as CNN's Lou Dobbs have begun to articulate more critical viewpoints with respect to economic globalization, although in Dobbs's case this has accompanied a more reactionary anti-immigrant discourse.

11. Although activists have continued to organize periodic mass actions, most notably against G8 summits, including protests in Gleneagles, Scotland (2005); St. Petersburg, Russia (2006); and Heiligendamm, Germany (2007), world and regional social forums have largely displaced mass protest actions as the primary vehicles of public expression among anti–corporate globalization movements.

12. In addition to representatives from the Brazilian Workers' Party, including then presidential candidate Luis Inácio da Silva, French politicians also had a visible presence at the 2002 edition of the WSF, including presidential candidates such as the left-wing nationalist Jean-Pierre Chevenement; Noël Mamère of Les Verts, the French green party; and the Trotskyist Olivier Besancenot. Many Spanish and Catalan leaders also made the trip to Porto Alegre, including Joan Clos, mayor of Barcelona; the socialist Jose Borell; Communist Party chief Francisco Frutos; and Joan Saura, secretary of Iniciativa per Catalunya.

13. See www.ussf2007.org (accessed January 26, 2007).

14. Calle 2004, 394.

15. According to Barbara Epstein (1991, 268), the U.S.-based direct-action activists she studied were influenced by similar visions but set aside strategic and organizational considerations in favor of a nearly exclusive focus on mass direct actions. However, the widespread emphasis on organizational and technological innovation among contemporary anti–corporate globalization activists suggests a much wider outlook.

16. Arjun Appadurai (2002) has similarly conducted ethnographic research among urban activists in Mumbai as part of an ongoing comparative study of how grassroots movements combine local activism with horizontal global networking. Appadurai's work

forms part of a larger project involving a network of individual researchers, each conducting fieldwork in a specific locale, rather than the kind of mobile yet locally situated ethnography I have outlined in this book.

17. Indeed, as Francesca Polletta (2002) has noted, "effective organizational forms are necessarily hybrids" (221).

REFERENCES

Aaronson, Susan A. 2001. *Taking Trade to the Streets*. Ann Arbor: University of Michigan Press.

Abbink, Jon. 1990. Preface to *Meanings of Violence*, ed. Göran Aijmer and Jon Abbink, xi–xvii. Oxford: Berg.

Abu-Lughod, Lila, and Catherine A. Lutz. 1990. Introduction to *Language and the Politics of Emotion*, ed. Lila Abu-Lughod and Catherine A. Lutz, 1–23. Cambridge: Cambridge University Press.

Agamben, Giorgio. 1998. *Homo Sacer*. Stanford, Calif.: Stanford University Press.

Altheide, David L., and Robert P. Snow. 1991. *Media Worlds in the Postjournalism Era*. New York: Aldine de Gruyter.

Alvarez, Sonia E. 1997. "Reweaving the Fabric of Collective Action." In *Between Resistance and Revolution*, ed. Richard G. Fox and Orin Starn, 83–117. New Brunswick: Rutgers University Press.

Alvarez, Sonia E., Evelina Dagnino, and Arturo Escobar, eds. 1998. *Cultures of Politics/ Politics of Cultures*. Boulder, Colo.: Westview Press. Introduction, 1–29.

Alvarez-Junco, José. 1994. "Social Movements in Modern Spain." In *New Social Movements*, ed. Enrique Laraña, Hank Johnston, and Joseph R. Gusfield, 304–29. Philadelphia: Temple University Press.

———. 1986. "El anarquismo en el España contemporánea." *Anales de la Historia Contemporánea* 5: 189–200.

———. 1977. "Los dos anarquismos." *Cuadernos de Ruedo Ibérico* 55–57: 139–56.

Appadurai, Arjun. 2002. "Deep Democracy." *Public Culture* 14 (1): 21–47.

———. 2001. "Grassroots Globalization and the Research Imagination." In *Globalization*, ed. Arjun Appadurai, 1–21. Durham, N.C.: Duke University Press.

———. 1996. *Modernity at Large*. Minneapolis: University of Minnesota Press.

Arquilla, John, and David F. Ronfeldt. 2001. *Networks and Netwars*. Santa Monica, Calif.: Rand.

Assens, Jaume. 1999. "La criminalización del movimiento okupa." In *Okupación, represión y movimientos sociales*, ed. Asamblea de Okupas de Terrassa, 57–78. Barcelona: Diatriba.

Auyero, Javier. 2002. "The Judge, the Cop, and the Queen of Carnival." *Theory and Society* 31(2): 151–87.

Ayres, Jeffrey M. 1999. "From the Streets to the Internet." *Annals of the American Academy of Political and Social Sciences* 566: 132–43.

———. 1998. *Defying Conventional Wisdom.* Toronto: University of Toronto Press.

Baiocchi, Gianpaolo. 2004. "The Party and the Multitude." *Journal of World Systems Research* 10: 195–215.

Bakhtin, M. M. 1984. *Rabelais and His World.* Bloomington: Indiana University Press.

Bandy, Joe, and Jackie Smith, eds. 2005. *Coalitions across Borders.* Lanham, Md.: Rowman and Littlefield.

Barker, Colin. 2001. "Fear, Laughter, and Collective Power." In *Passionate Politics*, ed. Jeff Goodwin, James Jasper, and Francesca Polletta, 175–94. Chicago: University of Chicago Press.

Barker, Colin, and Lawrence Cox. 2002. "What Have the Romans Ever Done for Us?" http://www.iol.ie/~mazzoldi/toolsforchange/afpp/afpp8.html (accessed July 17, 2005).

Barnes, John A. 1954. "Class and Committees in a Norwegian Island Parish." *Human Relations* 7: 39–58.

Barry, Andrew. 2001. *Political Machines.* New York: Athlone Press.

Bauman, Richard. 1977. *Verbal Art as Performance.* Rowley, Mass.: Newbury House.

Bauman, Richard, and Charles L. Briggs. 1990. "Poetics and Performance as Critical Perspectives on Language and Social Life." *Annual Review of Anthropology* 19: 59–88.

Beck, Ulrich. 1992. *Risk Society.* Newbury Park, Calif.: Sage Publications.

Benasayag, Miguel. 2001. "Fundamentos para una metaeconomía." In *Contrapoder*, ed. Toni Negri, John Holloway, H. Gonzalez, Miguel Benasayag, and Luis Mattini, 47–72. Buenos Aires: Ediciones de Mano en Mano.

Bennett, W. Lance. 2005. "Social Movements beyond Borders." In *Transnational Protest and Global Activism*, ed. Donatella della Porta and Sidney Tarrow, 203–26. Lanham, Md.: Rowman and Littlefield.

———. 2003. "Communicating Global Activism." *Information, Communication, and Society* 6 (2): 143–68.

Berezin, Mabel. 2001. "Emotions and Political Identity." In *Passionate Politics*, ed. Jeff Goodwin, James Jasper, and Francesca Polletta, 83–98. Chicago: University of Chicago Press.

Bey, Hakim. 1991. *T.A.Z.* Brooklyn, N.Y.: Autonomedia.

Blok, Anton. 2000. "The Enigma of Senseless Violence." In *Meanings of Violence*, ed. Göran Aijmer and Jon Abbink, 23–38. Oxford: Berg.

Boissevain, Jeremy. 1974. *Friends of Friends.* New York: St. Martin's Press.

Bookchin, Murray. 2004. *Post-scarcity Anarchism.* 3rd ed. Oakland, Calif.: AK Press.

———. 1998. *The Spanish Anarchists.* San Francisco: AK Press.

Bott, Elizabeth. 1971. *Family and Social Network.* 2nd ed. London: Tavistock Publications. (Orig. pub. 1957.)

Bourdieu, Pierre. 2001. *Masculine Domination.* Cambridge, UK: Polity Press.

Bourgois, Philippe. 2001. "The Power of Violence in War and Peace." *Ethnography* 2 (1): 5–34.

Bovè, Jose, and Françoise Dufour. 2001. *The World Is Not for Sale.* London: Verso.

Bowman, Glenn. 2001. "The Violence in Identity." In *The Anthropology of Violence and Conflict,* ed. Bettina E. Schmidt and Ingo W. Schröder, 25–46. Oxford: Routledge.

Brandes, Stanley H. 1990. "The Sardana." *Journal of American Folklore* 103: 24–41.

———. 1980. *Metaphors of Masculinity.* Philadelphia: University of Pennsylvania Press.

———. 1973. "Social Structure and Interpersonal Relations in Navanogal." *American Anthropologist* 75(3): 750–65.

Brecher, Jeremy, Tim Costello, and Brendan Smith. 2000. *Globalization from Below.* Cambridge: South End Press.

Breines, Wini. 1989. *Community and Organization in the New Left, 1962–1968.* New ed. New Brunswick, N.J.: Rutgers University Press.

Brenan, Gerald. 1943. *The Spanish Labyrinth.* New York: Macmillan Company.

Burawoy, Michael. 2000. "Grounding Globalization." In *Global Ethnography,* ed. Michael Burawoy, 337–50. Berkeley: University of California Press.

Burdick, John. 1998. *Blessed Anastácia.* New York: Routledge.

———. 1995. "Uniting Theory and Practice in the Ethnography of Social Movements." *Dialectical Anthropology* 20: 361–85.

Butler, Judith. 1993. *Bodies That Matter.* New York: Routledge.

Byrd, Scott C. 2005. "The Porto Alegre Consensus." *Globalizations* 2 (1): 151–63.

Calle, Angel. 2004. "Los nuevos movimientos globales." Ph.D. diss., Universidad Carlos III, Madrid.

Callon, Michel. 1991. "Techno-economic Networks and Irreversibility." In *A Sociology of Monsters,* ed. John Law. New York: Routledge.

Canetti, Elias. 1962. *Crowds and Power.* Trans. Carol Stewart. New York: Viking Press.

Canguilhem, Georges. 1989. *The Normal and the Pathological.* New York: Zone Books.

Carr, Raymond. 1966. *Spain.* Oxford: Clarendon Press.

Caruso, Giuseppe. 2005. "Open Office and Free Software." *Ephemera* 5 (2): 173–92.

———. 2004. "Conflict Management and Hegemonic Practices in the World Social Forum 2004." *International Social Science Journal* 182: 577–90.

Castells, Manuel. 2000. "Materials for an Exploratory Theory of the Network Society." *British Journal of Sociology* 51 (1): 5–24.

———. 1997. *The Power of Identity.* Malden, Mass.: Blackwell.

———. 1996. *The Rise of the Network Society.* Cambridge, Mass.: Blackwell.

Chesters, Graeme, and Ian Welsh. 2006. *Complexity and Social Movements.* London: Routledge.

———. 2004. "Rebel Colours." *Sociological Review* 52 (3): 314–35.

Clarke, John. 1976. "Style." In *Resistance through Rituals,* ed. Stuart Hall and Tony Jefferson, 175–91. Boston: Unwin Hyman.

Cleaver, Harry M. 1999. "Computer-Linked Social Movements and the Threat to Global Capitalism." http://www.eco.utexas.edu/Homepages/Faculty/Cleaver/polnet.html (accessed May 19, 2004).

———. 1998. "The Zapatista Effect." *Journal of International Affairs* 51 (2): 621–40.

———. 1995. "The Zapatistas and the Electronic Fabric of Struggle." http://www.eco.utexas.edu/faculty/Cleaver/zaps.html (accessed March 18, 2004).

Cockburn, Alexander, and Jeffrey St. Clair. 2000. *Five Days That Shook the World.* London: Verso.

Cohen, Jean. 1985. "Strategy or Identity." *Social Research* 52: 663–716.

Cohen, Jean L., and Andrew Arato. 1992. *Civil Society and Political Theory.* Cambridge: MIT Press.

Colectivo Situaciones. 2001. "Por una política mas allá de la política." In *Contrapoder*, ed. Toni Negri, John Holloway, H. Gonzalez, Miguel Benasayag, and Luis Mattini, 19–46. Buenos Aires: Ediciones de Mano en Mano.

Collins, Randall. 2001. "Social Movements and the Focus of Emotional Attention." In *Passionate Politics*, ed. Jeff Goodwin, James Jasper, and Francesca Polletta, 27–44. Chicago: University of Chicago Press.

Comaroff, Jean, and John L. Comaroff, eds. 2000. "Millennial Capitalism and the Culture of Neoliberalism." Special issue, *Public Culture* 12 (2): 291–343.

Conquergood, Dwight. 1992. "Performance Theory, Hmong Shamans, and Cultural Politics." In *Critical Theory and Performance*, ed. Janelle G. Reinelt and Joseph R. Roach, 41–64. Ann Arbor: University of Michigan Press.

Conversi, Daniele. 1997. *The Basques, the Catalans and Spain.* London: Hurst.

Conway, Janet M. 2006. *Praxis and Politics.* London: Routledge.

———. 2004. "Citizenship in a Time of Empire." *Citizenship Studies* 8 (4): 367–81.

Critical Art Ensemble. 1996. *Electronic Civil Disobedience.* Brooklyn: Autonomedia.

Csordas, Thomas J. 1990. "Embodiment as a Paradigm for Anthropology." *Ethos* 18 (1): 5–47.

Cucci, Maurizio. 2001. "Chronology of the Inter-continental Caravan for Solidarity and Resistance!" In *Restructuring and Resistance*, ed. Kolya Abramsky, 475–83. Distributed from resresrev@yahoo.com.

Cunningham, Hilary. 2000. "The Ethnography of Social Transnational Activism." *American Ethnologist* 26 (3): 583–604.

Danaher, Kevin. 2001. *Democratizing the Global Economy.* Monroe, Maine: Common Courage Press.

Daulatzai, Anila. 2005. "A Leap of Faith." *International Social Science Journal* 182: 565–76.

de Certeau, Michel. 1984. *The Practice of Everyday Life.* Berkeley: University of California Press.

Deleuze, Gilles, and Félix Guattari. 1987. *A Thousand Plateaus.* Minneapolis: University of Minnesota Press.

della Porta, Donatella. 2005. "Multiple Belongings, Tolerant Identities, and the Construction of Another Politics." In *Transnational Protest and Global Activism*, ed. Donatella della Porta and Sidney Tarrow, 175–202. Lanham, Md.: Rowman and Littlefield.

————. 1995. *Social Movements, Political Violence, and the State*. Cambridge: Cambridge University Press.

della Porta, Donatella, and Sidney Tarrow, eds. 2005. *Transnational Protest and Global Activism*. Lanham, Md.: Rowman and Littlefield.

della Porta, Donatella, et al. 2006. *Globalization from Below*. Minneapolis: University of Minnesota Press.

DeLuca, Kevin Michael. 1999. *Image Politics*. New York: Guilford Press.

Desai, Manisha. 2005. "Transnationalism." *International Social Science Journal* 57: 1468–2451.

Diamond, Elin. 1996. Introduction to *Performance and Cultural Politics*, ed. Elin Diamond, 1–12. London: Routledge.

Diani, Mario. 2003. "Leaders or Brokers?" In *Social Movements and Networks*, ed. Mario Diani and Doug McAdam, 105–22. Oxford: Oxford University Press.

————. 1995. *Green Networks*. Edinburgh: Edinburgh University Press.

Díaz-Salazar, Rafael. 1996. *Redes de solidaridad internacional*. Madrid: Hoac.

Dicken, Peter. 2003. *Global Shift*. 4th ed. Thousand Oaks: Sage Publications.

Díez Medrano, Juan. 1995. *Divided Nations*. Ithaca, N.Y.: Cornell University Press.

Diken, Bülent, and Carsten Bagge Laustsen. 2002. "Zones of Indistinction." *Space and Culture* 5 (3): 290–307.

Douglas, Mary. 1970. *Natural Symbols*. New York: Pantheon Books.

Downing, John D. H. 2003. "The Independent Media Center Movement." In *Contesting Media Power*, ed. Nick Couldry and James Curran, 243–58. Lanham, Md.: Rowman and Littlefield.

————. 2000. *Radical Media*. Thousand Oaks: Sage Publications.

Edelman, Marc. 2003. "Transnational Peasant and Farmer Movements and Networks." In *Global Civil Society Yearbook*, ed. Helmut K. Anheier, Mary H. Kaldor, and Marlies Glasius, 185–220. Oxford: Oxford University Press.

————. 1999. *Peasants against Globalization*. Stanford, Calif.: Stanford University Press.

Edles, Laura Desfor. 1998. *Symbol and Ritual in the New Spain*. Cambridge: Cambridge University Press.

Epstein, Barbara. 1991. *Political Protest and Cultural Revolution*. Berkeley: University of California Press.

Equip d'Análisis Política de la UAB i Universitat del País Basc. 2002. *Xarxes crítiques a Catalunya i euskadi*. Vol. 25. Barcelona: Fundacio Jaume Bofill.

Eschle, Catherine. 2005. "Skeleton Women." *Signs* 30: 1741–70.

Escobar, Arturo. 2004. "Beyond the Third World." *Third World Quarterly* 25 (1): 207–30.

————. 2001. "Culture Sits in Places." *Political Geography* 20: 139–74.

Escobar, Arturo, and Sonia E. Alvarez. 1992. Introduction to *The Making of Social Movements in Latin America*, ed. Arturo Escobar and Sonia E. Alvarez, 1–18. Boulder, Colo.: Westview Press.

Esenwein, George Richard, and Adrian Shubert. 1995. *Spain at War*. New York: Longman.

Farrer, Linden. 2002. "World Forum Movement: Abandon or Contaminate." http://www.nadir.org/nadir/initiativ/agp/free/wsf/worldforum.htm (accessed April 13, 2005).

Featherstone, Liza, and United Students against Sweatshops. 2002. *Students against Sweatshops*. London: Verso.

Feixa, Carles. 1999. *De jóvenes, bandas y tribus*. 2nd ed. Barcelona: Ariel.

Feldman, Allen. 1995. "On Cultural Anesthesia." *American Ethnologist* 21 (2): 404–18.

———. 1991. *Formations of Violence*. Chicago: University of Chicago Press.

Fillieulle, Olivier, and Fabien Jobard. 1997. *The Policing of Mass Demonstration in Contemporary Democracies*. Florence, Italy: European University Institute.

Fishman, Robert M. 1990. *Working Class Organization and the Return to Democracy in Spain*. Ithaca, N.Y.: Cornell University Press.

Foucault, Michel. 1986. "Of Other Spaces." *Diacritics* 16 (1): 22–7.

———. 1979. *Discipline and Punish*. New York: Vintage Books.

Fox, Jonathan A., and L. David Brown. 1998. *The Struggle for Accountability*. Cambridge: MIT Press.

Franco, Jean. 1985. "Killing Priests, Nuns, Women, Children." In *On Signs*, ed. Marshall Blonsky, 414–20. Baltimore: Johns Hopkins University Press.

Fraser, Nancy. 1992. "Rethinking the Public Sphere." In *Habermas and the Public Sphere*, ed. Craig Calhoun, 109–42. Cambridge: MIT Press.

Freeman, Jo. 1972. "The Tyranny of Structurelessness." *Second Wave* 2 (1): 20–25.

Furlong, Andy, and Fred Cartmel. 1997. *Young People and Social Change*. Buckingham: Open University Press.

Galeano, Eduardo H. 1973. *Open Veins of Latin America*. New York: Monthly Review Press.

Gamson, William A. 1990. *The Strategy of Social Protest*. 2nd ed. Belmont, Calif.: Wadsworth.

Gamson, William, and Andre Modigliani. 1989. "Media Discourse and Public Opinion on Nuclear Power." *American Journal of Sociology* 95 (1): 1–37.

"Gathering Food." 2001. In *Restructuring and Resistance*, ed. Kolya Abramsky, 456–61. Distributed from resresrev@yahoo.com.

Gedicks, Al. 2001. *Resource Rebels*. Cambridge, Mass.: South End Press.

Gerhards, J., and D. Rucht. 1992. "Mesomobilization." *American Journal of Sociology* 98: 555–95.

Gerlach, Luther P., and Virginia H. Hine. 1970. *People, Power, Change: Movements of Social Transformation*. Indianapolis: Bobbs-Merrill.

Giddens, Anthony. 1991. *Modernity and Self-Identity*. Stanford, Calif.: Stanford University Press.

———. 1990. *The Consequences of Modernity*. Stanford, Calif.: Stanford University Press.

Gilmore, David D. 1990. *Manhood in the Making*. New Haven, Conn.: Yale University Press.

———. 1980. *The People of the Plain*. New York: Columbia University Press.

Gitlin, Todd. 1980. *The Whole World Is Watching*. Berkeley: University of California Press.

Giugni, Marco, Doug McAdam, and Charles Tilly. 1999. *How Social Movements Matter.* Minneapolis: University of Minnesota Press.

Gluckman, Max. 1954. *Rituals of Rebellion in South-East Africa.* Manchester: Manchester University Press.

Goodwin, Jeff, and Steven Pfaff. 2001. "Emotion Work in High-Risk Social Movements." In *Passionate Politics,* ed. Jeff Goodwin, James Jasper, and Francesca Polletta, 282–302. Chicago: University of Chicago Press.

Goodwin, Jeff, James M. Jasper, and Francesca Polletta, eds. 2001. *Passionate Politics.* Chicago: University of Chicago Press.

Gould, Kenneth A., Tammy L. Lewis, and J. Timmons Roberts. 2004. "Blue-Green Coalitions." *Journal of World-Systems Research* 10 (1): 91–116. http://jwsr.ucr.edu/archive/vol10/number1/index.php (accessed September 9, 2006).

Graeber, David. 2004. "The Twilight of Vanguardism." In *Challenging Empires,* ed. Jai Sen, Anita Anand, Arturo Escobar, and Peter Waterman, 329–35. New Delhi: Viveka Foundation.

———. 2002. "The New Anarchists." *New Left Review* 13: 61–73.

Graham, Hugh Davis, and Ted Robert Gurr. 1969. *Violence in America.* New York: Bantam Books.

Gramsci, Antonio. 1971. *The Prison Notebooks.* London: Lawrence and Wishart.

Grass, Günther, and Pierre Bourdieu. 2002. "The 'Progressive' Restoration." *New Left Review* 14 (March–April): 63–77.

Green, Linda. 1999. *Fear as a Way of Life.* New York: Columbia University Press.

Greenwood, Davydd J., and Morten Levin. 1998. *Introduction to Action Research.* Thousand Oaks: Sage Publications.

Grupo Autónomo A.f.r.i.k.a et al. 2000. *Manual de guerrilla de la comunicación.* Barcelona: Virus.

Gubitosa, Carlo. 2003. *Genova per nome.* Milan, Italy: Altreconomia, Ed. Berti.

Guérin, Daniel. 1970. *Anarchism.* New York: Monthly Review Press.

Guidry, John A., Michael D. Kennedy, and Mayer N. Zald. 2000. "Globalizations and Social Movements." In *Globalizations and Social Movements,* ed. John A. Guidry, Michael D. Kennedy, and Mayer N. Zald, 1–34. Ann Arbor: University of Michigan Press.

Gupta, Akhil, and James Ferguson. 1997. *Culture, Power, Place.* Durham, N.C.: Duke University Press.

Habermas, Jürgen. 1989. *The Structural Transformation of the Public Sphere.* Cambridge: MIT Press.

Hale, Charles R. 2006. "Activist Research v. Cultural Critique." *Cultural Anthropology* 21 (1): 96–120.

Hall, Stuart. 1974. "Deviance, Politics and the Media." In *Deviance and Social Control,* ed. Paul Rock and Mary McIntosh, 261–306. London: Tavistock.

Halleck, DeeDee. 2002. *Hand-Held Visions.* New York: Fordham University Press.

Handelman, Don. 1990. *Models and Mirrors.* New York: Cambridge University Press.

Hardt, Michael. 2002. "Today's Bandung." *New Left Review* 14: 112–118.

Hardt, Michael, and Antonio Negri. 2004. *Multitude*. New York: Penguin.

———. 2000. *Empire*. Cambridge: Harvard University Press.

Hart, Gillian Patricia. 2002. *Disabling Globalization*. Berkeley: University of California Press.

Harvey, David. 1989. *The Condition of Postmodernity*. Oxford: Blackwell.

Hawken, Paul. 2000. "Skeleton Woman Visits Seattle." In *Globalize This!* ed. Kevin Danaher and Roger Burbach, 14–34. Monroe, Maine: Common Courage Press.

Hebdige, Dick. 1979. *Subculture*. London: Routledge.

Held, David, Anthony McGraw, David Goldblatt, and Jonathan Perraton. 1999. *Global Transformations*. Stanford, Calif.: Stanford University Press.

Herreros, Tomas. 1999. Introduction to *Okupación, represión, y movimientos sociales*, ed. la Asamblea Okupa de Terrassa, 13–32. Barcelona: Diatriba.

Hetherington, Kevin. 1998. *Expressions of Identity*. Thousand Oaks: Sage.

Himanen, Pekka. 2001. *The Hacker Ethic*. New York: Random House.

Holloway, John. 2002. *Change the World without Taking Power*. London: Pluto Press.

hooks, bell. 1990. *Yearning*. Boston: South End Press.

Inglehart, Ronald. 1977. *The Silent Revolution*. Princeton, N.J.: Princeton University Press.

Jacknis, Ira. 1988. "Margaret Mead and Gregory Bateson in Bali." *Cultural Anthropology* 3 (2): 160–77.

Jameson, Fredric. 1991. *Postmodernism, or, The Cultural Logic of Late Capitalism*. Durham: Duke University Press.

Jansen, Stef. 2001. "The Streets of Beograd." *Political Geography* 20: 35–55.

Jasper, James M. 1998. "The Emotions of Protest." *Sociological Forum* 13 (3): 397–424.

Johnston, Hank. 1991. *Tales of Nationalism*. New Brunswick, N.J.: Rutgers University Press.

Jordan, John. 2004. "The Sound and the Fury." In *Globalize Resistance*, ed. David Solnit, 481–85. San Fransisco: City Lights Books.

———. 1998. "The Art of Necessity." In *DiY Culture*, ed. George McKay. London: Verso.

Jordan, Tim, and Paul A. Taylor. 2004. *Hacktivism and Cyberwars*. London: Routledge.

Juris, Jeffrey S. 2005c. "Social Forums and Their Margins." *Ephemera* 5 (2): 253–72. www.ephemeraweb.org/journal/5-2/5-2juris.pdf.

———. 2005b. "Violence Performed and Imagined." *Critique of Anthropology* 25 (4): 413–32.

———. 2005a. "The New Digital Media and Activist Networking within Anti–Corporate Globalization Movements." *Annals of the American Academy of Political and Social Sciences* 597: 189–208.

———. 2004b. "Digital Age Activism: Anti–Corporate Globalization and the Cultural Politics of Transnational Networking." Ph.D. diss., University of California, Berkeley.

———. 2004a. "Networked Social Movements." In *The Network Society*, ed. Manuel Castells, 341–62. London: Edward Elgar.

Kalb, Don. 2000. *The Ends of Globalization*. Lanham, Md.: Rowman and Littlefield.

Kapchan, Deborah A. 1995. "Performance." *Journal of American Folklore* 108 (430): 479–508.

Kapferer, Bruce. 1973. "Social Network and Conjugal Role in Urban Zambia." In *Network Analysis*, ed. Jeremy Boissevain and J. Clyde Mitchell, 83–110. The Hague: Mouton.

Kaplan, Temma. 1977. *Anarchists of Andalusia, 1868–1903*. Princeton, N.J.: Princeton University Press.

Karides, Marina. Forthcoming. "Feminist Contentions at the WSF." In *World-Systemic Crisis and Contending Political Scenarios*, ed. Joya Misra and Agustin Lao-Montes. Chicago: Paradigm Press.

Katsiaficas, George. 2001. "Seattle Was Not the Beginning." In *The Battle of Seattle*, ed. Eddie Yuen, Daniel Burton-Rose, and George Katsiaficas, 69–72. New York: Soft Skull Press.

———. 1997. *The Subversion of Politics*. Atlantic Highlands, N.J.: Humanities Press.

Keck, Margaret E., and Kathryn Sikkink. 1998. *Activists beyond Borders*. Ithaca, N.Y.: Cornell University Press.

Khagram, Sanjeev, James V. Riker, and Kathryn Sikkink. 2002. *Restructuring World Politics*. Minneapolis: University of Minnesota Press.

Khan, Taran N. 2004. "Trio." *International Social Science Journal* 182: 541–50.

Khasnabish, Alex. 2005. "You Will No Longer Be You, Now You Are Us." Ph.D. diss., Department of Anthropology, McMaster University, Hamilton, Ontario.

Kidd, Dorothy. 2003. "Indymedia.org." In *Cyberactivism*, ed. Martha McCaughey and Michael D. Ayers, 47–70. New York: Routledge.

King, Jamie. 2004. "The Packet Gang." *Metamute* 27. http://www.metamute.org/en/The-Packet-Gang (accessed January 8, 2005).

Klein, Naomi. 2002. *Fences and Windows*. New York: Picador USA.

———. 2000. *No Space, No Choice, No Jobs, No Logo*. New York: Picador USA.

Kubrin, David. 2001. "Scaling the Heights of Seattle." In *The Battle of Seattle*, ed. Eddie Yuen, Daniel Burton-Rose, and George Katsiaficas, 59–68. New York: Soft Skull Press.

Lakey, George. 1973. *Strategy for a Living Revolution*. San Francisco: W. H. Freeman.

Lancaster, Roger N. 1997. "Guto's Performance." In *The Gender/Sexuality Reader*, ed. Roger N. Lancaster and Micaela di Leonardo, 559–74. New York: Routledge.

Laraña, Enrique. 1999. *La construcción de los movimientos sociales*. Madrid: Alianza.

Lasn, Kalle. 1999. *Culture Jam*. New York: Eagle Brook.

Latour, Bruno. 1993. *We Have Never Been Modern*. Cambridge: Harvard University Press.

———. 1987. *Science in Action*. Cambridge: Harvard University Press.

Lévy, Pierre. 2001. *Cyberculture*. Minneapolis: University of Minnesota Press.

Lichterman, Paul. 1996. *The Search for Political Community*. Cambridge: Cambridge University Press.

Linz, Juan. 2002. "Parties in Contemporary Democracies." In *Political Parties*, ed. Richard Gunther, Jose Ramon Montero, and Juan J. Linz, 291–317. Oxford: Oxford University Press.

Linz, Juan J., and Amando de Miguel. 1966. "Within-Nation Differences and Compari-
sons." In *Comparing Nations*, ed. Richard L. Merrit and Stein Rokkan, 267–319. New
Haven, Conn.: Yale University Press.

Linz, Juan J., and Jose Ramon Montero. 1999. *The Party Systems of Spain*. Working Paper
1999/138. Madrid: Instituto Juan March.

Linz, Juan J., and Alfred C. Stepan. 1996. *Problems of Democratic Transition and Consolidation*. Baltimore: Johns Hopkins University Press.

Little, Paul. 1995. "Ritual, Power, and Ethnography at the Rio Earth Summit." *Critique of
Anthropology* 15 (3): 265–68.

Lovink, Geert. 2003. *My First Recession*. Rotterdam: NAI PUBLISHERS/V2 Organization.

———. 2002. *Dark Fiber*. Cambridge: MIT Press.

Lovink, Geert, and Florian Schneider. 2002. "New Rules, New Actonomy." In *Cities of Everyday Life (Sarai Reader)*, ed. Sarai Media Lab, 314–19. Delhi, India: Rainbow Publishers.

Luhmann, Niklas. 1990. *Essays on Self-Reference*. New York: Columbia University Press.

Lynch, Cecilia. 1998. "Social Movements and the Problem of Globalization." *Alternatives*
23: 149–73.

Lyon, M. L., and J. M. Barbalet. 1994. "Society's Body." In *Embodiment and Experience*, ed.
Thomas J. Csordas, 48–68. Cambridge: Cambridge University Press.

Maffesoli, Michel. 1996. *The Times of the Tribes*. Thousand Oaks, Calif.: Sage.

Mahon, Maureen. 2004. *Right to Rock*. Durham, N.C.: Duke University Press.

Marcus, George E. 1995. "Ethnography in/of the World System." *Annual Review of Anthropology* 24: 95–117.

Martínez, Elizabeth. 2000. "Where Was the Color in Seattle?" *Colorlines* 3 (1).

Martínez López, Miguel. 2002. *Okupaciones de viviendas y de centros sociales*. Barcelona: Virus.

Massey, Doreen. 1994. "Politics and Space/Time." In *Space, Place and Gender*, ed. Doreen
Massey, 249–72. Cambridge: Polity Press.

Maturana, Humberto. 1981. *Autopoiesis*. Ed. Milan Zeleny. New York: North Holland.

Mauss, Marcal. 1973. "Techniques of the Body." *Economy and Society* 2 (1): 70–88.

McCarthy, John D., Jackie Smith, and Mayer Zald. 1996. "Accessing Public, Media, Electoral, and Governmental Agendas." In *Comparative Perspectives on Social Movements*,
ed. Doug McAdam, John D. McCarthy, and Mayer N. Zald, 291–311. Cambridge: Cambridge University Press.

McChesney, Robert W. 2001. "Global Media, Neoliberalism, and Imperialism." *Monthly
Review* 52 (10): 1–19.

McDonald, Kevin. 2006. *Global Movements*. Malden, Mass.: Blackwell.

McKay, George. 1998. *DiY Culture*. London: Verso.

Meikle, Graham. 2002. *Future Active*. New York: Routledge.

Melucci, Alberto. 1989. *Nomads of the Present*. London: Hutchinson Radius.

MetacOm. December 2003. "What Is Hacktivism? 2.0." http://www.thehacktivist.com/
hacktivism.php (accessed November 13, 2005).

Miller, Daniel, and Don Slater. 2000. *The Internet*. New York: Berg.

Mintz, Jerome R. 1997. *Carnival Song and Society*. Oxford: Berg.

Mische, Anne. 2003. "Cross-Talk in Movements." In *Social Movements and Networks*, ed. Mario Diani and Doug McAdam, 258–80. Oxford: Oxford University Press.

Mitchell, J. Clyde. 1974. "Social Networks." *Annual Review of Anthropology* 3: 279–99.

Moghadam, Valentine M. 2005. *Globalizing Women*. Baltimore, Md.: Johns Hopkins University Press.

Molinero, Carme, and Pere Ysas. 2002. "Workers and Dictatorship." In *Red Barcelona*, ed. Angel Smith, 185–205. London: Routledge.

Monahan, Torin. 2005. *Globalization, Technological Change, and Public Education*. New York: Routledge.

Moog Rodriguez, Maria Guadalupe. 2004. *Global Environmentalism and Local Politics*. Albany: State University of New York Press.

Myers, Fred R. 1986. "Reflections on a Meeting." *American Ethnologist* 13 (3): 430–47.

Nader, Laura. 1972. "Up the Anthropologist." In *Reinventing Anthropology*, ed. Dell Hymes, 248–311. New York: Pantheon Books.

Nash, June C. 2001. *Mayan Visions*. New York: Routledge.

Negri, Toni. 2001. "Contrapoder." In *Contrapoder*, ed. Toni Negri, John Holloway, H. Gonzalez, Miguel Benasayag, and Luis Mattini, 83–94. Buenos Aires: Ediciones de Mano en Mano.

Nelson, Diane M. 1999. *A Finger in the Wound*. Berkeley: University of California Press.

Nogueira, Ana. 2002. "The Birth and Promise of the Indymedia Revolution." In *Act Up to the WTO*, ed. Benjamin Shephard and Ronald Hayduk, 290–97. London: Verso.

Nordstrom, Carolyn. 1997. *A Different Kind of War Story*. Philadelphia: University of Pennsylvania Press.

Norris, Pippa. 2001. *Digital Divide*. Cambridge: Cambridge University Press.

Notes from Nowhere. 2003. *We Are Everywhere*. London: Verso.

Nunes, Rodrigo. 2005b. "Networks, Open Spaces, Horizontality: Instantiations." *Ephemera* 5 (2): 297–318.

———. 2005a. "The Intercontinental Youth Camp as the Unthought of the World Social Forum." *Ephemera* 5 (2): 277–96.

O'Brien, Robert, Anne Marie Goetz, and Jan Aart Scholte. 2000. *Contesting Global Governance*. Cambridge: Cambridge University Press.

Offe, Claus. 1985. "New Social Movements." *Social Research* 52: 817–68.

Olesen, Thomas. 2005. *International Zapatismo*. London: Zed Books.

Ong, Aihwa. 1999. *Flexible Citizenship*. Durham, N.C.: Duke University Press.

Orizo, Francisco Andrés. 1999. "Jovenes." In *Jovenes españoles 99*, 53–120. Madrid: Fundación Santa María.

Ortellado, Pablo. 2003. "Whose Movement?" http://www.nadir.org/nadir/initiativ/agp/free/wsf/whosemovement.htm (accessed April 13, 2003).

Ortner, Sherry. 1973. "On Key Symbols." *American Anthropologist* 75 (5): 1338–1346.

Osterweil, Michal. 2004. "De-centering the Forum." In *Challenging Empires*, ed. Jai Sen, Anita Anand, Arturo Escobar, and Peter Waterman, 183–90. New Delhi: Viveka Foundation.

Pagliai, Valentina. 2002. "Poetic Dialogues." *Ethnology* 41 (2): 135–54.

Paley, Julia. 2001. *Marketing Democracy.* Berkeley: University of California Press.

Pallares, Joan, Carmen Costa, and Carles Feixa. 2002. "Okupas, Makineros, Skinheads." In *Graffitis, Grifotas, Okupas,* ed. Carles Feixa, Carmen Costa, and Joan Pallares, 89–114. Barcelona: Ariel.

Parr, Hester. 2001. "Feeling, Reading, and Making Bodies in Space." *Geographical Review* 91 (1–2): 158–67.

Pastor, Jaime. 1998. "La evolución de los movimientos sociales en el estado español." In *Los movimientos sociales,* ed. Pedro Ibarra and Benjamin Tejerina, 69–87. Madrid: Editorial Trotta.

Patomäki, Heikki, and Teivo Teivainen. 2004. "The World Social Forum, an Open Space or a Movement of Movements?" *Theory, Culture and Society* 21 (6): 145–54.

Pérez de Lama, José 2004. "Geografías de_la_multitud." http://www.hackitectura.net/osfavelados/txts/sci_fi_geographies.html (accessed March 14, 2003).

Pérez-Díaz, Víctor. 2002. "From Civil War to Civil Society." In *Democracies in Flux,* ed. Robert D. Putnam, 245–88. Oxford: Oxford University Press.

———. 1993. *The Return of Civil Society.* Cambridge: Harvard University Press.

Peteet, Julie. 2002. "Male Gender and Rituals of Resistance in the Palestinian Intifada." In *Violence: A Reader,* ed. Robert Jackall and Arthur J. Vidich, 244–272. New York: New York University Press.

Peterson, Abby. 2001. *Contemporary Political Protest.* Aldershot: Ashgate.

Pi-Sunyer, Oriol. 1974. "Elites and Noncorporate Groups in the European Mediterranean." *Comparative Studies in Society and History* 16: 117–31.

Pleyers, Geoffrey. 2005b. "The Social Forums as an Ideal Model of Convergence." *International Social Science Journal* 182: 507–19.

———. 2005a. "Young People and Alterglobalisation." In *Revisiting Youth Political Participation,* ed. Joerg Forbrig, 132–43. Strasbourg: Press of the Council of Europe.

Polanyi, Karl. 1957. *The Great Transformation.* Boston: Beacon Press.

Polletta, Francesca. 2002. *Freedom is an Endless Meeting.* Chicago: University of Chicago Press.

Ponniah, T., and W. F. Fisher. 2003. Introduction to *Another World Is Possible,* ed. T. Ponniah and W. F. Fisher, 1–20. London: Zed Books.

Pound, Christopher. 1995. "A Look Forward." In *Technoscientific Imaginaries,* ed. George E. Marcus, 527–48. Chicago: University of Chicago Press.

Prazniak, Roxann, and Arif Dirlik, eds. 2001. *Places and Politics in an Age of Globalization.* Lanham, Md.: Rowman and Littlefield.

Pulido, Laura. 2003. "The Interior Life of Politics." *Ethics, Place and Environment* 6 (1): 46–52.

Rabinow, Paul. 1989. *French Modern.* Cambridge: MIT Press.

Ray, Raka. 1999. *Fields of Protest.* Minneapolis: University of Minnesota Press.

Reese, Ellen, Mark Herkenrath, Chris Chase-Dunn, Rebecca Giem, Ericka Gutierrez, Linda Kim, and Christine Petit. Forthcoming. "North-South Contradictions and Bridges of the World Social Forum." In *North and South in the World Political Economy,* ed. Rafael Reuveny and William R. Thompson. Cambridge, Mass: Blackwell.

Reyes, Oscar, Hilary Wainwright, Fuster I. Morrell, Mayo, and Marco Berlinguer. 2005. "European Social Forum." *Red Pepper,* January 2005. http://www.redpepper.org.uk/Jan2005/x-Jan2005-debatingESF.htm (accessed September 9, 2006).

Rheingold, Howard. 1993. *The Virtual Community.* Reading, Mass.: Addison-Wesley.

Rhodes, Joel P. 2001. *The Voice of Violence.* Westport, Conn.: Praeger.

Richardson, Joanne. 2003. "The Language of Tactical Media." In *An@rchitexts,* ed. Joanne Richardson, 123–28. Brooklyn: Autonomedia.

Riches, David. 1986. "The Phenomenon of Violence." In *The Anthropology of Violence,* ed. David Riches, 1–27. Oxford: Blackwell.

Riera, Miguel, ed. 2001. *La batalla de génova.* Barcelona: El Viejo Topo.

Riles, Annelise. 2000. *The Network Inside Out.* Ann Arbor: University of Michigan Press.

Ronfeldt, David F., John Arquilla, Graham Fuller, and Melissa Fuller. 1998. *The Zapatista "Social Netwar" in Mexico.* Santa Monica, Calif.: Rand.

Routledge, Paul. 2003. "Convergence Space." *Transactions of the Institute of British Geographers* 28 (3): 333–49.

———. 1997b. "The Imagineering of Resistance." *Transactions of the Institute of British Geographers* 22: 359–76.

———. 1997a. "A Spatiality of Resistance." In *Geographies of Resistance,* ed. Steve Pile and Michael Keith, 68–86. London: Routledge.

———. 1996. "Critical Geopolitics and Terrains of Resistance." *Political Geography* 15 (6–7): 509–31.

———. 1994. "Backstreets, Barricades, and Blackouts." *Environment and Planning D* 12: 559–78.

Routledge, Paul, and Jon Simons. 1995. "Embodying Spirits of Resistance." *Environment and Planning D* 13: 471–98.

Santino, Jack. 2001. *Signs of War and Peace.* New York: Palgrave.

Santos, Boaventura de Sousa. 2006. *The Rise of the Global Left.* London: Zed Books.

Scarry, Elaine. 1985. *The Body in Pain.* New York: Oxford University Press.

Schechner, Richard. 1985. *Between Theater and Anthropology.* Philadelphia: University of Pennsylvania Press.

Schein, Louisa. 1999. "Performing Modernity." *Cultural Anthropology* 14 (3): 361–95.

Scheper-Hughes, Nancy. 1995. "The Primacy of the Ethical." *Current Anthropology* 36 (3): 409–20.

Scheper-Hughes, Nancy, and Margaret M. Lock. 1987. "The Mindful Body." *Medical Anthropology Quarterly* 1: 6–41.

Schieffelin, Edward L. 1985. "Performance and the Cultural Construction of Reality." *American Ethnologist* 12: 707–24.

Schröder, Ingo W., and Bettina E. Schmidt. 2001. Introduction to *The Anthropology of Violence and Conflict,* ed. Ingo W. Schröder and Bettina E. Schmidt, 1–24. Oxford: Routledge.

Schwartzman, Helen B. 1989. *The Meeting*. New York: Plenum Press.

Seidman, Gay W. 2000. "Adjusting the Lens." In *Globalizations and Social Movements*, ed. John A. Guidry, Michael D. Kennedy, and Mayer N. Zald, 339–58. Ann Arbor: University of Michigan Press.

Singer, Milton B. 1972. *When a Great Tradition Modernizes*. New York: Praeger.

Sklar, Deidre. 1994. "Can Bodylore Be Brought to Its Senses?" *Journal of American Folklore* 107 (423): 9–22.

Smith, Angel. 2002. "Barcelona through the European Mirror." In *Red Barcelona*, ed. Angel Smith, 1–16. London: Routledge.

Smith, Jackie. 2004. "The World Social Forum and the Challenges of Global Democracy." *Global Networks* 4 (4): 413–21.

———. 2002. "Globalizing Resistance." In *Globalization and Resistance*, ed. Jackie Smith and Hank Johnston, 183–99. Lanham, Md.: Rowman and Littlefield.

Smith, Jackie, and Hank Johnston, eds. 2002 *Globalization and Resistance*. Lanham, Md.: Rowman and Littlefield.

Smith, Jackie, Charles Chatfield, and Ron Pagnucco, eds. 1997. *Transnational Social Movements and Global Politics*. Syracuse: Syracuse University Press.

Smith, Peter J., and Elizabeth Smythe. 2001. "Globalization, Citizenship, and Technology." In *Culture and Politics in the Information Age*, ed. Frank Weber, 83–105. London: Routledge.

Snow, David D., and Robert D. Benford. 1992. "Master Frames and Cycles of Protest." In *Frontiers in Social Movement Theory*, ed. Aldon D. Morris and Carol McClurg Mueller, 133–55. New Haven, Conn.: Yale University Press.

Speed, Shannon. 2006. "At the Crossroads of Human Rights and Anthropology: Toward a Critically Engaged Activist Research." *American Anthropologist* 108: 66–76.

Starhawk. 2002. *Webs of Power*. Gabriola, B.C.: New Society Publishers.

Starn, Orin. 1999. *Nightwatch*. Durham, N.C.: Duke University Press.

Starr, Amory. 2005. *Global Revolt*. London: Zed Books.

———. 2004. "How Can Anti-imperialism Not Be Anti-racist?" *Journal of World-Systems Research* 10 (1): 119–51.

Starr, Amory, and Jason Adams. 2004. "Anti-Globalization." *New Political Science* 25 (1): 19–42.

Stiglitz, Joseph E. 2002. *Globalization and Its Discontents*. New York: W. W. Norton.

Strathern, Andrew, and Pamela J. Stewart. 1998. "Embodiment and Communication." *Social Anthropology* 6 (2): 237–51.

Sturgeon, Noël. 1995. "Theorizing Movements." In *Cultural Politics and Social Movements*, ed. Darcy Darnovsky, Barbara Epstein, and Dick Flacks, 35–54. Philadelphia: Temple University Press.

Suárez-Orozco, Marcelo M. 1987. "The Treatment of Children in the 'Dirty War.' " In *Child Survivor*, ed. Nancy Scheper-Hughes, 227–46. Dordrecht: D. Reidel.

Subirats, Joan. 1999. Introduction to *Existe sociedad civil en España?* Fundación Encuentro.

Tarrow, Sidney. 2005. *The New Transnational Activism*. Cambridge: Cambridge University Press.

———. 2001. "Transnational Politics." *Annual Review of Political Science* 4: 1–20.

———. 1998. *Power in Movement*. 2nd ed. Cambridge: Cambridge University Press.

———. 1995. "Mass Mobilization and Regime Change." In *The Politics of Democratic Consolidation*, ed. Richard Gunther, P. Nikiforos Diamandouros, and Hans-Jürgen Puhle, 204–30. Baltimore: Johns Hopkins University Press.

Taussig, Michael. 1984. "Culture of Terror—Space of Death." *Comparative Study of Society and History* 26 (3): 467–97.

Taylor, Verta. 1995. "Watching for Vibes." In *Feminist Organizations*, ed. Myra Marx Ferree and Patricia Yancey Martin, 222–33. Philadelphia: Temple University Press.

Thayer, Millie. 2001. "Transnational Feminism." *Ethnography* 2 (2): 243–72.

Thomas, Janet. 2001. *The Battle in Seattle*. Golden, Colo.: Fulcrum.

Thompson, John B. 1995. *The Media and Modernity*. Stanford, Calif.: Stanford University Press.

Tilly, Charles. 1978. *From Mobilization to Revolution*. New York: McGraw-Hill.

Toussaint, Eric. 2005. *Your Money (or) Your Life*. Chicago: Haymarket Books.

Treanor, Paul. 2002. "Who Controlled the Florence ESF?" http://www.indymedia.ie/newswire/ (accessed April 13, 2005).

Trotsky, Leon. 1930. *The History of the Russian Revolution*. Vol. 1. http://www.marxists.org/archive/trotsky/works/ (accessed May 19, 2004).

Trouillot, Michel-Rolph. 2003. *Global Transformations*. New York: Palgrave Macmillan.

Tsing, Anna Lowenhaupt. 2005. *Friction*. Princeton, N.J.: Princeton University Press.

Turner, Victor. 1986. "Dewey, Dilthey, and Drama." In *The Anthropology of Experience*, ed. Victor Turner and Edward M. Bruner, 33–44. Champaign: University of Illinois Press.

———. 1982. *From Ritual to Theatre*. New York: Performing Arts Journal Publications.

———. 1969. *The Ritual Process*. Chicago: Aldine.

Turner, Victor, and Richard Schechner. 1986. *The Anthropology of Performance*. New York: PAJ Publications.

Van Aelst, Peter, and Steffaan Walgrave. 2002. "New Media, New Movements?" *Information, Communication and Society* 5 (4): 465–93.

Varela, Francisco, Humberto R. Maturana, and Ricardo Uribe. 1974. "Autopoiesis." *Biosystems* 5: 187–96.

Virno, Paolo. 2004. *A Grammar of the Multitude*. New York: Semiotext(e).

Wacquant, Loïc. 2004. *Body and Soul*. Oxford: Oxford University Press.

———. 1992. "Epistemic Reflexivity." In *An Invitation to Reflexive Sociology*, by Pierre Bourdieu and Loïc Wacquant, 36–46. Chicago: University of Chicago Press.

Wall, Derek. 1999. *Earth First! and the Anti-roads Movement*. London: Routledge.

Walton, John, and David Seddon. 1994. *Free Markets and Food Riots*. Oxford: Blackwell.

Walton, John, and Jonathan Shefner. 1994. "Latin America." In *Free Markets and Food Risk*, ed. John Walton and David Seddon, 97–134. Oxford: Blackwell.

Ward, Colin. 1973. *Anarchy in Action*. London: Allen and Unwin.

Warner, Michael. 2002. "Publics and Counterpublics." *Public Culture* 14 (1): 49–90.

Warren, Kay B. 1998. *Indigenous Movements and Their Critics*. Princeton, N.J.: Princeton University Press.

Waterman, Peter. 2006. "The Bamako Appeal." http://www.choike.org/documentos/bamako_appeal_janus.pdf (accessed September 9, 2006).

———. 2005. "Making the Road Whilst Walking." http://www.choike.org/documentos/waterman_wsf_comunic.pdf (accessed September 9, 2006).

———. 2002. "What's Left Internationally?" http://www.voiceoftheturtle.org/ (accessed September 9, 2006).

———. 1998. *Globalization, Social Movements, and the New Internationalisms*. Washington: Mansell.

Weber, Steve. 2004. *The Success of Open Source*. Cambridge: Harvard University Press.

Weiss, Linda. 1998. *The Myth of the Powerless State*. Cambridge, UK: Polity Press.

Wellman, Barry. 2001. "Physical Place and Cyberplace." *International Journal of Urban and Regional Research* 25 (2): 227–52.

Wellman, Barry, and Caroline A. Haythornthwaite. 2002. *The Internet in Everyday Life*. Malden, Mass.: Blackwell.

Welsh, Ian. 2004. "Network Movement in the Czech Republic." *Journal of Contemporary European Studies* 12 (3): 321–37.

Wert, José Ignacio. 1996. "Sobre cultura política." In *Entre dos siglos*, ed. Oscar Alzaga Villaamil, Javier Tusell, Emilio Lamo de Espinosa, and Rafael Pardo. Madrid: Alianza.

Wilson, Samuel M., and Leighton C. Peterson. 2002. "The Anthropology of Online Communities." *Annual Review of Anthropology* 31: 441–67.

Wood, Elisabeth Jean. 2001. "The Emotional Benefits of Insurgency in El Salvador." In *Passionate Politics*, ed. Jeff Goodwin, James Jasper, and Francesca Polletta, 267–81. Chicago: University of Chicago Press.

Wood, Lesley J. 2004. "Breaking the Chasms." In *Coalitions across Borders*, ed. Jose Bandy and Jackie Smith, 95–120. Lanham, Md.: Rowman and Littlefield.

Woolard, Kathryn Ann. 1989. *Double Talk*. Stanford, Calif.: Stanford University Press.

Wray, Stefan. 1998. "On Electronic Civil Disobedience." http://cristine.org/borders/Wray_Essay.html (accessed November 13, 2005).

Xarxa Ciutadana per l'Abolició del Deute Extern. 2001. *La consulta social del deute extern a Catalunya*. Barcelona: Editorial Mediterránia.

Ya Basta! 2001. "Victory." In *Restructuring and Resistance*, ed. Kolya Abramsky, 187–88. Distributed from resresrev@yahoo.com.

Young, Katharine. 1993. "Still Life with Corpses." In *Bodylore*, ed. Katharine Young, 111–33. Knoxville: University of Tennessee Press.

Youniss, James, et al. 2002. "Youth Civic Engagement in the Twenty-first Century." *Journal of Research on Adolescence* 12 (1): 121–48.

Zolberg, Aristide R. 1972. "Moments of Madness." *Politics and Society* 2 (2): 183–207.

Zulaika, Joseba, and William A. Douglass. 1996. *Terror and Taboo*. New York: Routledge.

anti–corporate globalization movements (*cont.*)

298, 300; organizational forms, 15, 290; repression and violence, 162–63; in Seattle, 9–10; sectors, 301–2

antiglobalization. *See* anti–corporate globalization movements

antimilitarism, 67–68, 81–82, 88, 322 n. 5, 324 n. 16

anti-NATO movement, 77, 323 n. 11

anti-roads movement, 43

Arato, Andrew, 290, 346 n. 2

Arnison, Matthew, 270–74

Arquilla, John, 35

Art and Revolution, 33–34, 43, 320 n. 16

ateneos populares, 62, 83, 91

ATTAC. *See* International Movement for Democratic Control of Financial Markets and Their Institutions

autonomous movements, 60, 88–92, 117, 167

autonomous spaces: in Barcelona, 113–18; cultural politics of, 233–35, 255–63; European Social Forum (ESF) and, 257; in London, 250, 258–61; in Mumbai, 258, 342 n. 39; Peoples' Global Action (PGA) and, 256–57; Strasbourg No Border Camp and, 256

autonomy: in Catalonia, 62, 65, 67–68, 322 n. 7; in Chiapas (Zapatistas), 39, 44–45; movements and struggles for, 44, 222; networking logics and politics and, 14, 16–17, 63, 111, 227, 261, 300; principles and politics of, 10, 15–16, 59, 63, 340 n. 39; spaces of, 255, 263; squatters and, 67, 322 n. 5

Aznar, José María, 151, 162

Babels, 251

Bakhtin, Mikhail, 140

Bakunin, Mikhail, 16, 346 n. 4

Bamako: Appeal, 265, 302; Polycentric World Social Forum, 51, 57, 247, 262, 265. *See also* World Social Forum (WSF)

Barcelona: anarchism in, 65; anti–corporate globalization movements in, 2–5, 15, 64, 71–92, 94–97, 100–104; Barcelona Campaign against the Europe of Capital (against EU), 110–18, 145–55, 192, 292; Barcelona Indymedia, 79, 109, 271, 273; Barcelona Social Forum (BSF), 72, 107, 116–20, 146, 150, 328 n. 24; Barcelona Trembles, 89, 105–6, 115; Barcelona 2001 Campaign against the World Bank, 15, 55–56, 61, 72, 97–100, 104–7, 125; ethnographic research in, 18–23; International Council meeting, 252–55; Peoples' Global Action (PGA) meeting, 199–201, 212–14; protests in, 10, 49, 54–56, 118, 125–27, 155–56; squatting in, 66, 323 n. 13. *See also* World Bank

Barker, Colin, 22

Barry, Andrew, 316 n. 22

Beck, Ulrich, 324 n. 27

Bello, Walden, 264

Bennett, W. Lance, 336 n. 7

Berlusconi, Silvio, 183–84, 192–93, 332 n. 2, 334 n. 22

Bey, Hakim, 31

Beyond ESF, 250, 259

Black Bloc, 44, 55, 58; debates on violence and, 194–97; in Genoa, 173–74, 176–78, 180–84; New Kids on the Black Block, 197–98, 267–68, 275; in Prague, 123, 136, 142–44, 155; in Seattle, 30–38. *See also* Blue March

Blair, Tony, 162

blockades: in Genoa, 192; in Prague, 124, 127–28, 130, 136–39, 142, 144, 147; in Seattle, 30–31, 33–34

Blok, Anton, 166

Blue March, in Prague, 123–24, 131, 142–43

Cohen, Jean, 290, 346 n. 2

Colectivo Situaciones, 24

Comisiones Obreras (ccoo, Workers' Commissions), 65, 76–77; Barcelona Social Forum (BSF) and, 116–17; critical sectors and, 324 n. 26. *See also* Partit Socialista Unificat de Catalunya (PSUC)

command logic, 25, 59, 94, 235, 245, 255, 259, 289, 298

communitas, 31, 139, 145, 154

complexity theory, 16, 260, 318 n. 36, 318 n. 37

Confederación Nacional de Trabajo (CNT), 65, 324 n. 26

Confederation of European Syndicates (CES), 36

Conscientious Objector Movement (MOC), 67

consciousness, contradictory, 81

consensus decision making: anti-corporate globalization movements in Barcelona and, 71, 77, 84, 98, 106, 116; autonomous spaces and, 259; cultural politics of networking and, 15; direct action and, 33, 37, 42, 52, 127, 172; history of, 324 n. 25, 338 n. 30; Indymedia and, 271; networking logics and, 11, 14; struggles within Peoples' Global Action (PGA), 208, 222–23, 227–28

Consulta: Consulta Social against the Foreign Debt, 68, 80, 82, 103, 113, 343 n. 34; European Social Consulta, 87, 282–285, 296, 327 n. 16, 343 n. 34; Zapatista National Consulta for Peace and Democracy, 345 n. 34. *See also* Citizens Network to Abolish the Foreign Debt

convergence center: in Barcelona, 147; in Genoa, 168, 172–73, 174, 179, 184–86; in Prague, 129, 130

convergence space, 15, 92, 105, 206, 218, 289, 298, 301

Conway, Janet, 319 n. 48

Correra, Rafael, 299

counterpower, 10, 26, 282–83, 295

counterpublics, transnational, 3, 201–4, 218, 220, 229, 245

countersummits, 39, 42, 52, 54, 90, 127–28, 155, 157–58, 220, 233. *See also* mass mobilizations; protests

Cox, Lawrence, 22

Critical Art Ensemble (CAE), 275, 280, 345 n. 21

critical mass, 150, 331 n. 31

critical sectors, 59, 71, 76–78, 110, 117, 145, 324 n. 26

culture jamming, 39, 274–75, 284, 344 n. 16

cyberspace, 12, 97, 220, 229, 270, 275, 280, 285

debt, 8–9, 34–36, 40, 58, 68, 75, 86, 185, 102–4, 293–95. *See also* Citizens Network to Abolish the Foreign Debt

de Certeau, Michel, 21, 343 n. 2, 346 n. 5

della Porta, Donatella, 121, 172, 180, 317 n. 28, 325 n. 33, 334 n. 20

democracy: direct, 9, 15–16, 59–60, 91, 119, 211, 223, 227–28, 254, 259, 270, 283, 285, 295, 300; participatory, 17, 68, 70, 86, 102, 284, 316 n. 17; power and, 211, 214; representative, 87, 118–21, 282, 295; Spain, transition to, 64–65, 98, 322 n. 4

Democratic National Convention (DNC) protest, 43, 47–48

Diani, Mario, 316 n. 20, 326 n. 5

Diaz School, 161, 186–89, 332 n. 2, 333 n. 19, 334 n. 21, 334 n. 22

digital divide, 13, 204, 281

direct action: anarchist-inspired, 15, 39, 42–44, 65; anti-corporate globalization movement and, 52–54, 57; in Barcelona, 145–54; cyberspace and, 275; Direct Action Network (DAN), 31, 33–36, 47, 130,

Free and Open Source Software (FOSS), 16, 211, 236, 250–52, 262, 272, 284–85, 318 n. 38

Freeman, Jo, 211, 228

free trade, 3, 291, 294–95; campaigns and struggles against, 12, 24, 37, 39, 41–42, 45–46, 200; Free Trade Area of the Americas (FTAA), protests against, 28, 49, 54, 57–58. *See also* globalization; North American Free Trade Agreement (NAFTA)

Friedman, Thomas, 6–7, 292

Gamson, William, 346 n. 6

G8 protests: in Evian, Switzerland, 50, 56; in Genoa (2001), 1, 10, 55, 161–98, 210; in Gleneagles, Scotland (2006), 9–10, 51, 347 n. 11; Global Days of Action and, 43, 46, 48, 202; in Heiligendamm, Germany, 51, 347 n. 11; in St. Petersburg, Russia, 51, 57, 347 n. 11

General Agreement on Trade and Tariffs (GATT), 41

Genoa Social Forum (GSF), 55, 108, 164. *See also* G8 protests

George, Susan, 37, 194–95, 335 n. 29

Gerlach, Luther, 14

Giuliani, Carlo, 154, 161, 179, 184, 334 n. 22

Global Days of Action. *See* Peoples' Global Action (PGA)

Global Exchange, 33–34

globalization: corporate, 2, 6–8, 28, 36, 38, 42, 53, 73, 245, 263, 288, 294, 300, 321 n. 24; dimensions of, 6–9; grassroots, 8, 297; grounded, 18. *See also* anti–corporate globalization movements; direct action; mass action; neoliberalism

Globalize Resistance, 170–71

Global South: grassroots struggles in, 37, 39–40, 62; Internet and, 12; Peoples' Global Action (PGA) and, 46–47, 157, 204, 207

Gluckman, Max, 332 n. 37

Goodwin, Jeff, 138, 329 n. 12

Gothenburg, protests against European Union, 49, 54–55, 146, 162, 193, 335 n. 29

Graeber, David, 22

Grajew, Oded, 245

Gramsci, Antonio, 22

Group of 19 (G19), at World Social Forum, 265

guerrilla communications, 197, 268, 274, 276

Habermas, Jürgen, 238, 255, 336 n. 4

hacking, 14; border, 280; hacking-in-the-streets, 280; hackitecture, 279; hacklabs, 277–81, 284; hackmeetings, 279; hacktivism, 278, 344 n. 20; reality, 279–80. *See also* activist-hackers

Hae, Lee Kyung, 50, 57–58

Hale, Charles, 319 n. 49

Handelman, Don, 139, 145

Hardt, Michael, 238

Hebdige, Dick, 181–182

Henshaw-Plath, Evan, 273

Herri Batasuna (HB), 146

Hetherington, Kevin, 218, 269

hierarchies, 17, 70, 126, 234, 273, 326 n. 11, 327 n. 13, 332 n. 37, 339 n. 38; informal, 18, 84, 207, 214, 217, 227, 230

Hine, Virginia, 14

horizontality: direct action protest and, 124, 131, 145, 196–97, 289, 301; horizontalism, 18, 87; "horizontals," 259; horizontal structures, 13–14, 84, 224, 300, 324 n. 27, 346 n. 4; independent media and, 268–71, 274–81, 284–85, 296; informational utopics and, 26, 282–84; political logics and cultural ideals, 11, 14–17, 59–60, 68, 79, 86–88, 165, 227, 259, 289, 300; Peoples' Global

Action (PGA) and, 207, 211–12, 224, 227, 229–30; World Social Forum (WSF) and, 235, 238, 244, 246, 255, 259, 262–63, 265. *See also* networking logic

identity: Catalan, 65, 73, 80; Citizens Network to Abolish the Foreign Debt (RCADE) and, 83, 102–4; collective, 111; Movement for Global Resistance (MRG) and, 70, 83, 93, 99–102; networking politics and, 92, 94; organizational debates on, 97–104; performance of during protest, 126, 128, 131, 143, 145, 151, 156, 158, 329 n. 9, 330 n. 24; protest violence and, 143, 166, 181–82, 193–94; social movement impact and, 290, 296; transnational anti–corporate globalization networks and, 201, 229, 263, 295, 300

image event, 42, 124, 135, 144–45, 155–56, 263, 300

immigrant rights, 1, 151, 215, 217–20, 224, 321 n. 28

Independent Media Center (IMC), 13, 34, 38, 71, 267–71

Indian Organizing Committee, 251

Indymedia, 13, 15, 26, 47, 267, 273–74; in Barcelona, 71, 79, 271–72; in Brussels, 268; in Genoa, 186–87; in Seattle, 34, 38; social forums and, 236–37, 252, 260

Infoespai (Infospace) (Barcelona), 13, 282, 284–86, 296

Iniciativa per Catalunya (IC), 74–75, 119

Initiative against Economic Globalization (INPEG), 127, 330 n. 15

institutional sectors or movements, 59, 71–76, 104, 107, 115–16, 147

intellectuals, 20, 22, 35, 37, 241–42, 264–65, 293, 302

Intercontinental Caravan for Solidarity and Resistance, 46, 202, 205, 334 n. 3. *See also* Peoples' Global Action (PGA)

Intercontinental Gathering against Neo-liberalism and for Humanity, 45. *See also* Zapatista National Liberation Army (EZLN)

Intergaláctika Laboratory of Disobedience, 233, 236, 242–43, 257–58, 261. *See also* Caracol

International Council (IC), 93, 246, 250–55, 339 n. 3, 339 n. 8

International Forum on Globalization (IFG), 34–35, 41–42

International Monetary Fund (IMF): corporate globalization and, 7, 27, 75, 292–93, 295, 329 n. 10, 342 n. 35; protests in Prague, 4, 37, 44, 48, 52–53, 123–24, 127–45, 291; protests in Washington, D.C., 47–48, 52, 293; struggles against, 39–41

International Movement for Democratic Control of Financial Markets and Their Institutions (ATTAC), 36, 53, 105, 120, 165, 170, 241

International Youth Camp (IYC), at World Social Forum, 236–39, 242, 252, 258, 261

Internet: anti-free trade campaigns and, 41; autonomous movements and, 90, 99; computer-supported social movements and, 12–13; Citizens Network to Abolish the Foreign Debt (RCADE) and, 68–69; critical sectors and, 78; ethnographic methods and, 19; European Social Consulta (ESC) and, 282–285; independent media activism and, 38, 268, 270, 278–279, 281; Infoespai and, 288; institutional sectors and, 76; media center in Genoa and, 168, 186; Movement for Global Resistance (MRG) and, 69–72; movements in Global South and, 204; network-based movements and, 85, 88; networking logic and, 10, 35; Peoples' Global Action

18–19; in Genoa, 55, 162–97; new technologies and, 12–13; in Prague, 52, 123, 127–45; in Seattle, 27–35; "unitary" mobilizations in Barcelona, 63–64, 66, 77–78, 80, 92. *See also* protests

master frame, 63

McDonald, Kevin, 316 n. 22

Meade, Margaret, 21

media: activism, 267–77; alternative, 159, 236, 270–74, 277–78, 281, 284, 346 n. 5; corporate, 13, 220, 270; events, 33, 45; framing, 291, 347 n. 8; global, 33, 124, 158, 161, 166, 179, 189; labs and hubs, 277–81, 284; mass media and protest, 47, 58, 124–27, 130, 135, 149, 155–59, 183, 184, 193–94, 289, 290–95, 333 n. 7, 336 n. 7; protest violence and, 161, 165–68, 183, 184, 193–94, 197–98; radical, 270; tactical, 219, 274–78, 284, 343 n. 2. *See also* image events; Independent Media Center; Indymedia

Melucci, Alberto, 60, 291, 296, 317 n. 34

Merten, Stefen, 285

militant activists: anti–corporate globalization movements and, 44, 60, 293, 301, 320 n. 21; in Barcelona, 4, 62, 68, 71, 88–92, 99–100, 104–18, 146; in Genoa, 164–67, 170, 173, 180–83, 191–94, 197, 332 n. 2, 333 n. 9; in Prague, 131, 136–43, 331 n. 33; in Seattle, 34, 38; in Strasbourg No Border Camp, 217–20. *See also* anarchists; anticapitalism; autonomous movements; Black Bloc

militant ethnography. *See* ethnography

Mische, Anne, 317 n. 24

Mitchell, J. Clyde, 316 n. 20

Monohan, Torin, 318 n. 40

Morales, Evo, 294

Movement for Global Resistance (MRG): activist background, 79–83; anti–corporate globalization movements

in Catalonia and, 93–98, 146; anti–corporate globalization networks and, 4–5, 295; Barcelona Campaign against the Europe of Capital (against EU) and, 107–18; Barcelona 2001 Campaign against the World Bank and, 104–7; Citizens Network against the Foreign Debt (RCADE) and, 4, 5, 47, 64, 74, 77, 87, 95, 98, 116, 326 n. 4; dissolution of, 93, 315 n. 3; founding of, 68; Infoespai and, 281–82, 288; militant ethnography and, 21–23; Multilateral Agreement on Investment (MAI), 41, 58, 322 n. 15; networking logic and, 69–72, 118, 165, 289; organizational practices and struggles, 83–85, 99–102, 327 n. 14; Peoples' Global Action (PGA) and, 199, 207–17, 222–28; political parties and, 120; political vision, 85–88; protests in Prague and, 63–64, 123; social forums and, 236, 243, 255; technology and, 69–70; World Social Forum (WSF) International Council and, 93, 252–55

multisited ethnography. *See* ethnography

Mumbai Resistance, 258, 342 n. 39

Nationalism, Catalan. *See* Catalonia

Negri, Antonio, 91

Nelson, Diane, 317 n. 33

neoliberalism, 3, 7–8, 28, 42, 45, 81, 87, 95, 244, 282. *See also* corporate globalization

network-based movements, 59, 71, 76–88, 104–5, 113, 117–18, 124, 127, 155–57, 211, 218, 249, 301

network-based organizational forms, 10–17, 68–72, 201–8, 245–52

networking: cultural logic, 3–6, 10–18, 25, 42, 58, 101, 118, 124, 235; cultural politics, 10–11, 15, 36, 72, 75, 92, 94, 118, 125, 165, 250–52, 299; horizontal logic, 38, 43, 94, 128, 212, 219, 230, 244, 246, 255, 263,

actions and, 155; networking logic, 4–5; organizational struggles, 211–17, 221–29; in Prague, 131; Strasbourg No Border Camp and, 220; technology and, 13, 201–8, 295; transnational activism and, 7, 201, 204, 229–30, 295; World Social Forum (WSF) and, 234, 255–58

Pérez de Lama, José, 279

Pérez-Díaz, Victor M., 325 n. 32

performance: cultural, 125–26; protest and, 123–59; terrain, 124–27, 141–42, 155; violent, 142–43, 162, 165–67, 180–83, 193–96, 333 n. 8

Peterson, Abby, 143, 181

Peterson, Leighton, 269

Pink and Silver March: in Genoa, 55, 170–76, 195, 199, 305–6; in Prague, 130–31, 136, 139–42, 145, 156, 330 n. 22

Pink March, in Prague, 123–24, 130–32, 134, 135–39

place, concept of, and social movements, 63, 201

Poletta, Francesca, 316 n. 17, 327 n. 13

political parties: anti–corporate globalization movements in Barcelona and, 59, 63, 71–76, 84, 87, 89; networking politics in Barcelona and, 94, 98, 105–6, 108–10, 113, 115–16; support for anti–corporate globalization movements, 293–94; World Social Forum (WSF) and, 241, 244, 256, 340 n. 18

Porto Alegre, and World Social Forum, 25, 53, 57, 233–66, 291–94

Prague, World Bank and IMF protests in, 4, 48, 52, 63–64, 95–96, 123–45, 291–93

prefigurative politics, 9, 131, 156, 266, 316 n. 16, 346 n. 3

protests, anti–corporate globalization, 48–51, 124, 126, 184, 192, 200. See also direct action; mass action; mass mobilization

Public Citizen, 33–34, 41

Rabinow, Paul, 12, 317 n. 25

Rainforest Action Network (RAN), 33–37, 40, 42

RCADE. See Citizens Network to Abolish the Foreign Debt

Reclaim the Streets (RTS), 43, 46, 48, 148, 209

red zone, 55, 169, 172, 193, 304

reformists, 36, 71–72, 75, 95, 99–100, 105, 113–18, 145, 150, 234, 236, 242, 293, 301

Refundazione Comunista, 165, 189, 340 n. 18

repertoire: of contention, 331 n. 27; of protest, 145–46, 159, 161, 180, 301

Republican National Convention (RNC) protest, 47–48, 51, 58

Rhodes, Joel P., 166

rhizome. See networks

Riles, Annelise, 318 n. 37

Rio Earth Summit, 41, 239

ritual: Carnival and, 140–41, 332 n. 37; conflict, 124, 131, 142–43, 166, 181; performative, 126; protest and, 125–27, 190, 193; of rebellion, 332 n. 37; of resistance, 182; World Social Forum (WSF) and, 238–39

Ronfeldt, David, 35

"Rose of Fire," 65, 110, 327 n. 20

Routledge, Paul, 21–24, 156, 207, 331 n. 32

Roy, Arundhati, 264

Ruckus Society, 33–34, 42–43

Sachs, Jeffrey, 9, 293

Salinas, Carlos, 45

samba band: in Genoa, 170, 173; in Prague, 130, 139, 140, 141; in Porto Alegre at World Social Forum, 234, 237, 240, 240

Sans-Titre Network, 209, 223, 225, 227, 338 n. 32

Santos, Boaventura de Sousa, 343 n. 53

scale: multiscalar ethnography, 18–19; multiscalar politics, 319 n. 42; shift, 319 n. 42, 336 n. 6

Scarry, Elaine, 191

Schengen Information System (SIS), 53, 218

Scheper-Hughes, Nancy, 23, 319 n. 46

Schneider, Florian, 277

Scouts. *See* Catalonia

Seattle: Seattle effect, 33–60; WTO protests in, 27–36

self-management, 15–16, 65, 67–68, 88, 90–91, 95, 219, 251, 284, 322 n. 5

self-organization, 16, 43, 89, 211, 216, 259, 278

Sen, Jai, 248, 265

September 11, 10, 53, 57–58

Shefner, Jon, 40

Shiva, Vandana, 37

Sikkink, Kathryn, 316 n. 20

Silva, Luiz Inácio da (Lula), 57, 241, 294

Sklar, Deidre, 21

social centers. *See* squatters

socialists, 56, 127–128, 244, 293; Socialist Workers' Party (SWP), 78, 105, 127, 170

social movements, 3, 5, 9, 60; assembly-based, 77, 87, 119; in Barcelona, 66, 73, 77, 83, 87–88, 90, 115, 252; computer-supported, 12–14, 271; cultural politics and, 15; emotion and, 126–27, 329 n. 12; impact of, 291, 296, 346 n. 6; militant ethnography and, 19–24, 299–300; networking logic and, 10–11; new social movements (NSM), 64, 117, 121, 290–91, 323 n. 11, 324 n. 16, 325 n. 33, 346 n. 2; political parties and, 119–21; Social Movement Assembly, at World Social Forum, 239, 243, 245; theoretical approaches to, 298–99, 317 n. 23, 317 n. 34; transnational, 201, 317 n. 23, 336 n. 4, 336 n. 5

solidarity: economic, 67; global, 1, 36, 39, 45, 62, 68; international solidarity movement, in Catalonia, 62, 67–68, 77, 236, 324 n. 16, 326 n. 4. *See also* affective solidarity

Soros, George, 9

Sosa, Mercedes, 244

Spain: civil society, 72, 94, 105, 319 n. 42, 323 n. 8, 325 n. 32; civil war, 64–65, 82, 91, 154, 173, 322 n. 4, 322 n. 5; history, 64–69; Second Republic, 64–65; Spanish Socialist Workers' Party (PSOE), 105, 117

spokescouncil meetings, 33, 35, 130, 136, 173, 175, 219, 223

squatters: autonomous movements and, 44, 60, 88–92; in Barcelona, 62, 95, 105–6, 109, 113, 115, 145, 322 n. 5, 322 n. 6; hacklabs and, 279–280; movement, 67, 83, 154; Movement for Global Resistance (MRG) and, 4, 64, 67–68, 83, 99–100, 105–6; in Prague, 131; social centers, 1, 44, 61, 67, 79–80, 163, 164, 168–72, 182, 216, 315 n. 2, 323 n. 15

Starhawk, 33–34, 158

Stevens, Philip, 295

Stiglitz, Joseph, 8–9, 52, 293

Strasbourg, No Border Camp, 56, 217–21, 256, 278

structural adjustment, 39, 41–42, 295

students: anti–corporate globalization movements and, 39–41; movement in Catalonia, 66, 73, 76–77, 79, 82, 89, 322 n. 6, 323 n. 11

submerged spheres, 124, 252, 299

summit hopping, 15, 157–59

swarm, 35, 123, 128, 130–31, 145, 147–48

"tactical frivolity," 141, 170–71, 305–6

tactics, diversity of: in Genoa, 161–62, 165, 170, 192–97; networking logic and, 25, 58, 124, 301; in Prague, 52, 128, 131, 148

Tarrow, Sidney, 319 n. 42, 336 n. 5, 336 n. 6

Taussig, Michael, 167

Teamsters Union, 30, 35

technology, digital: anti–corporate globalization movements in Barcelona and, 68–72, 78–80, 88, 90, 94; architecture,

Wood, Leslie, 207, 336 n. 2

Workers Party (Brazilian PT), 50, 57, 240

World Bank: anti–corporate globalization and, 7–8, 27, 75, 292–93, 295, 329 n. 10, 342 n. 35; protests against, in Barcelona, 15, 54–56, 61, 72, 97–100, 104–7, 118, 125; protests against, in Prague, 4, 37, 44, 48, 52–53, 123–24, 127–45, 291; protests against, in Washington, D.C., 47–48, 52, 293; struggles against, 36–41. *See also* Barcelona; International Monetary Fund

World Economic Forum (WEF), 9, 53, 293

World March of Women, 37

World Social Forum (WSF), 2, 9, 49–51; autonomous space and, 256–62; Bamako Appeal and, 265, 302; Charter of Principles, 264; Group of 19 (G19) at, 265; history of, 245–47, 337 n. 8; International Council Meeting in Barcelona, 252–55; International Youth Camp and, 236–39, 242, 252, 258, 261; media coverage of, 292; Movement for Global Resistance (MRG) and, 93, 236, 243, 255; in Mumbai (2004), 57, 238, 246–47, 250–51, 258, 340 n. 19, 342 n. 39; in Nairobi (2007), 7, 246, 248, 321 n. 29, 339 n. 6, 340 n. 19, 342 n. 44; networking logic and, 245–49, 302; networking politics and, 252–55, 256–58, 263–66; open space and, 206, 235, 245–49, 252, 255, 259, 262–66, 302, 340 n. 19, 339 n. 20, 341 n. 33; participants, 340 n. 19, 342 n. 35; Polycentric (Bamako, Caracas, Karachi, 2006), 57, 247, 262, 265, 302, 340 n. 19;

in Porto Alegre (2002), 53, 57, 233–45; in Porto Alegre (2005), 57, 261–62; technology and, 13, 249–52, 330 n. 23; transnational social movements and, 7. *See also* autonomous space; Group of 19 (G19); open space

World Trade Organization (WTO): corporate globalization and, 7, 75, 224, 293, 342 n. 35; culture jamming and, 275–76; Global Days of Action and, 46, 48–51; media coverage of protests, 291; protests in Cancun (2003), 10, 57–58; protests in Seattle (1999), 2–3, 9, 27–38

World Wide Web, 265, 271, 275–79, 282; weblogs, 274; websites, 3, 13, 68–69, 85, 87, 203–4, 229, 249–51, 275, 283; wiki and, 13, 250, 274

Ya Basta!, 44, 209, 233, 321 n. 19, 336 n. 2. *See also* White Overalls

Yellow March, in Prague, 123, 131–36

Yomango, 275

Zapatista National Liberation Army (EZLN): electronic civil disobedience and, 276; encuentros, 45, 83, 205, 207, 320 n. 19; Movement for Global Resistance (MRG) and, 64, 68, 82–83, 115, 323 n. 13; solidarity and support networks, 24, 45, 64, 68, 83, 115, 205, 321 n. 19, 321 n. 22, 321 n. 23; technology and, 12; uprising, 8, 28, 39, 44–47. *See also* Consulta

zone of indistinction, 162, 168, 177, 180, 190, 332 n. 13

Parts of the Introduction and chapter 8 have previously appeared in the *Annals of the American Academy of Political and Social Science* 597: 109–208; portions of chapter 4 in *Ethnography* 9 (1): 61–97; sections of chapter 5 in *Critique of Anthropology* 25 (4): 413–32; and portions of chapter 7 in *Ephemera* 5 (2): 253–72, all in modified form.

Jeffrey Juris is an assistant professor of anthropology in the Department of Social and Behavioral Sciences at Arizona State University.

Library of Congress Cataloging-in-Publication Data
Juris, Jeffrey S.
Networking futures : the movements against corporate globalization / Jeffrey S. Juris.
p. cm. — (Experimental futures)
Includes bibliographical references and index.
ISBN-13: 978-0-8223-4250-2 (cloth : alk. paper)
ISBN-13: 978-0-8223-4269-4 (pbk. : alk. paper)
1. Globalization. 2. Anti-globalization movement. 3. Globalization—Spain—
Barcelona. 4. Anti-globalization movement—Spain—Barcelona. 5. Capitalism—Social
aspects. 6. Capitalism—Social aspects—Spain—Barcelona. 7. Applied anthropology.
I. Title.
JZ1318.J86 2008
303.48'2—dc22   2007049448